Peter Biddlecombe is a travel-hardened businessman. His much-acclaimed first book, *French Lessons in Africa*, described his travels through French-speaking Africa, and has been followed by four more gloriously funny accounts of global business trips: *Travels With My Briefcase*, *Around the World – On Expenses* and *I Came, I Saw, I Lost My Luggage*, all of which are available from Abacus Travel, and *Very Funny – Now Change Me Back Again*, which is published in hardback by Little, Brown in 1997.

Also by Peter Biddlecombe

FRENCH LESSONS IN AFRICA
TRAVELS WITH MY BRIEFCASE
AROUND THE WORLD – ON EXPENSES
VERY FUNNY – NOW CHANGE ME BACK AGAIN
FASTER – THEY'RE GAINING

I Came, I Saw, I Lost My Luggage

Et tu, Royal Swazi Airlines?

PETER BIDDLECOMBE

ABACUS

An *Abacus* Book

First published in Great Britain in 1996
by Little, Brown and Company
This edition published by Abacus in 1997
Reprinted in 1997 (twice), 1999

A CIP catalogue record for this book
is available from the British Library

ISBN: 0 349 10812 9

Typeset by Solidus (Bristol) Limited
Printed and bound in Great Britain by
Clays Ltd, St Ives plc

Abacus
A Division of
Little, Brown and Company (UK)
Brettenham House
Lancaster Place
London WC2E 7EN

Contents

Introduction   1

Vienna   5
Copenhagen   20
Helsinki   39
Budapest   58
Warsaw   77
Bratislava   101
The Baltic States   115
The Caribbean   144
Reykjavik   165
Abidjan   183
Agadez   209
Dakar   235
Beirut   254
Taipei   272
Ho Chi Minh City   297
Havana   319
Dhaka   342
Mexico City   357
Managua   381
Panama City   402

I Came, I Saw, I Lost My Luggage

Introduction

Don't get me going on luggage.

I mean, here am I, I've practically bought three 747s the amount of money I've blown on airline tickets over the years, and will they let me take my luggage on board? Will they hell.

I say luggage. It's only one of those old canvas fold-up bags. But the guy in front of me who looks like Colonel Gaddafi's entertainments officer is allowed on with two huge briefcases, six plastic shopping bags and one of those great box-like multi-coloured bags that look as though they are used for smuggling businessmen back into Nigeria. Not to mention the fat lady with the kid – there is always a fat lady with a kid on every plane I go on. She's got about twenty-seven Harrods shopping bags each containing the complete set of *Encyclopaedia Britannica*, an ironing board and something that looks like a supermarket trolley.

'But . . . but . . .' I wave helplessly towards them.

'Regulations, sir,' grunts this antique smoking bimbo who's got a face like a wet weekend.

'But . . . but . . .'

'If you would like me to call the supervisor.' I get a long thin tight hairline smile that would set off every metal detector in the place. 'Sir.'

What do I do? I can't bribe her. At least, not at Heathrow I can't. Other places, maybe. I can hardly smack her in the gums. So I give in. Yet again.

Then what happens? You got it. Somehow they stick it on the wrong plane to the wrong place in the wrong part of the world and I end up sweating my way through Africa or freezing to death in the Far East wearing the same shirt, suit and tie for the whole week.

Sometimes, however, I get away with it. Like during the Gulf War, or on flights out of Dublin when Ireland are playing at home, when the planes are so empty you can practically pile all your gear in the pilot's seat and nobody objects.

Then what happens? It gets lost at the other end.

Change planes anywhere in Africa, India, the Middle East or South America and there's no way you are allowed to carry your own luggage to the next check-in gate, let alone the next terminal. Everything is thrown on to those enormous trolleys which just disappear behind huge swing doors. For ever.

Worse still, land in Atlanta, Georgia, where they have the craziest luggage system I've ever come across anywhere in the entire galaxy. You get your luggage from the carousel. You go through Immigration. You go through Customs. I'm not saying they're slow. It's just that the last time I went through my passport expired by the time I got up to the desk. Then what happens? Before you've even begun filling in the form for a new passport they grab your luggage and throw it on to a conveyor belt to another terminal where you are supposed to collect it all over again.

'No. No. That's okay,' you shriek. 'I'll keep it. I'm in a hurry. I've got—'

'No, sir. Sorry, sir. Pleased be advised, sir. Everything must go on the conveyor, sir. Do watch this out. Copy.'

That's how they speak. Honest.

'Yeah. But I can take this, can't I? I mean, it's hand baggage, I don't have to—'

'Regulations, sir. That's what they say. We're just the *donerers*.' (Whatever that means.) And it's goodbye to your luggage for at least a week, if you're lucky. For ever, if you're not.

'But it's a crazy system.' I've forgotten how many times I've tried to protest. 'I mean, what's the point? Why can't I just carry my own bag right out of the door there and into a cab like I do everywhere else in the world?'

'More efficient, sir.' They give you that putzy have-a-nice-day smile. 'It's for your own comfort and convenience. Enjoy.'

Comfort and convenience! How can it be for my comfort and convenience when I now have to struggle up and down God knows how many escalators, wait ages for one of those driverless shuttles, travel halfway across the southern States only to find when I finally get to the other terminal you-know-what isn't there.

'What did it say on the label, sir?' Some macho-homey who looks as though he's overdosed on honeydew melons starts giving me the third degree.

'There was no label.'

'But if there wasn't a label, sir, how can you expect—'

'Because it was hand luggage. In any case there weren't any labels at Charles de Gaulle. The whole place was on strike.'

'Yeah. But it should have . . .'

'And I'd got off the plane and you guys grabbed my bags. I didn't want to let go of them. But you guys said it would be—'

'But why didn't you put a—'

'Because nobody said anything about labels. In any case there weren't any labels around when they grabbed—'

'Because there should have been labels on it already.'

'There would have been if it wasn't hand luggage.'

'Well, it's not our responsibility then, is it?'

So what do I do? I start looking for a shop that sells shirts without gold tassels all over the place and a tie just a touch wider than a bootlace.

Take my advice. If you're going anywhere by plane and you want to stand any chance of ever seeing your luggage again:

1. Don't take any luggage with you.
2. If for some reason you don't feel you can survive a three-week round-the-world trip without at least a change of handkerchiefs, pack two suitcases. The odds on their losing two suitcases is about the same as there

being two bombs on the same plane: pretty reasonable.

3. But to be really, really safe – and I'm waiting to patent this idea – pack two suitcases and two briefcases. Put all the usual stuff in the suitcases, but put a complete set of essentials in each briefcase: razor, plugs, two shirts, three suits, two pairs of shoes. That way if the worst comes to the worst, and some Mrs Hitler with a personality bypass goes bananas and insists you check in everything except one measly item of hand luggage and they lose the rest, you're safe.

But whatever you do, make certain that if you're taking important papers with you, you also have a complete set in each briefcase. Don't do what I did recently. I was in a mad rush. I was working on these papers. I didn't have time to get them copied. So I just stuffed them all in one briefcase. What happened? You got it. They lost the briefcase, which means I've now got big problems trying to find the rest of . . .

Peter Biddlecombe
Luggage Enquiries
British Airways
Terminal 4
Heathrow

Vienna

It was Wednesday evening. I settled back in the famous couch. Draped all over it was a thick old-fashioned counterpane which looked as though Jo-fi, his favourite dog, had been using it as a mother substitute for years. My back was to the window. I lay my head down on the flat, dirty, lifeless, greasy pillow. There was a poor man's tapestry hanging halfway up the wall, presumably to stop me from hurting the wall when I started banging my head against it.

'Your Mutter. It is,' he began.

'I don't think I can blame my mother again,' I mumbled.

The beard and the glasses and the bald head nodded slowly. Jo-fi shuffled up to him, obviously suffering from some kind of neurosis.

'I mean, maybe it's just that I'm allergic to mountains of cream cakes, or Julie Andrews, or I'm suffering from sick building disease. Or perhaps it's ME disease. Or—'

'Your Mutter. It is, I am sure. Because . . .' The beard and the bald head nodded again. This time a little bit lower.

'Or maybe, between you, me and the bloke over there with the Schwarzwaldkirchentorte on his head, I just have this thing about Vienna. What I mean is, maybe I'm just schizophrenic about the place. I mean both of us are. If you see what I mean.'

'Your Mutter. Always it is die Mutter.'

Vienna – the big Apfel – makes me definitely schizophrenic.

Half of me loves the place. The whole time I'm there I'm in a Viennese whirl. The imperial grandeur. The baroque splendour. The unrelenting elegance. Never-ending corridors; Renaissance courtyards; crystal chandeliers; mile after mile of mirrors; lashings of marble. A thousand gilt-framed portraits of everyone who had anything to do with the Habsburgs, as well as probably everyone who ever shined their boots. Bookbinders; scientific instrument manufacturers; enormous, unbelievable cakes; music. Flowers cascading from balconies into immaculate gardens. Poetry in the trees in the Kartnevstrasse. Heavily scented magnolias. The old open air Naschmarkt. Cheese; coffee; a thousand different types and shapes and sizes of bread. Spiked helmets; medals; old soldiers. Turks selling spices; arabs banking all their money; Richard Tauber wandering carelessly through a cluster of tables and chairs.

Vienna is a beautiful middle-aged city. It is very clean, very classical, very pleasant, very, very civilised. Half of me is convinced they saw one of those old Hollywood movies of the Student Prince on his way through Vienna to meet Julie Andrews tripping around the hills and decided to make it look just like that – even down to the girls in white dresses with blue satin sashes.

It's one of the few cities I've been to in the world where even today I just know everybody, but everybody, instinctively maintains all the social graces and courtesies; where they still present their visiting cards on elegant silver plates; reply promptly to elegant invitations; spend their evenings at elegant soirées discussing Schoenberg's highly disciplined twelve-tone system, or chuckling about Beethoven's symphonies being written in one key and then suddenly switching into another, or giggling at the punchline in the final section of his Op.14 No.2 in G major, and deriding the English waltz which was only thirty beats to the minute compared to the Viennese which has sixty. Then afterwards, I'm sure they write pretty little thank-you-so-very-much notes to each other. Not because Mutter told them to – see Mother's influence again – or because they read about it in a book, but because it's in their blood. Blue blood, of course.

The more I wander around Vienna the more convinced I am that the centre is for wandering around, especially around Josefsplatz, probably my favourite baroque square in the world; and in the labyrinths of vast houses off Neutorgasse down near the river which are crammed with Bohemian crystal, Belgian tapestries and more marble statues than St Peter's in Rome; and the Hofburg, the sprawling complex of architectural treasures that was home to the Habsburgs and the seat of the Austro-Hungarian Empire, which not only ruled Europe from Spain to Transylvania, but did it with style.

And, mein Gott, did they have balls. Who wrote the music for the Society of Artists' gig in 1795? Some minor road musician called Ludwig van Beethoven. So impressed were the Viennese that a month later at yet another ball, meine Dame und mein Herr, back at the piano this time in person the one and only Ludwig himself playing selections from Haydn's greatest hits. Take it away Lud. So great was his success that he was back there in 1796 and again in 1814. He even launched his Eighth Symphony at another ball. A spectacular evening; it must have knocked spots off the last night of the Proms.

And what about the great ball after the Congress of Vienna in 1814 which, according to Jennifer of the *Tatler* – she must have been around at the time – was a dazzling affair attended by, can you imagine? in the left corner, Wellington, in the right corner, Metternich, and flitting backwards and forwards between the two, Talleyrand.

Just think what it was like in the time of the Hofbergs. The whole place must have been full of cavalry uniforms, fabulous horses, twenty-one-gun salutes, frock coats, crinolines whirling across polished dance floors and one imperial masked ball after another. Prince Rupert Ludwig Ferdinand zum Loewenstein-Wertheim-Freudenberg chatting up Princess Thing-of-Thing and Count-the-Spoons borrowing a fiver off the Duke of What's-it-called – that place-with-the-Big-Clock-in-the-middle-of-the-Town – and the Archduchess going on at the Archduke because he hadn't had any time off, as he promised, and what about a few days in this place called Sarajevo.

Waltzes. Military marches. Light music. Cabaret. Opera. Music is music in Vienna. It's not just something that hits you in swish elevators and luxury offices like in the States, where it is simply a means of increasing output by at least 25 per cent. It's serious stuff. Maybe not as serious as in the days of the Habsburgs when, if a ballerina slipped and fell or a poor tenor failed to hit the high note, they would be taken out and shot, or worse still made to appear on *The South Bank Show* with Melvyn Bragg. But serious enough actually to sit down and listen to. Damn it, they've even called the circular road that runs round the old city 'The Ring'.

And it's not just for the humans. In Vienna even the horses love music. Once when the fabulous Lippizaners, with their flowing white manes, performed outside the old neo-baroque City Hall, they tried to fob them off with muzak. It was a disaster. The horses refused to lift a hoof. They would only perform to the real thing.

Mozart, Strauss, Beethoven, Schubert: the four gods of Vienna; Haydn; even Wagner. You can hear them all in a single evening. *Parsifal*, *Fidelio* and *The Magic Flute*: you can see them all in a single week at the Staatsoper. Not to mention rare operas by Bartok; symphonies by Debussy; Gluck's *Alceste*; Lenny Kravitz, INXS and even the Black Crowes. In Vienna, music is music. There was once a time when Mozart was considered way out. Who knows, the same thing might happen to Lenny Kravitz. The Viennese might love their baroque but they like their roll as well.

Give or take Lenny Kravitz, Vienna is the top of the ops. Well that's how I heard one American describe it. Me, I would have said it was the Lieder of the Pack. Beethoven they love (sorry about that, Lenny). Although he was born in Bonn, he lived in Vienna for thirty-five years, in no less than sixty different houses and apartments. One of them, 8 Molker Bastei, was at the top of a spiral staircase with no less than 105 stone steps. Which makes you wonder whether they love him for his music or because he still owes them rent.

The problem, one Viennese culture-vulture who wore her wealth like a comfortable old spiked helmet told me, was that with so many productions pouring out one after another there was often little chance for rehearsal.

One of the big 'popera' stars, she said, rushed on stage one night straight from the airport completely unaware of what was going on. He sidled up alongside a chorus girl.

'Quick,' he hissed. 'Where is the tenor?'

'Mein Gott,' she snapped back at him, 'you are the tenor.'

'So who is your favourite tenor?' I asked the culture-vulture.

'Meinz Molecek,' she replied.

'Not Pavarotti?'

'My dear, no. He's so popular.'

Doctors, dentists, lawyers – even the old coffee-shop owners, they all have their own balls.

Once in the Redoutensaal, the old imperial ballroom next door to the National Library, a grand dame, who looked as though she had been around since Mozart started scribbling something he called *The Marriage of Convenience*, assured me quite confidently, 'This is where the president holds his balls and dances.'

First thing in the morning over a Wienes Frühstück; midday, taking a short cut along the pedestrian Karntnerstrasse; evenings dallying over an Indianerkrapfen, or even late at night, maybe especially late at night, walking back to the hotel trying to remember your way through the warren of old streets either side of Rotenturmstrasse after a long meeting at the office or, don't breathe a word back home, an evening at the opera, this, you feel, is an empire with no anger for its memories. It is at peace with itself. The whole place, I reckon, is like the Acropolis and should be rated – and treated – as such.

Then again, the other half of me feels as though whenever I am in Vienna I am squeezed between a baroque and a hard place.

Honest, Herr Doktor, I see nothing but the kitsch. Instead of beautiful furniture, sumptuous materials, paintings of mothers devotedly nursing their babies, children playing prettily in the sunshine, old women spinning away, clean, well-dressed peasants, I see grand but rotting seedy old baroque cafés and half-burnt museums. Instead of seeing everything in glorious Julie Andrews *Sound of Music* technicolour, I see it more in black and lime; Harry Lime.

Instead of going bananas over all the beautiful architecture, the silent squares, the long empty stairways, I have this phobia about all the dark, deep, mysterious courtyards and cellars. The Reisenrad, the giant wheel that has been doing the rounds in the Prater Fun Park since 1897; somehow it rings bells deep in my guilt-ridden, anxiety prone subconscious.

What about Hydrokultur? Does it really mean looking after goldfish? And those posters all over the place advertising what looks like a mini bed of nails which they say is for stopping cars from parking outside your house? This doesn't fool me one bit. I can recognise a masochistic fantasy when it hits me between the eyes.

I wander down the Karntnerstrasse, Vienna's number one shopping street where the tills are alive to the sound of cash. Coming out of Hanspeter Jucker, the big prestigious Swiss jewellers with their drooping eyes and hunched shoulders, are I imagine stand-ins for the Habsburg equivalent of Dad's Army.

And the dirty aluminium telephone boxes. Why do they look like one-man, self-contained padded cells? Is that why nobody in Vienna ever bangs on the side and tells you to hurry up, there's a queue outside?

Through a taxi's back window I once saw what I assumed was a house designed and built with absolute conviction by Wittgenstein. It looked as solid and as impenetrable as his *Tractatus Logico-Philosophicus*, the *Brief History of Time* of the 1920s. It made me realise that as a philosopher he wasn't much of an architect either.

And the sewers. Why is it that in Vienna I have this obsessional neurosis about sewers? Every time I go there I try to visit them. But I still haven't made it. They are always chock-a-block – with people, I mean. There are so many people visiting the sewers nowadays, hoping to catch a glimpse of Orson Welles disappearing round a corner, they are scaring the rats. In fact, I'm surprised some old English biddies haven't started a protection society to save the rats of Vienna.

And talking of sewers, everyone I ever meet seems to be an Archduke Dis, an Archduke Dat or a Count Nikolaus Bent Axel. I don't think I've ever met a plain, common-or-garden ordinary archduke. I'm not saying they're snobs, but if your name doesn't stretch to fifty-three syllables including the hyphens, and if your father was anything less than a grand duke, then I'm afraid you're not worth recognising in the Strasse, let alone crossing The Ring for. Don't call us, we'll call you. Titles are what counts. It's rank that is important. It doesn't matter whether some common-as-muck, less-than-human democrats voted out your titles a couple of hundred years ago, they are still yours by God-given right. And by God, in Vienna you will use them. And others will use them too.

Except for one man. Austria's most famous son. No, not Julie Andrews. No, not the housepainter, the only Viennese who didn't like Mozart (he preferred Wagner, and look at the problems that created). I mean the other Terminator, Arnold Schwarzenegger, whose philosophy in life is only slightly less complicated than Wittgenstein's: 'To defeat de enemy, to drive dem before you in baddle and den to hear not de lamentation of de womenfolk.'

Which is presumably why, whenever he flies home to see his liddle old mudder in Graz, he is welcomed by the Austrian president himself.

Am I being neurotic, Herr Doktor? Is our liddle old Arnie a mere vehicle for my prejudices? And that man over there, outside the seedy Hotel Regina opposite der Dom, the dark St Stephen's Cathedral (345 steps to the top of the south tower. You have to run up and down it six times to work off the effects of one Schwarzwaldkirschentorte); why he is wearing a hat and carrying an umbrella? I don't just mean carrying an umbrella. I mean carrying an umbrella like that. And that man in the Hauptbahnhof – why is he sitting like that, with his legs through the back of the bench? The old ladies who all look as though they were on intimate terms with Wagner; why are they wearing white? All over the world widows dress in black. You can't tell me that's not significant. What's more, whenever I see them they seem to be swallowing pills by the handful. Even walking down the Strasse.

And those choirboys. The Viennese always go on about their choirboys and how you must, but must, hear them singing 9.15 Mass in the marble and velvet royal chapel of the Hofburg. Which always makes me suspicious, for two reasons. Did you know Haydn's voice didn't break until he was sixteen? Until I knew that, he was my favourite composer. Not because of *The Creation*, but because he not only enjoyed hunting, he was also happy to be paid in wine. The other reason is that as far as I can see you only get good choirs where you get bad food. The best choirs come from the old universities and public schools which are certainly not famous for their good food. I mean how many famous American boys' choirs are there? In other words, watery cabbage, lumps of gristle and cold custard produce better choirs than hamburgers, hot dogs and triple chocolate milkshakes.

And, Herr Doktor, talking of choirboys, what about the Masons? There was I, sitting in my deckchair eating a chocolate éclair which the guy with the beard and the dog would obviously have described as 'long in shape but short in duration' and drinking a glass of a grossly pretentious dyethylene glycol to keep out the chill, when it suddenly struck me. Vienna is the Masonic capital of the world. I mean, it's obvious to anyone capable of rolling their trousers up and standing on one foot that Mozart was a Mason. His operas are all about the Masons. The guys who wrote the words were Masons. Look at the goings-on in *The Magic Flute*. That's all Masonic this and that. Sarastro is not your ordinary everyday ancient Egyptian kidnapper. Even Tamino thinks he is a high priest, a long way from home and way out of his depth. And what about the secret brotherhood? When was the last time you heard of a kidnapper having his own secret brotherhood? Come on. And what about the padlock? Who would possibly think of using a padlock to stop somebody from going on and on unless they were familiar with the Masonic Adoption and Initiation Rituals?

And why did he write the whole thing in four months? I know people who can't write an IOU in four months. Because Emanuel Schikaneder, who commissioned it, told him to, that's why. And he was also a Mason. Which brings me to another point.

Why did Mozart die so young? He was rich. He was famous. Look at all the CD contracts that were coming his way. I reckon, between you, me and him over there with the Schwarzwaldkirchentorte on his head, it was the Masons. Well, it's obvious isn't it? Once he spilled the beans about them in *The Magic Flute*, they had to get him. A bit like Mossad, today. All that business about Salieri being jealous and wanting Mozart out of the way because he was getting all the publicity is a lot of old nonsense. Think about it. If you're the grand secretary of the Masonic Lodge of True Unity (the Equity Branch) and you want someone out of the way, you hire your own guys to do it. Are you going to tell everybody what you've done? Of course not. You're going to shuffle the blame off on somebody else. Who better to point the finger at than poor old Salieri, Mozart's big rival. It's got to be them, hasn't it?

Of course, the other thing that could have got to poor old Mozart was the cholesterol. Thanks to Emperor 'I'm the Emperor and if I want dumplings, I'll have dumplings' Ferdinand and his neue Küche, Vienna is the cholesterol capital of the world. Cream cakes? In Vienna, whatever your complex, the last thing you can develop is a phobia about cream cakes. They have cream cakes designed for opera singers with cream on them as high as the Karwendel Mountains where the old farmers look as gnarled and weatherbeaten as the mountain itself and one village can be three, four or even five hours walk from another. They have great, big, round, soft, luscious cakes with more calories than the Viennese banks have illicit Arab dollars. They have croissants, bagels and coffee. In 1683 Vienna saw the birth of three of the greatest contributions ever made to Western civilisation; croissants, bagels and coffee. Where would we be today if we had jumped from 1682 straight to 1684?

Thanks to King Jan Sobieski of Poland and Duke Charles of Lorraine the Turkish siege of the city was lifted. The sultan's armies fled back across the Hungarian plains leaving behind their tents, their banners, their dead and sacks of mysterious brown beans. The croissant or, as the Austrians say, the Kipferl, is really, don't tell a soul, the Muslim crescent. The bagel is a roll shaped after the Polish king's stirrup. The mysterious brown beans they turned into every type of coffee you can imagine. Filter. Cappuccino. Melange, which is similar. Schwarz; plain black or espresso. Braun. Schwarz with cream. Mokka, the original Turkish coffee bequeathed to them after the Turks threw in their coffee beans. Einspanner, made in a glass with cream. Whipped. Maria Theresa, espresso with orange liqueur. Kaisermelange, melange with an egg added. Fiaker, black with rum. The next trick was to invent a machine for consuming them. This the Viennese did. They called it a café. As a result today there are more cafés in Vienna than there ever were Turks.

In Café Landtmann, which is the place for politicians and writers, I once heard a Frenchman, obviously a diplomat, boasting of the 'nombreuses serviettes de table' he had lifted from the 'Maison de Habsbourg'.

Demel, every Archduke claims, makes the best pastries in Vienna. And if they're the best in Vienna they're the best in the world. In Café Central, like Lev Bronstein – okay, Leon Trotsky – you can sit all day sipping coffee, staring into space and planning revolution against the people who worked hard all day long to earn a living for themselves and their families. I tried it once and gave up after five minutes. Instead I picked up the *International Herald Tribune*. On the front page was a story about a Viennese count. It said, 'Drunk gets nine months in violin case'.

Then there's Demel's K and K Hofzuckerbäckerei, sugar bakers to the Imperial Count. I went to Demel's once with one Wunderkind, a certain Herr Hoellrigt. I mean they are all so confident it makes you sick. By the time they're twenty-nine they think they've solved all the world's problems. For the rest of the world, of course, it's thirty-nine. I'm sure it must be all those marble staircases.

Herr Hoellrigt was helping a Dutch company get round the EC sanctions against Serbia by selling them half his factory so that they could make beds in Austria, which is of course outside the EC and supply everything they could possibly make to the Serbs. Did he have a guilt complex about it?

'No, no guilt complex,' he told me. 'I am the Claus von Bulow of the bed industry. I will never be found guilty. But I should never have done it.'

Wasn't he worried?

'Who talks about little Austria?' he said tucking into another Schneeballen, a huge, twisted mass of sugared pastry. 'Nobody. The only time they talked about us was when Waldheim was president.

I protested.

'Nonsense.' He stabbed his Schneeballen with his spoon and rummaged in his jacket pocket. 'See.' He waved a bunch of letters under my nose. 'Look for yourself. All my letters from the States go first to Australia. Then they send them to Vienna. Now you tell me we're important.'

The only thing that struck me as important at the time was, why does Demel put the jam on top of the chocolate while its butter-sweet rival, the elegant wood-panelled café in the Sacher Hotel, puts the jam inside its famous, rich, dark, Sachertorte. Why didn't Wittgenstein sort out that problem instead of worrying about less important things like logic, mathematics and metaphysics.

Then there is the whole question of food and drink. I've never known anybody wolf down as much as the Viennese. Home-made beef broth; blood sausages with sauerkraut; bone-marrow slices on dark brown bread; boiled beef with roast potatoes, beans and a glacier of horseradish; venison in juniper with a mountain of potato strudel; a slab of krusti brot, smeared with Liptauer, a lip-tingling, spicy paprika cream cheese, and Krauter Gervats, Austria's answer to cream cheese and chives washed down with a young white wine. Practically a whole pig's leg; a pile of potatoes as high as the Habsburg Palace and enough cream, salad, horseradish and mustard to float it halfway down the Danube; great huge dumplings; goulash; enormous Wiener Schnitzels. Roast pork and sausages served at a long wooden bench in an open-air wine garden to an accordion playing Schrammel music. Gigantic strudels; iced coffees in knickerbocker-glory glasses with more whipped cream in them than coffee.

This is no place for the weight-watcher, or the 'calorifically challenged', as I once heard an American describe himself in Figlmullers as he began tucking into a Wiener Schnitzel the size of a dinner plate.

Then there's all the booze. I'm no Freudian, but I reckon the Viennese must suffer not only from empty plate phobia but full bottle phobia as well. A deadly combination, at least in terms of cholesterol, if ever there was one. See an empty plate. They immediately want to bury it. See a full bottle. They immediately want to empty it. No wonder they do all that waltzing. It must help to keep their weight down. What am I saying? None of them look as though they are worried about keeping their weight down. They probably do all that waltzing just to stop themselves from getting even fatter so they can carry on eating and drinking as much as they like.

In the old days you'd no sooner get off a train from anywhere east of Vienna than you'd find yourself in a bar or café around St Rupert's Church, or near the casino, or in the cellars at Oswald und Kallo which has hardly changed since the kaiser was a boy, chatting to every Third Man in a trilby and trenchcoat and a funny accent about what you saw, what you didn't see and when you were going to go back again.

One evening in the Imperial, which seems to be one of the favourite business hotels, all *fin de siècle*, Carrara marble, and silk damask on the walls, one staid bowler hat and pinstripe suit – 'Two beers, allegro,' he said to the barman – told me that thirty years before when he was a wild, long-haired, bohemian student, he had got involved in a road accident just outside Prague and spent two nights in gaol. When he got back to Vienna he didn't have to buy a drink for a week, so many strange men in trilbies and trenchcoats wanted to talk to him about his experiences.

And the Habsburgs thought the Austro-Hungarian Empire was dead and buried. No way. Their melody lingers on. The old Habsburg Austro-Hungarian Empire, or the Austrarian-Hungry Empire, with its spiked helmet and droopy moustache, is not exactly going to strike back. But it's not exactly dead either. I kept stumbling over it. The Austro-Hungarian Haydn Orchestra. The Austro-Hungarian Hydrokultur Society which didn't have anything to do with goldfish. The Austro-Hungarian Preservation Society. And the more I stumbled over it the more questions I found one half of me asking the other.

Didn't they have a monarch who sat still and refused to move with the times?

Didn't one of their princes have an affair with a commoner?

Didn't they believe in old buildings and conserving everything that was ancient and crumbling?

Didn't they honour composers who wrote pop classics?

Weren't their politicians bumbling and incompetent and, well, always at the mercy of events rather than in control of them?

Didn't they have problems trying to, well, enforce law and order in parts of their empire?

Weren't they, towards the end, at the mercy of another, shall we say, force which dragged them kicking and screaming into the nineteenth century?

What does it mean? What does it signify? I mean, in Freudian terms. Does it mean what I think it means? Or does it not mean what I think it doesn't mean?

The last of the Habsburgs is a mild-mannered 81-year-old Euro MP with a grey moustache, known to his friends as 'Your

Imperial and Royal Highness, Archduke Franz Josef Otto Robert Maria Anton Karl Max Heinrich Sixtus Xavier Felix Renatus Ludwig Gaetan Pius Ignatius of Austria'. He lives in Germany, and is a member of the Bavarian-based Christian Social Union as well as leader of the Pan-European Movement, which thinks Maastricht is nowhere near tough enough when it comes to building a new Holy Roman Empire. But the shame of it. His son is – wait for it – the host of a television game show. Somehow, in spite of that, the family still harbours ambitions. Shortly after the Berlin Wall came down papa was invited to become president of Hungary. But he said nein. The president is elected by parliament. If he was going to be president he wanted to be elected by the people. The democratically elected parliament disagreed. So today he is still languishing amidst the gastronomic excesses of Brussels and Strasbourg.

A Euro MP he may be, but he wields real power. At least, before lunch. For years he has flatly refused all requests to allow scientists to examine the remains of poor old Crown Prince Rudolf who made such a name for himself at Mayerling. He has also refused to allow anyone to see a bundle of papers which are supposed to reveal – at last – the truth. Did the silly, impressionable Baroness Mary poison them both? Did he have a heart attack, as old Franz Josef maintained? Was it a bullet in the head, as the doctor said? Or did Rudolf realise Baroness Mary had mucked everything up, shoot her and then shoot himself? Some say the Archduke withholds the papers to protect the reputation of the Habsburgs. Others say it is because he is negotiating with *Hello!* magazine and the price is still not right. My theory is that the cheque never arrived. It is still in some post office in New South Wales.

Now don't get me wrong. Vienna doesn't, on the one hand, make me feel like the wolfman; nor on the other hand does it make me hysterically miserable. It doesn't depress me as much as it did Crown Prince Rudolf, with or without the help of a seventeen-year-old girl. And I don't pace up and down my hotel room for hours without saying a word. But I will admit,

Herr Doktor, it does make at least one half of me feel like doing something reckless like throwing away my tie, dissecting a cat and going off to live in a cottage in Norway. It makes the other half of me feel like going off to Sluka's under the town hall and gorging myself on Guglhupf.

Then suddenly Jo-fi leapt off the couch. The beard, glasses and bald head mumbled, 'It's always the . . .' The bloke with the Schwartzwaldkirchentorte on his head had disappeared. But I swear one of the funny old idols on his desk winked at me.

The whole thing must have been another of my diseased Freudian anxiety dreams dredged up from the depth of my subconscious.

Copenhagen

Many years ago there was a country that was so uncommonly fond of funny shapes and crazy way-out designs that everybody spent all their money on them without knowing what the hell they were. Clocks looked like knives and forks. Even a simple wristwatch looked like anything but a simple wristwatch.

'Wristwatch? That's not a wristwatch, that's a spoon,' I said, in fear and trembling. I was in one of those swish shops in the Stroget, the big shopping street in the middle of Copenhagen. I was wrong: it was a towel rail. Although how the hell towels would hang on it I do not know.

I once spent half an hour in an office in Kastelsvej, near the British embassy, looking for the telephone. In desperation, I asked a secretary to point it out to me. It was shaped like a sick hedgehog. I'd been sticking pencils into it all the time.

If the Dutch are obsessed with right angles and straight lines, the Danes believe everything should be like an inside-out, twisted-upside-down parallelogram in four dimensions, suspended halfway between the third and fourth astral planes. Circles are always square. Straight lines are always circular. Triangles come out looking like squares. It's as if every Danish designer is high on drugs. Which, of course, they probably are.

Actually, I'm convinced Kierkegaard wrote *Fear and Trembling* wandering around Copenhagen, not because he wanted to share the 'dizziness of freedom' but because he was wondering if what he had bought was a corkscrew or whether it was going to blow up in his face and prove all his existentialist ideas were a lot of nonsense.

You think I'm exaggerating! So who designed the Sydney Opera House with its flying roof and a stage too small for a grand opera even though the Australians never realised? And where did he come from? Who designed Mitterrand's drive-a-nuclear-submarine-through-the-middle-of-it Grande Arche? And where did he come from?

An English accountant told me that on his first visit to Copenhagen he had been given somebody else's office to work in. He had spent the whole of the first morning picking up his secretary's shoe and shouting, 'Put me through, put me through' at it. He only discovered the mistake when she came in at lunchtime and asked for it back.

It's as if all that raping and pillaging, or maybe all those single-sex marriages they go in for, affected their brains and sent them into a collective spin from which they have never recovered.

Don't get me wrong. God knows, if anyone yearns for good, practical design I do. Hardly a day goes by when my wife does not throw a fit trying to tear a simple packet of soap powder limb from limb shrieking, 'Designed by a man, I bet you anything it was . . . designed by a man.' Crash. One of the cats goes hurtling through the window. Bang. The fridge door shatters into a thousand pieces. Wallop. The two of them go spinning across the kitchen floor, down the steps into the sitting room and end up, thump, in a heap by the door, the packet of soap power still unopened.

Once I got back from a trip and found her wrestling a packet of turkey slices to the kitchen floor, one foot on one end, her teeth on the other. Still she couldn't open it.

Another time I got back to find her attacking one of those tiny boxes of milk on top of the red-hot oven. She had a six-inch knife in one hand. The other was precariously holding the poor innocent little packet of milk. Schung. The knife plunged at the heart of the box. Schunk. It missed. It was my fault. Again.

'Now look at what you've made me do. If it wasn't for you I could have—'

'But I've only just come—'

'So it's my fault, is it? It's always my—'

I tiptoed past. Schung. This time the knife was embedded in the top surrounding the – Schung. Now it was reverberating in the gap between the oven and the – Schschungung. I didn't have the courage to—

'Men. Designed by men,' she shrieked. 'It's always the same. The bloody men don't have to—' Thud. The milk carton shot across the kitchen floor. The cats – we have seven cats – leapt for the eighth of their nine lives. Smash. Right into the cats' dishes, it crashed. Kit-e-Kat, yesterday's leftovers, this evening's smoked salmon which would have been for me except that I deliberately made the plane seven and a half minutes late, all went splattering over the floor.

'Men,' she shrieked. 'Bloody men. They don't have to open the bloody—'

I bent down and, taking my life in my hands, picked up the packet. She had been trying to open the wrong end.

'Of course I don't expect you to agree.' She slammed the door. 'You're a man.'

A marketing manager I know, who lives with his French girlfriend, has the opposite problem. She does exactly what it says on the packet. Except, he told me, he has a hell of a time trying to find packets that say, Peel here. For a whole week he lived off Tesco's corned beef, but he wouldn't have changed it for anything.

Could the Great Danes make my life less, well, interesting? No way. Trouble is, nobody has the courage of a small child to tell them their designs are nonsense and will they please start taking the tablets and turning out sensible, practical things that we can all recognise and love.

Like fridge doors that close whenever you force your wife to accidentally leave them open. Like earrings that are not magnetically attracted to the bottom of electric toasters so that you spend days turning the house upside down because you did not understand the second law of domestic magnetism. Like keys that insist on finding their own way back to the fourth nail on the left of the barn door instead of jumping into someone's shopping bag and ending up in Broadcasting House.

So the Danes go on churning out the most beautifully designed load of old rubbish. Lamps that look like a cross between a wastepaper basket and a dustbin. I ask you. A lamp. You have to stand it in the corner; it's so big it takes up half the room; and to switch it on you have to scramble around on your hands and knees searching for the beautifully designed, oh-so-concealed switch because a normal switch would upset the practical functionalism of the design. And KD or Knock Down furniture which seems to me to be nothing but a mass of beautifully designed shapes in a beautifully designed box never to be assembled unless you've failed a degree in post-modern deconstruction for the third time.

And of course – you've got it! – Lego, those wretched pop-and-pull bricks from the Danish 'leg godt' which I'm convinced means, You'll never believe how many parents buy these stupid little coloured plastic bricks for their kids because they think they're educational and then refuse to let them play with them in case they swallow them. Who on earth could come up with something called Lego but a repressed sect of fundamentalist Danish Christians motivated by a sense of love and community? Love of money, that is, because I cannot think of any other reason why anyone should want to devote their lives to building models of London, linked by models of trains to a model of the Channel Tunnel linked by another model train smelling of models of garlic to a model of Paris full of models going around doing what models always go around doing in Paris.

Community because, damn it, if it takes 2,702,197 bricks to build a Dutch windmill you'll need some help or you'll have no life left to live by the time you get to brick number 2,702,196, if you haven't choked on one by then.

I once spent a morning being dragged around the Royal

Museum of Scotland in Edinburgh by a Danish banker. The exhibition featured a nuclear submarine made of 270,000 pieces of Lego. It symbolised, he told me, 'human values'. To me all it symbolised was a complete waste of time. For the designer. For the poor guy who built the thing. And especially for me when I could have been doing something far more useful, like making with the Danish pastries or comparing the relative merits of a 12-year-old MacCallan with a 13-year-old with a 14-year-old with a . . .

For all the claims that Lego is not a toy but a 'universal concept of play embodying creativity and self-expression', to me it's been responsible for creating misery and poverty all over the world. If I was Russian, or Chinese, or from any fast-growing developing country, I'd be busy building my own real-life 102,981,500-piece nuclear bomb to drop on Lego's headquarters in Billund, Jutland. For I reckon they are all living and working and dying in buildings that look as though they were designed by Danish architects who got hooked on Lego at an early urge and have been unable to break the habit.

Some unkind people I have come across actually refer to Denmark itself as Lego Land. Which is unfair. Because I wish I had said it first. But the more I go there, the more true it becomes. As for the Danes, I reckon they are the most isolated, insular and homogenous people in Europe.

They lost one war after another. They have had one chunk of territory snatched from them after another. They even lost their fleet to the likes of Nelson and Wellington. Instead of fighting back like any sensible nation would have done and getting killed in the process, they decided to stay at home, build a giant Lego wall around their magic land and disappear up their own Lego turrets. As a result, today they seem to be living in a world of their own, with their own values, standards and logic which, even a child can see, is completely unrelated to the real world.

Take their so-called progressive welfare system. In order to reduce unemployment, the state not only pays the fiercely egalitarian Danes £6 an hour to hire domestic servants, they encourage dustmen to volunteer to go unemployed at different times of the year to give their jobs to their unemployed colleagues.

Education. The Danes have the most chaotic educational system in the world. Because if any two or three parents want to get together and start their own school, the government will give them all the money they want to do their own thing. Ask them if there is any connection between that and the high crime rate among children and they will tell you it's because they suffered from complications at birth and neglect because the parents were too busy going round opening new schools with government money. Not that they're not tackling the problem. In Nysted, in order to keep children off the streets the town council has come up with a solution that only a Danish council could dream up. They've asked the children to re-write the minutes of their council meetings because, they say, nobody can understand the reports written by the officials. Presumably they suffered complications at birth and neglect from their parents who were too busy setting up new schools, and, therefore, were never taught to write properly.

Prisons. The toughest thing a prisoner in Denmark has to decide is whether to run – what am I saying, run? I mean stroll casually through the open gates – or hang around for a couple of hours until he's locked in and go through all the bother of turning the key and letting himself out.

I tell you, two days in Copenhagen and even I'm looking for their popular do-it-yourself family guide to suicide. The only thing that's stopped me so far is their bicycle laws. A country that has the toughest bicycle laws in the world has got to be a country to be admired.

Accidentally turn into one of their bicycle lanes and in a split second you'll feel the wrath of their ancestors, who between the eighth and tenth centuries terrorised Europe, discovered America and plunged deep into Russia. I don't recommend it.

Given all this, you'll be surprised to hear that Denmark is

the one country in Europe where women have more than their fair share of the action. They have six months' maternity leave; child-care facilities, open from 7 a.m. to 5 p.m., that make the Savoy look like a Holiday Inn; free choice over abortion; and deliberately high prices on everything that even looks like booze and so that the fellas have no choice but to go home early for dinner. And if the fellas don't go home early for dinner, no problem. Denmark was the first country in the world to legalise same-sex marriages.

'Heidi, do you take Heidi to be your lawful partner?'

'Heidi, do you take Heidi to be your lawful partner?'

That's it. You're married. But don't invite me to the reception because they'll all be at it as soon as they get there – smoking, I mean.

While they insist that taxi drivers refuse tips, hotel porters help with your luggage, shop assistants actually serve you in the shops, and you don't get skin cancer – throughout the summer Danish radio broadcasts special bulletins telling you how long it is safe to stay outside in the sun *au naturel* – they think nothing of engulfing you in great clouds of nicotine. Finland banned smoking in public in 1976. Norway banned it in 1988. Sweden toughened up its already tough law in 1993. But in Denmark there are fags everywhere. In fact, I can't quite remember seeing so many fags in one place anywhere else in the world. Queen Margrettine does it, apparently at the rate of sixty a day, even though she has already had one tumour removed. Which had nothing, of course, to do with smoking.

One woman, a member of the Smokers' Rights Association, did it on television. Immediately after giving birth. The baby was said to be coughing well and asking for a pipe.

And as in any organisation where women want nothing but their fair share, they always end up by dominating the place. Which is why, I reckon, for forty years, while the outside world wrestled with the problems of the Cold War and got involved with nasty things like nuclear weapons and missiles and Richard Nixon, the Danes were happy to smoke their cigarettes, sip their half glasses of organic elderflower juice, enjoy the protection of

NATO and watch other people fighting their battles for them without ever letting those wicked foreign soldiers let alone even more wicked nuclear missiles on their soil.

Similarly the European Community. It existed purely for their advantage. They had no duty or obligation to contribute to it. NATO had been a one-way street; so should the European Community. For twenty years they enjoyed all the good things the Community had to offer. They were happy to see the wicked witches of Brussels casting their spells and making everybody else buy their butter and bacon and cheese. But did the Danes let the Germans buy their pretty little country cottages? Did they change their rules on VAT? Did they open up their market to the rest of Europe? Did they allow even their fellow Scandinavians to come into their pretty little rose-tinted paradise without a passport? Did they hell.

You think the British are one-sided about Europe. Try talking to a Dane, especially a Danish woman, about Europe and you'll realise that the British are models of European enlightenment and understanding.

The Danes are convinced there is only one good fairy, even though she might be waving a cigarette instead of a wand and have nicotine up to her elbows, and that is Denmark. The rest of the world is full of hunchbacked old crones whose duty it is to love, honour, and keep the good fairy supplied with fags. The amazing thing is that the whole place is not covered in crèches and cigarette smoke. Instead it all looks as if it has been put together using a giant box of Lego: Scandinavian, clean and tidy. Economy edition.

The streets all look the same; bright and spotless. Nobody crosses the road until the lights change because they're scared of being knocked over by the Queen, who is usually out scouring the city on her funny old-fashioned big green bicycle smothered in clouds of cigarette smoke, looking for a missing dachshund, while hubby, *le très grand* Comte Henri de Laborde de Monpezat, is back home cuffing the kids and everybody in sight for leaving the door open and letting the dog escape.

The traffic, when it arrives all looks the same; five million bicycles and two Mercedes. The bicycles are always the same funny old-fashioned big green bicycles no midwife would be seen dead riding through the back lanes of Barchester. Perched on the back is always the same pretty mini-Heidi. Riding alongside her is always another pretty mini-Heidi or a Heidi with a haircut.

The buildings all look the same. All the royal palaces look as though they have been well scrubbed. The parliament building looks calm and unruffled. The old churches look bright and clean and innocent. The office buildings look as if they've hardly been used. Even the Little Mermaid, who really is a little mermaid, looks as though she has had a good wash behind the ears.

The bars in the brightly painted old houses along Nyhavn overlooking the canals look as though not so much as a molecule let alone a drop of beer has been spilt on the floor since they were built over 200 years ago. Leave your credit card behind in a restaurant, it is still there when you go back; unused, untampered with, uncopied; completely dust-free.

The food is all the same; herring, herring and more herring. In France, they boast of the variety of their food. In Denmark they boast that it is all the same: 'Herring. We serve it in thirty-two different ways,' says one restaurant.

'Herring; the way you want it; thirty-five ways to choose,' says another.

'Herring; hundreds of recipes. The choice is yours,' says another.

They've obviously been so successful blackmailing other people to take bacon they've got nothing but herring for themselves.

Well, that's not quite true. They've got a few bits and pieces, but not enough to make a full meal. These pieces they slice into even smaller pieces, allocate sparingly to huge slices of bread and call a smorgasbord or smorgas-bored, depending on whether it is your first or second attempt. At the first attempt, it tastes of plaster. At the second attempt you just get bored.

And the people, they all look the same; one half look like Heidi, take care of the house and do the shopping; the other half look like Heidi with a haircut, take all the decisions and are virtually all priests. They're the women.

But I saw none of this on my first trip to Copenhagen.

Vroom. Vroom.

Gobble. Gobble.

Slurp. Slurp.

Vroom. Vroom.

That was my first visit to wonderful, wonderful Copenhagen.

How long did I have to soak in 800 years of history? About 80 minutes. Including the taxi from the airport into town and a taxi out of town and back to the airport. Including a slap-up three-course meal at the swish Hôtel d'Angleterre near the Royal Theatre. I've had many gastronomic blurs in my life, but this was the first one caused by the clock. Usually there are more exciting reasons.

I had been invited to speak at a conference in Aarhus, the second city in the country and the home of Denmark's famous Women's Museum, which along with the Erotic Museum is high on my list of places not to visit, especially as a few days earlier *The Times* had carried a report saying, 'Home Secretary to act on Danish video nasties'. The organisers insisted I came via Copenhagen, which struck me as odd. But then many things in this life strike me as odd. When I got to Copenhagen I discovered why.

I was met by the managing director of the company organising the show who looked less like a strapping great Viking and more like another interior designer, complete with long blond hair and earring. 'Quick. Quick!' he said. 'I need you.'

My mind boggled. Did he want my advice on some yellow curtains he was thinking of buying to go with a purple what-on-earth-is-it in the corner? No way. He wanted me for my body. As an excuse for a very late lunch or a very early dinner.

'Here in Denmark everything is so frightfully expensive,' he gushed shaking my hand and making a grab for my briefcase. 'I can't afford to go to a restaurant on my own money. I can only go for the company. If you would be so kind as to . . .'

Never one to refuse to help a poor struggling interior designer in his hour of need, I immediately agreed. Although I admit I might have been a little bit more forthcoming if it hadn't been for the long blond hair and earring.

'Lead on, Hamlet,' I said.

A car appeared. We were off. Vroom. Vroom. Out of the airport we zoomed, past the building works – there are always building works at airports. On to a tiny motorway, past some scrubby-looking trees. Oops, that's the end of the motorway. Lego roadsigns shoot past. That way there's a church. How do I know? Because there is a silhouette of a church on the roadsign. Clever designers, these Danes. A field. No, it's a football pitch. Are they playing? I couldn't see.

The taxi driver tells us he isn't really a taxi driver. He is a flower farmer. With his father, he grows sweet peas. They are the only ones left in the whole of Denmark growing sweet peas on a commercial basis. Prices, as a result, are high. But not high enough to support him all year round. For two months of the year he has to work as a taxi driver to make ends meet.

'Times are hard,' he says. I begin to feel sorry for yet another poor farmer. 'But, of course, I have three months holiday,' he adds.

We now shoot past some nondescript Lego houses. Are they offices or flats or just more great slabs of Lego? Quick. A tricycle with two children sitting precariously in a giant box on the front two wheels. Now we're in the Centrum. Another tricycle. A jogger. More traffic. A big square. Past the Danish Industries headquarters. Bet that's the town hall. Along by a canal. This is just like Amsterdam. Tall, thin, narrow homes. That's probably the Opera . . . We're there. The Hôtel d'Angle-terre. We're out of the taxi, across the pavement, in through the door. Our coats we hang up ourselves – it's quicker – and make straight for a window seat looking out directly on the square outside.

Everything is very discreet, very elegant. Certainly not your typical Danish smorgasbord outfit: black suits, long white aprons, black bow ties. The maître d' looks like a kindly home secretary in a video nasty. He is wearing a dinner jacket, striped pants and a striped tie. It's a warm, almost clubby atmosphere. 'A menu, sir.'

But we're there for business. None of the social pleasantries you get in Italian restaurants when you go in for a quick lasagna and come out five hours later 2,300 calories heavier, over £100 lighter and a lifelong friend of the family. These guys were obviously geared up to the eighty-minute airport rush.

Wonder about the lobster. Hesitate over the prawns. Ask whether they've been sautéed in wine. No way. I was looking at the roulade d'anguille farcie (stuffed eel swiss roll).

'Have the lobster,' the waiter said.

'Okay,' I agreed immediately.

'Followed by Chateaubriand,' said Hamlet.

'Okay, okay,' I nodded.

He ordered lobster and the Chateaubriand for two people. For himself. And the same again. For me.

'The wine list, please,' he gasped.

My eyes were spinning. An ordinary bottle of Sancerre was over £30. A Chablis nearly £50. Champagnes were higher still. And the clarets? A bottle of Château Lafite 1985 was £199. A bottle of Château Mouton Rothschild, £229. A Haut-Brion? I couldn't bear to look.

'Quick. Quick.' He called back the wine waiter almost before he'd left the table. 'We'll have a bottle of champagne.' Fantastic, I thought. 'And a bottle of Chablis.' Wow. 'And two bottles of Château Lafite.' Oh la la. This was going to be an occasion to try and remember. On a £-per-minute basis it was already the most expensive meal I'd ever eaten – and I hadn't even seen the food yet.

Back came the waiter. 'A small appetizer,' he smiled. 'On the house.'

An appetizer. Free. This guy must have been a regular. The

champagne arrived, was uncorked and poured gently, lovingly into two enormous balloons. Hamlet grabbed the glass, took a quick gulp. 'Fine,' he gasped. 'Fine. If you would be so . . .'

Our glasses were topped up. We were off. Before I'd taken a sip, the lobsters arrived. They were the size of a Danish longboat. Two minutes 35 seconds, we finished. There were skidmarks all over my plate.

'Would monsieur like one . . .?' the wine waiter arrived with the Chablis.

'Yes, of course. Please.'

Into the same glasses it went. There was no time for frivolous social niceties like clean glasses. This was raw survival in a high price economy. The Chablis was gone.

'And now,' Hamlet called to the wine waiter, 'the Lafite. We'll have the . . .' Vroom. Straight into the same glasses.

The Chateaubriand arrived. Vroom. It was gone. So was the Lafite.

'Dessert,' he was now saying. 'What shall we have for . . .?'

'Well, I must admit,' I groaned.

'No, no, nonsense. You must have dessert. You cannot come to Copenhagen and not have dessert.'

It was now three and a half minutes to five. We had been eating for exactly thirty-five minutes. We had shifted in half an hour what would normally take in, say, a London restaurant, allowing for the poor service, three weeks, two days and as long as it takes to attract the wine waiter.

Once, in the Bow Wine Vaults just off Cheapside in the City of London, we waited so long for the girl who was in charge of the wine that the guy I was with pulled out his mobile telephone and dialled the restaurant's switchboard.

'Hey,' he barked into his mobile, 'I'm on the table by the window. I'd like the wine waiter, please.'

It was brilliant. It was the first time I appreciated the real value of mobile phones.

I looked up. Our waiter was busy on the next table mixing something with two slices of orange and half a gallon of Grand Marnier.

'A small rest before the next . . .?' he smiled across at us.

'No.' Hamlet practically leapt out of his dark pinky-cream striped chair. 'No. We'll—' He tried to relax as best he could, bearing in mind the pressure he was under. '. . . We'll carry straight on.'

'We have crêpes suzettes . . .' Vroom. There they were on the table.

'Well, perhaps I'll have some cheese,' I hesitated. 'Danish. Do you have any Danish?'

The waiter looked at me. Hamlet didn't bat an eyelid. He was buried in his crêpe suzette, the funny Grand Marnier thing, and some kind of chocolate cake as well.

My cheese arrived. 'This is Danish,' the waiter said, pointing to the Edam.

'Port. Would you . . .?' There it was, on the table, in a chilled glass.

I gobbled down my Danish Edam. I glugged back the port. Hamlet looked at his watch. It was ten past five. We had been there all of 46 minutes. My plane to Aarhus was leaving in 25 minutes. It was time to move.

'Just one more port,' he said.

'No, no,' I protested. 'I'm afraid . . .'

'But it would only take . . .'

'Only one? Are you . . .?' I hesitated.

'Sure,' he said. Vroom. They were on the table.

I gulped down my port as though it was Coke. 'Okay, let's go,' I burbled.

I looked at my watch. We'd been there for $48\frac{1}{2}$ minutes. My plane left in $22\frac{1}{2}$ minutes.

Hamlet leapt up and went chasing after the maître d'. 'The bill, the bill,' he was screaming.

I looked at my watch. We had been in there exactly 51 minutes. The couple behind had arrived before us, but they were still on their lobster.

In the distance, I saw him signing the . . . I leapt up and . . . ran out . . . taxi . . . Vroom. Vroom. Skid. Screech.

'This is the final call for Aarhus. Will passengers go straight to the departure gate. The plane is ready to leave.'

I got there as the door was closing. My stomach arrived three days later.

Trips since then – Copenhagen is the ideal jumping-off point for southern Sweden – have not been so hectic. Either my body has lost its appeal or the rate of inflation has eased back. But they have no way changed my mind.

I am also convinced that every time I go there, the place is more overrun with crazy designers. But it does, as they say, make life very entertaining, especially as they all seem to compete to make the craziest, most way-out, most useless designs you cannot possibly imagine. What's more, all their crazy, way-out designs seem to have the wonderful knack of making anyone who looks at them abandon their critical faculties and go ape about how fantastic and functional and modernist they are. Which is not surprising, I suppose, bearing in mind the whole place literally hero-worships a neurotic misfit like Hans Christian Andersen, the most politically incorrect writer of all time, who came from a town called, appropriately enough, Odense, and made up daft stories about a Little Mermaid who for love traded her voice for a pair of legs. What amazes me is that a country which is supposed to worship straightforward functional shapes and designs selected as their national emblem a mermaid whose shape is neither straightforward nor functional for either one thing or the other.

But don't take my word for it. Wander along the Nyhavn canal. It is lined with beautifully restored nineteenth-century tall ships. All the houses are painted in rich ochres and pale marine blues. I see some antiquarian bookstalls and stroll across to them. A group of Danes are looking at the strangest of shapes in a shop window nearby. It could be anything from a cocktail stick to a set of traffic lights.

'Oh, er – it's different, quite the finest thing I've ever seen,' says Claudius.

'The design and the colours – oh yes, they please me immensely,' gushes Gertrude.

Nearby is Amalienborg Palace, home of our chain-smoking, bicycle-loving, fairly average book illustrator who in her spare time doubles up as Queen. I head for the palace. Maybe there's another search party going out for another missing dog. Maybe Henrik is thumping somebody else round the ears.

I pass another shop. In the window there is what looks to me like a pile of nuts and bolts.

'The space. Just look at the space that encompasses. Isn't that remarkable?' says Polonius.

To me the remarkable thing isn't the nuts and bolts but the fact that these Danish pastries are now so sophisticated they no longer appreciate the designs themselves. Instead they just adore the space the designs occupy. I know it's rude, but I couldn't help it. I stopped and stared at them.

'Fabulous,' they were whispering to each other outside a shop called Bogmarked, which had huge signs in the window saying 'Lavpris'.

I passed another shop called Holme Gaard of Copenhagen. 'This will divide the wise men from the fools,' I heard a middle-aged Laertes say, pointing to the lush glassware inside.

It was the same all along the Stroget from Kongens Nytorv down to Town Hall Square and the Tivoli Gardens – the world's longest continuous shopping precinct, say the Great Danes. Everywhere everybody is ooh-ing and ah-ing at designs in shop windows. Not the products. Just the designs. I begin to feel like the kid in that story by what's-his-name.

'A lovely piece of stuff, isn't it?'

It looked like a three-week-old pizza. Honest!

'Quite the finest thing I've ever seen,' said a blond Laertes with an earring in his eyebrow!

'It has my very highest approval,' said ... said ... whoever was with him.

Everybody else agreed. 'Oh, it's very beautiful. Magnificent. Delightful. Excellent,' they purred.

I couldn't tell you whether it was a lawnmower, a box of

dates or a cat's liver. Now, I ask you, it's got to be a con hasn't it? I mean all those crazy designs. All those crazy people ooh-ing and ah-ing at all that stuff in the windows. I mean, you can't even tell what it is, can you? Then it hits me. If I can't make any sense of these crazy designs, then I need help. On the basis that drugs give you a completely opposite picture of reality, the only people who can help me make out what the stuff is all about are the guys on drugs. To them it probably all looks serious and sensible and terrible practical.

I get a cab to Christiania, the way-way-out hippie Free State from drug addicts, drug pushers, drop-outs and nice cleancut Danish students who cannot afford the high rents for flats in the city. This time the taxi driver grows orchids and can only afford four months holiday a year, one month of which he spends at an old Nazi prison camp at Frosler in the south of Denmark which apparently does a roaring trade as a bed-and-breakfast hotel for German tourists.

When I get there, Christiania is empty. Only in Denmark could it happen. All the drug dealers are on strike. Instead of buying their supplies openly everybody is racing round town trying to get their daily fix on the black market.

I'm left with no alternative but the Tivoli Gardens, the idea of a creepy Danish journalist who wanted to suck up to King Christian VIII. 'People who are enjoying themselves do not complain,' he told him. Such a startlingly original thought had never occurred to the poor old king, who sounds as if he was another creation from the diseased mind of Hans Christian. But there and then he gave orders for the military grounds outside the city's western gate to be cleared. The Tivoli was born.

To the Danes it's the cultural and religious equivalent of the Great Wall of China, St Peter's and the Wailing Wall rolled into one. So much so that during the war, when the Nazis wanted to retaliate against the Danish resistance, what did they do? They bombed all the tulips in the Tivoli Gardens.

I thought, naturally enough, that it was going to be a park, like the city centre parks you find all over the world. No way.

If I tell you it's the world's oldest amusement park and it's run by women, does that tell you what it's like?

First, to go in costs DKr 35. Yet to buy nine shares in the company which runs the park and is quoted on the local stock exchange, costs only DKr 25 and you can get in free as many times as you like. I ask you, does that make sense?

As for the amusements; Walt Disney is supposed to have said it was the inspiration for his Disney World. Well, if that's what Walt Disney said he was talking like Donald Duck. It's nothing like Disney World. It's not even an inspiration for a Disney World. You don't get Magic Castles. You don't get a Hans Christian Andersen roundabout. And you don't get a Soren Kierkegaard Existentialist big dipper especially designed to make you feel alone and unhappy. Instead you get trees. There are nearly 1,000 fun-packed trees. You get 150,000 riveting, side-splitting tulips. You get 250 million death-defying, stomach-turning bedding plants. You get about two and a half million coloured lights.

As for fun, squeezed in between the tulips are two boring but no doubt very safe roundabouts and something called a Flying Trunk ride which at first I thought was something to do with elephants. Then there was the dubious pleasure of sitting in a box in the dark surrounded by hordes of shrieking kids and chugging your way past a chimneysweep, a shepherdess and three dogs. Which would no doubt be heaven for some people. But not for me. I can't stand chimneysweeps.

There was a wooden roller-coaster, which claimed it was the oldest in the world; I thought that was one hell of a recommendation, especially from the safety point of view. And there were a few shooting galleries and a couple of dozen bars where you could sit with half a glass of weak beer and be stared at by chainsmoking women who believe that alcohol is bad for your health.

So successful has this formula been that after 150 years of fun-packed existence the only place in the world that has decided that it too would like to bore everybody to death is Kurashiki, a place I'm determined not to visit, somewhere in the middle of Japan. But then the Japanese were so taken with Danish culture that in 1990, for some reason known only to themselves, they decided to build a complete of Egeskov Castle, thirty-five kilometres south of Odense, in Hokkaido, to house a dolphinarium.

The following day I had a meeting down past the Tuborg brewery and its enormous elephant gateway. As I left, the chairman, who looked like all the others except he didn't have an earring, said he wanted to give me a souvenir of Copenhagen. Now in France, though never in Villefrance, I've been given bottles of Krug as souvenirs. In Holland, Delft china and sometimes a lump of Edam. In Ghana, I was once given a traditional Kente cloth which, if I had the courage to wear it, would make me look like a tribal chief. This time I was given a, well what I mean is, it looks like a, you know what I mean. It's about ... I mean, when you pick it up it, it kinda ... For the life of me, I couldn't tell you what it is.

Suggestions, please, in purple ink on an octagonal postcard to:

Danish Designs,
What the hell are they?
Hans Christian Andersen House
Legoland NO1 DEA1

Helsinki

I just knew it was going to happen. Heathrow was packed. The queue for the hand-luggage-only section was longer than for the normal check-in. I chose the longest check-in queue on the basis that the shortest queues always take longest. Especially when I'm in them. This time, of course, the longest queue took the longest. Some fat lady with a kid held us all up for twenty minutes because she insisted on taking her twenty-three suitcases through as hand luggage. And got away with it. If I try to take a copy of yesterday's newspaper through with me, they raise hell and I have to leave it behind.

I practically got thrown off the flight because my ticket said, Biddelcombe and not Biddlecombe. Which is one of the less serious mistakes people have made with my name over the years.

'It's a typing error,' I said. 'They are always making—'

'It's all right for you to say that, sir. But what if it's not?' Mrs Hitler growled at me.

'Then why am I showing you my passport? Surely I would have—'

'There's no need for you to take that attitude, sir.' Now she was sneering at me.

'Attitude,' I gasped. 'What attitude? All I said was—'

'If you persist in being unreasonable, sir, I shall have to call the manager.' She growled again, slammed the ticket back on the desk and started shuffling her papers around.

'Time of the month,' the American behind me was whispering. 'I usually get them. Best of luck.'

I didn't even blink. Whatever I did was going to be wrong. I just stood there. One. Two. Three ... Twenty-six. Twenty-seven. Suddenly she was smiling at me. She picked my ticket up, checked me in and was wrapping the sticker around my suitcase.

'Pack your bag yourself, sir?' she smiled.

'Who else is there to pack my bag for me?' I whispered.

'That's what I say,' she positively purred.

'Time of the month,' the American was saying. 'It's usually me. I usually get them.'

Security was the usual chaos. This time I chose the shortest queue. Which, of course, took the longest.

'Keep metal objects in your pocket,' said the sign by the archway. So naturally I did. I walked through. The bell rang like hell.

'You should have taken your keys out of your pocket, sir,' said the security guard who looked as though he could have been a Mossad agent – thirty years ago.

'But the sign said—' I began.

'Security, sir. Just doing my job.'

'But there's a ...'

'It's a serious matter, sir. Safety of all passengers.'

I got taken apart. I swear I've had medical examinations that were nowhere near as thorough. And all in public as well. As I was trying to regain what little dignity I have, an old lady waddled through the archway pushing a trolley. On top of the trolley were three of those large metal suitcases.

'Young man,' she squawked at the Mossad agent, 'I'm late. If you would be so kind ...'

'Of course.' The creep jumped to attention. Through she went. Not even the slightest attempt to check ...

'Hey,' I couldn't help saying. 'What about her? How do you know that's not a fake trolley? What about the—'

'Trying to be funny, sir?' he growled at me.

'Yes, but how do you know she's not ...?'

'Are you saying I'm not doing my job properly, sir?'

What could I say? I didn't fancy the rubber-glove treatment.

'Thank you, thank you,' I grovelled. 'Thank you very much. Thank you.'

Through passport control. No problems. No problems! Something had obviously gone wrong.

'. . . Helsinki. Gate 25. All passengers . . . Gate 25.'

I went to Gate 25. It was Gate 28. Which was empty. Everybody on the flight was in the little bar round the corner topping up on the cheap booze before they hit Helsinki. When finally we were told to board a massive thundering herd came galloping, heaving and panting out of the bar. It swung down the centre of the aisle, sweeping the final check-in counter aside, through the door to the plane, down the stairs and into three waiting coaches. So many came through at the same time that the girls were unable to push the boarding passes through their little machines, so we all had to get off the coaches while they double-checked us through again.

Finally we all got back on. What happens? The coach takes us to the wrong plane, and we spend another twenty minutes wondering why on earth they are not letting us on the plane. I am, of course, standing next to a Finn with a bald head and a long blond pigtail who dances up and down all the time. When the coach finally discovers its mistake and takes us to the right plane, as soon as the doors open he is out and up the steps.

I settle in to seat 11A, next to the emergency exit.

'I'm sorry, sir. You can't put your briefcase . . .'

'I know, I know. I just want to get some papers . . .'

'Regulations, sir, forbid . . .'

'Just two seconds . . .'

'I'll have to take your briefcase, I'm afraid, sir.'

I hand it over. There's no fight left in me. Then – you guessed it – who comes and sits next to me? The fat lady with the kid. For the next three weeks, the kid is screaming and bawling and pawing me and dismantling the seat.

'So adventurous,' the fat lady smiles. Snap. Off comes the top of the armrest. That's before we've even hit the runway. 'Very enthusiastic.' Off comes the ashtray as we begin to take off. 'So much energy for his age.' He is now pulling the cushion off the seat. We're barely into the North Sea. 'Good for them,' I think. The dirty yellow lifejacket is now being unrolled before my eyes. 'Like to see them doing . . .'

The kid is now throwing everything all over the cabin. Zunk. The armrest hits an old man three rows behind us. The ashtray goes spinning down the centre of the aisle. The cushion bounces off two old ladies huddled together reading the *Sun*. The lifejacket. I cannot tell you where the lifejacket ended up. All I can say is, it meant a lot of money for some hairdresser somewhere.

The only good thing I can think of is that it's a relatively short flight. If we had been flying to Tokyo, this kid would have dismantled the whole plane.

I'm trying to finish my glass of red wine without spilling it. Impossible, of course, with the turbulence inside the plane let alone outside. Everybody around me is on the hard stuff; vodka, Bloody Marys, whisky. One man in a red jacket and a loud yellow tie, who looks as though he has been drip-fed on vodka since Pierre Smirnoff was a tot, keeps going to the back of the plane and returning with a tray full of plastic glasses – inside each glass, a miniature bottle of vodka, gin or whisky. These he distributes amongst his friends. Again. And again. And again. He's better at serving drinks than the air hostesses.

Finally we arrive at Helsinki. The plane thumps down on the runway, overshoots the turn-off, slams on the brakes, does a sharp left-hand turn on two wheels which practically melts the tyres and skids to a halt at the arrival gate with clouds of burning smoke coming up from the wheels.

And what happens next? You got it. My luggage has disappeared. Into Finnair. Or at least I think it has. The trouble with going to Finland is that they're so heavy on the booze that you no sooner arrive than – Cheers. Nice to see you. Well just one. Gulp – you're in there with them. And I don't mean kids' stuff. They might go on about how eating too many liquorice pastilles makes you turn blue, but this is Yeltsin country. Even the fresh air I reckon is 65 per cent proof. At least. It's the only place I've ever been which has more handrails and benches, even in the toilets, than zebra crossings. In fact, I bet you a bottle or three that when the Russians staggered in, way back in 1807, so that Tsar Alexander I could have his buffer zone against Napoleon, they were led by a tall, swaying, tired and emotional figure with a shock of white hair. I'll go a stage further. I'll bet you another bottle that the tall, swaying, tired and emotional figure with the shock of white hair should have been there in 1806 but he was still sleeping it off.

Make no mistake, the Finns are not just drinkers. They are professionals. Olut, or beer, is for boys. Whisky, especially Irish whisky, is for men. But he who aspires to be a hero of the Finnish people drinks vodka, especially Koskenkorra, which not only blows your brains out and turns you blind, it also melts not just the lining but the whole contents of your stomach.

Which is presumably why, all over Helsinki, in hotels, in bars, in restaurants, even in lifts, they have carpets with the day of the week displayed proudly in the centre, on the basis that if – what am I saying, if – when you crash out, the only way you'll know how long you have been under is by checking the day on the carpet when you come round. It's obviously the Finn end of a very subtle anti-drinking wedge they are trying to drive between those who enjoy life, good company and good food and drink and those who are non-smoking, non-drinking vegetarians, who are obsessed with E-numbers and worried about their weight.

After that, before you start getting hallucinations about Russian Foxtrot class submarines popping up along the Finnish coast, it's off to the drying-out chamber – the sauna, which I was told stands for So much Alcohol Ugh Never Again. Me, I've always avoided saunas on the basis that they make you sweat like a pig which gives you a raging thirst which makes you want to drink a lot which is why you've got to have a sauna in the first place. Why go through all the pain and agony of lashing yourself with dirty great branches and rolling around in the snow when you're going to end up having a couple of drinks afterwards in any case?

Then, you've guessed it, it's Kippis, Cheers – back to the bar again. Even the mini-bars. Finland is the only country I know where in the mini-bars the Coke bottles are covered in dust but all the vodka bottles are shining bright, fresh from the distillers that morning.

The charm and the whimsy of alcohol? The grape that cheers; the flagon that stays me? Forget it. Take a Finn to an English garden party and he won't touch a glass. He'll put his head straight in the punchbowl. I promise you, they don't begin to function until the balance of their mind is disturbed, their liver is throbbing and they are coughing up blood.

An alcohol-free lunch? Are you out of your mind? Even the mention of it could bring on an acute attack of alcohol deficiency paralysis.

'Glass of mineral water, old man? Sparkling or flat?' Can you imagine a bunch of Finns making the rounds of merchant banks in the City today? There would be skidmarks all the way to the Channel Tunnel. More time to drink going by train.

Believe me, I've been in some sessions in my time: from hour-long cognac tastings in Wimbledon town hall to day-long benders in practically every bar from the Travellers Club in Pall Mall around the world in 80 hangovers and back to the Travellers again.

One of the deadliest cities I vaguely remember was Manchester, of all places. Not the Manchester of today with its trams and G-Mex Centre, but the Manchester of the old days when everybody was wheeling and dealing; fortunes were being made every which way and the police and the crooks were virtually operating hand-in-hand. Well, at least drinking together, with one side buying more drinks than the other side. If you get my drift.

Double vodkas were the order of the day. Nobody could think of having lunch without at least five or six vodkas inside them. Lunch was always at least two bottles of wine. Good wine, nothing cheap. Followed by, say, half a bottle of port. Each. At the minimum. When I die, I'm certain that if I have any liver left, any kindly, non-smoking, non-drinking vegetarian pathologist who has to cut me up will see Manchester engraved all over it.

Years ago, I used to go there every Tuesday by train from Euston. Every Tuesday at 5 p.m. I used to catch the Pullman back. This time I had to go to Leeds first. Because I was going to Leeds, then on to Manchester, then back to London, I decided instead to go by car and take my wife. It was one of the rare times I've taken her on a trip. We drove first to Leeds. I had meetings in Leeds. We stayed the night at the Post House. The following morning I drove across to Manchester and left her at the Midland Hotel while I visited a client.

'I'll be back at five,' I said. 'No problem.' I got that look. 'I promise,' I grovelled, the way we all do. 'Honest, I promise.'

What happened? You got it. The client had just landed a big deal. He wanted to celebrate. Who was I to argue? Across the road we went to the pub. Double vodkas all round. Then off to the Midland Hotel. Champagne, oysters, the works. More people joined us. More champagne, more oysters. Still more people joined us. More champagne, more oysters. At 4.30 I can remember thinking: the Pullman leaves at 5.00. I must be on the Pullman. I must be on the Pullman. I must be on the Pullman. At one minute to five, don't ask me how, I was racing across the station, onto the platform and into the train as it pulled away. I'd made it.

I can remember slumping down in my usual seat. But something, something kept telling me something was not quite right. At Stockport I realised. My wife was at the Midland Hotel. Waiting for me. Since five o'clock. I leapt off the train as it pulled away. How I did not break both legs, both arms and everything else of value, I do not know. All I know is by the time I got a train back to Manchester, got a cab to the Midland and staggered through the door in an advanced state of refreshment, as they say nowadays, my story about having to work late, lots to do, an important client, did not exactly

ring true. The result was a painful decision: to take my wife
with me on business trips in future or to go alone. There and
then I naturally chose the most difficult, the most self-
sacrificing and personally most inconvenient alternative. I
decided to go everywhere on my own.

Then there was the time in Prague when I learnt to drink
vodka the Russian way. I was with an old Czech mate. We had
been threatening to do business together for years, but neither
of us wanted to spoil a beautiful friendship. Early one evening
we ended up in a tiny Chinese restaurant near the big
roundabout in Dejvice.

'Why Chinese?' I said. 'Surely we could go to a—'

'Shh,' he put his finger to his lips. 'You will see.'

As soon as we went in he ordered the essential ingredients
for an evening to completely forget: a sheet of dirty newspaper, a chilled bottle of vodka, a plate of tiny pieces of bread
and a dish of the foulest smelling fish you could imagine.
'Now,' he said, 'we drink vodka Russian-style.'

He laid out the newspaper on the table and smoothed it
with both hands. He poured the vodka into the glasses. He
picked up a piece of bread, stood up, put the bread into his
mouth, put his hand behind his back, shouted out at the top
of his voice, 'Na zdarovie' and slugged the vodka back in one
go. I did the same. Not quite as fluently. Not quite as
professionally. But I didn't feel guilty. In fact, I was quite
prepared to sign on for a long, long apprenticeship.

'And the fish,' I can vaguely remember asking sometime
between whatever time we went in and whatever time the
chair moved as I was about to sit down. 'What's the fish for?'

'The fish', he said, 'is to make us sober. When we finish the
vodka we smell the fish. If the fish is really bad it will sober us
up. That', I can remember him grinning, 'is why I always drink
vodka in Chinese restaurants.'

Helsinki, if you can still remember after all you've had, is
like that. But all day, every day. It is literally a drinker's city.
They are not just the heaviest drinkers in the world – whisky,
paraffin, liquid nails mixed with snake's-head juice followed

by paint-stripper chasers, but especially vodka – they are the fastest drinkers as well. Take my word for it. No, don't take *my* word for it. Take my liver's word for it. They just seem to throw it down: glass after glass, bottle after bottle. They don't even know there are any sides for it to touch. In fact, the amount of stuff they drink, any sides they had must have rotted away years ago. Trouble is they expect you to keep up with them. Which I could have done in my Manchester days, but now as a weak, pathetic, housetrained vegetarian confined to Diet Cokes, at least when I'm at home, I'm out of training. I can actually remember what happened the night before.

Trouble is, it's not just the drinking. Helsinki is like being in the land of the everlasting firm's Christmas party. Because once they have finished boozing, everyone begins throwing up. If there was a gold medal for throwing up, the Finns would win by a very large bucketful. First, because of the quantities involved. Second, because there is no word in Finnish for, 'I'm sorry. Excuse me.' Honest. As a result, they throw up to their hearts', or stomachs' content without being embarrassed or guilty or anything.

In any other country, everybody dreams of seeing their first swallow in springtime, their first honest politician – whichever is the rarer – or, even more difficult, their first British car. Not in Finland. Everybody wants to spot the first guy throwing up. Not that I like bringing up this kind of thing myself.

Aaaggh. In the bushes. That was just outside the airport.

Yaaaaaaagh. Outside the jazzy-looking Finlandia Hall.

My own personal record is three and a half seconds. I fell off the plane one Sunday afternoon and there at the bar opposite the walk way was – yah. Too late. I stepped right in the middle of it.

'Why do they drink? Ask yourself. You're living in a country miles from anywhere. It's the seventh largest country in Europe. It stretches more than 1,000 kilometres from the tip in the Arctic circle down to Helsinki in the south. In between there is nothing but trees, trees and water. Probably because of all the throwing up that's been going on for generations, it has more swamp land – 37 metres of water per head of population – than any other country in the world apart from Russia and Canada. And look at the size of Russia and Canada compared to little old Finland.

They do their best to boost what they call their *suomi kuva*, public image. One businessman told me that Finland's mountains are higher than the Alps.

'Higher than the Alps?' I wonder nervously.

'Higher than the Alps,' I am assured. A pause. 'Before the Ice Age, of course.'

'Of course,' I murmur.

'Then, of course, the Ice Age wore them down.'

'Of course.'

'Of course.'

'Hic.'

'Yaargh.'

After lunch nobody understands a word you say or, worse still, even tries to understand a word you say. Or maybe it's just that they are all bombed out of their minds and everybody goes around slurring at everybody else not understanding a word anyone is saying.

'Huhtl baalhunstant,' a banker said to me one afternoon as we crossed the square in front of the main railway station.

'Froh zu cho my knee,' I replied. Which was obviously the wrong thing to say whatever it meant for he put his arm around my shoulder. 'Zu los moy tee,' he grinned.

'Noh, noh.' I tried to back off. 'Zec ham busi ziz evening.'

On the other hand, I was told once by a British sales manager who boasted that he came to Helsinki to drink for Britain, that apart from Saturday night Glaswegian, Finnish is the most difficult language in the world. It's by far top of the Finno-Ugrian impossible-to-speak group of languages. Its grammar makes nuclear physics seem kids' play. Each noun apparently has 15 cases. Each verb has 207 declensions. And each adjective 2,721 ways of being spelt backwards.

I've been there nine times – one over the eight – and all I've been able to discover is that it's full of double letters. Stop is

Stopp. Hotel is Hotell. And a Baari is not a Baari. It's a snack bar. Something to do with them seeing double all the time, I suppose. Which is obviously why only 40,000 foreigners live in Finland, the lowest percentage of foreigners for any country in Europe. Most of them, surprise, surprise, are Japanese; not because the Japanese can speak Finnish – they can't. They are only there for one reason – business – but there is something about the Finns that makes them good Japanese speakers. Apparently the Japanese accent is so difficult any real Japanese speaker can immediately tell where any foreigner learnt their Japanese. But not with the Finns. They speak it like natives.

Nobody, however, not even the Japanese, can begin to pronounce a word of Finnish. Years ago I kept coming across Outokumpu, one of these enormous unknown Finnish companies that is into everything: engineering, steel, construction, anything so long as it can be done with vodka. Could I pronounce their name? I couldn't even pronounce the name of the guy I was working with, which was Jatkuu Seuraavallaa Sivuulaa. Or at least, I thought it was. It was only after two bottles of vodka I discovered that Jatkuu whatever-it-was actually meant More to Follow. When he sent me his first fax confirming the meeting only the first page came through. I thought the mumbo jumbo at the bottom was his name so I kept faxing him back. Attention: Mr More to Follow.

How was I to know it wasn't his name? Although, I must admit, after about twenty-three faxes and no reply I did begin to get a little suspicious.

As for Helsinki itself, there's nothing to do. Which is obviously why everybody drinks so much. Actually, the Finns go on and on about their culture so much they drive you to drink: the Golden Age of Gallen-Kallela, Edelfelt and I-forget-the-others; passalballi, whatever that is; and, of course, Sibelius or 'Old Sib' as Sir Thomas Beecham used to call him. I'm all for promoting your cultural heritage, but can you believe it, they've had a series of programmes on Sibelius on radio that has been running non-stop for nearly twenty years.

I was once stopped by a bunch of innocent, wide-eyed American matrons by the central station. They were off to Turku down in the south-west to pay homage to Sibelius. I didn't have the heart to tell them that even though it boasts a Sibelius Museum, pumps out Finlandia at the drop of a fur hat and scours the world for the great man's manuscripts, notes and even cigar butts, Old Sib had nothing whatsoever to do with the place. They've just latched onto what they think is a good way of bringing in the punters.

As for Finnish architecture, it's not bad in a not-bad sort of way. In fact, it's a bit like the Finns themselves: solid; straightforward; built to last forever; and on the rocks.

All over Helsinki there are enormous rocks – in parks, in gardens, supporting buildings. There is even a complete church built inside the rocks in the middle of a big residential square which, Finland being Finland, is regularly used for, would you believe it, rock concerts because it has the best acoustics in town. Either that or they don't want to disturb the neighbours.

All the flat, square, granite office blocks tend to put you off a bit. Then here and there you spot some interesting modern buildings. Then some old buildings again. Some people say it's a country cousin of St Petersburg. Others say it's Russia with a human race.

The parliament building, for example, is massive. Which I suppose is what a parliament building had to be with the Russians living on your doorstep.

I like the Senate Square; I suppose everybody does. It's clean, uncluttered. The hugh Lutheran cathedral on top of all those thick granite steps. The Senate House itself along the eastern side. The waterside market is fun. Especially in a force nine gale.

All over the place there is plenty of green which, I suppose, is necessary if you have a drink problem like the Finns. There are also lots of thick, heavy statues of presidents, politicians and soldiers who are the only upright men you'll ever see in the city. My favourite is Kyosti Kallio, tucked away along by the parliament building. He is built like a mountain and looks positively out-to-lunch, out-to-tea and out-to-dinner as well. What puzzles me is, if all Finns were built like him, how come it took them so long to throw off the Russians.

Oh yes, the weather. Winter is winter – it's so cold even the trucks get hypothermia – and summer is just sixty-seven days when the sun never sets, the temperature soars to an unbelievable 30° centigrade, offices close at 3.15 and everybody packs their rods, reels and flies and heads for their own personal 37 metres of water scattered over 188,000 lakes to find the necessary for their interminable crayfish parties.

So it's no wonder they drink.

I've been in Helsinki early in the morning watching them queuing up outside their state-run Alko liquor stores. Sure there are a couple of winos there. But most of them are serious, clean-living, healthy ordinary people. Like – hic – you and me.

Years ago I used to organise conferences in London. Regularly we would have Finnish speakers. First, because they immediately gave an international air to the event. Second, because they were cheap. In those days they were practically paying me to invite them to speak at conferences just so that they could come to London and get smashed out of their minds. Ordinary guys. I had a team of people I had to send round their hotels every morning to make certain they got up and were at the conference pretty much on time. Or at least, before lunch. When, of course, they would start all over again. In the end I gave up. I was spending more money getting them to the conference on time than I was being paid by the delegates.

I was once – I think – at the Saslik, one of the best Russian restaurants in Helsinki, with a group of Finnish businessmen: Mr More to Follow, Mr Please Send that Page Again and Mr This is a Wrong Number Please Try Again.

We were supposed to be having a vodka-tasting session. We had a bottle of Viru Valge Vin, which is 34 per cent proof, from Estonia; a bottle of good old Gorbatschow vodka at 40 per

cent; some bottles of Koskenkorva, the fancy-flavoured vodkas; Pealinna Viin eln Stolitshnaja from Poland; Black Death
vodka from Armenia; a Monopol a Moen Pirtu, the Terminator
vodka from the US; apricot-flavoured Yuri Gagarin vodka
which, I was told, actually fired him into space. Or at least, if
it didn't it could have done.

Rasputin; Selikoff; Petrov; Starorusskaya; Fyodr; Setinov;
Rubiskays; Tolstoy: there are over 170 different vodkas in
Russia alone. Old diehards maintain that Russian vodka tastes
better. It is made with soft water from the springs around
Moscow. Other vodkas from the River Vazuza deep in the
Russian forests, or made from cereals from the scanty soils in
Nizhny Novgorod, are much harsher. Others just go for the
nearest bottle. Either way good vodka is never supposed to
give you a hangover. In theory it is supposed to be out of your
blood in twenty-four hours, whereas beer and other spirits can
be there forever.

The discussion began like any tasting. It's the grain: only the
finest grain makes the finest vodka. It's the water: Finnish
water is the best water, not Russian. Mr Please Send that Page
Again said he'd been at Saariselka, in the far, far north of
Lapland for the Finlandia Vodka International Drinks Competition. Finlandia was produced by Alko, the state drinks
company. The turnover was over US$ 3 billion. They accoun-
ted for nearly 10 per cent of all state revenues.

'Niet, niet, niet,' a Russian grunted who had red maps of
Bordeaux etched deeply on both cheeks. 'The Cristal factory
in Moscow. Hic. The spiritual home, hic, of vodka. Home of
Stolich-hic-naya.'

Good vodka, I seem to remember him saying, should never
go to your head. Only to your stomach. 'Drink as much as you
like then go straight back to the office or driving a bus or
piloting a plane,' he slurred. 'It having no effect whatsoever.'

I tried to mention all the bus drivers and airline pilots I'd
seen slumped in corners at railway stations all over Eastern
Europe. But nothing came.

'Got a cold – a glass of vodka with plenty of pepper.

Following morning, you on top of the world.' I nodded weakly. 'Stomach ache. Glass of vodka with spoonful of salt. The following morning. The following morning. The following . . .' He crashed to the floor.

Another Russian, obviously a drinkers' drinker, then gave me a lesson in drinking vodka. 'To sip it is wrong. It is made to drink so.' He lifted the glass to his lips. 'Na zdarovie.' The whole glass he emptied in one go. 'There,' he gasped. 'That is drinking vodka. Now,' he handed me a glass. 'Now you try.'

Gulp. Down it went.

'You must not drink it chilled,' he continued. 'Chilled, it is not good. It loses its goodness. You must drink it cool.'

Zunk.

'No. You not breathe properly. Not like this.' Zunk. Down went another one. 'Like this.' Zunk.

'Before you drink, out-breathe like this.' He out-breathed as if he was going to implode. 'Now like this.' He gasped. He picked up the glass, put it to his lips. Zunk, it was gone. 'Now out-breathe like this,' he gasped. 'Is good. You try.'

'Yes. Yes.' I out-breathed for all my life was worth. 'How much do you drink a week then?'

Gulp. Down went another. 'Nothing at all. Maybe two or three.'

Every Russian, man, woman and child, drinks an average 15 litres of the stuff every year. Gulp. Down went the however many it was.

'Glasses?'

The next, I seem to remember, tasted of cranberries. Or maybe it was peaches. Or what the hell.

'Bottles.'

'Show, how much d-do you drink in w-w-one go?'

'Maybe one, maybe two.'

Sheventeen.

'B-b-bottles?'

Fifty-sheven.

'But not all at once.'

Two hundred and sheven.

'No. Over an evening. Say two, maybe three hours.'

ZZZzzzzzz.

The government, like governments all over the world, has tried to ruin everybody's fun by ignoring a million years' uncontested evidence of the sobering effects of a cold shower, cup after cup of boiling hot coffee and five minutes slapping yourself on the face, by trying to crack down on drinking in the first place.

First, in between sessions, the hard-drinking Members of Parliament introduced tough drink-driving laws. Which is why one taxi driver told me he would never drink more than half a bottle of vodka in the evening. Another driver told me the laws were tough but the police never enforced them. A policeman told me it didn't make any difference because, with all the government cuts, they only had one breathalyser kit in any case and somebody had broken the mouthpiece three New Years ago and they had never bothered to replace it. An earnest Dutch Member of the European Parliament told me, however, over his two glasses of mineral water – see; I do drink the stuff if I have to, although I can remember my liver trying to reject it – that Finland had been reported to a special Council of Europe Committee on the Prevention of Torture because the Finnish police laid out drunks on white lines on the floors of police cells instead of taking them to official 'detoxification centres'.

I must admit even the mineral water couldn't stop me from laughing. Which is just what I shouldn't have done.

'This is serious,' he said very sharply. 'They are suffering loss of human dignity. They are being treated like white lines in a car park. It is not—'

This time I just couldn't help it, I promise you. Even though it meant losing a valuable contact.

Then, in order to stamp out drinking on the roads, the Finns decided to do everything they could to encourage drinking at sea. As a result, every shipowner in town – and Helsinki, don't forget, is surrounded on three sides by water – now devotes themselves heart and soul to making everyone, but everyone, drunken sailors.

If you could go down to the sea again, I promise you, you wouldn't want to. Night after night cruisers, car ferries, even huge nine-deck passenger ships complete with saunas, discos, cabins for 2,000 people and enough duty-free to float the US Seventh Fleet, push off into the sunset full to the lifeboats with your serious drinkers determined to roll along on the crest of the waves. Come the following morning, if they can remember where they've been and what they've been doing, they haven't enjoyed themselves.

Well, I say everyone. There is, my wife will be pleased to hear, a bunch of dull, boring, miserable, serious, sober fanatics who go around advocating no smoking, no drinking and clean healthy living. They also go on about saving the world from the threat of over-population, dwindling resources and environmental destruction by; first, actually cutting off aid to developing countries so that they all just die off like flies; and then introducing compulsory abortions for every woman who has more than two children. Which is the best argument I've ever come across for being bombed out of your mind.

Philosophers, the Finns call them. They live miles from anywhere in wild, remote, empty places, usually by ponds – Thoreau fans, please note – refuse to have electricity, would not dream of having a telephone and do nothing but fish. I know what I'd call them, under the influence or not.

Yet there is a growing body of opinion in Finland that takes them seriously, is prepared to discuss not only their proposals but also the most practical, cost-effective ways of implementing them. My only hope is that once they realise the effect their proposals will have on the ozone layer they will back off and go back to terrifying the fish.

The other factor you would have thought would have turned the Finns off their booze is money. Or rather the lack of it. No way. Not even their current economic problems created by the collapse of the Soviet Union. Almost as soon as the Berlin Wall came down the economy did not just slam into reverse, it shrank by 15 per cent. In spite of 17 per cent interest rates, capital fled the country. The currency lost a third of its value. Unemployment soared to more than 20 per cent compared to an average 3 per cent before. The welfare system shuddered violently. Banks started tottering.

The government, of course, took decisive action as only Finns can do. After some uncertain footwork, even the President began stumbling and falling over at receptions and slumping over the table at official receptions as proof of how he was standing up to solving the problems, then turning up the following morning with a large plaster on his forehead.

Drunk?

'The President does not have a drinking problem.' He went on prime-time television to set the record straight. 'The recent sanctimoniousness is pretty revolting.' Which immediately scotched that rumour.

Today as a result, just when they are needed most, hand-outs, unemployment, sickness and housing benefits have been slashed. Politicians were not worried. They thought this was only going to affect those who needed them most. Not so. There was an outcry from those who you would have thought needed them least: businessmen looking after their elderly parents; professional people struggling to support relatives who had fallen on hard times, and industrialists going without themselves to try and keep their companies going. But in vain. Gone is the cradle-to-grave social security system. Gone are all the no-questions-asked government hand-outs. Gone forever is the safety net that protected so much of the population for so long.

Instead there is the new Mrs Thatcher reality. Everybody is supposed to stand on their own feet. If they can't exactly make it on both feet, the government will come up with the readies to enable them to keep at least one foot precariously on the ground.

The problem, however, is it's not working. More and more people are tottering helplessly, wondering what to do. The streets of Helsinki, for the first time for over a hundred years, are now full of tramps and down-and-outs.

The government then had another idea. They gave the army

a month's holiday. Some said they were frightened they might take over, although heaven knows why. The government said it was to save paying their wages for a month. The result; the streets of Helsinki were full of down-and-outs – and half the Finnish army.

Sure, the Finns always had big problems with the Russians. But whether they got telephone calls or not from Moscow, there is no denying Communism was good for Finland. First, directly or indirectly, it gave them their freedom, which they had never had before. Then for forty-three years it gave them prosperity, a guaranteed market for everything they could produce, and cheap oil. Finland was number one supplier to the Soviet Union, in much the same way as, say, the Netherlands is the number one supplier, sub-contractor, virtual workshop for Germany today. During the 1980s its economy grew faster than anybody else's in either the EC or EFTA.

Now they've got to try and stand on their own two feet. Which is difficult for them at the best of times. Are their problems over? Can they give up the booze? Depends who you try and talk to.

The feeling, at least before the second vodka, seems to be that with a 1,300-kilometre border with Russia; Soviet attack helicopters still stationed at Alakurtti, less than 100 kilometres from their borders; a gunship unit north of St Petersburg; two helicopter transport regiments closer still, and Vladimir Zhironovsky, the wild man of the Russian right, blathering on about Finland being reincorporated in the homeland, it is probably safer to forget all about it and have another drink.

Did I really lose my luggage?

I can remember getting off the plane. I can remember waiting by the carousel. I can remember meeting this guy and going off for a quick one while we were waiting for the luggage. After that – nothing. Zilch. Total blank. It was the Finnish. Again.

Budapest

I first discovered Hungary a million years ago in the downstairs bar of the old Piccadilly Hotel, a Tokay bottle's throw from Piccadilly Circus.

While the rest of the world rushed off to the Gay Hussar in Greek Street to have a spat with Roy Hattersley and goodness knows what with Tom Driberg, for some reason or other, I can't possibly think why, I was adopted by a group of old Hungarian emigrés who were determined to become more British than the British. They used to meet every Tuesday lunchtime to relax, chat amongst themselves in their ever-improving upper-class English accents, and gossip about inconsequential things like the problems of translating *Tractatus Logico-Philosophicus* into Urdu, the intricacies of algorithmic complexity theory, and how easy it was to take over the British Establishment.

'The best Hungarians are either dead, in prison, or drinking champagne in the downstairs bar at the Piccadilly Hotel,' they used to chuckle to themselves in varying shades of a throaty John Gielgud accent; first John Gielgud as Attila the Hun; then John Gielgud as St Stephen, whose coronation on Christmas Day in the year 1000 marked the foundation of the Hungarian state, and finally John Gielgud as John Gielgud – with a Hungarian accent. In fact some of them spoke such good English that they could read an optician's chart and make it sound like Henry V doing his bit on St Crispin's Day.

Hungarian, on the other hand, sounds like eating yesterday's dried-up goulash on toast. Experts say it's of Finno-Ugric origin. To me it sounds as if it has been marinated in Turkish, mashed in German and chewed up in Russian. As far as I can gather it has a number of Chomskian generative structures – you can tell I've been talking to Hungarians – and the style, syntax and resonance of Shakespeare. Except that as far as we are concerned, Shakespeare is seventeenth century, whereas for the Hungarians he is today. Apparently they love the way Shakespeare rolls his sentences, the way the words rise and fall and then sweep you up until without realising it you are standing on your chair in the middle of that downstairs bar along the Vaci Egyetem with the steamed-up mirrors and the broken glass all over the floor, crying God for Harry and St Georgius. Which, I suppose, is a bit like the French who go round and round *les maisons* to try and find what they obviously think is an elegant expression for a mundane fact. For instance, one day I was halfway through a four-page article in *Le Monde* about the consequences of the European intercourse under the sea before I realised they were going on about the Channel Tunnel.

The problem is, when Hungarians write or, worse still, speak English they just can't switch to our flip, casual style. As a result, the words come out like extracts from some medieval book of quotations.

'Hey, whaddya reckon. Summat er drink then?' you will say to them.

'Good wine is a good, familiar creature if it be well used,' they will reply.

'What about one of these old bottles then?'

'Good wine needs no bush.'

'You wanna taste it or just hit the bottle straight?'

'The wine of life is drawn and the mere lees is left this vault to brag of.'

'So is it any good then?'

'I am known to be one that loves a cup of wine with not a drop of allaying Tiber in it.'

I remember talking to a Hungarian who was trying to translate the intricacies of logical positivism into Latin. He kept on about the need for inserting a special structure into the totality of the modern world. This would, as a result of a cognitive mapping process confirming existential data, produce an empirical position endorsing his theoretical hypothesis.

I could only think of one thing to say. 'Er, yeah. You goin' have a double then?'

When I first got involved there must have been about twenty of them altogether. Most of them elderly. A few very elderly. They all wore pinstriped suits, collars, regimental ties and waistcoats with a gold watch and chain looped through the middle button. A number of them even turned up from time to time wearing the black jacket and striped trousers which I always thought was the uniform of a head waiter at a pretty swish restaurant, but which they insisted was the ultimate symbol of being accepted by the British Establishment. It was like MI5, or is it MI6, in reverse. MI5 or MI6 is trying to break into Establishment circles in overseas countries, to find out what's going on, so that they can snatch their secrets. These guys were trying to break into our Establishment circles to discover the greatest secret of all; what makes a true Englishman.

To do this, they needed advisers, just as the Russians obviously had people advising them how to infiltrate enemy lines and establish secure positions so that they could feed back to their colleagues vital intelligence from deep inside enemy territory: like from the Foreign Office, the British embassy in Washington or even the Queen's Gallery. These Hungarians had their advisers, too, judging by the way they all rolled their umbrellas, brushed their bowler hats, polished their shoes, creased their trousers, debated the state of the economy, discussed the relative merits of the metaphysical poets compared to the Lakeland versifiers and always knew what was going to win the 3.30 at Haydock Park on Saturday.

Me? Heaven only knows why, but I was their adviser on what they called 'England's quaint olde English customs'.

Why are the stripes on a maypole red, white and blue? Why

aren't they red, green and gold? How many bells does a Morris man have round his knees? Which sheep produce the best woolly jumpers? Why do we no longer eat peacock?

For hours on end I would stand in the bar discussing everything from point-to-points to why there is an Eastbourne but no Westbourne. Never have I had such an appreciative audience, for anything. They lapped it up. If Budapest University awarded a doctorate in superficial knowledge, I'd have got it.

One of them became my star pupil. He would insist on going to the Athenaeum to discuss writing a book about England's quaint olde English customs. In the Naval and Military we talked about politics. Once in Bucks we downed a couple of bottles of champagne trying to avoid talking about religion. How he ever got into these clubs I don't know. He obviously had all the right connections in all the right places. Like with restaurant managers. They always just happened to come from his next village back home, and wherever we went he was greeted like a longlost friend. His bowler hat and umbrella were collected at the door. He was ushered to the best table. Porters, waiters, barmen always turned towards him and gave that slight, deferential bow. Head waiters and maître d's practically grovelled at his feet. He was either the richest man in London or he owed them all a fortune. The crispest serviettes were swished flamboyantly in the air and presented to us for our consideration. Tablecloths were always the whitest or pinkest you've ever seen. The glasses sparkled so much the only way you could stop them from blinding you was to fill them very quickly with champagne. Menus? I don't think we ever saw a menu. There was always something special that was not on the menu that was out of this world.

What he did, how he made his money, I have no idea. All I know is he lived in Prince of Wales Drive overlooking Battersea Park. He used to go to Milton Keynes a lot. Apart from that he spent a lot of time helping what he called his 'chums'.

At the end of every meal we would talk about how one day we would have dinner together in Budapest. These were the coldest days of the Cold War. Eastern Europe was in the grip of the Communists. Khrushchev was facing down Kennedy. So any idea of having dinner together in Budapest was about as likely as the Berlin Wall coming down and the whole of MI6 hot-footing it to Moscow.

But it happened.

Shortly after the Wall came down and news broke that practically the whole of MI6 had, in fact, hot-footed it to Moscow, I was in Vienna at a conference. He was already back in Budapest. I dropped him a line. Back came a business card giving his private address.

Forget the flannel. Depending on where you are standing Budapest is either the filthiest or the cleanest place on earth. In other words it's the hot bath capital of the world.

Feeling down? You need a hot bath. A touch of rheumatism? A hot bath. Worried about the old gout? A hot bath. Circulatory problems? Digestive disorders? Nerves? The old urinary tract playing you up? A hot bath.

There are over twenty spas in Budapest compared to only two casinos. More than anything that tells you how much they believe in hot baths. Three of them are your genuine Turkish bath. Fifteen are in the open air, including the famous Szecheni pool where your bottom half can marinate to Kingdom Come, your middle half can play chess and your top half can freeze to death in the biting cold and wind. But the most famous of all is the spa in the Gellert Hotel where in the old days before the Revolution when they had nothing to do, and presumably nothing to hide, the entire Budapest City Council used to hold their meetings. Nowadays, of course, they are all rushing around doing deals, making a fortune, growing fat, getting heart attacks and having plenty to hide.

Now I'm no expert on hot baths. I've spent most of my life in cold ones for one reason or another, but I gather each spa is ideal for something different: for having your face lifted; for having your nose straightened; for catching double pneumonia; for getting your teeth fixed. Last time I was in Budapest, I was told lots of Hungarian doctors and dentists were doing a roaring trade in the spas. But then lots of Austrian doctors and dentists will tell you, beware. The Hungarians don't know what they are doing. They are using technology that was out of date when Attila the Hun hit town and their fillings and crowns are so full of cadmium that it is touch and go whether your hair will fall out before the rest of your teeth. Others will tell you they are no better and no worse than doctors or dentists anywhere, that whole villages along the border with Austria have become vast medical and dental clinics with busloads of Austrians coming across every day of the week for treatment that is just as good as they get back home but for a fraction of the price. ·

But for those who can get the soap out of their eyes and put their clothes on, or who are allergic to water, like me, Budapest is also one of the most beautiful cities in the world. Or rather Budapest are one of the most beautiful cities in the world. For it is really two cities, not one: Buda, the old, medieval, respectable bit with the palaces, the castles and the cobbled streets, and Pest, which is where the action is: as well as all the multi-coloured advertising hoardings, the fast-food outlets and all the other signs of freedom. Which, when you think about it, makes a lot of sense. For no single city could give us, on the one clean hand, Franz Liszt and Bela Bartok, and on the other dirty hand, Zsa Zsa Gabor. Not even Milton Keynes.

In between the two is the Danube which, contrary to the publicity, is definitely not blue. It's more a dirty, muddy, My-God-where-did-they-bury-the-dog type of colour. Europe's second longest river, it is probably also the most polluted. You think the Rhine is bad. In Budapest, cars can drive across the river, there is so much gunge and stuff in it. In fact, the only people who regretted Jacques Attali jumping the European Bank for Reconstruction and Development

were the Hungarians, for he reckoned cleaning up the
Danube was as important as overhauling the Gabcikovo Dam
on the Hungary-Slovakia border, introducing safety procedures in the Kozloduy nuclear plant in Bulgaria and cleaning
up the huge Danube delta itself. But it was not to be.

Over an enormous dish of goulash – which isn't exactly a
stew; it's more like, well, goulash – any Hungarian will tell you
Budapest is almost slap bang in the middle of Europe. It is
exactly halfway between Portugal and the Urals. Stand with
your towel outside the Gellert, in front of you is Europe with
all its wonders of Western civilisation; the sewers of Vienna,
the Cinéma Latin on the Left Bank and Mr Blobby. Behind you
– careful with the towel – are the Great Plains, which stretch
between the Danube and Romania, the everlasting steppes of
the Ukraine and the Hindu Kush where Thesiger kept going
on about Eric Newby and his what-do-you-call-him being a
couple of pansies because they didn't sleep on the ground, but
insisted on being tucked up in a couple of puffy sleeping
bags.

Where you are actually standing, clutching you towel, is
where the Turks arrived back in 1541. They must have been
pretty professional visitors; they stayed for only 150 years, but
their influence is everywhere. Churches they turned into
mosques. Streets were lined with tanneries. Baths and dervish
monasteries were built all over the place. Then, of course, the
Habsburgs defeated the Turks and immediately set about
building the city of Budapest. Not that there is much left of
their hard work because the place was almost flattened when
the Germans held out against the Red Army in the winter of
1944–45. The famous Chain and Elizabeth bridges across the
Danube were destroyed. The whole of the royal palace was
destroyed. What wasn't destroyed then was destroyed during
the uprising in 1956. As a result, maybe as much as 75 per cent
of the old city of Budapest is in fact the brand new city of
Budapest, although to look at it you wouldn't think so. Huge
new areas of it look more derelict and destroyed than the old
bit. But this has not stopped it being hailed as the Paris of the

East by international sophisticates, *bon viveurs*, all lovers of the good life, and the occasional businessman who can snatch the odd twenty minutes between meetings for a quick look-see.

It has the bars, the clubs, that certain *je ne sais quoi* and most important, I suppose, plenty of people under seventy years of age, which came as quick a shock to me. I expected everyone to be ancient, like all the Hungarians I met in the downstairs bar of the Piccadilly Hotel. The whole country, I was convinced, spent the mornings taking the baths, lunch-time meetings at the Muvesz opposite the Opera, afternoons playing bridge and the evenings at the opera. It was quite a shock to discover there were actually such things as young Hungarians. It took some time to adjust.

Wandering around after another hectic day of meetings, it really is like wandering around Paris, the Paris part of Paris. The broad sweep of the Danube looks like the Seine. The parliament building is a dead ringer for Notre Dame. *Mon Dieu*, they even drive on the pavement the way they do in Paris. But then, I think Dundee looks like Moscow; Liverpool looks like Leningrad; Cheltenham with its Cotswold stone looks like Warsaw before the Nazis moved in, especially the bit around Nowy Swiat, the main shopping area; Wandsworth town hall looks like the old headquarters of the East German Communist Party; and Glasgow City Chambers looks like the British embassy in Moscow.

All the same, you stand more chance of bumping into Inspector Maigret in Budapest than in Paris. Because just as New York film-makers prefer to make authentic New York films in Toronto, so French film-makers prefer to shoot their authentic Parisian locations in Budapest.

Usually the switch works, but occasionally you hit a googly. Normally I never watch television in France. There is usually too much to do. But once in Villefrance – if you've been to Villefrance you'll know why I watch television in Villefrance – I switched on the box. There was Karl Marx, strolling casually through Soho on his way to the Reading Room in the British

Museum: past a shop painted Pawn Shop; past a shop painted Green Grocer – except it wasn't Soho. I swear it was Prague. On another occasion, I was watching some American film when the hero came out of Claridges Hotel in London, walked round the corner and straight into the House of Commons.

To members of the Old Bags' Club, of course, Budapest is also 'That p-p-place'. Or that 'rat hole'. Or 'That that that . . . God I HATE that man.' All because some silly woman at some cocktail party went on about how her husband no longer comes home to be shouted at at weekends and has instead decamped to Budapest, where apparently one can still live in some style on a less than inflated expense account with a luxury flat near the fashionable Vorosmartyr Ter; take cocktails at Gellert's; eat at Gundels, one of the great restaurants of Europe, and be looked after by a slim, blonde Hungarian English teacher whose only demand in return is to go to Gerbaud's twice a week for a cup of coffee. Which you've got to admit is one hell of an incentive to do business in Eastern Europe.

Either way, with or without an English teacher, the castle area is nowhere near as impressive or extensive as the castle area in Prague, but it's worth a few minutes before hitting the bars, if only for the statues. There is one celebrating not the death of a stag but the triumph of the hounds which brought it down; one is easing his thirst; another is ever-alert and the third, with an eye to his master, is ready for the next cry to the chase. Another shows a poor old retainer trying to gain control of his master's horse. The Magdalene Tower is enough to make you weep. Originally part of an old Gothic church, it was destroyed during the last war. Matthias Church, which was rebuilt in 1896, has so much colour everywhere the architect must have been either Italian or colour blind.

Then there are the old neo-Gothic, neo-Renaissance, neo-Habsburgian and neo-modern buildings. The neo-Italian style opera house, a scream and a nightmare away from the old Gestapo and then the Communist KGB headquarters, majestically surveys what I reckon is one of the most impressive

avenues or boulevards in Europe. The neo-parliament building looks to me as if it should be the parliament for the whole
of Eastern Europe. Stroll across the bridge in front of it – it was
the first bridge, built by a Scotsman in the 1840s – and you are
where it all happened. Here first the Reds, then the Whites
fought each other backwards and forwards after the First
World War. Here also on October 23, 1956, Soviet troops fired
on demonstrators and sparked off the Hungarian Revolution.

On top of Gellert Hill high above the city is still the giant
monument to their liberation by the Communists, your typical
proletarian heroine flanked by two workers holding aloft the
palm of victory.

'But why,' I wondered, 'after everything you've been
through, is it still there?'

'Because it's beautiful,' an old lady told me. 'And because
we'll never ever agree what should replace it.'

In the bad old days, Hungary had its own form of goulash
Communism which enable them to have closer ties with the
West than anyone else in Eastern Europe and a degree of
freedom undreamt of east of Berlin. In fact, they've always
been a bit of a Budapest to the Russians. They abandoned
central economic planning way before the rest of Eastern
Europe. They introduced incentives and – horror of horrors –
efficiency payments before the rest had even heard of the
idea. By the 1970s they had virtually their own economic
policy, but were still loyal to Moscow. The result shows. When
the final break came, they were off.

Today, as a result, even though they don't have the natural
resources of Poland, the Czech Republic or Slovakia, they are
streets ahead. Or, maybe, *because* they don't have the natural
resources of Poland, the Czech Republic or Slovakia they are
streets ahead. They concentrated on doing what they do best;
wheeling and dealing. The best Hungarian traders are among
the best in the world, whether it is in Wall Street, London or
the corner of Bajcsy-Zsiliinszky üt and Rudas Laszlo utca,
under the lamp post.

Their economy is a bit like their national dance, the

unpronounceable czardas. It began slowly. But it's going to get quicker and quicker and quicker. Already you can see the signs. Roszadomb, the up-market area of Budapest, is wall-to-wall Mercedes. It's also wall-to-wall Romanian gypsies, on the basis that the rich always attract the poor.

One local told me that since the government had started fining farmers as much as £7,000 for keeping Romanian gypsies as slaves to work the land, they had all left and moved into Roszadomb, where according to the Hungarian Economics Research Institute the disparity between the top 5 per cent and the bottom 5 per cent was already astronomic. Greater than in France; greater than in Germany; almost as great as in the United States. To hire a Ferrari for a day costs the same as the state pension for a whole year.

But wander around the back streets. It is a secret world of crumbling façades, dirty bullet-scarred old buildings and secret courtyards. Some are plain, functional and as filthy as anything you would see in, say, Naples or Moss Side or, I suppose, Paris. Others are almost luxurious. Damp maybe, crumbling quite a bit here and there, but, well, *Parisien*. Some are choked with rubbish. Some are used as short cuts. Some even boast little stalls and shacks selling everything from matches to well, more matches.

And the traffic. One second it's chaotic. The roads are blocked. Cars and trucks and buses are slotted together this way and that. It doesn't take much imagination to guess where Rubik got the idea for his cube. The next second they're all gone.

In the past they were all Trabants. Not any more. For every filthy, loud, foul-smelling two-stroke Trabant you saw in the old days, you probably see two Mercedes today. Which I think is a shame. Not that I'm about to launch a Trabant Protection Society. All I know is that they might have been old, broken-down, and powered by coal judging by the clouds of smoke they belched, but they had their plus points. They were easy to repair. A slight dent and you could beat it out yourself with a hammer. After all they were only made of plastic, or that's what it felt like. They didn't corrode. The engine might have been the filthiest, most polluting engine in the world but it didn't affect the car itself. It only destroyed any town on the receiving end of its toxic fumes. They were cheap to run – and re-repair. You don't believe me; there's a million Trabant owners who would tell you it's true. They spend more money on facemasks to keep out the fumes than they do on the engine. Probably most important of all, Trabants were the place to be if you were involved in a road accident. If you're in a Mercedes or Volvo and you're involved in a road accident, because of all the super safety precautions they have, you'll be trapped for hours until you're cut free from the wreckage. In a Trabant you avoid all that. You'll be killed outright.

So what's the first thing the Hungarians do when they get their freedom? They pick on the Trabant. I mean, just because it's probably the most dangerous car ever built, that's no reason to launch an extermination programme against it. Hand in your old Trabant and you get a free three-year season ticket on what is probably the most efficient transport system in Eastern Europe. I ask you. Is that democracy?

After the lack of Trabants, the other thing you notice, apart from Germans returning in their camping buses from a week at Lake Balaton, Europe's largest lake and Hungary's playground, is all the re-émigrés. Most of them are middle-aged. They fled with their parents when they were children, when the Communists seized power or looked as though they were going to. Now they've come home to do their bit for the old country. Lots of them, mostly statisticians, have come from Canada. In the Baltics most civil servants seem to have come from the United States. Estonia's privatisation programme is run by a re-émigré from Sweden, whose training for such a key position for the country's future was managing the pop group Abba. It's the same in Hungary. In business nobody is anybody unless they've either been expelled from some US business school or made a million by the time they were fourteen.

But helping the old country is not easy. The ones who

stayed behind are still wedded to the old ways. They find it difficult to adjust, to do things on their own, actually to do things without an official letter of authorisation; even harder to do things without some kind of rubber stamp on some kind of piece of paper.

'I wanted my office decorated,' one re-émigré, another Canadian, told me. 'My father was out of work. He needed money. I asked him to do it. He refused. He said he needed an official permit. I couldn't give it to him. Therefore, he couldn't do it.' His secretary's boyfriend did it instead over a weekend and walked away with a bundle of dollars in his pocket.

One evening I was wandering along Vacifuta, their Fifth Avenue, where they apparently used to cruise in their funny old Eastern bloc cars. Today it's bursting with expensive stores and shops selling everything a struggling young economy needs, such as foie gras, caviar, crystal, expensive chocolates.

If any car made a mistake, or forgot to signal, the other drivers would all scream 'Poland' at the driver. Which made me wonder.

In one of the big stores, I noticed a young couple discussing something that was obviously going to change their lives for ever; their first Western sit-down, as opposed to squat-down, toilet. The husband told me he still had the same job with the same engineering company as before, but now they were making money. He was also being paid more. His wife was working in a stationery shop. Both also had part-time jobs. He worked as a driver in the evenings and at weekends. She did cleaning work. They had three children and lived in a small flat. They had got rid of their Trabant. They were thinking of holidays. But their first priority was a sit-down toilet. To see the gooey look in their eyes you'd have thought they were buying something soft and dreamy and mildly embarrassing like a pair of motorbike gloves.

As for the bars and restaurants, you don't need me to tell

you that this is a country where chefs have always been honoured members of society. In the old days they were rated higher up the social scale than even landowners. Today, of course, everyone is rated higher up the social scale than anyone to do with land or property. Especially estate agents.

At the turn of the century Budapest had as many cafés as Dublin had pubs. It was the café capital of the world. For my money, I reckon it hasn't got far to go to get back there. All I know is, a Hungarian's idea of heaven must be to break the fast at Gundels, lunch in the sleek Garvik's, have a quick snifter of the old world atmosphere of Gerbeaud's Café at Vorosmartyr ter or, if that's chock-a-block with tourists as it usually is nowadays, the Muvesz opposite the opera house, grab something to eat at the New York, a spectacular old-fashioned nineteenth-century coffee house full of cherubs and gold leaf and marble curlicues and cartoons of famous writers, and then spend the rest of the evening wandering in and out of the bars along the Belgrade rampart, the embankment on the Pest side of the river where, I'll let you into a secret, everyone is supposed to drink standing up. Until, of course, you're dead drunk; then it is perfectly good Hungarian manners to collapse all over the floor until it's time to break the fast again at Gundels.

As for the food; in most parts of Eastern Europe you spend your time leaping over the sewage seeping across the pavements, basking in the warm glow of radioactivity leaking from the local power station, and trying to work up an appetite for another dinner of marinated parrot. Not in Budapest.

I've spent enough of my life in the Gay Hussar – downstairs, of course – to know that real Hungarians don't eat salad. They eat, or rather guzzle, gallons of chilled wild cherry soup, huge plates of rich, spicy food laced with paprika, mountains of creamy dessert, washed down with gallons of Bulls Blood and sweet Tokay, in order to have another heart attack as quickly as possible.

As if that is not risky enough, whatever you eat comes with an enormous dollop of gypsy music, gypsy music and still more gypsy music: out in the streets; in terrace cafés; in the swish, exotic restaurants.

'I'll have porkolt chicken, galushka dumplings, stuffed cabbage followed by a beautifully rolled strudel.'

'Yes, sir. With a large helping of gypsy music?'

'Yes, of course. Thank you.'

'Thank you, sir.'

Then it comes. Your typical Hungarian soup. As thick as a boar's head with great lumps of dumpling the size of the Albert Hall all around it.

I've had goose and gypsy music; duck and gypsy music; pheasant and gypsy music; wild boar and gypsy music; pressed boar's head and gypsy music. Not to mention capons, beef, lamb, pork and fish all cooked and stewed in a million different broths plus, you said it, gypsy music. I've had borju porkolt, a veal goulash, although you would never have guessed it unless you had been told, with gypsy music; toll tott marhatekexes – stuffed beef rolls – with gypsy music; gyu-moles pudding nyirsegi szilvamartassal – fruit pudding with plum sauce – with gypsy music, and even somloi delice, a fantastic cakey mixture of rum, cake, more rum, cream, even more rum, walnuts and still more rum, with gypsy music.

I've even had kangaroo and gypsy music. In one rather up-market pub near the Forum Hotel, I could have whatever I wanted, so long as it was kangaroo: kangaroo tail soup, curried kangaroo, grilled rack of kangaroo or just plain kangaroo sandwiches. For some reason I didn't quite under-stand, it was their local kangaroo week. But whatever I had, had to be with – you got it – gypsy music.

One evening I was on the way back to the hotel from Szentendre, north of Budapest, which is pure tourism: artists, art galleries; two and a half thousand tourist shops; over fifty-six million bargains. The only good thing about it was that the museums were free on a Wednesday. If, of course, you go on a Wednesday. I went on a Friday. On my way into the hotel I was handed a leaflet saying, 'Should you wish to dance or entertain yourself come to the VD Club.' I didn't go because

I thought I would catch some gypsy music.

Instead I spent the evening in the Gellert, drinking glass after glass of sweet Tokay, trying to get rid of the taste of kangaroo – to the sound of gypsy music. Which, as far as my busted eardrums are concerned, means Hungary is the only country in the world with more violinists than bus conductors, more guitarists than engineers and more zither players than brain surgeons.

Just think of the joy they would create if instead of churning out violinists and guitarists and zither players they churned out bus conductors, engineers and brain surgeons. They'd probably double their earnings from tourism overnight. That's not to say what it would do to their industrial sector.

The consolation, however, is that it's cheap. Budapest is the kind of city where you think they have given you the wrong change. But in Budapest they always seem to give you too much change. A bottle of Coke at a street stall costs, wait for it, 15p. Yes, 15p. In the centre of London it costs you about £1.50 just to look at the bottle, another £1.50 to ask the stallholder if you could have one, £1.50 for the price then another £5.50 because he hasn't got change for a £10 note. A meal – with gypsy music – will cost you all of £5. Without gypsy music, I'd be prepared to pay ten times as much. A night out in any halfway respectable bar will cost you the price of a couple of Cokes. Everything included. Which is about the cost of a taxi across town. What the cost of going to the VD Club would be, I shudder to think.

When I got to my pupil's house, it was not what I expected. It was not up near the castle in one of those bright, clean buildings with a fountain playing in the courtyard. It was a dirty bullet-scarred old building overlooking the railway line. Romanians had occupied the first three floors. He was living in a flat at the very top. But inside, for all the world, it could have been in the Quai Voltaire overlooking the Louvre and the Tuilleries Gardens across the Seine. In the nineteenth century.

There were heavy velvet curtains everywhere. The sitting-room walls looked as though they were painted leather. Everywhere there was thick, heavy, almost Gothic furniture. If Miss Havisham had an elderly uncle living somewhere in central Europe this was him. In one corner was an enormous globe, about the size of a radio telescope; in another corner, an ancient harpsichord or clavichord which looked as though it had given sterling service to Bach during his many recording sessions. There were paintings all over the walls; nothing special or striking, lots of landscapes, the occasional icon. Piles of books. A handbook on tortional vibration rubbed spines with a book called *Physikund Technix*. There was a book on the problems of industrial logic, another on approx-imate linear algebra equations. There was a grand piano along one wall. There were candles all over the place.

But it was cold; so cold that I felt like opening a window to let in some warmth.

In the far corner, deep in the gloom facing the window, was a long, heavily embroidered sofa that looked as though it had come out of a waiting room in a Mogul palace. There was my pupil.

Gone were the pinstripe suit, the starched collar, waistcoat and regimental tie. Instead of a black jacket he was wearing an old blue sweater with holes in the sleeves, greasy black trousers, thick multi-coloured woollen socks, and a pair of slippers held together by prayer and sticking tape. His face was thin and sallow. His cheeks were hollow. A couple of strands of hair streaked across his head. His eyes were all milky. And he was deaf. Not your ordinary deaf; the fat old motherly babushka who seemed to be looking after him said – this is true – he could only hear if you shouted up his nose.

'Shouted up—' I couldn't help exclaiming in English, not exactly having been prepared for this eventuality by my Hungarian phrasebook.

'This way. Like me,' she grunted and turned to him. 'You hear, yes?' she bellowed up his nose as if he had shaken his head too violently, sending his eardrums spinning round to block his nasal passages. 'Yes. Okay. Understand. Yah,' she hollered up at him. Now she turned to me. 'You. You now talk like I show. Yah.'

I spent the evening shouting up his nose about the joys of being in London. 'London. Yah. Good.'

He nodded.

'Good old days.'

Another nod.

'Piccadilly Hotel.'

Another nod.

If he hadn't looked so obviously old and ill and weak I would have bet everything I won betting on the 3.30 at Haydock Park all those years ago that I was being set up by a Magyar Jeremy Beadle for some kind of Hungarian *Candid Camera*.

Once, when Babushka left the room to prepare the only meal I've ever had in Budapest without gypsy music, I accidentally on purpose tried speaking normally. Nothing happened. I tried shouting in his ear. Nothing. But when I went back to shouting up his nose he seemed to react. 'Mrs Thatcher. Yah.' I couldn't tell whether he nodded or shuddered. 'Good. Yah.' This time it was definitely a shudder.

When she came back, she brought a tray with a plate piled high with tiny pieces of bread, a bottle of vodka and three glasses. She sat on the sofa and poured three glasses.

'He's one of the Nomenklatura bourgeoisie,' she told me.

How or why he went back to Budapest I never discovered. Babushka told me a man had stopped her in the street near the Grand Hotel and asked if she would like to look after a friend of his. She said yes. She needed the money. It wasn't hard work. Every month the money was left for her in an envelope at the nearby bank. Who paid, she didn't know. All she knew was she was paid. That's what counted.

We finished the bottle of vodka between us. I stood up to leave, but he didn't react. I said I would call in again to see him next time I was in Budapest. But the next time I was in Budapest he had disappeared.

I telephoned. There was no reply. A couple of times I went to the flat. The first time there was no reply, the second time it was empty. I still think about him whenever I come across any quaint old English customs.

Warsaw

Psst. Wanna buy some civil reactor grade plutonium? Powder, liquid or solid? With all the international legal bits of paper? No? So what about some highly-enriched weapons grade 239? About five to six kilograms? I give you a good price.

I could also get you the tube and detonators. All you need to make your own nuclear bomb.

Just over fifty years ago plutonium did not exist. Now it seems to be everywhere. In Britain, France, Russia, China and the US; in Canada, Germany, Japan, Italy; in Kazakhstan; in the Ukraine. And most of all, in a mercury mix in lead canisters being smuggled in and out of Poland.

From the Kurchatov Atomic Energy Research Institute in Moscow; from the Sverdlovsk 44 Research Centre in the Urals; from Uncle Vanya's cherry orchard in Chekhov: it all seems to have a strong attraction for the magnetic Poles.

There's so much radioactive material being smuggled backwards and forwards across the borders that the border guards already have second-degree burns.

Poland is fascinating. Far and away the largest and most densely populated country in Eastern Europe, it's religious. Not wishy-washy religious, but rough tough religious. More fisherman religious than tax collector religious, if you see what I mean. As befits the homeland of Papa Wojtyla, as he is known locally, it's probably one of the most Catholic countries on earth.

It's violent. You think the Bronx is tough. Or South Central Los Angeles. Or Little Cuba in Miami. All the men here look like Lech Walesa or out-of-work kneecappers. Or both. All the women look like Ivana Trump with sensible shoes or out-of-work kneecappers. Or both. Try refusing to pay the unofficial entry tax to the gangs on the Moscow–Brussels express as it comes into Warsaw East station and you'll soon be on your knees praying like mad to the Black Madonna with the rest of them, because when they come to collect, they come to collect. Men or women.

It's riddled with crime, corruption, deceit, lying and cheating. It is the only country I know where the bars, restaurants and even the snack bar in the Central Station actually closed for three days in protest at the amount of protection money they had to pay, until they were forced to re-open by other security firms promising to protect them from having to pay so much in the future; providing, of course, they paid them a little extra. Those free, independent, honest, upright businessmen who refused to give in to such blatant criminal capitalist blackmail are, I am told, making good progress and should be able to use their zimmer frames very shortly. Poland seems to be the only country in the world that worries about the sixth commandment but couldn't care less about the fifth and seventh.

It is one of the most rip-roaring, wheeler-dealing, buying and selling countries in the world. Everyone is a millionaire, or at least a zloty millionaire. A cup of coffee costs a pocketful of notes, vodka an armful, and a car a whole furniture-van load. You name it, they're doing 'bizniz' in it.

It's also as polluted as hell.

As the country that started the break-up of the Soviet Empire and the end of the Cold War, in many ways it's the country that seems to be doing its best to start the break-up of the post-Cold War peace and the collapse of everything the Soviet Empire didn't stand for. It's not whether it's right or wrong; it's whether it's possible. That's what seems to count in today's swinging, wheeler-dealer, anything goes 'I'm all right Jerzy' Polish economy.

You want to smuggle cheap shoes into Denmark? No problem. There are at least three factories turning out any type of shoe you want – with any name on it you like. You want spare parts for a Mercedes or a BMW? No problem. You want the car itself? No problem. Poland is the largest market for stolen cars in the old Eastern bloc, with over 400,000 stolen cars going through the system every year, around 10 per cent of all cars on Polish roads.

You want raw aluminium ingots fresh from the back door of the Mg-29 assembly plant in the north of Moscow; some low-grade uranium pellets; a few kilograms of uranium 238 from the Arzamas-16 plant near Nizhny Novgorod in central Russia, or some highly enriched 235? How about a little bit of caesium 137 and a dash of strontium thrown in? No problem. You want to build a nuclear bomb? There's tons of the stuff in Kazakhstan. You only want six kilograms? I'll talk to one of my friends.

You think I'm exaggerating. During one trip, the Polish press was exploding with stories about how even the highly cautious, secretive Vundeskriminalamt, the German Federal Investigation Office, had admitted they had only traced four cases of radioactive material being smuggled across the border in 1990, whereas in 1992 the figure had soared to a terrifying 158.

Get any train out of the country and I guarantee it's virtually a smuggler's paradise on wheels. I once got a train from Warsaw to Vilnius, Lithuania. Behind the walls, under the seats, inside the lights, even underneath the toilets, there were cigarettes.

It's the same by coach. Behind the panelling, under the seats, in special boxes between the springs, inside thermos flasks, in the middle of loaves of bread, inside bags and hold-alls with false bottoms, in moon boots (50–100 packets), inside T-shirts (100–150 packets), sewn into pockets inside coats (150–250 packets), strapped inside corsets (I shudder to think).

Everywhere, wherever you go, the Poles are wheeling and

dealing. Outside the Central Bank in Charles de Gaulle Square in Warsaw on an old cardboard box were a pile of rusty old tools: screwdrivers, hammers, pliers. An old man was trying to sell what looked like the contents of his grandfather's garden shed. Opposite the clock on Castle Square, which was restarted in July 1974 at the very second it stopped when the Nazis invaded thirty-five years earlier, spread out on a dirty cloth on the pavement were a selection of buns and cakes. An old lady was selling what she had presumably cooked in hope that morning. Round the corner from the big red-brick Barbakan gate, in a hole in the wall, a man in a leather jacket was selling watches.

From inside rusty old Trabants parked in front of the old Communist Palace of Culture, which everybody calls St Josef's Cathedral, people were selling books, raffle tickets, cigarettes, boxes of matches, sweets, gums and jellies and as many different home-made chocolates as you can imagine. Outside the National Philharmonic Hall on a series of cardboard boxes another old lady was selling – or trying to sell – single cloves of garlic, sprigs of privet hedge and some bits of coloured tape.

Once at Central Station waiting for the 14.17 to Moscow I was hustled by three very eager young entrepreneurs, as they call them, who were offering me everything from a packet of cigarettes to the Empire State Building. If I had asked them to get me Michelangelo's *Lady with a Dead Ferret round her Neck*, Poland's most famous painting, I bet you any money you like they would have got it, and probably by the following morning.

And not just in Warsaw. The Poles nowadays seem to be hustling all over the world. In Italian restaurants in Chicago; on cab ranks in Vilnius; sitting outside vineyard gates early in the morning all over Germany. Waiting outside building sites in France and Belgium. Arriving by the busload outside semi-conductor plants outside Frankfurt. Even in Brussels I've come across Poles hustling vodka, caviar, foie gras and, of course, cigarettes. On the train from the airport, wandering across the

Grande Place, and once even waiting downstairs in DG VIII, a couple of very friendly, persuasive entrepreneurs kept offering me a box of Marlboros for a couple of Belgian francs or even fewer US dollars.

But why the Poles? Why not the Czechs, the Hungarians, the Romanians, or whoever? Because, an old Polish businessman told me, for generations the Poles have had to learn to survive. If it wasn't possible, they found ways of making it possible.

'The Czechs. They said to the Russians, you leave us alone we leave you alone. Okay. We Poles, we say to the Russians, yes. Then we do it our way. When the Wall come down we already have lots of practice,' he explained.

The Czechs became very institutionalised. They were reluctant to act on their own, let alone bend, or even, perish the thought, ignore the rules. Not so the Poles. If a rule exists, it is there to be broken.

'A Czech, he will not take a new job because of what the neighbours will say. Not the Pole. He will take the job. He will buy new BMW. He will put it outside his neighbour's house,' he added. 'The Czechs, they come here. They will spend Czech crowns in Poland. No problem. Money is money. We go to Czech Republic. They refuse to accept Polish zlotys. They only want Czech crowns.'

To Muscovites, Warsaw is Paris. To Parisians, it's Moscow.

At one time it was the intellectual, cultural and social centre of Europe. Ambassadors used to complain bitterly if they were transferred to London. Not any more. Warsaw today looks like one vast council estate with the occasional community centre thrown in for lectures by the Workers' Educational Association.

Wherever you turn the place seems heavy with memories. Bad memories. The Royal Way is full of huge, splendid, spacious buildings of a long gone era when Poland and Polish society practically dominated Europe. On Krakowski Przedmiescie is the Hotel Bristol where Napoleon, on the nights he was not with Josephine, used to develop his various strategies (not to say tactics) with his Polish mistress Countess Walewska.

Everywhere, of course, there are memories of the Nazis. The ghetto is gone, but you can still see where the Jews were herded up and sent off to Auschwitz. There are memories of the uprising in 1944 when over 200,000 people died trying to overthrow the Nazis, while looking on all the time from Praga, across the Vistula, were the Russians waiting to move in when it was all over. In retaliation, the centre of Warsaw was effectively razed to the ground by the Nazis. Amazingly, the entire Old Town – all the seventeenth- and eighteenth-century houses as well as the cathedral – has been rebuilt brick by brick, from memory of the few survivors that are left and from paintings by Bernardo Bellotto, a nephew of Canaletto. Even the Hotel Bristol, for forty years a pile of rubble, has been rebuilt and refurbished, although there is still apparently a desperate shortage of countesses to go round. At least, that's what I was told when I was looking for someone to discuss my strategies and tactics with.

The Palace of Culture, the old Communist Party headquarters, is still there, although it looks nothing like a palace and less cultural than anything else in Warsaw. It towers thirty-two storeys high above the city centre. It looks like a copy of the Empire State Building as seen by a hack Moscow architect with poor eyesight working from an old postcard. In the bad old days, I was told, that's where all the telephone conversations were bugged. The Poles decided the only way they could fight back was to make as many long, boring telephone calls as possible, so that in the end the building was crammed so tight, floor to ceiling, with reports of reports of reports of telephone conversations that it just toppled over with the weight. Today it is home to long, long, empty corridors, dirty, dusty conference rooms, and their new stock exchange. In the basement is a casino. Which seems to tie in nicely.

In the yard of the Church of St Stanislaw Kostki is the red granite tomb of Father Jerzy Popieluszko, one of the martyrs of modern Poland. A great champion of Solidarity, he used to give fierce anti-Communist sermons, and for his troubles was murdered by the secret police.

Then there is the famous Narodowy Theatre. Anywhere else in the world, theatregoers are only concerned during a performance with getting to the bar first at the interval and afterwards getting a cab and not missing the last train home. In Warsaw it's different. In 1968, at the end of the final performance of *Forefathers Eve*, a stirring national drama written in thirteen-syllable standard metre about the day-to-day struggles of the Lithuanians against the Russians, they rushed not for the last train but for the monument to the author, Adam Mickiewicz, one of Poland's great writers, on Krakowskie Przedmiescie Street. Even though the play was anti-Russian as opposed to anti-Soviet, the censors had decided that it should close. The protesters demanded that it should continue. Several students at Warsaw University who were among them were arrested, and even though the magistrates could not believe the censors had been foolish enough to ban the play, they were still thrown into gaol. Demonstrations took place at the university to free the students. At first plain-clothes police tried to pull the ring-leaders out of the crowd. Eventually the police moved in, truncheons at the ready. The official press referred only to 'disturbances in road and communications traffic'. But it was the beginning of the end. The press began blaming everything, as they always did, on the Jews. More protests took place. More police charges. More arrests. The rest, as they say, is history.

Maybe it's the thought of all this; maybe it's all the other memories; maybe it's the atmosphere; maybe it's just the mood of the place, but the more I go back the more I am convinced Warsaw is what the world would be like if the Reformation had never taken place and Lech Walesa was the Holy Roman – oops, I mean, Polish – Emperor. I mean it's full of churches: not empty churches like Venice, or, I suppose, the City of London. But full churches, in full working order, packed not with old ladies in black shawls and broken shoes but with everybody: young, old, men, women, entrepreneurs, non-entrepreneurs, kneecappers and non-kneecappers.

What's more, everybody recognises they are churches and behaves as if they are churches. Which, incidentally, is how you spot the tourist. Once I was in the Church of the Holy Cross, where the heart of Fryderykow Chopinowi – Frédéric Chopin to you and me – is revered in the second pillar on the left-hand side, even though he left Warsaw when he was twenty and died in Paris of TB when he was nearly forty.

A group of Americans were ushered in by a serious-looking tour guide. They shuffled down the nave to the pillar.

'So it's a musical ashtray,' I heard one of them grunt. 'Let's go and have a beer.'

A similar thing happened to me once back home in St Paul's Cathedral. Between meetings in the City I dashed in to catch an exhibition in the crypt. I'd no sooner got inside than I was stopped by some big guy, American, with his Havana still jammed between his teeth.

'Excuse me, sir,' he bellowed. 'How much of all this is now offices?'

Warsaw is also serious. Hong Kong is serious: but serious about doing business. Rio is serious: but serious about having fun. Warsaw is serious about being serious. You don't have to be in town longer than it takes to walk from your cab into your hotel to feel it. In the air; in the look in the eyes of the hotel porter; in the manner of the girl on reception. By the time you get to your room, you can feel it bearing down on your shoulders. In Warsaw it's practically impossible to straighten up, let alone hold your head high. It's a bit like going back to the house after a funeral. There is no gossip, no bantering, not the slightest smile. The men look as though they have just survived three weeks studying Wlodarczyk's book on social realism. The women all look like widows or the Archduke's grandmother, even the ones who look less like grandmothers than the others. Cab drivers, as soon as you clamber in, immediately switch their radios to a pop music station as if they are embarrassed to be found listening to Henryk Gorecki's harrowing Third Symphony, which in Poland far and away outsells Michael Jackson and Madonna. And chatty they are not. All they seem to say is, 'You're the boss.'

'Nice day.'

'You're the boss.'

'OK, let's go to the ministry of finance.'

'You're the boss.'

'Forget the ministry of finance. Let's go to the nearest bar.'

'You're the boss.'

The restaurants think nothing of turning you away, not because you might not have a tie but because they think you're badly dressed. And there's nothing frivolous about the food. It's just one boar after another: good old-fashioned plain simple boar; boar cooked hunter-style; or boar cooked with venison. The wine list is ambitious. In most restaurants you can have beer, beer or even, on special occasions, beer. The service is definitely not collar-and-tie and a decent suit.

Conversation is as likely to be about a Papal encyclical as the best way to kill a pig. Honest. One evening in a restaurant in the Market Square in the Old Town I was invited to dinner with a group of businessmen from different steel companies. The wild boar was no sooner on the table than they were off.

'A yoke, that's the best thing.'

'We always used a hammer.'

'Never. That's cruel.'

'It bruises the head, makes it all black and blue. Then you can't sell it.'

Then from the other end of the table I began to catch the odd phrase.

' . . . The right to act according to one's conscience.'

'Eat the head?'

'But the order of things must be subordinated to the order of people.'

'Why not? Some people eat the cheeks, the ears, everything.'

' . . . active part in political life . . .'

'Fat that thick around the neck.' The man sitting opposite me held his hands up like a fisherman exaggerating the size of a goldfish.

' . . . personal responsibility . . .' said somebody somewhere.

'But first you should weigh the head. A pig always weighs ten times the weight of its head.'

' . . . social interchange . . .'

Or they go on about priests. I once spent a fun-packed evening in the restaurant in the Forum Hotel, the old Intourist hotel opposite St Josef's Cathedral.

'Four priests there were,' they started as soon as we sat down. 'But one morning Father Henryk did not come down for breakfast. They went up to his room. His bed wasn't slept in. Eventually they found him outside. Under a tree. Dead.'

Which is one hell of a way to start an evening off – even in Warsaw.

The funfair outside St Josef's Cathedral is serious. I know nothing about children, but I know I've never seen so many serious-looking kids having the time of their lives as I saw on the swings and roundabouts. I reckon if you showed them even a postcard of Disney World, it would blow their minds.

What's more, even the graffiti is serious. Warsaw is the only place in the world where I've seen rival graffiti praising different saints. And I mean saints saints. Not football or baseball teams.

If you're planning once and for all to crack algorithmic complexity theory or even what the wife wants for her birthday, Warsaw is the place to go. You'll be able to work from seven in the morning until ten at night. Non-stop; no distractions; and definitely no temptations. But first you would have to grow a big droopy moustache, get yourself an old sports jacket, some baggy trousers and a pair of scruffy shoes.

In fact the only mildly frivolous thing I thought I came across in the many times I've been there was muzak in the Forum, which once was what sounded like non-stop wobbly old Cilla Black records. Every time I heard 'Make it easy on yourself', it wobbled on a different word giving the whole thing a totally different meaning to that which I am sure was intended.

The only people I ever saw not seriously laughing and joking in a Warsaw restaurant were a group of German tourists. And they were not serious because they were rolling up their towels, escaping Cilla Black and going home the following Morgen. Either that or they had just bought a load of weapons grade 239 plus the tubes and detonators in return for a couple of packs of Marlboros.

Wherever you go in Warsaw, whether to Zabke, on the east bank of the Vistula River which cuts right through the middle of Poland, which is a bit like Chicago's south side or Moss Side, Manchester, or to Pruszkows on the up-market west-side-story side, it always looks as though it has just finished snowing. There is hardly any traffic. There is plenty of space to park. The pavements are wet, there are piles of slush everywhere, and it's empty. Like old-fashioned Sunday after-noons between Mass and Benediction. You feel as though either there are not enough people to go around, or they are frightened of coming out in the open, or they're all up at Trakiszki, near the border with Lithuania, hustling cigarettes or nuclear missiles.

If you see any policemen, they're like nuns; they always travel in threes: one who actually has a job to do, one to keep him company, and one to keep the other company if one of them has to be left behind somewhere for some reason. The only people who seem to go around by themselves are the kind of people who always seem to go around by themselves.

If you are lucky enough actually to see anybody they tell you to go to the Blikle bakery which is famous throughout the Polish-speaking world for *paczki*, jelly doughnuts. Not me. For excitement I make for the football stadium in the suburbs of Braga early on Sunday mornings where, as the wind whips across the river and around the stadium, it can often be as warm as –20°. Originally built to mark the tenth anniversary of the Communist Revolution, it is now home to Warsaw's biggest street market.

More rusty old screwdrivers, more wooden drills, more piles of old but old clothes that even Oxfam would not accept for the poorest, warmest countries. Bits and pieces of guns, knives and forks: everything is for sale, in whatever currency you care to name – zlotys, roubles, Czech crowns, dollars. Everybody prefers dollars. This is the real economy. This is how people keep body and soul together.

A pile of old books; an old man who looks as though it's a million years since he had any food for thought let alone for his stomach is asking only two dollars for the lot. And this French tourist in all his flashy gear is arguing, but arguing about the price. The old man told me he used to be a miner, one of St Barbara's finest, after the patron saint of mining. Under the Communists, miners earned twice as much as doctors. They were the élite. Everybody wanted to jump over the miner's apron, as they say, and drop straight into the pit. Not any more. The only way he could live now was to sell, literally, everything he had. He had already sold the clothes off his back. Now he was selling the books off his shelves.

Next to him an old lady, as thin as half a rake, was selling icons. For some reason throughout Eastern Europe they have this thing about icons, which are, I suppose, religious pin-ups. On the one hand most of them are pretty primitive primitives. Almost childlike. But on the other hand, many are strangely moving. Maybe it's because they are still more religious than art. Maybe it's because the artlessness in itself makes it art. Maybe just because they're different. I'm no expert. But to me they seem to recall an event or a person. They set the scene. They tell a story. There is nothing clever about them. They are straightforward, head-on reporting. Like taking family photographs; you don't want anything arty, just a straightforward shot to put on the wall or keep on your desk. Swirling colours, vast contrasts might be all very well for Michelangelo, but in the east the icon painters were interested only in keeping things plain and simple. They produced icons the way they always produced icons: wide-eyed saints, dragons and devils out of all proportion.

Most of the ones you see around today are fifteenth- or sixteenth-century. The seventeenth and eighteenth centuries produced some superb examples. The nineteenth-century ones are somewhat indifferent. The modern ones are, well, modern. Some are produced by genuine icon painters following the traditions laid down over generations, but – be warned – some, maybe most, are fakes. But, as the old lady knows if she still has any feeling left in her body, there is big business in icons, genuine or fake. There are tiny ones, three to four inches square. There are even small travelling brass icons a bit like a spiritual Filofax which, tucked away in the breast pocket, stopped many a bullet during the First World War. Then there are big ones, like paintings, which hang on the walls of churches, homes and even offices. I went into one office in Warsaw where the walls were positively dripping with them.

Big or small, the most popular icon of all is the Black Madonna, which was supposed to have been painted by St Luke himself on a bit of old wood he found in a carpenter's shop in Nazareth; passed on by St Helena to Constantine for the new city he was building on the edge of the Bosphorus; handed on to Charlemagne, then lost and found again and, since the thirteenth century, has been the centre of worship in Jasna Gora in Upper Silesia in the south of the country. Next seems to be St George and the Dragon. Then for some reason St Demetrios of Thessalonika, an early Christian martyr famous for defending Thessalonika against the marauding Roman armies of Diocletian and Maximian. It's misshapen, unreal; there is no attempt at light relief or narrative – practically no attempt at making it even artistic. He just kind of stares at you, a cross in his right hand, a sword and a tiny shield in the other.

The feeling seems to be, if it's important, stick it on the wall.

Lech Walesa? Well, yes, I suppose so. The Pope? Sure. Linda Evangelista? Well, maybe. But Jacques Attali?

At the Ministry of Finance, I met an economist, a mumsy woman in a cardigan, who told me she no longer believed in the European Bank for Reconstruction and Development. They were spending too much money on decorating their offices and not enough on Eastern Europe. As a result she had decided to take Jacques Attali's picture off her bedroom wall. Me, I'd only stick a picture of Jacques Attali on the wall if there was a hole in it and I wanted to stop the draught getting through. Then again, maybe I'd rather stick a picture of the wife's mother up there instead.

The old lady, by my calculation only wanted $3 to $5 for her icons. Which was crazy. The trouble is being able to tell the real from the fake. For, as with civil reactor grade plutonium, weapons grade 239 and tubes and detonators to make your own nuclear bomb, the Poles have moved in and completely fouled up the market.

From secret midnight exchanges in Gorky Park or Ishmaalovo Park in Moscow via Sheremetyevo Airport with a little bit of assistance from you-know-who or in secret panels in cars or trucks or in diplomatic bags from all over Eastern Europe, icons are all channelled through Warsaw. Church wardens; museum curators; clergy; picture restorers: they're all in it. Years ago I knew one of McGraw Hill's top men in Europe. He was a Pole. Whenever he went to Poland he drove back to London with the boot as well as the back of his big Mercedes packed with icons which he then sold at Sotheby's.

Today, icons are big business. There are icon galleries everywhere. Berlin is full of them, most of them on the Kurfürstendam. Others I've seen in Milan, Zurich and, of course, London.

Some icons can be worth anything from US$5,000 to US$50,000. Rare ones can go up to US$100,000, really rare ones way over that. But only to a specialist collector. Find an icon produced by Andrei Rublev, a Russian Orthodox monk who after St Luke is credited with starting the whole business, and you'll be worth more than a zloty millionaire.

But as if she hasn't got enough problems, what has the old lady got to put up with now? A German is threatening to tear the city apart unless she reduces the price of a fabulous little icon of St George by a whole 10 cents. Worse still, a group of – oh no! – Englishmen and women are just walking past smiling vacantly the way we do and mumbling, 'No thank you, not today thanks.'

I didn't want another icon. I've only got one so far. It's about the size of a beer mat. It shows three shadowy priests or monks. I bought it in a tiny shop in Vilnius. At first I thought it was going to pay for my retirement, but when I got back to the office and worked out that it had barely cost me £3.70 I began to have doubts. But I feel so ashamed. Here are these once proud people reduced to selling – nothing. I buy a whole table-load of icons from her for twenty dollars. And then give them back to her. I mean, what would you have done?

If Warsaw is grey and serious and Stalinist, Cracow is fantastic. It's Venice, Salzburg and a bit of Oxford rolled into one. If you promise not to laugh, I'll almost go as far as to admit that it is one of my all-time favourites. Like, I suppose, boring old Auckland is to New Zealanders.

There's nothing cheap or crass or superficial or touristy about the place. It's almost as if it stands four-square for what's right and honest in this world. You can almost breathe the medieval atmosphere and hear the divine office wafting over the rooftops.

Everyone you see or talk to is, you feel, either a moral theologian, the world's leading authority on St John of the Cross, or the bishop's housekeeper. People bless themselves whenever they get on a train or bus which, I admit, is not reassuring until you get used to it. They carry prayerbooks under their arms on weekdays. They sit on doorsteps, in cafés, in bars reading books of meditation. Everybody, I swear, meditates on the Four Last Things before they go to sleep at night. When husbands die, wives don't sell the family silver and head for Rio, they seem more than happy to don their weeds and spend the rest of their lives polishing the candle-sticks, sweeping the church and praying for the souls of the faithful departed.

You can bet your bottom zloty they are the only people in the world who could spin through the Pope's book, *Crossing the Threshold of Hope* (which I admit I first thought, judging by the title, was about his trips by dodgy airlines in Third World countries) without stumbling over common everyday words like soteriology, ateopagi or apocatastasis.

As for the rationalisation of the last century, well it's as obvious in its Anglo-Saxon expression as in its continental expression in Kantianism, Hegelianism, as well as the German philosophy of the nineteenth and twentieth centuries up to Hüsserl and Heidegger, that it's a continuation and an expansion of Cartesian positions. Isn't it? Well to them it is.

'Be not afraid.' That, the Pope said, was his message. (See what I mean about travelling by dodgy airlines in Third World countries.) Me, I'm afraid that even if I studied philosophical ethics at Lublin University for twenty years I still wouldn't understand half of what he was saying. Which is why, I reckon, it will be like Stephen Hawking's book, *A Brief History of Time*, one of the great unread bestsellers. That is, if I'm allowed to say such a thing without being suddenly struck down by lightning. (Phew. So far so good.)

Cracow, Pope John's home town, is unreformed, unrecon-structed, 100 per cent genuine back-to-basics pre-Vatican II Catholicism. Everywhere there are priests, friars, nuns and monks: sitting waiting for trams; strolling up and down reading their prayerbooks; wandering along the narrow streets gossiping, I swear, in Latin. The place is even full of priests' and nuns' shops selling priests' shoes, priests' socks, priests' vests, priests' pants and presumably, behind the black curtain, nuns' this and thats as well. One nun, I was told, in the Convent of the Enclosed Order of Poor Classes, is well over a hundred years old and has been behind the curtains so long she has never seen a tram, let alone a broken-down Range Rover.

Go into offices. On the desk, alongside the pocket calculator, the electronic notebook, a pile of print-outs, a diary crammed with meetings, is the Daily Missal.

Get a taxi. Instinctively you feel taxi drivers know it's a mortal sin to overcharge deliberately. Accidentally, of course, is another matter. Because as any moral theologian will tell you, especially a Jesuit, to commit a mortal sin it must not only be a serious error but you must be fully conscious of what you are doing; and if for whatever reason you were in a rush you could not have been fully conscious, so maybe it was okay to slap an extra six billion zlotys on the bill. Which is only about 27p anyhow.

You get the feeling in this place that nobody, but nobody, eats meat on a Friday. If they did you are in no doubt that the clouds would part, there would be this awful, terrifying rumbling sound and – zap – a shaft of lightning would send them to Kingdom Come.

Dammit, they even banished McDonald's to a side-street and there are not many places that would do that. Until the city fathers change their mind, therefore, the most historic site in Polish history still remains the Gothic castle on top of Wawel Hill, the seat of Polish kings from the eleventh to the seventeenth century. The Royal Cathedral alongside, built in the fourteenth century, is full of ornate side chapels and works of art.

But the centre of the town is, of course, Rynek Glowny, the market square which has got to be one of the largest and best preserved in Europe. In the centre is the Renaissance Cloth Hall. In the old days it was the great cross-over point between East and West. Furs from the north and east; honey and fruit from the warm south; carpets from Turkey; clocks from the west, and everything else from everywhere else, would all be traded there. Today it is full of stalls selling everything from religious statues and rosaries and prayerbooks – I told you this was pre-Reformation country – to the usual T-shirts and postcards. But all in the best possible taste.

On one corner is the town hall tower, built in the fifteenth century. On another corner is the tiny tenth-century church of St Adalbert. On one side is an enormous statue of the poet and playwright Adam Mickiewicz. Towering over everything is the dark, sombre, brooding, eternal presence of St Mary's with its twin spires. Inside is what many people say is the most splendid Gothic altar in Europe. All around the square are cafés and bars and restaurants.

The cultural, intellectual, almost spiritual, capital of Poland, Cracow escaped almost unscathed during the last war. But it has not been so lucky in peace. During the days of Soviet rule, it was the only city in the whole Eastern bloc, I was told, that actually closed down its Lenin Museum (Lenin lived in Cracow in 1912) because nobody ever went there. And, of course, it paid the price. Today in retaliation it is surrounded by sprawling factories, giant refineries and massive industrial plants, a punishment by the Communists for the way its citizens refused to give in. The result is that for years it's been subject to industrial pollution which, I know, is nowhere near as bad as moral pollution, but is all the same slightly irritating to say the least.

It has also suffered grievously. Kazmierez, the old Jewish quarter, was home to 65,000 Jews in 1938. Today there are only around 600 left. From November 1940 to 1943 it was bound by ten-foot high walls. Inside there were 40,000 people, the world's largest concentration of Jews, desperately trying to continue to live as normal. Shops had sales. Printers printed wedding invitations. Lawyers argued about property rentals. Children studied for their exams; their parents continued to worry about whether they would find a job when they left school.

In the first year, they were decimated by starvation and disease. From July to September 1942 over 30,000 were deported to Treblinka where they were gassed.

In January 1943 came the uprising. The Nazis withdrew. But in April they returned with a vengeance. What they did, the horrors they perpetrated, the untold suffering they caused will live forever. Not because it happened but because, unfortunately, it was the raw material for *Schindler's List* which as far as I'm concerned should be renamed *Spielberg's List of Mistakes*.

What Spielberg said happened in Kazmierez didn't. It happened across town in the Podgorze ghetto on the other side of the Vistula River. But Spielberg thought Kazmierez looked more like the real thing and used it as his substitute film ghetto.

You remember the little boy who was shot in the square? He wasn't. It was somewhere else. But who's interested?

Not the Spielberg tourists, who are beginning to pour in not to remember the true horrors of Kazmierez, but to shed quiet tears at the fictional deaths that took place in the film.

'The boy. That little boy. You remember. He died here, at this very spot.' I forget how many times I've heard American matrons say that.

Not the Spielberg tourist industry that's grown up, backed inevitably by local businessmen.

'And this is where Mr Spielberg himself came to discuss the film. This is where the Hollywood producer himself decided . . .'

Where Mr Spielberg went in the evenings to discuss the film was the Ariel Café. Except today there are now three Ariel Cafés, each claiming to be the one and only original; each claiming to know whether he drank two cups or three, with or without sugar; and each competing for the tourists.

'And this is where Mr Spielberg bought his morning newspaper.'

'And this is where Mr Spielberg decided to look at the strip cartoons.'

'And this is where Mr Spielberg blew his nose and decided to . . .' Well, never mind.

No mention of the sixteenth-century synagogue, the oldest synagogue in Poland. No mention of the Remu'h synagogue further down the road which is still in business. No mention

of the Poper, the sixteenth-century Jewish cemetery, one of
the oldest in Europe. No mention of the black curly Hassidic
Jews with their black coats who, in spite of everything,
survived. And no mention of Auschwitz, probably the biggest
concentration camp ever built in the history of the world and
probably the biggest extermination camp of all time.

There are some things I shall never understand and
Auschwitz is up there near the top of the list. I mean, how on
earth could the Nazis actually murder four million innocent
people in the Auschwitz–Birkenau concentration camp? It's
just way, way, way beyond me. Four. Four hundred. It's bad
enough. But four million. It's just unbelievable. How could
human beings contemplate, let alone do such a thing. On such
a scale. And over so long a period of time.

If that's not unbelievable enough, how could they presumably sit down and cold-bloodedly plan it all, in all its
horrifying detail? Knowing the Nazi mania for planning, for
organisation, for efficiency, there must have been committee
meeting after committee meeting: memos, reports, proposals,
counter-proposals, costings, estimates, budgets, procurement
orders, delivery notes, dockets. Sign here, Herr Kommandant.
Initial here, mein General. It beggars belief.

For years I deliberately avoided visiting Auschwitz. Somehow it didn't seem right that it should be a visitor attraction.
But on one trip I was running ahead of schedule. I had driven
from Trinec in the Czech Republic, across the border and all
through Silesia, Poland's rust belt and Cracow's crown of
thorns, over eighty miles of non-stop steelworks, chemical
works and everything else that pumps gas, fumes and smoke
into the atmosphere. As we headed towards Katowice I went
to open the window.

'Damage it will your lungs,' the driver told me firmly.

'But I need some fresh air.'

'Fresh the air is not. Please to close window.'

'But I can't . . .'

'Please to . . .'

I wound the window down. 'Aaaaraghhhh.' It was my own

fault. In three seconds I'd probably swallowed a couple of tons of soot, three hundred gallons of acid rain and God knows what else.

The air is so thick, it sticks to your teeth. If the factories could only produce sharp enough knives you might be able to cut it into small lumps and export it. But they can't, so it smothers the whole area like some massive thick sulphurous blanket that can be seen over twenty miles away. Most places look better when it snows. The snow covers everything in white. Not Silesia. In Silesia it snows black snow. There is so much soot in the air it just comes down to earth again. Similarly, it rains black rain.

One young manager in Jaworzno III power station, which every year belches out over 75,000 tonnes of sulphur dioxide and nearly 10,000 tonnes of dust and ash, told me that they all had to keep clean shirts in their desks so that if they had to go out and meet a customer they could change. 'It's the only way to look clean,' he said.

As for the water, so much chemicals and waste and sewage had seeped into the soil over the years that nobody would drink so much as half a glass even if it had been boiled four times.

'You know why the Pope never comes back?' he said. 'He's frightened he's going to have to kiss the ground again.'

As a result, I was in Cracow a day earlier than I had expected. Auschwitz – Osweizcim in Polish – was only fifty kilometres away to the west of the city. I decided I had to go. But I wish I hadn't.

Auschwitz is the world's largest cemetery. Four million people, ordinary people like you and me, suffered such agonies, such unimaginable pain, and died the most horrifying of deaths here. But it's not like a cemetery at all. I was expecting, I suppose, long empty corridors, dark empty rooms. Stillness, silence, respect, memories. Small groups of people hushed, huddled together trying to remember – and trying to forget. Instead it was . . . different.

From the outside, you could be visiting any minor stately

home or major garden centre north of Tunbridge Wells. The car park is practically full. Coach after coach after coach is unloading hundreds of people.

'Una ora,' an Italian tour guide was lilting away to her flock. 'Everyone back on the coach by 2.30 p.m. We have to be in . . .'

My God, call me old-fashioned, but surely this is not the way to visit a place like Auschwitz.

Another coach was unloading local schoolchildren. 'Children, children,' the teacher was saying in a stage whisper. 'Now, remember what I said. I don't want to hear or see anyone . . .' But, of course, Karola in the back row was already making Katarzyna giggle.

Inside the reception centre, which had obviously been built to handle visitors, it was bedlam. The noise was deafening. Kids were running backwards and forwards. A film? You want to see a film taken by the Russians immediately after the camp was liberated? Sorry, not possible. They need fifteen people, minimum. Move along, please. Next. On the wall is a sign saying, 'Because of the thrilling character of exposition children under 13 are not admitted.'

I heard a group of French visitors asking if there was a restaurant. And there was! Even a hotel. As part of the complex. Which is definitely not what I expected.

Just outside Vilnius in Lithuania is the Paneriu Memorialas, a simple stone monument in Hebrew, Lithuanian and Russian in a clearing in the centre of the forest. No posters; no giant photographs; no audio-visual displays; no crowds of people being herded by guides in six languages; no hordes of kids, running around and shouting and screaming or looking bored or making funny remarks and smirking at each other. Just the monument. Just the silence. Just the surrounding forest where over 100,000 people were massacred between July 1941 and July 1944, most of them Jews.

Auschwitz, I had thought, would be like that.

I walked outside and into the camp itself which looks like, I suppose, an army barracks, or your typical council housing estate. There are roads up and down the camp. Along each road are long, two-storey brick buildings. At first it was a concentration camp for Polish political prisoners, Jews as well as non-Jews. Then Soviet prisoners were held here as well. Towards the end of 1941 it was converted into one vast, non-stop death machine. In a single day, up to 20,000 people could be gassed, cremated and their ashes either buried, used as fertiliser on the surrounding fields or just thrown in the river.

I walk slowly up and down each roadway. I go into the buildings. In Block 5 they still have the suitcases left by the Jews on the unloading ramps with their names and dates of birth still legible. There is a cabinet. Inside there are baby clothes and dummies, a teething ring, tiny shoes, clasps of hair . . .

I go into the block where they were taken for medical experiments; into the final extermination block. It's clean today. But the benches and the stalls are still there. I go into the gas chamber itself. You walk inside, you see everything. But somehow it seems wrong – it is wrong – to tramp all over the floor where how many people lay gasping for breath and choking and dying in agony. Why is it wrong? Maybe it's me. Maybe it doesn't make any difference, so long as we remember and make certain that it never, ever, ever happens again. Or maybe it does.

I then went to Birkenau, the adjoining camp which could hold up to 200,000 people. There there is no big car park, no visitors' centre, no restaurant. It is extremely cold, and it is beginning to rain.

I climb the tower straddling the railway line. On the left are a collection of low, squat buildings. On the right, still there, are row after row of wooden sheds. Down there, not so many years ago, men, women and children were bundled out of trains, herded, sorted and led away to you just cannot imagine what horrors.

Suddenly hordes of kids come clambering, shouting and screaming up the stairs and rush to see the view. I go back downstairs and walk up and down through the camp. Hell, it's cold now. What on earth was it like then?

I go in and out of the huts. I try to imagine what agonies, what horror went on there day after day. It's impossible. You can't imagine such things. If anything, you feel numb: it's too much, too horrendous. And yet it happened.

At the back of the camp are the ruins of the gas chambers and crematoria. They are enormous, each capable of handling 2,000 people at a time. There are even electric lifts to shift the bodies from the gas chambers to the crematoria as quickly as possible ready for the next batch. The chimneys must have been continually pumping out smoke. You must have been able to smell burning flesh for miles. Good God, if hell did not exist, it would have to be invented for the people who did such things.

I walk back to the entrance, to the reception, across the railway lines to the railway platform. Of course. That's what I would do to commemorate the horrors of Auschwitz and Birkenau. I'd wipe Auschwitz off the railway maps of the world. I'd rip up the railway lines in the whole area. Sure, it would cause a lot of people a lot of inconvenience. But nowhere near as much inconvenience as Auschwitz itself created. In any case how anyone could think of travelling by train to Auschwitz beats me. I'd pull down the railway station in the centre of town.

The only lines I would leave would be lines inside the camp. That, I think, would be a better memorial to all those who suffered and died there.

Bratislava

The collapse of the Berlin Wall; the break up of the 'Evil Empire'; the death of the Trabant. The opening up of Eastern Europe opened up for me a whole new world of intrigue, double-dealing, lying and cheating. In other words, opera.

The more travelling I do, the less excitement I seem to get from staring out of hotel windows at the traffic lights changing in the rain or, where there are not even any windows, listening to the whine of the Xpelair unit in the bathroom next door. Wherever I go, therefore, I try to force myself to observe, share or even take part in some local cultural experience, although in some cases over the years I admit some of them have tended to be less cultural and more experience. But that's another story.

In Amman, the goody-two-shoes capital of Jordan, for example, I go to the ballet which, whatever the production, makes me marvel at the intricate footwork, the superb sense of balance and the amazingly precise timing needed to get from your seat to the bar and back again before the curtain comes up for the second half. The last time I was there I saw the *Nutcracker*. The male lead was a big, butch Iraqi business-man, complete with Saddam Hussein moustache, who, I was told, was always looking for an opportunity to dress up in tights and prance around in public. At least, I think it was the *Nutcracker*; from where I was sitting I saw more nuts than crackers.

In Vilnius I went to see *Death of an Anarchist* in Lithuanian. I didn't understand a word, but it didn't matter. It was fantastic;

the characterisation, the delivery, the timing, the staging, the sheer absurdity of the story. The whole thing was absolutely hilarious. If anything it was easier to follow than when I first saw it in London in, I think, English.

Somewhere, I can't remember where, in the middle of France – it was one of those days – I once saw *The Carmelites*, the story of a group of nuns sentenced to death in the last days of the French Revolution. The stage, I vaguely remember, was practically bare. I can't remember the music at all. What I do remember, what is etched forever on my soul, is the final scene: the nuns lined up on the scaffold one behind the other waiting to be guillotined singing the *Salve Regina* and at each crash of the blade, a head rolled, one voice disappeared, until in the end – silence.

Oh yes, and once outside La Scala in Milan I saw a lorry unloading crates of cheese, big boxes of sliced grilled chicken, great piles of toasted club sandwiches and a whole ton of fresh lemons for Big Lucy, which is the nearest I've ever come to grand opera.

The result is that today I am to culture what a violinist is to the derivatives market.

Now I admit, music is not my hammer. I forget how many times I've heard the Humming Chorus and I still can't remember the words. Instead of going to a concert I'd rather spend a couple of hours mucking out the stables. But when I first started going through Eastern Europe, there was not much else to do – or at least, not if you excluded helping to make home-made videos for the KGB. Now, of course, it's all changed. If they want videos, they have to pay for them like the rest of us. But in those days it was a case of either hunt the microphone, spot the camera lens or go to the opera.

I decided to go to the opera, and now I'm hooked. But only in Eastern Europe. Not because of their stunning inter-pretations of age-old dramas, the luxurious settings or the fact that the opera houses are invariably the warmest place in town. But because of the price. For less than half the price of an ice cream cornet in Covent Garden, or half a glass of champagne at the Châtelet in Paris, I can forget all my worries and wallow in glorious luxury all evening.

The scene of my conversion: Bratislava.

Since then I have been to the opera all over Eastern Europe, including Chicago. Which as far as I'm concerned is Eastern Europe. There are always more Poles at the opera in Chicago than there are in Warsaw. Not because the Warsaw Poles don't go to the opera, but because the Japanese tend to get there first.

My favourite opera city is probably Budapest. I remember once seeing *Tosca* there, shortly after the Wall came down. The place was packed. Everybody was in their finery – smart suits, smart jackets, strapless dresses. Even a few dressless straps. Everywhere there was a smell of mothballs.

The story of *Tosca* is pure, gorgeous, beautiful ham. I mean how many of your lovers would not only be prepared to commit murder to save your life but would then go home, get changed, do her hair and fix her make-up before finally getting round to delivering the official pardon to secure your release from gaol? The whole thing is a nonsense.

But from the moment the curtain went up everybody, but everybody, was on the edge of their seats. The atmosphere was electric. As the story unfolded you could practically feel the emotion. Tosca, the world's most dangerous art critic, came in looking like Audrey Hepburn's mother. Cavaradassi was a pot-bellied Peter Bowles in riding boots. Scarpia was like an elderly overweight Peter Cushing, brilliant in black and white, leather boots up to his thighs, a sweeping black cloak, looking every inch the most evil pantomime baron you could imagine. Every time he took a step forward I expected lightning to strike down at him and every grown-up kid in the audience to hiss. Instead there was that total almost tangible silence gripping your throat.

Sometimes you see Tosca and you can't wait for her to throw herself over the balcony so you can go off and have a drink. Not here. This was for real. Everyone knew a Cavaradassi. Everyone knew a Tosca. Everyone knew a Scarpia.

Everyone knew what it was like living under a reign of terror. Everyone would have loved to have plunged that knife into his back if only they had the chance. Believe me, it was one of those evenings when the whole theatre is one, when everybody practically stops breathing. By the time Tosca got round to throwing herself over the battlements, there wasn't a dry eye in the house. It really was an evening to remember.

I've never experienced an evening like that in Bratislava, but it is still my first love, at least as far as opera is concerned. Compared to Vienna where tickets even for the B-team at the Staatsoper cost an arm and a leg, you just can't afford not to go there. Tickets in the stalls cost a mere £10, a programme £1.50. It's ridiculous. Admittedly, the opera house, at the end of a little square down near the banks of the Danube, doesn't have the vast staircase, all that fancy interior decoration, the three long galleries or that glorious terrace they have in Vienna where you can sip sekt and practise your German. But who cares.

Probably best of all, to go to the opera in Bratislava you don't have to actually stay in Bratislava. You can get there from Vienna, forty miles up the road. To go to the opera in Vienna, or rather to be seen at the opera in Vienna, you don't need to take out a second mortgage. All you have to do is sell your house, the contents, the car, everything you've ever owned. What could be better, therefore, than to stay in Vienna on expenses and get a bus or, better still, the hydrofoil down the Danube and go to the opera in Bratislava?

I hate to say it, but apart from the opera and a couple of exhilarating micro-seconds listening to the clock ticking in the bus station, Bratislava, the northern border of the edible chestnut, is hardly worth a first visit let alone a second, even if you're between jobs, marriages or nervous breakdowns.

It has a thousand-year-old castle which in the sixteenth century was home to the Habsburgs. Like all women, Empress Maria Theresa was not satisfied with it and started adding on extensions here, a conservatory there, central heating and probably double glazing as well. It has more than its unfair share of churches and monuments. There are very few bars, hardly any open-air cafés. Roland Café, near the Michael Tower, looks like the typical intellectual café you find all over Eastern Europe, but it isn't. There is no hub let alone bub. All people want to do is drink coffee and look at the tractors tearing up the square outside.

The shops are small and dusty. The merchandise seems out of date. One fashion shop actually tried to liven up its swinging window display by scattering books about Tomas Morus and copies of the *Anglicko-Slovensky Dictionary* among the merchandise.

Gee whiz, they don't even have a McDonalds.

There's little advertising, although I did spot one display card which, I was told, said, 'We have a wide selection of ladies' and gentlemen's aftershaves.'

There's not much colour. The only excitement seems to be the cranes and trucks modernising yet another old building back to its original eighteenth-century condition.

One morning I went to a group of lawyers' offices just off the main square down towards the Danube; Bratislava's answer to Lincoln's Inn. It was packed with floor after floor of tiny, scruffy offices that needed a lick of paint when Jarndyce v. Jarndyce first started. The office I went to was piled with Carpathian mountains of dusty paper. Before the revolution I'm convinced they just stockpiled paper. They didn't even bother to think about trying to solve legal disputes. With justice itself a highly moveable concept they obviously felt it was safer not even trying to find a solution to anything. With the result that today they are not only literally buried in their past, they have also forgotten how to find an equitable solution to anything.

The streets are almost empty. There's always lots of parked cars but hardly any traffic. Even at what should be busy crossroads, and in main streets, there's little traffic. The occasional tram trundles along followed by maybe a Skoda, maybe a

Trabant. Until, of course, you want to cross the road. Then they suddenly appear from everywhere. Especially if you're at a zebra crossing. Bratislava is the only place I know where the traffic actually speeds up as soon as anybody steps onto a zebra crossing. It's as if Slovak motorists realise they lack practice knocking down pedestrians and are desperate to improve their skills. I can't remember how many years of my life I have wasted trapped in the middle of zebra crossings rather than walk 100 metres up the road, go down the underpass, up the other side and back another 100 metres on the other side.

That's Bratislava. Apart from Auckland, New Zealand, it's the quietest city I've been to.

Offices are basic. Most seem to be at the end of dusty, mysterious courtyards, behind broken doors and up three flights of crumbling stairs. No, I tell a lie. Up one and a half flights. Half the stairs are usually missing. The offices themselves, however, are a delight. Remember those old Remington typewriters? Believe me, they don't die. They go to Bratislava. So do old telex machines. And do you remember those purple trays of jelly we used before the days of photocopying? They are still alive and well and being used regularly in offices all over Bratislava.

The factory estates outside of town are a tribute to the Marxist School of Economics, the Stalinist School of Architecture and the superb skills of a rusty screwdriver. In one factory, where they made old-fashioned heavy weaponry, they could only operate the lift by unscrewing the safety catch and jamming a screwdriver in the works wherever they wanted it to stop.

As for the managers, it's easy to tell the young, thrusting, dynamic, professional types. They are the ones who hobble through the door unaided. The secretaries look like KGB generals who took early retirement and are still learning how to apply their lipstick in the dark.

The most exciting thing I think I've ever seen in Bratislava was a postman trying to push-start a Lada outside the main post office.

The Slovaks have none of the Czech humour or sense of fun, and definitely none of that wry satiric outlook on life. If Kafka had been a Slovak he would have spent his life writing technical catalogues and the Good Soldier Schweik would probably have been content jamming screwdrivers into bits of old machinery that didn't work.

Everyone looks middle-aged, even the children. Everyone looks the same. Men and women look the same. It's like a nation of plumbers worried about their S-bends. The whole place looks as though it relies on the hand-me-downs of their better-off relatives in Bulgaria. All the men seem to wear pullovers and thick, heavy, double-breasted suits, even in summer. The occasional fashion-conscious brat will wear what looks like a Russian lightweight woollen suit with open leather sandals. Not that I know anything about women's clothes, but most of them seem to want to be fashion-conscious but lack the courage. Instead of all the wild, crazy colours and designs you see all over the world, the United Colors of Bratislava are dark greens, browns and – shock! horror! – light grey.

Everyone behaves the same way: slow, deliberate, plodding, as if their brains send messages by carrier pigeon and it takes them a long time to respond. They queue up outside shops without speaking. They clamber on buses without speaking. They walk along the streets, heads down, going from A to B. Hardly anyone seems to recognise anyone. If they do, they mutter something quickly under their breath and move on. There's none of the French or Italian hugging and kissing. There also seems to be little idle chatter and gossip. Couples walk along together in silence. Businessmen just talk business. Taxi drivers don't talk at all.

Put it another way: Bratislava still looks and feels and almost behaves pre-liberation. It's as if they can't believe they're free. They can't believe the liberation took place. They can't believe it's going to last.

An Austrian businessman told me that of all the places he's visited in Eastern Europe, Bratislava still had the feel of the old days. 'It's strange,' he told me in the Roland Café. 'It's in their eyes. It's as if they don't know how to relax. They don't want to.'

The Hungarians, the Czechs, the Romanians – they all seemed to embrace the liberation with open arms. The Slovaks are still thinking about shaking hands. Maybe it's something the Russians used to put in the Slovak beer; maybe in the rush to get away they've forgotten to take it out.

The Slovaks would be ideal running an English hotel where that studied degree of indifference to guests is more highly rated than a belief in giving service, satisfaction and value for money.

And yet everything should be so different. Bratislava is the Mittel of Mitteleuropa. It should be a hiving, thriving, thrusting crossroads city like Vienna. It's the ideal location for any company trying to do business in Eastern Europe. It's on the banks of the Danube: look one way and you can practically see Austria; look the other and you're in Hungary. It's cheap. In Austria the average industrial wage is US$3,200 a month; in Slovakia it's US$200.

But they've blown it. Not content with getting rid of the Russians, they decided also to get rid of the Czechs. Canada; Turkey; Sri Lanka; Yugoslavia: you name it, tribal warfare, official or unofficial, is everywhere. Slovakia is where not tribal war, but tribal peace broke out – and the tribe lost. The Slovak prime minster simply told the Czechs he wanted to quit Czechoslovakia. In the time it took the Czech prime minister to work out how much money he was going to save by dumping the poor, underdeveloped, heavily subsidised Slovaks, it was done. It was the fastest, most peaceful War of Independence in history. There was no real discussion, no real analysis, no vote. The deed was practically done by the two of them. In private.

For the Czechs, it was a dream come true. They had just gained their freedom from the Russians. They needed funds to invest in upgrading and modernising their already fairly modern industries. Bingo, they were free of the Slovaks without as much as a bad word in public let alone a long-drawn-out slanging match, separatist campaign, or worse. The US$1.5 billion they were pumping into Slovakia every year could now be diverted to their own use.

For the Slovaks, it meant they had won their independence. But they lost practically everything else in the process. The economy collapsed. Inflation hit 25 per cent. Unemployment soared to 15 per cent. The koruna had to be devalued by 10 per cent.

Were the Slovaks pleased with their leader and his glorious victory? Were they hell. His popularity plummeted. His party bombed. From at one stage holding 74 out of the 150 seats in parliament, it crashed to 14.

To me Slovakia is like a gambler who bluffed and lost. They obviously thought they had a good hand. They obviously thought the Czechs would object and protest and throw money at them to stay put. But they didn't. The Slovaks called and lost, disastrously. They not only got taken to the cleaners, they had to leave everything there as well. But like all gamblers who go down, they won't admit it.

'We kept asking for our independence because we thought the Czechs would try to buy us off,' one of the lawyers in his dusty office told me from behind a mountain of paper. 'But they didn't. They called our bluff. It just shows you, you can't trust the Czechs.'

I believe in minority rights as much as the rest of the majority. But Heaven help us, there must be a limit, otherwise 53 Acacia Avenue is going to want to declare its independence not only from the local nuclear-free town council but from the rest of the avenue as well. Then 52. Then 51, and so on. Whether you are in the Ukraine, Spain or the local chamber of commerce, everybody living on the edge of any area feels neglected, wants to be loved, and demands their God-given right to the extra cash.

In the old days, the minority would be bought off: extra funds here, a new bookcase for the library, a memorial to the previous major's mother-in-law there. It always worked, until now. Today for some democratic reason minorities seem to think they should be treated as more equal than the majorities.

Try asking for a beer in a Montreal bar in English and you'll very soon see how minorities impose their will on the majority, even though a minority is still a minority and not a majority in spite of the majority pretending it is the minority and the minority, the majority just for the sake of peace and quiet. Not that I expect you to agree with my minority majority or majority minority point of view.

Try the same thing in Sri Lanka, in Turkey, and in I suppose the United States, which is the home of minorities. I'm not saying minorities have no right, should be ignored and driven out into the cold. Not at all. What I am saying is that a minority is a minority is a minority. But the minority and the majority should accept it.

Wherever you go in Slovakia today, even though polls show that, given the democratic chance to vote, over 60 per cent, the majority of the minority of Slovaks would say No, for heaven's sake No, to the minority of one prime minister who undemocratically negotiated and accepted their independence from the Czechs, everybody is desperately trying to justify the decision.

Except funnily enough in Komarno, the centre and virtual capital of Slovakia's 600,000-strong, well-rounded Hungarian community which inhabits the flat lands of the rural south; well-rounded because they are all fat, middle-aged and bearded thanks to the salami and beer. Here, you see Hungarian and Slovak signposts all over the place. Here everybody you meet is called Attila, Lazlo or Miklos. Here you don't have to be reminded the Magyars ruled Slovakia for a thousand years up to the First World War. Post-1918 Hungary was cut back to a third of its size leaving three million Hungarians out in the cold in Ukraine, Romania, Serbia – and Slovakia. Come 1939 Hitler gave them back the flat lands of southern Slovakia. Come Stalin and everything changed again.

But Attila, Lazlo and Miklos maintain that what's right for one minority in a majority is right for another minority in another majority although, of course, in this case the majority of the minority of that majority maintain that their minority in their majority is different from their minority in their majority – if you can follow the minority, or even the majority, of what I am saying.

My own simple view is that whatever the rights or wrongs of their argument, this particular minority is backing a lòser. Not because I have some secret information, but because of geography. The Danube is the natural boundary. It's simply not possible to cut a chunk out of another country just across the river. Countries are not made like that. Greater autonomy, that's another matter. That I can see happening. But then, I'm only a minority.

Before I went to Bratislava I used to think opera was fantastic – until the fat lady began to sing. The colour; the atmosphere; the stage; the costumes – even the music. Everything was great until some fat old Wagnerian goddess started firing off enough decibels to constitute a disturbance under Schedule 4 of the Local Government Miscellaneous Provisions Act 1982.

What on earth are they going on about? So the bass baritone dwarf has got the ring. So what? I've had bigger problems than that in my time and the last thing I would think of doing is riding my horse through flames. In any case, what's the poor horse done to deserve that kind of treatment?

What are they actually singing about? Love? Death? The price of cabbages? Or an everyday story of incest among a bunch of weirdos who go around pulling swords out of trees, making love to their sister, killing their father – or was it their uncle? – and then, if that's not bad enough, falling in love with auntie – or was it their uncle?

My God, what language are they singing in? Italian. German. English. Serbo-Croat. Cockney rhyming slang. It's all the same to me. And the subtitles didn't help either. Take *La*

Bohème. Towards the end of act one, there's poor old Mimi, wracked with consumption, going at full throttle, '*Ah! Sventata, sventata. La chiave della stanza, dove 'ho lasciata?*' My heart is soaring to the heavens even though some Mimi's I've seen must have weighed over twenty stone. I'm ready to die for her. I look up. What do the subtitles say? 'Oh dear. I have lost my key. I must have dropped it somewhere.' Although, I admit, as soon as Musetta hits the Café Momus, I don't need any subtitles to know what she is up to, or rather down to. And what about poor tormented Marschallin in *Der Rosenkavalier*, terrified of growing old, wandering around the palace in the middle of the night crying out, according to the subtitles, 'Stop the clock. Stop the clock.' It works the other way, of course. I swear I once saw Siegfried stumble across Brunnhilde asleep on a mountain top and, scared out of his life, shriek at the top of his voice, 'Das ist keiner Mann.'

Then there are all those blokes poncing on and off stage with no elastic in their underpants. What on earth are they supposed to be doing? Are they really meant to walk like that?

I'd love to have been in New York when what's-her-name, instead of throwing herself onto a mattress tucked away at the bottom of the parapet, hurled herself straight onto a trampoline substituted by a malicious tenor and bounded up over the top of the parapet fifteen times before the audience finally died of exhaustion. Or in San Francisco when the firing squad shot the wrong man then threw themselves off the battlements one after the other.

As for the acoustics, it doesn't make any difference to me, it doesn't make any difference to me, it doesn't make any difference to me. I'm usually a few bars in front of the rest of the audience in any case.

Then I went to the opera in Bratislava. The tiny opera house is not exactly Bayreuth – the seats are more comfortable. Or Glyndebourne – they serve sekt, not champagne. There's not too much gilt, just enough to remind you it's an opera house and not a palace of culture. No deep red velvet curtains or chairs or carpets. No snooker players. Just smart suits and dresses, apart from the occasional Austrian dentist who is making so much money in Vienna he can only afford a very smart suit. But to me it's the best in the world.

The first time I went there, I didn't know what to expect. The orchestra struck up, the curtain rose, they were off. I didn't for the life of me know what they were singing, what language they were singing in, who was going to do what to whom or who was complaining because you-know-who was not going to do you-know-what to whom. But it was spectacular. I just sank back into my seat, suspended any sense of judgement I might have and let the whole thing wash over me. It was *Don Pasquale*, which I know many people regard as somewhat less than the greatest opera ever written. But to me it could have been *Don Giovanni* popping into the *Barber of Seville* before going off to the *Marriage of Figaro*. I couldn't have cared less. It was fantastic.

The audience, by London standards, was completely uncivilised. They didn't snore. They didn't scratch themselves. They didn't smoke. They didn't eat crisps. They didn't cough every twenty-seven seconds or worse still suck sweets loudly for twenty-six seconds and cough on the twenty-seventh. (In some opera houses, to try and solve the coughing problem they distribute sweets free to everybody who comes in. Which is worse. For the whole of the first act nobody can hear what anyone is singing for the sound of a whole opera house sucking sweets.) And they didn't, as they do in Chicago, take their lap-tops and mobile phones with them. Once in Chicago the orchestra hit a particularly twiddly bit and the whole of the stalls reached for their mobile phones. And they didn't keep on about drinky-poos and dropping the barman something so that he'll have the drinks waiting for them in the second interval.

Instead everybody sat lost to the world, totally enthralled by the action, completely immersed in the music. At first it was almost unnerving. I kept turning round to make certain they were all still there and hadn't sloped off to the bar. Then I realised. The secret to enjoying opera is to forget everything:

the plot, which is usually pretty absurd; the characters, who are usually as pretentious as hell; what they're singing, which is generally pretty meaningless, especially in German when it takes them fourteen hours to say nothing at all; the language they are singing in; even the music, which can often be jerky, overblown and sometimes as irritating as hell.

If the costumes are old-fashioned, ostentatious, if the props are falling apart, so what? If every note is not in place, if every upper octave is not perfectly polished, if the fat lady fails to hit the top C, what the hell? If the orchestra fails to keep up, what difference does it make? I couldn't care less. I'm hooked. But only in Eastern Europe, where opera is still old-fashioned, traditional and out-of-date. None of this modern stuff, like *Rosa* with its rough sex, animal torture, bestiality and various forms of degradation, or Rodion Schedrin's *Lolita* in Swedish, or even Harrison Birtwistle's *Gawain*.

As far as I'm concerned, after a hard day's travelling, a never-ending series of visits to bars and restaurants, all I want to do is sit back, soak up the atmosphere, slip into a different world. I'll even quite happily sit through women's lib-y *Cosi fan Tutte* if there is nothing else on offer. But then I admit I am comparing it to the joys of looking through hotel windows at traffic lights changing in the rain or listening to the whine of the Xpelair unit in the bathroom next door. But, I warn you, you won't find me at Covent Garden. You won't find me at Glyndebourne even though it's just down the road from where I live. Partly because I've got more important things to do when I'm home, like exercising the horses. Partly because I don't like dressing up as a snooker player.

But go to the opera in Budapest, Prague, Warsaw, Buchar-est, Moscow, all points east of Vienna, I'll be there. I might be the last one in, a pile of papers under my arm, a silly grin on my face, a handkerchief in one hand ready for the end of act three. But I'll be lapping it all up. The colour. The excitement. The atmosphere. The music. Even the fat lady singing. Not understanding a word of what's going on. But what the hell.

So I'm a philistine. Don't blame me. Blame Bratislava.

The Baltic States

Beaches so polluted that nobody goes near them any more.

Tap water that on some days is literally inflammable.

A Chernobyl-style nuclear power station – the biggest ever built – so leaky that three times a day a single engineer has to carry out the world's most sophisticated nuclear detection procedures on no less than 10,000 different cooling pipes by holding in front of each one a stick with a rag tied around the end of it. If the rag starts waving it means that a microscopic jet of radioactive steam has escaped. If the stick is sliced in two it means the jet is not so tiny and you'd better start putting the suit on. If the engineer doesn't come back, it means it's only a matter of time. For all of us.

The Russians are coming. At one time the phrase struck terror the world over. Whether they had snow on their boots or not. Now striking even more terror into people's hearts is the opposite: the Russians are going. Especially in the Baltics. For behind them, the Russians are leaving the most God-awful, soul-destroying mess anyone could imagine. What's more, in some cases the mess they are leaving behind is going to destroy not just this generation but maybe untold generations to come.

Jurmala, about five miles west of Riga, the capital of Latvia, was in the old days a bustling seaside resort for the Soviet military. It was the Baltic's answer to Odessa on the Black Sea. Every summer all the old brass used to head for its hydro-therapy clinics and baths and sanatoria to soothe away the cares of office until their office was no doubt soothed away from them. Today it is practically deserted. Jomas Street, once packed with visitors, is empty. The day I was there the ice-cream seller hadn't sold a cornet for hours. The little boy with the pet monkey couldn't remember the last time he had his picture taken. All the wooden summer homes were falling down, their gardens choked with weeds. On its beach, which stretches for about thirty kilometres, I could see one or two people. Nobody but nobody was in the water. A big cellulose factory at the western end of the beach was discharging its waste straight into the sea. The water was polluted as hell. When the sea is rough, I was told, it looks like a . . . well, never mind.

Sillamae, on the north coast of Estonia towards the Russian border was in the bad old days a military city sealed off from the rest of the world. Today every visitor is guaranteed a warm welcome. Because the number one tourist attraction is a huge lake of 50 million cubic feet of virtually raw radioactive sludge, comprising pure uranium, radium, thorium and every other -ium produced by its once secret uranium processing plant. But just to set your mind at rest, there are only a few acres of ground radioactivity. Guaranteed to keep the feet warm during the coldest summers.

Paldiski, about fifty kilometres west of Tallinn, was founded by Peter the Great. In the old days it was a fashionable seaside resort. The Russians turned it into one of their top two nuclear submarine training bases. They built not one but two nuclear reactors to provide fuel for the subs. Above ground today it is crumbling into the dust. Buildings are collapsing. The roads have more potholes than a teenager's face. Below ground, the whole place is choked with pipes full of radioactive waste.

Ventspils, further along the Latvian coast, has never stopped cursing the fact it has one of the few harbours that do not ice over during the long Arctic winter. Because of this, the Russians turned it into one vast industrial complex. They built oil and gas refineries, chemical works, a big fertiliser plant and an ammonia works in the area. Today it has the unenviable reputation of being the worst of the worst. Not only is the air polluted but the soil as well. The whole area is saturated with hundreds of tons of liquid rocket fuel that is not just toxic but mega-toxic, mega-volatile, mega-carcinogenic and if that doesn't blow your mind, acts as a mega-nerve gas as well.

The harbour at Liepaja, Latvia's third largest city, is practically silted up with crude oil so deep the whole place will have to be dredged if it is ever to be cleaned up. Except dredging is impossible. At the end of the Second World War, the Soviet navy dumped all their unexploded bombs just outside the harbour and the protective casings are expected to start decomposing any day now.

At Tapa, east of Tallinn, the capital of Estonia, so much jet fuel has seeped through the soil into the water supply that some days the tap water is highly inflammable.

'The Soviet pilots, they were told, fly so many flights a week. But planes cannot fly because need spares. What they do? They throw fuel on ground to pretend they fly. That what they do. Now we have problem,' I was told by a local businessman who had come back from London to help the old country.

He went on to tell me the particular nature of their problems. 'Today,' he said, 'nobody in the Baltic countries stands in front of toilet to flush it. Just in case.'

As for the Ignadina nuclear power station in Lithuania, up near the border with Belorussia, it's a nuclear nightmare. It's not waiting to happen. It probably already has. It is running on stone-age technology. The people in charge are completely inexperienced. Yet one tiny leak in only one of those 10,000 pipes and we could have another Chernobyl on our hands. You think I'm exaggerating. There had been four leaks the year I was there. None of them serious – at least that's what they say. Of course, leaks could be a good thing. The more leaks there are the more the inexperienced engineers become experienced. On the other hand, you could also say the more leaks there are the more vulnerable the plant becomes, the more casual the engineers become, the more chance that we all end up . . .

'It's like trying to survive a nuclear war – without the bombs,' a horribly frail and thin woman told me in a roadside snack bar on the outskirts of town.

But that's not all. All along the coast from Klaipeda, close to the border with Kaliningrad, up to Sillamae, the whole Baltic Sea is littered with cannibalised warships, sunken battleships, rotting hulls, massive nuclear submarines not only blocking harbours and making the area dangerous for shipping, but also leaking God knows what into the sea.

In the countryside, huge areas of farmland which had been confiscated for military exercises, target practice, even practice missile drops, are now seeping fuel, oil and God knows what else. Great swathes of forest have been smashed to pieces. Vast stretches of open country are full of unexploded bombs, mines, rockets and probably huge quantities of live ammunition.

In the cities, even worse, the Russians left behind enormous, anonymous-looking buildings with miles of underground passageways and hundreds of tiny little rooms, as well as parks and open spaces which are now either closed or blocked off from public view. Here volunteers are engaged in the gruesome task of unearthing another legacy of the Soviet occupation: the countless victims of Stalin's troops after the war as well as those of the KGB.

The Tukum airforce base in Latvia; the Tapa military base in Estonia; the Zokniai airfield in Lithuania: when the Russians finally pulled out they took just about everything that wasn't locked, bolted or nailed to the floor. Doors; toilet seats; even their radioactive light bulbs. In some cases where things were locked, bolted and nailed to the floor, they took the floor as well. Windows were broken, wiring was ripped out. Gaping holes were smashed in roofs, buildings were partly or wholly destroyed. It was as if they held the biggest acid house party in history, except they smashed the houses to smithereens and left the acid behind.

In Estonia, at the Tondi barracks in Tallinn, I saw buildings stripped bare of anything of value. In Lithuania, I saw the big

Red Army barracks on a fifty-hectare site slap bang in the centre of Vilnius. Originally, it had looked like your usual rough and ready barracks: vast bunkhouses, training areas, guardrooms, football pitches where, I was told, everybody did nothing but lie, cheat and swindle everybody else. Officials would order food and alcohol for the whole camp, then resell the lot on the open market. Officers would order television sets, hi-fi units and alcohol for the troops, then resell the lot on the open market. The stores, engineering depots, maintenance units and garages would order oil, spare parts and alcohol to keep everything going. Then – you got it – resell the lot on the open market.

When I went there it had been smashed to pieces. In one block there was not a single pane of glass. Doors, furniture and equipment were piled in huge mounds as if waiting to be set on fire. Toilets were blocked with concrete – either that or the Russians had developed the most powerful curry known to mankind. The whole place was a disaster area. In some cases I was told the clever guys had even stripped out the printed circuit boards from everything from electric kettles to nuclear missiles, melted them down and sold the gold, platinum and other precious metals they recovered to international gangs who retailed them round the world.

Down the road, in Jermoyne, the officers' quarters were not so badly affected. There, they left the light fittings. Everything, however, was still pretty primitive. What wasn't falling apart was probably only being held together by the radioactivity in the air.

The last time I swung through the Baltics everyone was hosing down the fish in the market places. Railway tracks were buckling, and trains had been ordered to cut their speed by 50 per cent to 14 mph. At first I thought it was the radioactivity, but it wasn't. It was the heat. Since the Russians had left they had had nothing but glorious sunshine.

'The worst house guests in history,' a Vilnius banker told me. 'At least the Romans left behind some pretty decent buildings, a legal system, a sense of order, discipline, culture.

All the Russians left behind was a complete mess.'

And the pity of it is, first of all that it happened, and second, the poor Baltics are being left to clean it all up.

The Lithuanian government was one of the first to take decisive action. They immediately built a block of luxury flats for Members of Parliament so that they could sit up all night discussing the problems without worrying about catching the last bus home. They also, I was told, established a special investigations unit to search out and bring to justice the people responsible for such unspeakable behaviour. Headed by an ex-KGB officer.

Although given the choice between the Russians and clean beaches, clean water and clean nuclear power stations, and no Russians and the filthiest beaches in the world, inflammable tap water and leaking nuclear power stations nobody is really complaining.

Medical experts have started moving in and begun checking the health of the population. In some areas they have discovered alarmingly high death rates among babies and children. In some areas they have even started issuing gasmasks just to be on the safe side. In Ventspils, for example, the death rate among children is twice the European average. In Klaipeda, Lithuania's major port, I met one woman who was deathly pale, as thin as a rake and almost unable to walk. She had two children, both severely deformed. The whole town, she said, was full of walking uranium rods. One evening in a Riga bar a very nice man in a black leather jacket warned me to beware, not of *les femmes fatales* but 'les femmes toxiques'.

As if the danger of radioactivity is not enough, they are also having to cope with enormous dangers from conventional weapons. Live ammunition and explosives are everywhere. Partly because the Soviets just dumped them wherever they could. Partly because some of the more capitalist-oriented officers sold everything off in the last few days to dealers who stashed it all over the place for safe-keeping. Partly because the dealers then found there was so much explosive on the market, they either dumped their stocks or sold the copper artillery shells to be melted down, resold as part of another deal or converted into souvenirs. The rest they just dumped. All over Vilnius there are shops selling old Russian shells. The big ones they sell as straight souvenirs; the smaller ones they have converted and are selling off as cigarette or cigar lighters.

I can only think that the whole place hasn't exploded either because they keep their six fingers crossed or because three times a day the entire staunchly Catholic nation of Lithuania gets down on its knees and prays to Our Lady of Perpetual Protection from Radioactive Fall-out from Dodgy Soviet Power Stations.

On the other hand, the one with five fingers, the fiercely atheistic Communists also left some pretty impressive monuments to their presence – in Tallinn, in Riga, in Vilnius, out in the countryside. People keep pointing them out to you. They are always at key locations and always the centre of attention. Churches, I mean.

While we were building nothing but supermarkets the Russians were rebuilding and restoring churches. Such was the difference between the Christian West and the Communist East. What's more the Russians were also developing and perfecting their skills in areas in which we in the Christian West are mere beginners: turning churches into entertainment centres – museums, planetariums, art galleries, concert halls. The wonderful old Orthodox church in the middle of Riga they turned into a planetarium. The splendid cathedral in Vilnius which, with its row of enormous columns, looks more like a stock exchange, was an art gallery.

This, I'm convinced is something they should capitalise on. After all, think of the number of archdeacons and canons and bishops who are desperately trying to do the same thing in this country but lack the necessary expertise and experience. What could be better than hiring Russian experts to do the job? There'd be no problem getting that past the Deanery Committee on Conservation or the Diocesan Council for Preservation. A solid battery of fat old ladies demanding money for coming in; an art gallery down the centre of the nave; a planetarium in the sanctuary. A lift to the top of the church tower. A snack bar in the crypt. Book shops at the church door. Piped muzak or, perhaps, massak everywhere. Bound to bring in the crowds. And if there's any time available on Sunday mornings perhaps a quick – what did they used to call it? Oh yes – a quick service. But it'll have to be finished by 11.00 because the television cameras have to be set up ready for a special edition of *Gladiators*. In the Lady Chapel with the new stained-glass windows in the background. Which are sponsored by Tesco.

Not that all the Russians have gone. There are still plenty of roadsigns about. Maybe it's the policy in different countries to leave up 40, 50 or just 10 per cent of all Russian roadsigns in proportion to the number of Russians who have stayed behind.

Most of the statues have disappeared. Well, maybe 40, 50 and 10 per cent of them. Only the plinths are left, although some of those have gone as well, particularly if, like the one of Lenin in the centre of Riga, it was in too prominent a position.

But there are still plenty of people suddenly standing up in crowded restaurants between the radioactive soup and the radioactive main course and bursting into song. Except they are no longer called Russians. They are now called non-ethnics, at least in polite society. Trouble is, most of them seem to be the kind of Russian the Baltics would rather be without; the junior, second-rate, inexperienced managers, engineers and technical experts; the unskilled, untrained and unsociable drop-outs; and, of course, all the junior KGB agents; the blonde, elegant, slightly faded women who used to sit opposite the lifts in hotels; the taxi drivers with smart suits and good teeth and the heavies with cheap black leather jackets and good shoes.

'They overstayed their welcome before they even arrived,' one Lithuanian businessman told me.

In Tallinn I kept being told that there were still as many as 2,000 KGB agents in town, but instead of working for the

Soviet Union, they were now working for Russia.

Anywhere in the Baltics if someone breaks into your house, steals your car or even beats you up, the last thing you do, I was told, is call the police. 'Why not?' I asked in all innocence. 'I thought the police—' Everybody just fell about laughing.

In Estonia, which was occupied by the Soviets in 1940, invaded by the Wehrmacht Nazis the following year, then reoccupied by the Russians in 1944, they reckon there are still over 500,000 non-ethnics, about a third of the population, in the country.

After the local Estonian population had been reduced to around 250,000 as a result of successive purges, the Russians started shipping in their own people. Later, lots of other Russians, Belorussians and Ukrainians fled there of their own accord for a better life working in their offices, factories and mines. The result is that today they are everywhere. Kopli, a suburb of Tallinn, about five kilometres from the centre of town, and Lasnamae, about seven kilometres in the other direction, are both virtually self-contained Russian towns. Dull, drab, squat; vast blocks of flats; everything looking desperate; potholes and enormous puddles everywhere. It makes you wonder how bad things are back home if they prefer living or rather existing in these conditions.

'You cannot replant an old tree,' an old man with a heavy Slav face and a beard told me outside the cinema in Kopli.

Estonia said they could stay and even become Estonians, provided that they spoke the language. A reasonable point, you would have thought, for any country to make. The Russians, however, said Niet. If they lived more or less all together in Russian-speaking enclaves like Kopli and Lasnamae, why should they learn Estonian? Which, of course, made the Estonians doubly annoyed. But the Estonians are the masters now, so most of the Russians who want to stay are frantically trying to learn one of the world's more difficult languages so that they can apply for citizenship. If they don't, they will be registered as visitors and have to apply for a permit every five years.

Latvia saw all this going on and, with an even bigger Russian population, maybe even a majority, decided to do nothing, which was probably practical politics although in many ways they suffered worse under the Russians than the other Baltic States. When the Russians seized the country in 1940, they say the drains at the police headquarters were choked with the blood of their victims. Thousands were executed. Others were shipped out by cattle truck, thousands per day – sometimes as many as 14,000 – to God knows what in Siberia. This means that even today, in some parts of Latvia the SS is actually held in the greatest respect, because when the Germans arrived in July 1941 they effectively liberated them from the Soviets. What could be more natural than throwing in your lot with your liberators? The problem, of course, was that so enthusiastic were the Latvians for their liberators that many volunteered for Schutzmannschaft units, many of which were responsible for rounding up Jews; the Waffen SS, and even the Arajs Commando death squads that went around killing Jewish babies.

Lithuania was lucky. Their Russian troops went back home in 1993. Well not exactly back home. They moved next door into Kaliningrad, a Russian enclave sandwiched between Lithuania and Poland. The Russians left behind account for maybe around 10 per cent of the population. Their problems, they say, are the Poles. But that's another story.

In the old days, to while away the time between being photographed going into your hotel and being arrested on trumped-up charges of spying, everyone used to play Spot the KGB man – or woman, a kind of grown-up version of I . . . Spy . . . a . . . Spy. Today the game is much more straightforward, though it varies depending on which country you're in. In fact, in Latvia I often thought we should be playing Spot the Latvian, but didn't have the courage to suggest it.

The rules are simple. Spot two Russians and you get one glass of vodka; five Russians, two glasses of vodka; ten and you get the whole bottle. Guess the wrong one and you buy the vodka. Anyone can play: businessmen, secretaries, waiters, taxi drivers with bad teeth; even taxi drivers with good teeth. First to spot the Russians simply shouts out Russian, Russki, or various alternatives which I didn't quite understand.

I was introduced to the game while hanging around in the freezing rain outside the cinema in Kopli. My driver, a stiff, upright, very military-looking man, kept barking out something or other at nearly everybody who came by. At first I thought I'd landed a right one. But as we drank some foul-tasting coffee (at least, I think it was coffee) from a nearby stall, he revealed all. 'Everybody does it,' he said. 'Now you try.'

A tiny, shrivelled-up old lady hobbled along, wearing what looked like bedroom slippers, a thin coat, no hat. She was trying to avoid the puddles which were about the size of the Black Sea. But in vain.

I nodded. The driver gave me a quick military grin.

Behind her came a rather brisk, middle-aged man – blue raincoat, briefcase, sensible shoes, and what looked like a commissionaire's hat.

Another nod. Another quick grin. I'd made a glass of vodka already. This was too easy, so we agreed to put Kopli and Lasnamae out of bounds, otherwise there wouldn't be enough vodka left in the country to gulp down.

The centre of Tallinn was more difficult. A short man, brown wellingtons, a long blue sweater, standing soaked to the skin.

'Russian,' I shouted.

'Wrong, Latvian. Countryman.'

A security guard dodged in front of the car as we pulled up near the bus station.

'Russian,' I shouted.

'Wrong. He's American. I know him. Here on a special mission.'

Now we were quits. A bunch of fair-haired kids came racing along the pavement as we drove towards the town centre. They all had sensible hats and coats on, and those funny old-fashioned satchels strapped to their backs.

'Russians,' I exclaimed. 'That's—'

'Estonians,' the military man bristled with pride. 'The future of Estonia.'

It might never come, but that night the future of Estonia cost me well over a bottle of vodka, I can tell you.

In Riga, I found it much easier, because there are many more of them.

A young girl rushing into a bank along Brivibas Street; blonde, make-up, fancy coat.

'Russian.'

The businessman I was with nodded. 'There are lots of Russian girls here. They work in the office in the daytime,' he said. 'At night . . .'

'Femmes toxiques,' I said.

We careered across the road and almost hit a truck.

I went to call on a contact in one of the art nouveau buildings along Sinilsu Street. A very smart middle-aged woman who looked as though she was either a shop assistant or a colonel in the KGB crossed the road in front of us. She had on a red hat, black raincoat, sensible shoes.

'Russian.'

'Polish,' he said. 'She's not looking for a nanny.'

'A nanny,' I began. 'What's that got . . .?'

'If they're looking for a nanny, they're Russian.'

So eager are the Russians in Latvia to stay there that, like their fellow countrymen in Estonia, they are also desperately trying to learn the language. The quickest way, they decided, was to hire a Latvian girl who could teach them and the kids. Hey presto, they fulfil the regulations and can sign on as Latvian citizens.

We crossed the road outside the Riga Hotel, on the edge of the Old Town. There was a tall, thin young man getting out of a car. He had one of those old-fashioned leather jackets on with imitation fur around the neck.

'Russian.'

'Belorussia.'

'Minsk?' I wondered.

'No. Somewhere out in the country, farmer's son. They all come here to earn money. Probably a taxi driver. Unofficial, of course.'

A few days later I was in the Metropole Hotel, which is supposed to be the most expensive hotel in town. Two men walked into the bar. They had heavy coats on. They took them off and threw them over the chairs. They were wearing expensive suits and a couple of jazzy ties.

'Russians,' I whispered.

The Latvian I was with shook his head.

'Latvian?'

Another shake of the head.

'Estonian?'

Another shake.

'Lithu—'

Another shake.

'So who are they then?'

'Mafiosi.' He stood up and grabbed his coat. 'Come on,' he said. 'Let's go. I know somewhere else where we drink.'

I climbed into the car.

'Now,' he said switching on the engine. 'You owe me two bottles. If you do not guess mafiosi, you know nothing. You pay twice.'

'But that's not in the rules,' I protested.

'It is now,' he said. 'Now we make the rules.'

The Baltics – or the Balts, as the professionals say – are, I always think, a dress rehearsal for Russia, although the Baltics themselves probably think they are a dress rehearsal for Sweden or Finland or anywhere but Russia.

Sure, they have a history that stretches all the way back to the Garden of Eden. Sure they have their own languages and culture and traditions. Sure the place is littered with medieval cities and churches. But, to me at least, the whole place looks like a job lot from a Russian Oxfam shop.

In the countryside, it's galoshes and woolly hats and threadbare jumpers; men with fingers chopped off whose only dream is to marry a woman whose family has a part-share in a tractor; women who look like babushkas by the time they leave school; empty roads and deserted country lanes; ploughing with horses; harvesting by hand and humping everything home on your back if the village horse and cart is tied up elsewhere; cattle with their front legs tied together or tethered to the ground because nobody can afford fencing; wages ranging from nothing to next to nothing and whatever you want to eat so long as it is radioactive potatoes.

In the towns, it's smoke and mist and overgrown railway tracks; streets full of broken-down old cars; empty, desolate factories; offices with all the windows smashed; electricity men who repair power lines by strapping a pair of tin leggings to the inside of their legs and clambering up the telegraph poles. No ladders. No safety harness. No Health and Safety Regulations. Families living four, five, six, even more to a single room; no heating, hardly any lighting, maybe indoor toilets, and if they have sewers, the sewers probably won't be able to take paper. Salaries ranging from nothing to maybe as much as US$100 a year and whatever you want to eat so long as it is potatoes; except in the towns it's radioactive potato pancakes.

In Riga people sit all day long in parked cars, reading, playing cards, talking, falling asleep. It's the ultimate supply and demand situation. People with flats and cars need money. People without flats and cars need to keep warm. The result: people with flats and cars rent out their cars for the hour, for the half day or for the full day while they are at work. The money they make pays for their flat and the car. The people who rent the cars get out of their single rooms, cut down the cost of any heating and keep warm simply by being cooped up inside a car all day. What's more, nobody steals anyone's car.

The hotels are Russian. In fact, I always try and stay at one of the old Intourist hotels. Not because they are usually the only place in town to have tepid running water and sheets that are less than jet black, but because they are the only place in town where you don't have to look at Intourist hotels. And they are all run the Russian way. Every floor has its ex-KGB lady sitting opposite the lift checking you in and checking you out. Every room has its own unique collection of sizes, shapes, colours and thicknesses of towels as if they have been gathered over the years from jumble sales all around the Eastern bloc. And every second floor is a brothel.

The service is also quite deliberately appalling, because they know that in desperation for a crust of black bread you'll drop the waiter half a month's salary, which will save them paying him a decent wage. To conceal the fact that there's a shortage of water in the hotels, they ensure that it takes two days before the water drains out of the sink and a whole week to empty the bath. And nobody complains because – this is where the Russians are clever – everybody thinks they are the only ones affected and what's the point anyway. It's only when you get on the plane home and see that everybody has a four-day growth and is smelling slightly suspect that you realise it's happened to everyone. By then it's too late. Again this means they don't have to spend money they don't have renovating the hotels and putting in a decent hot-water – what am I saying? – putting in even a decent cold-water system.

Their planning is Russian. When the bread is not delivered, the butter is not delivered either. When your car does not arrive, your driver does not arrive either. When the plane is cancelled, there is always a mistake with your ticket which would have meant you wouldn't have been able to get on it in any case.

What technology they have is Russian: mobile telephones the size of a telephone kiosk complete with a queue of people waiting to use them; abacuses alongside electronic calculators. In bars, coffee bars, restaurants, shops, even in banks all over the Baltics you see large, medium and small abacuses. What happens? You order six different things; they add up the individual items on the abacus – and then ring up the total in their super, modern, hi-tech cash registers.

In Riga I met one Russian Einstein who told me he was working on a plan to check whether the food left on the side of the plate in restaurants is thrown away or freshened up and served to somebody else. He was developing, he said, a special radioactive powder which people could sprinkle on the food they sent back. All the next customer had to do was use some special gadget he was developing to see whether the food contained any traces of the powder.

I must, however, say in fairness that nothing beats the technology of a Russian alarm clock. I mean, after spending a lifetime trying to master a Japanese electronic alarm clock, let alone wristwatch, a Russian electronic alarm clock is a dream. You just wind it up – and that's it. The following morning you wake up bang on time. Because this enormous great Russian maid is outside your room, smashing the door down, wanting to get in and clean it so that she can get home before the sun comes up and spend all day in the fields picking potatoes.

Dammit, the Balts are so Russian I can hardly drop in for a quick meeting without being smothered in flowers. Although I suppose bringing them to me at my hotel would make me even more nervous.

The Balts are, however, crazy in their very own, non-Russian ways. One old, crinkled taxi driver I came across in Riga was wearing fancy pink Dame Edna glasses. 'My wife's,' he said. 'My eyes are bad. No money to buy new glasses. Wife go to office. I use her glasses. She come home. Her glasses are there. No problem.'

No problem, I thought, as we swerved in front of trams, shot up one-way streets, straddled the line in the middle of the road and ended up at the wrong office, in the wrong street at the wrong end of town.

Of the three Baltic States, Estonia, which describes itself as a pluralistic, liberalised, democratic market economy, is the smallest, the most northerly, the most Lutheran, probably the least Russian, and the most successful. When they gained their independence in 1991, as ex-socialists they very quickly realised that the only way to succeed under capitalism is to do the opposite of what capitalists tell you to do.

You're too small to have your own currency, everybody from the World Bank down to the manager of the duty free shop at Tallinn docks told them. It'll never work. What happened? They were the first of the old Soviet states to launch their own currency and, surprise, surprise, it's been a roaring success. The shops are full. Unemployment is down to around 3 per cent, compared to, say, 15 per cent in the other old Soviet republics. Privatisation is hotting up. Inflation is high, but falling.

The Finns, as a result – Helsinki is only eighty kilometres away – have come flooding back shopping for booze, like the British flocking across to Calais for their cheap duty-frees. Which is just as well because Finns are probably the only people in the world who can understand Estonians. While the Lithuanians and the Latvians are descended from Indo-European stock, Estonians come from Finno-Ugric. Their language is very Finnish. Most Estonians, especially shop-keepers, speak Finnish, especially phrases like, 'No you can't have another containerload of whisky,' and 'Why on earth did you have to do that right in front of the doorway?'

Tallinn, an old merchant and trading centre – it was once the gateway to Central Russia – is fantastic. It's like a down-at-heel, much junior version of Prague: the medieval alley-ways; the church spires; those big, sturdy towers, especially Fat Margaret Tower. It's like walking back into the fifteenth or sixteenth century. The streets are all narrow and cobble-stoned. There are lots of old merchant and guild houses. The city gates are older still; they go back to the twelfth and thirteenth centuries. Above them, up more narrow, winding cobblestones are the cathedral and the castle.

Outside Tallinn there seem to be nothing but islands – over 1,500 of them, where apparently life is still so steeped in tradition and the old ways that they probably still listen to Vera

Lynn. Tartu, nearly 200 kilometres to the south, I feel sorry for. They don't know whether they are coming or going. They've been razed to the ground and rebuilt no less than fifty-five times, so people are frightened to go out in case it's not there when they get back. And nobody bothers to print a map of Tartu. The streets have been renamed so many times nobody can remember what they were in the first place. In any case if they print a map, they'll probably all be changed again before they are in the shops.

But whether you're in the town or the country, costs are nothing. The managing director of a Finnish company told me his new Estonian plant, including management, was costing him less than a third of what it cost to run a similar one outside Helsinki. 'How can I afford not to come here?' he said.

The whole place, in fact, is still pre-tourist country. If you like your countries untouched by tourism now is the time to go. And I mean now. Leave it another day and Coca Cola ads will be all over the place, there'll be an American Express office in the centre of every historic square, and you won't be able to move for backpackers looking for the nearest drug dealer, travel incentive programme and free ticket to Madame Tussaud's.

And it must be said, the Baltics are not yet ready for tourism. People are genuinely pleasant and friendly and helpful. There is none of this automatic 'Have a nice day' stuff. Ask someone the way and if they can't tell you they will actually take you there. None of this waving and shouting about the tourist information office being down the third turning on the left under the soap factory and, in any case, I don't live here.

Queue up at a bank to change some money and they actually change the money for you. None of this filling in forms so the ministry of tourism can bury you in mail shots until you've forgotten where on earth their country is. None of this where's your passport and can I have your mother's thumbprint. And what's more, they give you a good rate.

Catch a train or a bus and all you do is get a ticket and catch your train or your bus. No way does some Red Coat want to see your travel permit. No way do you have to tell them whether you're coming back on Tuesday morning, Thursday afternoon or the middle of next year under cover of darkness. No way do they give you a stack of leaflets, three feet high and full of useless information.

On a fine day, from the top of Toompea, the hill in the centre of Tallinn, you are supposed to be able to see across the Gulf of Finland to Helsinki. What you don't see is coach after coach disgorging fat old ladies, bored old men and a million kids in search of a toilet, somewhere to sit down or a place for a quick drag before being herded back on the coach. What you might see is a little toy tourist train called Toomas. But it won't last. It won't last.

Riga, the capital of Latvia, on the other hand, is culture. Symphony orchestras – yes, two of them; seven different concert halls; chamber music; the largest pipe-organ in Europe. Over twenty different museums. A library bigger than the cathedral, and not because the cathedral has gone out of business; it hasn't. It's just that the library is so big. It covers a whole block and is packed from the bottom to the top shelf with nearly six million books, including Martin Luther's catechism.

They are even blowing US$24 million on a facelift for their opera house, although God knows how they are going to make it pay, with a home market of just 2.7 million people on an average income of US$120 a year who do nothing but read books, when Covent Garden can't survive without massive government hand-outs. But it doesn't seem to worry them.

Riga is the largest city in the Baltics, with a population of around a million. It's a solid, worthy, respectable, bustling port, full of Romanesque, Gothic, Renaissance, Baroque, Classical and Soviet architecture. There are even lots of art nouveau buildings built by Mikhail Eisenstein, the father of Sergei who made all those wonderful Russian family classics like *Battleship Potemkin*. Because his son was unable to keep him in the manner to which he wanted to become accustomed, poor old Mikhail had to scrape along as a civil engineer in Riga. Which is probably why the city is such a picture. It's full of private, expensive shops, stuffed to overflowing, where everyone is cheerful, pleasant. Can you believe that? Cheerful, pleasant staff? Well, they're only beginners. Wait until they're experts. There are pavement cafés everywhere and lots of tiny restaurants, especially around the medieval town. They even boast the original hangars for the old Zeppelins, which now house the central market.

That's Riga living. But for Riga mortis nothing beats a visit to the Riga Motor Museum. Normally nothing on earth would drag me anywhere near anything that even smelt of a motor museum, but this one has got to be one of the greatest alternative tourist spots of all time. It's virtually a black museum of the Soviets' love affair with the motor car.

Quick, there's Stalin – yes, a waxwork of Stalin, the saviour of his people – sitting somewhat awkwardly in the back of his 1949 Zil, almost a copy, I was told, of a Packard Clipper except this one is literally built like a tank. The whole thing is made of armoured steel. The windows are bullet-proof. To lift it takes not just a jack but a Boris, a Mikhail, a Leon and a heavyweight crane. My guess is that the Russians made such heavy cars because even in those days they realised that the worst hazard they would face was being smashed up by another car, because they would never be able to produce enough to make a traffic jam. During the recent upheavals, an attendant told me the museum offered the car to the Latvian government in case things got out of hand. But they turned it down. They were frightened that if it broke down, there wasn't enough lifting gear in the country to pick it up and get it to the nearest garage.

Hey, there's – no it's not. Yes it is! – Khrushchev himself tripping lightly out of his 1965 Zil, which was apparently the first Soviet car to have a V8 cylinder overhead valve system, whatever that is. He's only got one foot on the ground. Presumably because they could only find one shoe. He must have left the other one behind at the United Nations.

And along there it's good old Brezhnev, complete with bushy eyebrows, looking more askew than ever, sitting slightly dazed behind the wheel of his smashed-up 1966 Rolls Royce. Apparently when he wasn't invading Czechoslovakia or putting down the Hungarians he enjoyed nothing better than a drive in the park backing on to the Kremlin. Except this time he smashed into – oops, I mean a truck smashed into him and wrecked the front offside wing. Which proves that, in the car stakes at least, no way did the KGB rate him anywhere near as important as Stalin. Everybody asks after the truck driver. But what I want to know is, why has it taken Rolls Royce so long to repair the damage? If this is how they treat Brezhnev, what hope have I got if I ever decide to swop my broken-down Volvo – it's so old even the lights don't come on automatically – for a Rolls Royce Silver Shadow?

Hey, look. Back there. Would you believe it, there's Molotov's lethal 140 bhp cocktail of a car: an aluminium coupé built on top of a 1939 Rolls Royce Wraith chassis capable of doing up to 140 kph, which obviously ensured he got out of all those tight corners he encountered so quickly.

And there – no, I can't take any more – is Maxim Gorky complete with hat, droopy moustache and walking stick standing alongside his 1934 Lincoln, just like any other working man returning from twenty hours slaving for next to nothing over a clapped-out grinding machine trying to build heaven on earth.

Lithuania, the largest of the States, and once a Grand Duchy with a proud bunch of aristocrats and a grandeur all of its own, is the birthplace of one of the greatest Englishmen of all time. At least as far as the British housewife is concerned. A fanfare of cash registers, please, for Michael Marks, the Marks in Marks & Spencer. He fled Russian Poland, which is today's Lithuania, as a nineteen-year-old because of anti-Jewish persecution and, with all the world to choose from, ended up in 1884 in

Leeds Kirkgate market. Some people say that his English was so bad the only way he could do business was to put up a sign saying, 'Don't-ask-ze-price. Zits-alla-dahpenny.' My guess is that, like all Lithuanians I've ever met, he spoke perfect English. It was just that to t'Yorkshire folk perfect English is a foreign language so they marked him down as a foreigner straight away. And the story just caught on.

Probably thanks to Marks, a booming Lithuania was at one time a big supplier of bacon and dairy products to Britain, much the same as Denmark is today, with enormous ships ploughing between Liepaja and Tilbury. Now it's all gone: a booming Lithuania; the bacon; the dairy products; even Tilbury. Only Marks remains. Which must mean something.

Today Lithuanians can barely afford to buy a Marks & Spencers bacon, lettuce and tomato sandwich. The whole country probably couldn't raise the cash for a frozen lasagna, and there's no way Marks's well-trained descendants would allow the country to have an M&S credit card. There is virtually no cash in the entire country.

No country in the world relies on nuclear energy as much as Lithuania. Their leaky old power station at Ignabina – Our Lady of Perpetual Protection from Radioactive Fall-Out from Dodgy Soviet Power Stations, protect us – supplies virtually all their electricity. But they can't afford to run it. Or, at least, not at full tilt. Which is probably a good thing for us, but tough on the Lithuanians. When I first went there they had just survived a winter in the dark and the cold. There were almost no lights; there was no hot water. People had to struggle in the pitch dark to offices and factories that couldn't work because they had no power and then struggle back again to homes that had no heating and practically no lighting. All there was to eat was radioactive cabbage; cabbage, red; cabbage, pickled; cabbage with shredded carrots; cabbage with gherkins; cabbage without gherkins; cabbage with gherkins hot; cabbage with gherkins cold. In the markets they were selling cheap supplies of food and milk, but few people bought any because they claimed it was only cheap because it was contaminated by the fall-out from Chernobyl. And nobody at all went to the only Chinese restaurant.

When the Swedish minister of defence arrived for an official visit, the only guard of honour they could afford to lay on was the crack Lithuanian Cycling Corps. A couple of dozen gawky young soldiers in ill-fitting overcoats and tin hats lined up in two straggly rows to welcome him with their bicycles at the ready. And they weren't even modern bicycles. They were those old-fashioned boneshakers. Some with high handlebars, others with the very sensible, very level handlebars favoured by midwives. But everyone had those very sensible dynamos attached to the front wheel. Only one had a bell. Which didn't work.

People, however, managed to survive. A Swede who at the time was staying at the slablike twenty-two-storey Hotel Lieuteva, the old Intourist hotel, which looks like a Spanish nuclear power station, told me that suddenly late one evening there was a knock on his door. 'I opened it. This girl was there. I thought ... Then she pushed this fat little old lady into my room. "Quick," she said. "This is my mother. Can she have a bath in your room?" What could I say?'

Today things are oh-so-slowly getting better – or worse, depending on how many fingers you've got and whether you can avoid standing in front of the toilet when you flush it. The power station is leaking – oops, I mean working – more than it used to. The lights are coming on all over Lithuania, although at night Vilnius is still almost pitch black. Hot water is still in very short supply. Offices, shops and factories are struggling back to normal. Radioactive cabbage soup is still pretty standard, although one or two up-market establishments have started throwing in the odd beetroot and calling it borscht. The crack Lithuanian Cycling Corps has bought another bell. Which works. There is a little more traffic around. Few cars, hardly any motorbikes, plenty of buses. In the hotels there is plenty of radioactive pork and sausages and pickled salads and Danish lager. People are still knocking on hotel doors. Except now it's fat little old ladies who then push their daughters into the room.

In the countryside too, things are slowly improving – just. In the bad old days of collectivisation and state planning, just as the Ukraine was the breadbasket, Lithuania was the dairy cow of the Soviet Union. They only had to produce milk and dairy products. Everything else was shipped in from other parts of the Soviet empire. Now Lithuania has to produce its own grain – and can't.

Latvia and Estonia avoided the problem. There they didn't sell the land back to the former owners. Instead, as compensation, they gave them shares in industrial companies. The land they sold off to the highest bidder. Not the Lithuanians. In 1991 they started breaking up the collective farms. They wanted to return the land to its former owners and increase production. All simple, obvious, textbook stuff. Except it hasn't worked. Partly because there were too many former owners, so that by the time they had shared everything out, the farms were too small to support the farmers themselves, let alone produce anything to sell on. What was sold on was so expensive nobody was prepared to pay for it. The other reason was the disastrous state of the market.

In the towns, at the bottom end of the market, it's impossible. Nobody owns property, rents are expensive, so most families live in two, maybe three rooms. Which can still cost 200 lits a month. Some live in one room in their parents' flats. But to live for a whole month, after paying rent, they only have on average another 100 lit, maybe 150 lit. Which is impossible. At the top end of the market, Lithuania has the usual selection of rich and very, very rich wheeler-dealers that you find in any poor country.

The stock exchange, the first to be opened in the new Eastern Europe, is based on the Paris Bourse, so that trading begins just before lunch with a glass of champagne. There are more brokers than there are stocks, but that doesn't matter. They are all wearing Yves St Laurent suits and Hermès ties. All transactions are cash, which means cheques, credit cards and IOUs from French farmers are accepted. Settlements take four days unless there is a reception at the French embassy or the Brittany fishermen are about to wage another riot. When I was there trading was thin. Only five securities were traded. Turnover was around US$400. They blamed the primitive banking system, the shortage of funds, worries about insider trading and fears about the companies going bankrupt. But they didn't fool me. I knew it was because, French-style, they were all desperate to get off to lunch.

There is also a wide selection of swish bars and restaurants, such as the Stikliai, the best and most famous restaurant in the whole of the Baltics, which has been patronised by the likes of President Mitterrand; a flashy champagne bar and a strange chrome and enamel restaurant underneath an office block.

The one thing I don't understand about Lithuania, is what they call the Polish Question. On the face of it, of all the countries in the new Eastern Europe, these two should be the best of friends. They are both intensely Catholic. Pope John, when he comes to Vilnius, actually speaks Lithuanian and calls the country his second home. They are both fiercely proud of their history. They are both determined to put the past behind them and build a new future. But do they get on? Do they hell, if you'll excuse the expression.

The problem seems to be a series of recent events stretching as far back as 1385. The countries were then one: the Polish Lithuanian Commonwealth, which ran everything from the Baltic to the Black Sea. By the 1920s Vilnius was full of Polish and Jewish residents. There was hardly a Lithuanian to be seen. A Polish general, Lucjan Zeligowski, promptly claimed that if it was full of Poles, it must be Polish and seized it for Poland. Lithuanians ever since have maintained that what he did was wrong, an act of aggression and what's more, illegal. The Poles, they say, must admit it was wrong, aggressive and illegal otherwise they won't play. The Poles don't seem to be prepared to say it was wrong, an act of aggression and illegal.

'We can easily admit it was wrong. That's not the problem,' an old Polish soldier told me. 'The problem is, where does that leave the legal rights of the Poles who are still living in Vilnius?

If the annexation was illegal, does that mean everything that the Poles have done in Vilnius since then has also been illegal, that the Poles have no legal rights today and have had no legal rights before? What happens to their property, the contracts and agreements they have signed, their membership of the local golf club? It is very complicated.'

Today, therefore, what should be a thriving two-way street between Vilnius and Warsaw is a huge bottleneck with cars and trucks queuing for days, sometimes weeks, at the border.

'The situation, it is shocking. All those people. All that waiting. And there are no toilets there. In the summer it is, phew, how do you say?' a Lithuanian banker told me.

Even the Germans, the modern master-roadbuilders of Europe, have given up in despair. They wanted to build a super autobahn of 1,000 kilometres all the way from Germany to the Baltics and on to Finland. Not any more.

But that hasn't stopped even more Poles from moving into Lithuania and grabbing a slice of the action. Around 30 per cent of the population of Vilnius, and 50 per cent of the taxi drivers, I reckon must be either Polish or of Polish descent. The Poles have lived through the traumas of switching from a command economy to a free-market wheeler-dealing open economy where everything goes. They know the tricks and the dodges. They know what to avoid. And they know how to make money. For as little as US$5,000 to US$10,000 they can be in business in Lithuania, running a shop, a small workshop or even a bakery. Costs are minimal; wages are 25 per cent of those in Poland, which are definitely not the highest in the world. Profits can be anything from 15 to 50 to think-of-a-number per cent. Taxes, if you pay them, are 29 per cent for nationals and only 7 per cent for foreigners. Poles, as a result, are the third largest investors in the country after Russia and the US.

For anyone who has even a nodding acquaintance with Betjeman, Vilnius is fabulous. An old baroque university town, it's got so many old churches – Napoleon said he wanted to take one of them, the tiny sixteenth-century Church of St Anne, back home with him in his pocket – that it's almost like Venice without the canals. In the Old Town alone, you could spend a week happily church-crawling from one Gothic church to another, from one classical church to another and from one wildly rococo church to another. My favourite has to be St Peter and Paul's. Outside it's plain and pretty non-descript; the whole of the interior is covered with hundreds and hundreds, if not thousands of sparkling white baroque statues. There is St Mary Magdalen dressed in the latest medieval court fashions; a very bored-looking St Catherine complete with wheel who looks as though she'll be glad when the whole thing is over. It's as if the interior designers were on one of those open-ended contracts and somebody just forgot to call them off.

The other thing I shall never forget in Vilnius is the old KGB headquarters in Gedimino Prospektas which is now, would you believe, a museum. At first, I admit, I thought it was the ultimate cashing-in. But not any more. Just to wander along the long, dark, dank, underground corridor, to look inside the tiny green cells that held up to twenty prisoners at a time, to see the isolation cells and, my God, the torture chamber padded to stifle the screams and still stained with blood is unforgettable. To think that for over fifty years here, in this very spot, thousands were maimed, tortured and shot . . .

It probably makes it all the more horrifying that they have left it as it was. There are still notices on the noticeboard. There are still, in the officers' room, books on Marxism and venereal disease. There is still hanging in the torture chamber the straitjacket the poor helpless prisoners were strapped into. Climb the stairs halfway along the corridor and outside in the yard are open cages where troublemakers were herded, stark naked in freezing temperatures for days, weeks, months on end.

Go back down into the corridor. On the wall are photo-graphs of what the KGB did to people, here in this building. Along this corridor. You can see mashed-up faces, skulls smashed to pieces, people reduced to a bloody pulp. Below them is a tiny fresh bunch of flowers.

And it's all, how shall I say? – real. It's not a tourist attraction. There is no official entrance, no ticket office. There are no charges. You just push open the door, follow the signs and there it is. It's unbelievable.

After that there was only one place to go: Tuskulenai Park in the centre of town. On one side of an ordinary-looking wooden fence people walk their dogs, picnic on the grass and watch the kids playing tennis. On the other side they are unearthing the remains of one of the biggest KGB burial grounds in the Baltics. Again it's unreal. I mean, how can people just line up hundreds and hundreds of other people and just shoot them? And yet here, on the other side of the fence, this is what they did, day after day, week after week, month after month.

I am now in the middle of nowhere, way past Kaunas, Lithuania's second largest city which, apart from a pretty, central square, a baroque town hall, a single towered cathedral and a few scattered remains from a castle is Lego Land: one faceless modern tower block after another.

An old man who looks like an ex-KGB general tells me it was known as Sausage Village, 'Because it's next to the meat plant. In the old days people said it was built with all the meat smuggled out of the Kaunas meat plant and sold on the black market for sausages.'

The countryside is flat and uninteresting. But surprisingly, there are lots of small fields, unlike in other parts of the country.

'I thought all the farms were collectivised,' I asked an old farmer who had two fingers missing and hardly a tooth in his mouth. He told me that in this part of the country they were lucky. The local commissioner was a Lithuanian and he only *encouraged* them to collectivise. Elsewhere they were forced to. Fences disappeared, boundaries disappeared, whole villages disappeared. And, of course, anyone who stood in the way disappeared as well. 'We were lucky,' he said.

Backwards and forwards we drove through Tauragè, a tiny village on the banks of the River Sesuve. In the old days people here grew a special herb which was supposed to cure skin cancer, drank nothing but sour milk and lived to be 110. Not any more, although today things couldn't be more basic. The horse and cart is still the order of the day. If somebody has a battered old Lada they don't let the dog inside. He has to run along behind it.

Outside what looks like a derelict farm building we come across another group of old farmers standing around in the biting cold looking at a decrepit HTZ tractor made across the border in Minsk, Belorussia.

'It is good,' I said.

'It is not good,' a short bullet of a man said to me in English. 'It is Russian.'

On the way back to Vilnius we stop at a cepelinai, a tiny roadside café the size of a garden shed, where you can eat whatever you like so long as it's potato. It's packed with Lithuanians, Poles, Belorussians, a lorry driver from Kaliningrad and a group of mysterious heavy-set men in black leather jackets.

I talk to a tiny, fragile woman as thin as a matchstick who says she wants to practise her English. She is from Klaipeda, Lithuania's major shipping port. Her husband is a journalist and a photographer. She has two daughters. They all live in one room in her parents' house.

'I want my daughters to be big woman,' she says. 'Not like me. Me small, small, small . . .'

Two Lithuanians join us. We talk about the future.

'The one thing the Russians did was build good roads. We can now get out and travel and export our goods all over Europe,' says one of them.

'But it means the Russians can also come back in again,' says the other.

For their sakes, I crossed my fingers. All eleven of them.

The Caribbean

You're not going to believe this.

I'm not a finance director. I'm not a director of an in-house insurance scam, oops, I mean company. I'm not even a member of a senior executive remuneration review committee. But I have been to Bermuda, Barbados, the Bahamas and most places within laundering distance of what I maintain is the true capital of the Caribbean – Miami.

There, amigo, I knew you wouldn't believe me. What's more I hated it. Somehow it's just not me: kicking back and sipping Mai-Tais in totem-filled, thatched-roof, Tonga-style theme restaurants, full of dim lights and even dimmer waiters with hibiscus in their hair, watching 63-year-old teenagers wiggle and jiggle around on stage with geriatric Dorothy Lamours on artificial hips.

And shorts! You're as likely to see me wearing shorts, funky or otherwise, as you are to get your luggage through Miami airport without it being lost, re-routed to Papua New Guinea or simply disappearing off the face of the earth. The only shorts I fancy come in tiny glasses and have practical, down-to-earth names like 'a large one' or even 'a very large one'.

Which is probably why I'm not a finance director, a director of an in-house insurance – I nearly said it – company or a member of a senior executive remuneration review committee.

To listen to hardworking, results-oriented, cash-conscious finance directors and assorted financial whizz- and not so whizz-kids when they drag themselves back to the office, the

Caribbean is lush, exotic, tropical. It has a fabulous climate. It is sensuous, laid-back, bathed in warm, rich, golden sunshine with sparkling translucent turquoise water, and you breakfast on coconut bread, water melon and papaya all drowned in maple syrup, lunch on cocktails, fresh minted banana daiquiris, and have chargrilled lobster night after night for dinner. But to me, it's the land of transplants. Of hair. Of hearts. Of lungs. Of bank accounts. Of cash. Especially cash.

Admittedly, I've never been to the French Caribbean. I'm saving myself for it. I've only been to the English- or, should I say, American-speaking Caribbean, but I get the distinct impression that it's all pretty much the same, give or take the accent and the chilled champagne. Especially at night. During the day, I'm told that from underneath a coconut palm beside the beach with a perfectly chilled rum punch in your hand, it can be quite boring. At night the wild animals come out to play. Wearing loud suits with broad shoulders which not even gangsters would be seen dead in (this applies to men, women and whoever else happens to be around), they slip quietly ashore from their yachts and, posing as tourists, look around for somewhere to do their laundering; preferably casinos, especially in Nassau.

'No, I'm sure mine is longer.'

'Five hundred dollars on the black.'

'Longer? No way. Impossible. Mine is longer.'

'A thousand goes on the . . .'

'But how long? We're supposed to be talking about *long* beaches, not any old beaches.'

The wheel spins.

'Well, what about Barbuda? It's much longer than yours in Grand wherever it is.'

The croupier rakes in his winnings.

'Grand Anse.'

'Where the hell is Grand Anse?'

'On Grenada. Where the . . .'

'Cayman Islands has a long beach. Six or seven miles or something.'

'Five hundred again on . . .'

'Grand Cayman.'

'Grand Cayman what?'

Again the wheel spins.

'It's not what anything. That's where the beach is. Grand Cayman. And it's not Seven Mile Beach. It's Six Mile Beach. They just call it seven because they say it sounds better.'

'Hell. I just won another 50,000 bucks. What's wrong with this table?'

During my first visit, I had hardly been on the island long enough to open a string of bank accounts in different names before I was confidentially taken to one side by what I thought was a respectable British banker to be told that he could do me a favour. For every US$1 million cash they had to count before putting it into the system he would only charge me US$20,000. Say what you like, you don't get that kind of service in Heathfield.

Jamaica is different. When I think of Jamaica, I don't know whether to put on a dressing gown or a bullet-proof jacket and mix myself a deadly cocktail of malaria, bilharzia, conjunctivitis and a shot of lead. Usually from a Glock 17 semi-automatic. Shaken, not stirred. Me, that is, not the drink.

A million more people go to Hawaii every year than to the Caribbean. You would have thought, therefore, that Jamaica would be more exclusive, more select, more up-market. But it's not. Which, as they say, is a shock-up. Jamaica is down-market, bargain-basement; not so much working-class, as people who are prepared to sing banana boat songs all night and limbo dance under flaming poles far closer to the ground than is humanly possible. Especially with a pot belly full of Mai-Tais. Somehow, to me, it seems to lack that *aloha*, which as far as I can discover means whatever Hawaiians want it to mean, neither more nor less.

To 'dear Noël' and Errol and darling Ian – something of a disappointment to us all, y'know – and, of course, Larry and Cecil, it was, my dear, the only possible place in the world where one could oh-so-casually throw on a silk dressing gown, tie a cravat loosely around one's neck and languidly pour oneself another glass of Dom Perignon with no one to worry one, no one to hurry one. They were all so busy having the time of other people's wives or husbands or butlers or whatever, they just had to find somewhere where they could recharge their batteries as well as the cost of it all to someone else. Jamaica it was. Before you could say, 'Man, woman or dog, throw it on the bed,' they were all off to Firefly Hill, the house with a view, 1,000 feet above Blue Harbour.

To the rest of the world, Jamaica is the last country anyone should go to who is a coward, Noël or otherwise.

Kingston, the capital, is tucked into a valley surrounded on one side by the lush, tropical, misty Blue Mountains and on the other by one of the world's largest natural harbours. It is shame up, as they say, most definitely not laid-back. Unless you call lying back in the gutter outside your yard with a bullet through your head, laid-back. In the days of the pirates, it was the richest and wickedest city in the world. Today, thanks first to ganja, the country's biggest cash crop, produced in the north of the island, and now to the heavy stuff, it almost still is. The murder rate is almost as high as in New York. A walk round the mean streets of Kingston is, well, nearly as dangerous as a walk round the mean streets of New York. The heat is oppressive. There is rubbish rotting everywhere. Music blares straight through you from all directions. Most of the men are carrying knives or even guns. The women, I was told, carry tiny jars of acid to throw at anyone who attempts to ask them the time, let alone the best place to buy a jar of acid to protect yourself against anybody who stops you in the street and asks you the best place to buy a jar of acid.

For years the European Union has been trying to persuade Jamaica's farmers to break the habit of growing boring old ganja and switch to exciting things like carrots, potatoes and mixed veg.

On one trip to Washington I met a US diplomat who told me he was an expert on ganja.

'You mean you're working with the European Union,' I said,

'trying to get the farmers to switch to carrots.'

'No,' he said. 'It's what you get downtown when you go to a party or anything.'

Whenever I go to Jamaica everybody is either sticking little bits of powder up their nose or heading for the beach or the golf course. Not me. I like to grab a passing Centurion tank and make for the suburbs, or rather garrisons, of Angola, Tel Aviv and Southside to see how much more mashed up they've become. I'm never disappointed.

Angola is not Angola the desperately poor ex-Portuguese colony in Africa wrecked by years of civil war, but Angola the desperately poor part of Kingston, next door to Beverley Hills in the foothills of the Blue Mountains, that has been wrecked by years of civil war between the People's National Party and the Jamaican Labour Party.

Tel Aviv is People's National Party territory or, as the slogans scrawled on every square inch of available wall say, A Jamaica National Party Death Zone. Walk down Gold Street – if you dare – and you're into Southside, another Jamaica National Party territory and another Jamaica Labour Party Death Zone. It's a bit like Belgium, but without the violence.

Tivoli Gardens belongs to neither side. But no way is it a mini Switzerland. It is ruled by the biggest drugs baron or Don on the island, who again and again has faced charges for rape, multiple murder and robbery but has been released each time after vital witnesses failed to appear to testify against him.

Montego Bay, the island's second city, I've never fancied, since I discovered it practically means Lardsville. It was where the Spaniards used to offload all their animal fats way back in the seventeenth century.

But I once ended up at Ocho Rios on the north coast with its Dunn's River Falls which cascade 600 feet down to the sea. It has two claims to fame. First, it was the hideaway of the legendary pirate John Davis, who was virtually, if that's the right word, a headhunter for the big plantation owners in the eighteenth century. Second, it is one of the few places in the world where I have actually loosened the top button of my

shirt and sat on the beach. Not, I hasten to add, with hibiscus
in my hair or a string of flowers around my neck.

If Jamaica is dangerous for visitors, Bermuda is safe for
visitors unless, of course, you happen to be a visiting police
commissioner, a governor-general or even ADC to a governor-
general. Way back in the 1970s all three were murdered within
six months of each other. So, if nothing happened on the
island between 1503 when it was discovered by Juan de
Bermudez, and 1972 when the murders took place, don't go
anywhere near the place in the year 2463. Take my word for
it, these things repeat themselves. Until then you're quite safe.
I hope.

Bermuda is serious. It's responsible. It keeps itself very
much to itself. A bit like an elder sister treading that thin line
between being unmarried and being a spinster. It drinks
English tea and has muffins at four, served on the very best
Wedgwood. Everybody wears a collar and tie; English collar
and tie. None of this Ralph whatever-his-name-is stuff. And
you can bet your life or your annual subscription to the golf
club, whichever is worth more to you, they write little thank-
you letters for the slightest reason and say please, and thank
you awfully so much, all day long.

There is no illiteracy, no income tax, no graffiti, no
vandalism, no dirty fingerprints. And nobody bites their nails.
They have full employment and high wages, and I mean high.
Salaries are almost double those in the US. They have British
postboxes. They drive on the left-hand side of the road.
Genuine English Wedgwood is always on sale at Trimming-
hams and everything else any Englishman could possibly want
at the English Sports Club. It's so laid-back you're not even
allowed to think of doing anything. Perish the thought. Pass
me another gin and tonic, old chap. Awfully good of you.
Thank you so much.

Curtain Bluff or Jumby Bay on Antigua? Young Island off St
Vincent in the Grenadines? Mustique? You can hardly walk for
people eager to rent Princess Margaret's so-called hideaway
home and romp between her sheets for £6,000 a week. Sam

Lord's Castle in Barbados on the east coast, which is constantly pounded by the Atlantic, is fun. I once spent a whole day there in the middle of an enormous tropical storm, huddled under a beach umbrella with an American construction engineer getting bombed out of our minds on rum. Sandy Lane Hotel with its soft golden sand and palm trees is not bad providing you're prepared, without really trying, to blow £1,000 a night for two. And that's without the Mai-Tais. Which to me is crazy. I think it's run by Italians on a busman's holiday from running hotels in Sicily. But don't tell them I said that.

Bridgetown, the capital, I like. It still has the feel of an old pirate haunt, a fishing port and a colonial outpost; or was it just the rum piña coladas? Still, they built their statue to Lord Nelson a hundred years before we got round to doing it in London.

I have not been to Cuckold Point. And I don't intend to be in that position if I can help it.

Now listen up, you guys; forget what the maps say, the capital of the Caribbean has got to be – Miami. Right? Right. First, there are more Caribbeans there than there are in the entire Caribbean. Not to mention Mexicans, Salvadoreans, Nicaraguans, Panamanians and everything north of Patagonia.

Second, it's practically the world, let alone the Caribbean, capital of sun, fun and everything you can think of doing for 900 days a year. That shimmering sand. That tropical sunlight. Those over-exuberant smiles. Those exhilarating pouts. Those radiant teeth. Those acres of bronzed, bachelorette perma-tan. Those ... those ... My God, the wonders of modern silicon technology.

Third, it's the world capital of lost luggage. Wherever I go to, through or from within a million miles of Miami, somehow they always seem to lose my luggage. London to Miami to Panama. They lose my luggage. San Salvador to Miami to Boston. They lose my luggage. How the Americans can suddenly airlift troops to Grenada, to Panama, to Haiti, and not get my luggage from gate B18 to gate B19 without losing it I do not know. And I'm not talking about five minutes between flights. I'm talking about three, four even six hours between flights with great red 'Transfer bag outside USA' signs slapped all over it. My theory is that it's the CIA. It's always the CIA. They think the only way they can maintain US influence in the region is to stop British businessmen from getting in there, distributing their literature and signing up the deals. Lose enough luggage and we'll soon get the message and avoid the place altogether. Right? Right.

But that's not why I like Miami. I like Miami because I don't get robbed there. I don't get beaten up. I don't get killed. At least, not yet. On that basis alone, it's got to be a great place. As far as I'm concerned. You, of course, might have different ideas.

In fact the most dangerous thing that has ever happened to me in Miami was one evening outside Tavernier, the sports fishing capital of the world where landing an evening meal works out at around US$350 per plate, not including the chips. There was I, minding my own business wondering whether I could disguise the bill on my expenses as Entertaining the whole of the North American sales force, when for no reason at all this very nice, friendly, goddamn air-brain, who looked like a rice pudding on heat with size-12 Doc Martens and a T-shirt saying 'I'm not Nucking Futs', came thumping up to me, *Madre de Dios*, and started calling me, of all people, Eurotrash. Which I must admit I took as a compliment. He could, I suppose, have gone on to demand my loney or my mife. But he didn't.

That apart, the most dangerous thing that happens to me in Miami is being forced to shop until I drop, which I've always reckoned is a crime against humanity, or at least male humanity. The only reason they've never been able to make it stick is because under the guise of justice they pack the juries with women probably on the basis that it's the only subject they truly understand.

My wife won't agree with me – she never does – but I reckon I've done more than my fair share of shopping in my time, if only because I still haven't perfected my I've-got-a-broken-leg-but-I'll-be-all-right-by-dinner routine.

In Paris, I've been up and down the rue St Honoré as many times as President Clinton's trousers in an Alabama motel room. In Rome, I've dragged myself in and out of everything with a door and a shop window in the via Condotti. In Singapore, I've trailed the length of Orchard Road, spiritual home of the rich and super-rich Indonesians and Malaysians, particularly those not involved in receiving aid from the British, not involved with building huge dams in the middle of nowhere and not involved with not putting Britain last, if you don't see what I mean. Many happy hours I've wandered around Revolution Boulevard in Belgrade. Before the troubles began, it was packed with hundreds of stalls selling American cigarettes, Swiss chocolates, Japanese cassette players and television sets and Italian suits. Since the troubles began, I'm told, it is still packed with hundreds of stalls selling American cigarettes, Swiss chocolates, Japanese cassette players and television sets and Italian suits. They might be a lot more expensive, but they are still there.

In Eastern Europe, there is nothing like U, the old-fashioned department store in Vilnius, which is still firmly rooted in the days of Stalin. On each floor, grim female prison wardens sit by the escalators counting them up and counting them down again. Just think of smiling at one of them and you'll be packed off to the gulag before the next till rings. A tie? Sure, if you are going to the annual reunion of the Apostles. A suit? No problem, if you don't mind looking like a Cambridge undergraduate circa 1930. A fur hat? Certainly, comrade. Second floor. Turn left at the lift which doesn't work, first right by the counter which should sell cakes but doesn't and right opposite the counter selling postcards of happy, smiling, well-fed Soviet citizens which five years after the collapse of Eastern Europe they still haven't managed even to give away. The only good thing about it is the price of everything. A tie? A snip at 17 cents. A suit? Not a penny over US$16. And that hat? For you, just $6. Trouble is they look as though you paid $6 – for the lot.

Flea markets, you name them, I've had them as well. Antigo Mercade by the Niteroi Bridge in Rio which, last time I went there, was full of Portuguese candlesticks; the infamous Marché aux Puces near Port de Clignancourt in Paris, with its mountains and mountains of le junk, le rubbish and le this-could-be-worth-a-fortune-if-only-I-knew-what-I-was-buying; the football stadium in Warsaw. In the Piata Amzei in Bucharest I narrowly missed being trampled by a herd of stampeding fat old ladies when a rickety van arrived full of fresh eggs for sale. I've been swindled by Moroccans selling old clothes, watches and plastic flowers. I've been cheated by Senegalese in Harvard selling old books. I've been in a jewellers in the gold market in Amman called Al-Shark; a shoepurmarket in Cardiff, and once, in Paris – again – I was going to a meeting in the Académie Française when I got dragged into a shop with what I thought was, to say the least, an interesting name; Nauti Store. Inside I quickly discovered it was, in fact, a nautical equipment centre.

But shopping in Miami is as different from all that as a supermarket trolley is from a Porsche.

I'm not old enough to remember but I keep being told by crusty old colonels beached in seedy hotels in Tunbridge Wells that there was a time when, if anybody anywhere in the Caribbean needed as much as a box of matches, they would automatically think of going back to Blighty for it. Nowhere else existed. Now, however, Miami is the centre of the world. For wall-to-wall sun; for wrap-around shades; and especially for non-stop you-want-it-we-got-it shopping. In fact, I reckon unlike any other beach in the world, Miami is famous for the three S's; sun, sea and – shopping. It's in a class of its own for shops, shoppers, and the actual mechanics of shopping.

In the dim and distant past when culture was more than the top of a yoghurt, people used to do cultural things like visit cathedrals, tour art galleries, wander aimlessly around museums, get lost trying to find the house where Tchaikovsky wrote the 1812 and get bombed out of their minds at every corner bar in town. Not any more. Americans visit the nearest shopping mall. The aim now seems to be to visit as many shops as possible, tour all the department stores you can, wander aimlessly around one shopping centre after another and get lost trying to find the cheapest detergent in the Western world.

'Gee, Elmer, d'ya see the size of that yah, yah . . .?'

'Yah. Sure, honey. That's right. I'll take it.'

'Take two. It'll be cheaper.'

The only reason I decided to check out the shopping malls in Miami was that there was a distinct shortage of cathedrals and art galleries. And I didn't fancy pushing anything up my nose. In any case I thought it would be less dangerous, more socially acceptable and cheaper. Now I'm not so certain. What I am certain of is that in Miami there are three different types of shopping centre: hugh, huge and my-God-I'll-never-remember-where-the-hell-I-parked-the-car. Call me unbiased, unprejudiced and totally objective but to me they all look like huge great glistening white splodges of 75 per cent pure coke with gaping chunks missing where everyone and their lawyer has been gouging out lumps to melt down in only the bluest part of the flame to make the softest syrupy goo possible to inject into their left arms with only the cleanest of syringes.

Come to think of it, the shoppers themselves also looked huge, huge and my-God-the-springs'll-never-take-it. In fact, the first time I went to a Miami shopping centre I thought being fat was a qualification for entry. You think I'm kidding. In one shopping centre, I was once asked, 'Can I see your ticket, sir?'

'Ticket?', I said. 'Why do you want to see a ticket?'

'Because we have a coupon malady,' the security guard said in that slow deliberate tone they all pick up from watching too many John Wayne movies in the afternoon while the rest of us are at work, 'created by a malfunction occasioned by an over-endowed . . .'

'Coupon malady,' I began, 'what's a . . .?'

Then I noticed this big, beefy, eighteen-stone security guard was wearing a namebadge that said 'Mandi J. Armitage' so I just gave in like I always do although I still don't know what he was going on about.

Inside the shopping centres the first thing that amazed me was that they were so full of people. I thought everyone would have been on the beach, or rolling up twenty-dollar bills, sticking one end up their nostril, inhaling masses of white powder and then snorting like a herd of rhinoceros.

Second, was that everybody was shopping with their own Platinum American Express cards. With somebody else's Gold American Express card. Gee whiz, even with real money if they had to, which I admit was a shock. Usually I find people only go into shopping centres to get out of the rain, fall asleep on the benches by the fountains or play hide-and-seek with the store detectives.

Third, there seemed to be as many different types of shoppers as there are of coke.

There was the shopaholic, the addict who is so stuffed with shopping chromosomes that their DNA comes in carrier bags. Designer carrier bags, of course. You can see them like zombies bombed out of their minds – I shop, therefore I am. I shop, therefore I am. I shop, therefore . . . – clutching carrier bags bulging to bursting point as they rush to fill the car with another load of clothes they'll never wear, hats which will never leave the box and shoes that will never see the light of day. They all seem to wear the same designer clothes, carry the same Coco Chanel handbags with semi-automatics hidden in the lining, and look as though they only had children to compensate for not being a success in their career.

I was once in Dade County, which includes the actual city of Miami. It was around midday. I had been to a meeting. I was hopping up and down on the burning hot concrete sidewalk, waiting to cross the 250-lane highway to get to my car which was melting on the other side of the street. Cars were screeching past with their air-conditioning howling like banshees.

A woman came up to me pushing a supermarket trolley stacked with every designer carrier bag you can imagine.

'There's supposed to be a full moon tonight,' she said. 'Can you see a full moon?'

Can I see a full moon? There am I, in the middle of Miami, in the middle of the day, hopping up and down on the hot concrete, cars hurtling past, looking up at the sky trying to see a full moon. I tell you, these Americans can get to you.

Then there's the business shopper. You know the type; unless they've got their own range of clothing named after them, they're a failure. Ralph Lauren, forget it. You're not exclusive, but I mean exclusive, until you've got your own Art Finkleburger range of jockstraps. They can't walk past a duty free shop in any airport without buying something.

'What do you want another briefcase for?'

'It's a good price.'

'But you've already got seventy-three.'

'It was a bargain. What's more I beat him down by . . .'

I know one big American wheeler-dealer with pockets as deep as a Texas oilwell. Deeper. He spends more time buying a tin of boot polish in a backstreet in El Salvador than he does negotiating to purchase an electronics company in Silicon Valley.

'Is this the right colour? Will it go with my . . .? Does that match . . .?' Dammit, it's only a tin of boot polish. How long does it take to buy a tin of boot polish?

I know another American who's just the same. We were in Kinshasa, in Zaire. He offered me a lift to the airport. Kinshasa is the kind of place where, if anyone offers you a lift anywhere, you take it. What he didn't tell me was that on the way he was visiting some famous Zairian sculptor. I ended up by carrying home the Zairian equivalent of a Henry Moore bronze because he wanted to avoid paying excess baggage. Moral of this shopping story: don't accept lifts from people you know. You're better off with strangers. They don't buy the Zairian equivalent of a Henry Moore statue.

As for the actual mechanics of shopping, these guys are not just eager to exercise their purchasing power. In the old days they had to out-shoot everybody in town; now, they want to out-shop everybody in town.

'You buying that lifelike automated baby tyrannosaurus rex with the darting eyes and moving head, legs and tail and the mouth that opens and closes?'

'Sure. I thought, a little souvenir, perhaps.'

'I'll have two.'

I was once coming through Miami with another big American wheeler-dealer. He wanted to buy some Davidoffs. We went into the duty free. A Dutchman was buying his cigars.

'Gee, they look great,' the American beamed. 'I'll take the same. But double it up.'

The assistant immediately grabbed box after box and slid them fast as greased lightning into the oh-so-elegant carrier bag.

'American Express?' he smiled at the American.

'Sure,' he replied, handing over his card and grabbing the bag.

'And that, sir,' said the assistant, whizzing the card through the machine, 'will be US$4,995.'

The American went white. Obviously for the first time in his life he had been out-shopped.

Then there are the run-of-the-mill supermarket shoppers: the browsers; the indecisive; the friends; the mothers and daughters; the sisters; the in-laws. And I swear that was Elvis Presley I saw by the shoe counter with all those little green men.

I wandered into the home furnishing section of this enormous shopping mall. There was this typical, God help us, all-American family. They were going on about shower curtains. What colour they should be, what length they should be. The one in the middle had a red neck, sawn-off shorts, Tom Sawyer throwbacks with a T-shirt saying, 'Help me. Don't dis me.' That was the mother, I assumed. The one on the left was wearing the usual T-shirt emblazoned with 'My folks went to Miami and all I got was this lousy bullet-proof vest and their ashes.'

'Gimme AC. I want AC,' he was screaming.

'Mellow out,' the father or perhaps I should say the most elderly looking person in the group was screaming down at him. 'Mellow out. Mellow . . .'

The mother ignored all this. For some reason she kept going on about spaghetti. 'Raw spaghetti, that's what I use. Light the end of it, it will light any candle.'

In the food hall everybody had trolleys with their own built-in calculator – not to calculate the cost; nobody is interested in the cost of anything in Miami – but to calculate calories. One woman, who was extra heavy on the blue tint, was so busy calculating she ran into a stack of tins. They crashed every-where.

I heard one very pleasant, civilised, down-trodden guy like the rest of us, mutter something in his partner's ear about her being 'hormonally challenged'. Did she go bananas!

'That is harassment. Verbal harassment,' she screamed in a naturally non-harassing manner, her moustache twitching violently at both ends. The white end and the blue end. It wasn't her fault, she screamed. It was because the trolley didn't have a 'correctural facility'.

Sitting by the fountain – there's a fountain in every shopping mall in the US – were two old dears. With their coats on. Other coats were folded neatly in their laps. They were surrounded by a million carrier bags.

'Ice cubes never. A steam iron is your answer. Hold it just above the carpet, ruffle it up with your fingers. It will take out any creases,' one was saying.

'Nah. Yo donna wanna usa de olda commona Bermuda. Usa dis new Tifway instead. Itsa da best for da golf coursa,' the other was saying.

At least they weren't doing anybody any harm.

I wandered into a book shop. I was riffling through their classics and wondering why I still hadn't read *Jonathan Livingstone Seagull*, when this guy came in, not wearing socks, who looked as though he did his heavy thinking before breakfast.

'Hey kid,' he shouted at the anaemic boy behind the counter who looked more non-living, as they say, than alive. 'I'll take fifty dollars' worth.' This guy was buying books by the price, nothing else.

'Got this new house. Wants some books on the shelves,' another assistant whispered to me. 'It's great. We get rid of all the old stock. Everybody's happy.'

I decided I still wasn't ready for *Jonathan Livingstone Seagull*.

Then, in a class entirely of their own are the professional shoppers. I was once in the El Cheapo Fuel Stop – garage to you and me. I met an American hooterama, a blowdried dilettante with a ring through his nose, who told me he was in videography! In a big way. He was the world's greatest living expert on, well, on everything. At least that's what he said. He was an expert on neolithic stone axes. He was the world's leading expert on eskimo ivory. He was the intergalactic expert on buying everything. Was he the intergalactic expert or was he not? He could recognise the toes of a stuffed kiwi from the teeth of a boa constrictor at twenty paces. And often did.

We went back along the street. Within about fifteen minutes we came to this antique shop which to me looked as though it was full of junk.

'There,' he said pointing urgently to this thing under a pile of, well, junk at the back of the shop. 'Can you see it?'

I peered into the gloom. 'No. Can't see a thing,' I admitted. 'What is it?'

'What is it?' He practically passed out. 'It's a commode. But not your ordinary commode. This is a Louis XIV commode,' he whispered. 'I've got to have it.'

'It'll cost a fortune,' I ventured.

'Cost a fortune,' he exclaimed. 'You have not seen Elmer Winvitz, the second generation. Just watch this.'

He sauntered in, wandered through the piles of, well, junk, trying to look uninterested. 'So how much is this?' he mumbled, picking up some old curtain tassel.

'Twenty bucks,' grunted the old man behind the counter.

Over to the other side of the shop. He picked up what looked like lumps of some ancient Buddha, turned them over in his hand, looked at them again. 'And these?'

'Fifty.'

'Cheap.' He gave the old man a big smile.

'Thank you, sir.'

Across to the worst painting in the shop. He picked it up, looked at it, put it back, picked up the dusty old vase alongside it, turned it over, put it back. Now he wandered across to the . . . 'No,' he said suddenly, 'tell you what, I'll take that commode thing. How much is that?'

'Twenty-five thousand dollars,' the old man said briskly. 'It's the only good thing I've got.'

Collapse of professional shopper.

But don't get me wrong. People don't just go to Miami for the shopping. Outside the malls in the real world, believe me, happiness is needle-shaped.

One New Englander who puts on his best threads and goes to Florida Keys every spring for the golf, told me Miami was balmy. Boy, was he talking. There are not many slam-dunk certainties in this life, but that I can guarantee. Visiting Miami is not like entering a different State or country; it's like being plunged headlong into a giant McDonalds carton of warm saliva, fruit cakes, frazzle brains, deadhead goofs, dumb zombies, crack crazy teeny boppers and other perhaps less obvious forms of jail bait, all loading it on coke, popcorn and anything that's high on crythorbic acid to combat the tendency of nitrites to become nitrosamines. Or is it the other way round? Here they have syringes the size of the Statue of Liberty and enough white powder to make the Himalayas look like the foothills of the Andes.

A group of Buffaloes from Massachusetts told me that nothing, but nothing, would stop them from taking their spring vacation in Miami now that they had discovered how to pump 50,000 volts through the bodywork of their car.

'Through the bodywork of the car? You're kidding me.'

'No way José,' they said, proving I suppose that they had at least picked up some culture during their annual trips. 'Trouble is, we have to wear rubber shoes the whole time. Touch that car without rubber shoes on and you're a dead man.'

I first went to Miami when it was a retired Jewish suburb of New York, where in the old days the kilo-advantaged, or is it unsympathetically constructed, who put off being young until they retired, would flock in in order to block off those cancer-inducing rays from their less advantaged compatriots. The blue rinse in the hotel dining room was bluer than the blue rinse in the sea.

The whole place was falling apart. Hotels were going downhill as fast as their residents. Pick up a copy of the *Miami Herald* in the street and underneath would be five retirement homes. Sales of hot milk and denture powder far and away exceeded sales of Harvey Wallbangers or Absolut Bloody Marys.

Today it's all changed. Practically the whole of the southern side of town has been renovated and, because it contains so many twentieth-century historical and architectural buildings, not only renamed Art Deco District but slapped on the National Register of Historic Places as well. In fact, so art deco is it that some of the most aerodynamic curves and sleekest shapes in town are to be found lining the sidewalk rather than stretched out on the beach soaking up the cancer-inducing rays of the sun. The kilo-impaired now flock there in order to stay out of the sun in case the cancer polyps they get are too big for their bodies to carry. The only blue rinse you see is the blue rinse worn by the Golden Girls. And they're all fellas.

For filling in times between meals, there is all the usual seaside entertainment; carjacking, trying to get into Joe's Stone Crab, and wandering leisurely around South West Eighth Street.

I'm not saying carjacking is a problem. It's just that if you don't want to be carjacked, you'd better get yourself a four-wheel battering ram with tinted windows, a battery of mobile phones and, wherever you go, floor it, fishtail style, like the natives. Once I floored it all the way from Miami Beach to Coconut Grove to Coral Gables and back again without once using the indicator, getting rammed, carjacked by a rival carjacker or killed. But I don't recommend it. Even if you are adventure-impaired.

Alternatively, grab a cab and try to find Joe's Stone Crab. If you don't, don't worry about it, because whatever time of the day or night you get there the place is full, there are a million people queuing up to get in and however long you wait you'll never make it. Which is probably just as well because the place is always full of celebrities, or rather 'incognito celebs' as everyone whispers to everyone else behind their shades. At least that's what I was told. I never managed to get in.

Then there is the scenic tour up and down South West Eighth Street, or Calle Ocho as it is known to the Spanish-speaking majority. Where you'll be delighted by all the sacrificial goats hanging from the trees, thrilled by the screams of live chickens as they are about to be sacrificed and can marvel at the crowds of homeless Cubans and Haitians hanging around the piles of rubbish in the streets discussing the best way of slitting throats. Goats' that is. That is, I think it's goats' throats they were talking about.

After that you'll be ready for South Beach.

South Beach must be the hippiest strip of sand in the world. Who says so? Not me. To me every strip of sand looks like every other strip of sand. But people who know about these things tell me it is: like finance directors, directors of in-house insurance companies and members of senior executive remuneration review committees. Apparently it's got something to do with the ratio between the number of great hulks who are heavy on the smiling and low on the salsa and meringue and what's known as seasoned singles.

But be warned. Not everything you see is genuine. In fact, very little of what you see is genuine. I mean, such unrelenting perfection has got to be fake, or the result of plastic surgery. The shimmering sand is fake. It was imported from the

Bahamas because it looked more like the real thing than the real thing. The real thing, probably like everything else in town, most likely left with the Indians. The grass either side of the highways is fake. It's been dyed green by a group of businessmen worried that all those vicious lies and rumours about Miami being a drug-infested city of guns, drugs, killings and carjackings is putting off the tourists. Their solution: gallons of green paint.

Those happy smiling 'have a nice day' guys at the airport and hotels who escort you through the officials then shepherd you to your waiting bus or taxi? They're fake. They're really happy smiling 'have a nice day or else' security men hired by another group of businessmen worried about those vicious lies and rumours putting off the tourists.

That bunch of Norwegian tourists over there, getting off the hotel courtesy bus, who've just been to a big shindig on how safe Miami is, organised by some Discover America International Pow-wow. Now they're real. And so was the gang who hijacked them on the way back from the conference.

So, okay. How safe is Miami?

'Very.'

They practically grab you by the throat, hurl you to the ground and fill you full of statistics until you agree. No, I mean, until you put your hand in theirs and give in. Then you hand over the contents of your wallet to the hotels, bars, ice-cream parlours and whatever. Except that even going on the lowest possible crime statistics they give you, and the highest possible tourist figures, it still means every year over 5,000 people end up staring down the wrong end of a gun.

Now I might not be a finance director, a director of an in-house insurance scam or even a member of a senior executive remuneration review committee, but – wait a minute – that means that every week a hundred people end up staring down the wrong end of a gun.

Go on the figures, they don't give you and – Help! HELP! Get me outta here. GET ME OUTTA HERE FAST, D'YOU HEAR, FAST!

Maybe there is something to be said for those lush Caribbean beaches after all. I mean, what's the occasional polyp? Better than a hole in the head any day.

Reykjavik

'If you're ever passing, you must drop in.'

Some people, believe it or not, actually like my company. Not many, I admit. A few have even asked me to drop by and see them. They were not exactly on their bended knees, but at least they asked. Which is how, one bitterly cold Saturday morning, I ended up in the middle of a screaming force-12 gale, being lashed by hail, sleet and torrential rain, steel hawsers around me snapping like bits of string, in Grindavik, a tiny fishing village on the edge of the Arctic Circle, God knows how many frozen miles from the frozen centre of frozen solid Reykjavik.

The wind was howling like a banshee. The hail was slicing through me. The sleet was coming down like stair rods. Ships trying to get into the harbour were being hurled backwards and forwards by the huge black seas. I hadn't exactly been expecting a warm welcome, but I hadn't expected the atmosphere to be so, well, chilly. I've been cold many times in my life; even frozen almost to death. But this was a different kind of cold. This was right-through-you-to-the-marrow-of-your-bones cold. Like staying in a Scottish hotel. In summer.

'Truly the wrath of the North Atlantic winter,' my driver kept telling me all the way from Reykjavik, which is probably the only English phrase they have to worry about in Iceland. Wrath of the North Atlantic, I thought. This guy has never had to stand on Buxted Station in the middle of an English winter waiting for the 6.09 which doesn't arrive until 6.27. And that's on a good day.

In Japan there are eight words for shadows; in England, fifty-three words for rain, fifty of them unprintable. In Iceland there are eight words for wind and all of them freezing cold. That Saturday I froze to death in every single one of them.

Vast petrified lava fields; huge volcanic craters; deep crevasses. Creaking glaciers, some 1,000 metres high and 1,000 metres thick, covering more than 10 per cent of the country. Weird lava formations; giant bubbling mud pools; huge steam jets; and everywhere the stench of sulphur. To drop by for my meeting I'd driven through some of the bleakest country I've ever seen; so bleak and desperate that it is blasted by the winds and gales for 364 days of the year. The other day the occasional shaft of sunshine pierces the thick grey cloud cover for a split second and temperatures soar to as low as 50° Fahrenheit and it's summer. *Summer.* The rest of the year it's around minus 15°. Go outside without a hat and your hair drops out.

I was in a Jeep with more advanced telecommunications equipment stacked into it than on an aircraft carrier. Miss the switch for the windscreen washers and I reckon we could have started World War Three. But even inside the Jeep, it was bitterly cold.

Outside it looked as though World War Three was over. We edged our way against the wind, the rain and the hail across an enormous barren, black, pitted landscape full of deep fissures and vast gaping holes. This is where American astronauts train for landing on the moon, which must be a walkover by comparison.

We drove past tiny little huts; swung through clumps of three or four cottages; skidded past storm shelters where people could hole up for days waiting for the world to end. Then nothing, nothing and more nothing.

If you don't know what it's like for the earth to move, head for Iceland. They have so many earthquakes it's dangerous to put your plate not just close to the edge of the table, but on the table at all. In fact they have so many earthquakes that they no longer get any publicity. The last really big one, in 1991, didn't warrant a paragraph anywhere in the world. Some people say it's because they are not as newsworthy as those in Chile. Others say it was because that was the day the Gulf War broke out and everybody was too busy watching CNN to take any notice. I didn't take any notice of it either. Partly because the earth moving is no big deal as far as I'm concerned. And partly because I've been to enough countries which seem to be falling apart. Iceland is no exception, except that it is falling apart literally. All along a line running roughly south-west to north-east.

There seemed to be deep gashes everywhere: in the road; along the ground on either side; even in the sides of mountains.

'An American, he tell me the earth, here it is splitting its pants,' said the driver in a deadpan voice that told me this was his second phrase in English.

It's all to do with the American plate and the European and African plates not exactly seeing eye-to-eye. A bit like the United Nations. Iceland apparently sits slap-bang in the middle of the mid-Atlantic Ridge, which runs all the way from the Arctic down to the Antarctic. Whatever happens anywhere along the ridge affects Iceland. Drop a teacup on the floor in Tristan da Cunha or slam a door in the Azores: by the time the shock waves hit Iceland, they practically split the country in two.

Admittedly it's only – only! – splitting apart at the rate of two centimetres a year, but that, I would have thought, was more than enough to make a difference between joy and despair. Give or take another couple of thousand years and not only will Iceland be Icelands but, with or without President Clinton's help, America and Europe will be even further apart than they are today.

We drove past two or three more tiny cottages whose only advantage must be they are too far away for the wife's mother to drop in for a seven-day weekend. Along the edge of the swirling seas with waves crashing against the coast. Through another moonscape. If the Americans use this place as a dummy run for landing on the moon, UFO freaks use it for dress rehearsals to welcome the first little green men from outer space. Regularly they gather on the tip of the Snaefellsnes peninsula at the base of the magnificent Snaefellsjokull glacier for iced coffee mornings, expecting to see the odd flying saucer drop by, fooled by the landscape into thinking it has reached home. Although why beings from outer space should want to come all this way to land on a lump of ice in the middle of nowhere is something only an intelligence greater than mine would appreciate.

For me this is a land fit only for trolls. Or for ogres. Or for American students with backpacks. Definitely not little green men from outer space.

Finally we got to Grindavik, a cluster of buildings clinging like limpets to the edge of the coast, hammered, battered and torn to shreds by the gales.

Past the tiny auction house we edged. Past the harbour we crept. Past the 'Bar Restaurant Pizzeria Pub' on the very edge of the coast we slid. Past a sign which said, Sjomanna Og Velstjorafelay, which was either the name of the restaurant or a warning not to drive on the very edge of the coast in a force-12 gale.

High above us was a mountain which you could see was already splitting its pants. In front of us, in the tiny harbour the seas were heaving. Fishing boats were practically being thrown out of the water.

I scrambled out of the Jeep and fell and stumbled and skidded and ran to the door of a tiny, dirty green hut.

'If I was passing, you said to drop in,' I gasped.

At the time I was working on a project to build fish farms in Africa. Plan A was a typical African plan: enormous Olympic-size concrete swimming pools, miles from any water; huge pumping stations, miles of pipelines, purification plants, processing plants and the biggest fleet of freezer lorries the world has ever heard of to distribute the fish all over the country. It would take years to build, cost a fortune and no doubt keep teams of Swiss bankers happy for years handling the transfers from one numbered account to another.

Plan B was – surprise, surprise – to find a stretch of land close to the sea, scoop out a string of pools, line them with plastic, pump in seawater, throw in a couple of fish and you're in business. A refinement was going to be a chicken farm on top of each tank. The droppings from the chickens would fall through the slatted floor into the water to feed the fish. The whole thing would take months not years and probably only keep one clerk at the Trustee Savings Bank busy for maybe half an hour.

Then I came across this Icelandic company which made me realise there is more to fish than fish. Icelanders in the race to survive decided they should widen their production capacity and increase their range of services and skills. So they went into every type of fishy business you can think of:

    fish processing
    frozen fish blocks
    fish stock assessment
    fish statistical assessment systems
    on-board fish processing techniques
    fish catch storage
    fish catch product storage
    oven-ready fish entrées
    fresh fish production for France
    saltfish production for Spain
    fishing gear manufacture
    fish navigational equipment
    design and production of fish processing equipment
    fish tub production
    fish freezing plants
    fish canning
    fishing processing
    fish distribution

And, oops, I nearly forgot, fishing. They still manage the odd catch or two, though nothing like the old days when no chip was complete without a lump of Icelandic cod.

My friend at the frozen end of the world was studying ways of converting old oil tankers into brand new fish farms. Old oil tankers were going cheap. We'd buy one for next to nothing, tow it round the coast to where it was needed, anchor it alongside the port wherever the fish farm was needed, line the tanks with plastic sheets, pump in the seawater, throw in a couple of fish – hey presto, an instant fish farm.

Trouble was, of course, that it was too simple, too quick to install and, worst of all for Africa, too cheap. If you get my drift.

'If you're passing by and you want to make it more expensive,' he told me on the phone, 'drop in, we can discuss it.'

I was in Pittsburgh. In the previous week I'd had four different invitations for the weekend:

– a self-guided Mount Pleasant log cabin tour in Steuben-
  ville, Ohio

– a Barbie Doll through the Ages exhibition at the West-
  moreland Museum of Art, Greenburg

– an Oglebay Institute Mansion Museum Christmas wedding
  and Miniature Train Race in Wheeling, West Virginia

– the 28th Annual Show Shovel Riding Contest in Economy
  Park, Ambridge, West Virginia

So I decided to take him at his word. I got a plane to JFK, then the flight to Reykjavik. I arrived, God help me, in the middle of the night. At least I think it was the middle of the night. The winds were howling, snow was everywhere, the place was deserted. It was bitterly, bitterly cold.

Reykjavik, which is exactly halfway between Washington

and Moscow, which is probably why the Reagan–Gorbachev meetings went so well – either that or the vodka – is supposed to mean Surprise City. But as we drove through the dark, silent city, it held no surprises for me. More shock. Thermal shock.

First, it was one of the cleanest cities I had ever been to. There was not the slightest bit of rubbish in sight. Because everything was buried deep in the snow. What it would look like if the snow ever melted was something else.

Second, it was full of street signs saying No Entry for Snow Ploughs. Even in 20° Fahrenheit the bureaucratic mind can come up with objections to put the most sensible proposals on ice.

To the Icelanders, this is Cod's own country and they themselves are Cod's frozen people. For breakfast they eat yoghurt and cod. For lunch, cod. For dinner, cod. Then for a complete change as a nightcap, hot milk and cod.

Forget all this cod about poor, chilly old Iceland. Iceland is hot. At least in money terms. Because nobody is interested in Iceland, nobody bothers to look at the figures. If you check the figures, however, you very soon warm to the fact that there may be only about 250,000 of them living squeezed up in the corner of a near barren rock, about the same size as Ireland, far from everybody, on the edge of the Polar Circle, but they have their own language – forsooth, the oldest living language in Europe, their own culture, their own way of life, their own currency, their own international rock star and their very own Hard Rock Café. They also have their own university, their own daily newspapers and magazines, their own theatres, their own two television stations and their own three radio stations.

They also have their own three major industries: fish, fish and fish. For centuries, Iceland was blessed with some of the richest fishing grounds in the world. They've even gone to war to protect them, the last time in the 1970s with I forget who. By comparison everything else is tiny. They are just about self-sufficient in meat. Energy is booming: because of all their natural resources, they can generate electricity more cheaply than almost anybody else. There's none of this 'Please turn the lights off when leaving', or funny doorkeys which turn the lights on or off in your room. Iceland has so much hydro-electric power it doesn't know what to do with the stuff. It fell over itself to build an aluminium plant just to use up some of it even though it meant bringing the bauxite all the way from Jamaica. Now it is trying to build a steelworks, even though the steel will probably have to be shipped in from the other end of the world too. In fact, it's got so much hydro-electricity it heats some of the pavements in town. So what's a couple of 100-watt bulbs? I left them all on in my hotel room all day. I was tempted to leave them on all night as well, but it was already difficult enough to tell the difference between day and night.

Economic growth is a chilling 4-5 per cent a year. Inflation is practically frozen. Unemployment is zero, apart from one or two huskies who've gone soft because of all the vegetarians who pour in to see the baby seals and insist on taking environment-polluting snowbikes rather than exploit the dogs by letting them do what they were bred for. Income, per head of population, is an unbelievable US$24,000, more than that of the United States, the richest country on earth. They have more video cameras and personal computers than Japan, the most technically advanced country on earth. See what I mean about looking at the statistics.

On everything else, from infant mortality to the number of telephones per 1,000 inhabitants, it's definitely in the top five. What's more, due to the stresses and strains of living on a lava-blasted, glacier-gouged barren lump of rock which is covered in snow eleven months of the year, life expectancy is an unbelievable 74 for men and 80 for women, probably the highest in the world.

Icelandic may sound like Benny Hill speaking Swedish but – eat your heart out Luxembourg, San Marino, Monaco and all the other mini-states – at least it's their own language they are speaking, not somebody else's. Similarly their culture. Admittedly Iceland's famous writers are only known in Iceland but at least Icelanders, who read more books per head of population than anyone else in the world, are reading Icelandic books, not Jackie Collins or Jilly Cooper, or, heaven help us, Barbara Cartland or Jeffrey Archer.

There may be more public lavatories listed in the tourist guide than art galleries and museums but at least they are still reading the 1,000-year-old Icelandic sagas with the rabid attention of anyone forced to spend eleven months of the year locked up against the elements. After all, eleven months doing nothing but rehearsing for a part in the Icelandic National Human Body Percussion Championships must begin to take its toll eventually.

Trouble is, as far as I can tell, all the sagas are about women, which is probably not surprising, until you realise that the woman all Icelanders dream about has three heads. At least. Three eyes in each head. At least. A swollen black eye in the back of each head. Goat horns. Ears falling down in great loops over her shoulders which then curl round and disappear up her nose. Teeth the size of rocks. A beard on each chin. And giant black claws on every finger.

The wife's mother? Wrong. It's good old Gryla, the friendly, baby-eating mother of the trolls who, before Walt Disney smothered everything in sugar and spice and all things nice, used to do Icelandic parents a favour by eating any kid who dared to even think of screaming its head off because it wanted to watch *Zombie Flesh Eaters* or *The Mutilator*, an everyday story of death by pickaxe and chainsaw, on igloo television when the grown-ups wanted to watch *Mary Poppins* again. Suddenly Gryla would appear in all her glory, pop them into her big grey shopping bag and whisk them off to the mountains for lunch. Her lunch.

Like some kind of unreformed, unreconstructed Snow White, with the Seven Dwarfs to help her in her work, she had thirteen lucky kids of her own: Sniffer, who could smell cakes a mile away. Shorty, who could only smell them half-a-mile away, so had to be content with licking all the pans and plates, and was so busy doing so he forgot to grow up. Pot-scraper, and Boot-licker, the next on the scene. Spoon-licker, who had the leftovers. Window-peeker, who could only stand outside cursing that he couldn't get in. Sausage-stealer, who was fed up with the whole business and decided to do his own thing. Meat-snatcher, who was a bit more ambitious. Noise-maker, because there is always one in every family. Poor old Stiff-Leg, who presumably didn't get there at all and missed the whole thing. And three others whose names I can't for the life of me remember.

Today Old Mother Gryla is no more, but not because there are no longer any naughty children left to eat in Iceland. Instead mothers try to tell their unruly kids, if only they will turn their video nasties down a bit for a few seconds, that she had a slow, lingering death and finally wasted away and died. Which I would have thought would have had a more profound effect on a child brought up in a world of malnutrition, vitamin deficiency and famine. But I don't know anything about children, Icelandic or otherwise.

As for the trolls, who used to spend their lives terrorising travellers by jumping out at them whenever they turned a corner, barging past them in hotel bars and climbing through their bedroom windows, they've all gone as well. Which means there's nothing stopping you travelling round the country any more. If, that is, you thrill to the hail battering twenty-four hours a day; glory in fresh winds that can reach 70–80mph and marvel at snow and ice twelve months a year.

In the capital, Reykjavik, the most northerly city in the world, the temperature hovers around a bracing $-5°$ centigrade up to a sweltering zero. Even in the middle of summer, it never gets over $10°$ centigrade. And that's on the coast. Inland, high up, it's like living in Manchester on a rainy day in the middle of winter all the year round with your mother-in-law.

The only advantage I can see of the sun setting after midnight is that you can play golf through the night; which, when you think of it, is a big advantage. You can get home at three in the morning and your excuse, I was playing golf with the guys from the office, is at least plausible. It's better than sitting in the car with your wife arguing about why you would have taken the last turning on the left if only she had been reading the map properly so that you wouldn't now be sitting in a ten-mile traffic jam.

Spring? The only way you can tell it's spring is when the snow turns green and the rain – they have over 500 millimetres a year – soars to a staggering –4° centigrade.

The one month of the year that they can spend like the rest of us, they spend like the rest of us – providing of course they have not exhausted themselves rehearsing for their National Human Body Percussion Championships and sleep all the way through it. Except that they can't take the dog for a walk, because dogs are banned in Reykjavik. They can't watch television on Thursdays. Because there is no television on Thursday. And they can't eat a nice, big, fat, juicy prime rib of beef because they've still got all that fish to finish before they stock up again for next year.

But that doesn't mean there's nothing to do. There is the seventeenth-century cross-stitched bedcover, one of Iceland's greatest treasures, to visit yet again in the National Museum. There is the great national pastime of licking lamp posts. Goodness knows why, but when I was standing freezing to death in the snow outside the airport, an old man shuffled up to warn me never on any account to go around licking lamp posts. Lick a lamp post at –15°, he told me, and your tongue will stick to the metal. Something to do with cold fusion. In the interests of Anglo-Icelandic relations I thanked him profusely, and promised that no matter how bored I got I would not spend an afternoon in Reykjavik licking lamp posts.

There was no alternative, therefore, to Plan A. If you're in a foreign city and you're bored out of your mind, I always find there is only one thing to do; queue up outside a Hard Rock Café for a week or two. But in Reykjavik even this was not possible, because their Hard Rock Café is the most famous Hard Rock Café in the world. There is nothing particularly outstanding about it; it's just easier to get into than any other

Hard Rock Café. You can even, I was solemnly told, get in without queuing. Without queuing! Do they realise what a national asset that could be? Not in the same class as seventeenth-century cross-stitched bedcovers, I admit, but all the same, they could organise flights from all over the world. In the time it takes queuing to get inside a Hard Rock Café in London, Tokyo, Chicago or anywhere else, people could fly to Reykjavik, walk straight in, have their fix of hamburgers, beer and ear-shattering music, ogle at Eric Clapton's underpants and fly back again just in time to get into their local HRC.

So what do Icelanders do to fill in time in all that ice? After all, there is a limit to the number of snow-covered hill rocks they can ski down, the number of spare rooms to be turned into indoor driving ranges and the amount of time they can spend cranking up the thermostat. Having thawed out after my trip to sunny Grindavik I asked the hotel receptionist what there was to see in Iceland.

'Our famous glacier,' she said. 'Everybody goes to see the glacier, Vatnajökull, the biggest in Europe. It's three times the size of Luxembourg.'

'Don't fancy glaciers,' I said. 'Anything else?'

'You must see our Blue Lagoon,' she said.

If your idea of heaven is to sit outside in a pair of shorts in sub-zero temperatures choking on the smell of sulphur and with your feet dangling in a giant puddle of boiling hot water, then the Blue Lagoon is for you. It is not, I can tell you, for me. Even though it's obviously Iceland's hottest tourist attraction. They seem to think the best way of encouraging people to travel halfway round the world to bathe in it is to promote it as the miracle cure for any skin disease you care to mention. Each to his own, but as far as I'm concerned I'd rather lick lamp posts than leap into a puddle of hot water visited each year by over 100,000 people suffering from skin diseases.

'Don't fancy the Blue Lagoon,' I said.

I thought of trying to resolve once and for all one of the biggest problems facing mankind: how to read the Iceland telephone directory. You think I'm joking. No way. Trouble with the Iceland telephone directory is that, first of all, their names are complicated. At least, to me they're complicated.

If Fred, for example, has a son, the son is called Fredsson. If Fred has a daughter the daughter is called Fredsdottir. Which is straightforward, okay. But what with the long winter nights and so on, three out of four children are born illegitimate. So nobody knows whether they should be taking the father's name or the mother's. As a result sons have different names than their fathers. Daughters have different names than their mothers. Dammit, even mothers have different names from fathers. Confused? Good.

The second problem is that, wait for it, people are not listed in the phone book by either their mother's name or their father's name. They are listed according to their first name. Which complicates things even more.

But I decided the telephone directory could wait. In the end, to show you how desperate I was, I decided to go on a tour. Normally I never go on tours. I like mooching around by myself, wherever I can catch a quick few seconds between meetings. But in Iceland! What is there to do in Iceland, especially when it's not the Body Percussion season?

I took a cod tour of Reykjavik. We assembled in the snow outside the hotel, instead of waiting in the relatively warm lobby. I say, relatively warm, because every time somebody opened the door, in came great 30mph gusts of freezing snow.

While the occasional visitor is practically buried alive inside half a dozen snowjackets, a pair of giant mitts, a balaclava helmet complete with its own air-conditioning unit which reaches down to the waist and a pair of moonboots each the size of Westminster Abbey – that's just to go into the hotel dining room – your average Icelander strolls around in sports jacket and open-neck shirt searching for the best cod piece they can find. For the next two days we did the same. We went into one restaurant after another sampling the cod. We even saw a church built like a cod. As we came out, there was your typical American couple.

'It's about one and a half metres.'

'I don't understand. What's a metre? Harold, will you tell me what one and a half metres is?'

We climbed back on the bus.

'It's about that wide,' Harold said, barely opening his arms.

She looked at him in amazement. 'I know that,' she shrieked. 'Whaddya think I am, stupid or something?'

The bus pulled up outside another cod restaurant.

'What is it in inches? I can understand inches. Everyone understands—'

'Well, I don't exactly know,' he drawled. 'I guess . . . I guess . . .' He pulled himself up to attention and looked her squarely in her blue rinse and her double chins. 'Well, say a metre is a dollar, right?'

'Right,' she nodded.

We all got up to get off.

'So one and a half metres is one and a half dollars. Right?'

That's it, I thought. This guy is some kind of rocket scientist or something. His unfailing ability to master the most complicated concepts and immediately turn them into something everybody can . . .

'Naw,' she shrieked as we clambered off and waited in the ice for our leader.

'Okay,' Harold took a step back and punched his right fist into his left hand. 'Don't let's say dollar and a half. Let's call it six quarters. Now do you . . .?'

Did she get it? She was suddenly all smiles and grinning and handshaking. 'Why couldn't that dumb guy have said that in the first place?' She beamed all over me. 'Always tries to make things difficult so he can show me up. I don't know why I stay with him.'

With that they linked arms and walked together into the restaurant.

I headed for the nearest lamp post.

The man I blame for all this is a Norwegian, Isolfur Arnarson.

He was so fed up kowtowing to all the other Norwegians he decided, like any self-respecting Viking, there was only one thing to do. Run away. With a couple of dozen other rough, tough drop-outs who were prepared to stand up for their rights, including his wife, Hallveig, he upped and headed for the open seas to establish his own little kingdom, where presumably he would make all the others kowtow to him. Except, of course, his wife.

Nobody actually lived in Iceland till around the year 850, when Mr Arnarson, his band of rough, tough disciples and his wife arrived. Some people say that Irish monks got there 200 years earlier, in the sixth century. My own feeling is that if they did they got the hell out as soon as they arrived and headed for Boston, but kept quiet about it because they didn't want to take the blame for discovering America.

Like all early settlers, Isolfur Arnarson and his merry band managed to hit the best spot first time and landed at Reykjavik where they set up home. Why Reykjavik is called Reykjavik and not Arnarson or even Hallveig I have always thought unfair. After all Sydney is Sydney and not Germaine, Kev, Clive or any other aboriginal name.

Poor old Arnarson obviously had Irish blood in him. First, because of all the islands in the world to choose from he chose not only the coldest but the one with the least arable land: less than 1 per cent was capable of growing any crops. Second, because the rough, tough Vikings who ran away with him were obviously so exhausted with all the raping and pillaging they had been doing they only had enough energy left to talk about it. The result is that Iceland probably has more sagas about the goings-on of the trolls and the little frozen people than people to read them.

Third, because with all the sitting around and writing they were doing, his loyal followers, obviously led by his wife, very quickly realised that there was more in life than kowtowing to old Isolfur in the Big White Igloo on the top of the hill. So they came up with the idea of a Thing, or, you know, a Thingvellir, or parliament, which meant in order to stay leader he had to pander to everybody under the midnight sun to get their votes. Which means the Icelandic parliament is probably not only the first but also the coldest parliament in the world. Except during debates. (When Mrs Thatcher was in her prime, nothing could be chillier than the atmosphere at Westminster, especially when she was tearing into some poor innocent leader of the opposition.) Although to be fair, to try and raise the temperature a little, the Icelandic parliament did introduce a rule that once a year every member has to stand up and make a speech in rhyme. Had Westminster introduced the same rule it might have raised the standard of debate. But it was not to be.

In the tenth century the first Christian missionary arrived. Two Icelanders promptly made up a funny song about him. Instead of turning the other cheek the holy man killed the pair of them. He ended up being exiled to a monastery in Kiev which must have been a good move on his part. As for the Icelanders, I suppose it was bound to leave an impression on them.

Iceland remained buried in snow for another 1,000 years until the start of the last World War, when they suffered another major setback. Not from the Nazis, but from the Allies. The Nazis moved into Denmark in 1939. But amazingly, in spite of their admiration of Iceland, not only for its racial purity, but for its right kind of Aryan racial purity, they failed to follow up. Not so the British. Soon afterwards the non-racially-pure British moved in.

In April 1940 the British requested permission to use Reykjavik as a military base. Iceland said no, just as before the war they had said no to the Germans when they requested permission to use Reykjavik as a halfway stop for transAtlantic flights. In May, in order to help defend small independent nations against the mighty onslaught of huge military empires, the British invaded. Except, of course, it wasn't an invasion. It was a protective occupation. A bit like the Americans, I suppose, going into Grenada or Panama or Haiti or wherever they fancy next.

The Nazis had invaded Denmark. Iceland at the time was a colony of Denmark. It was obvious, therefore, that before long the Nazis would be using Iceland as a hideaway for their U-boats trying to blockade the UK. What better than to get there first? Churchill gave the order. The Allies went in. And the Americans followed afterwards. As usual.

For the length of the war, as if they didn't have enough problems, the 120,000 Icelanders had to put up with no less than 60,000 Americans. Which must be a world record for something or other. B-17 bombers; P-38 fighters; C-47 transports: suddenly Reykjavik had more firepower in their backyards than igloos. At one stage in the build-up for the Normandy landings they were being protected by over 1,000 flights a month shipping goods in and out.

One of the results was that poor old Iceland ended up with US$100 million in the bank; but they suffered more casualties per head of population than any of the countries actually fighting the war. Although precisely what type of casualties I've never been able to discover.

Come the end of the war, the Americans decided that it was obviously in the best interests of the poor, defenceless, isolated, innocent Icelanders if they remained there, thrust them into the front line, put the cold into the Cold War and, in the event of Europe being overrun, make them an advanced staging post for any attack on Moscow.

Invasion or protective occupation, the results are there today: Coca-Cola, Madonna and a huge NATO airbase at Keflavik, the birthplace of Icelandic rock and roll, presumably because it is also home to 5,000 US airmen and their families, although, I must say, you never see them in town. They're probably all chained to their air-conditioners trying to get the warmth back into their number 5 irons.

In the event I never went back to Iceland. Our fish farm scheme was rejected. The last I heard, they were into their third feasibility study, with each study proposing a bigger and bigger project, further and further from the sea. In any case, somebody else asked me to drop in the next time I was passing. They had a permanent suite at the Negresco in Nice.

Guess how long it took before I happened to drop in there for a long weekend.

Abidjan

The shelves are piled high with fromages. The camembert is fresh. The Mont d'Or is, well, Mont d'Or. An elegant homme d'affaires is sifting through the pâtés. A matronly dame d'un certain âge is selecting the perfect caviar russe. Two secretaries are giggling over the tuiles pâtisseries. Something to do with the shape of them – you know how sophisticated they are! Sacks of herbes de Provence are everywhere. The selection of wines is fantastic. Every château you can think of. Every clos in the world. Every hermitage known to man. The gossip at le check-out is serious gossip. About books. About art. About politics. About music. About whether Lâncome's Blush Subtil is better than Chanel's Joues Contrastes.

Paris? Nice? The Dordogne? The Loire? Or that secret, hideaway world of Provence which is now wall-to-wall with two and a half million Brits clutching that damn book.

Jamais de ma vie. I'm in Abidjan, the capital of Côte d'Ivoire, the most French city of all French Africa. It's so French that even the poodles bark with a French accent – partly, I admit, because their darling devoted owners would not dream of giving them anything but the very best French dogfood flown in fresh from Paris every day.

The old president of Côte d'Ivoire, Felix Houphouet-Boigny, the No. 1 Peasant, le Vieux, le Sage, who was in power for thirty years, was also really the father of franco-phone Africa, the voice of moderation and of everything calm, quiet and peaceful. After champagne and caviar, I reckon he did more than anybody to make Africa French.

Try and imagine the opposite of a revolutionary and there you have Houphouet. Immaculately groomed: black jacket, striped trousers, white shirt, oh-so-discreet tie, the shiniest black shoes you've ever seen. Yet, to me, he was really the true revolutionary. For while the rest of Africa was falling over themselves to go Communist and out Marxist-Leninist the next man, he was the only one to insist on doing it his way: the French way.

He is dead now. Something he postponed as long as he possibly could, because it meant never seeing Paris again, sipping chilled champagne and nibbling those tiny sweet biscuits. He even blew over £130 million of his own money – now, now, that's what he said – on building the biggest church in the world in his home village of Yamoussoukro in order to stay on a bit longer. Which seemed to work, because he was well into his nineties before he finally headed off for obviously the very much second best Champs Elysées.

Everybody said he would go when he was ready and not before. They even told jokes about his having built the church, which looks exactly the same as St Peter's in Rome, then going off to see the Pope and asking him whether he was going to go to a francophone heaven or an anglophone hell.

'Come back and see me tomorrow,' the Pope tells him.

He goes back the following day.

'Okay,' the Pope says. 'I've got good news and I've got bad news. The good news is, you built the church, you're going to heaven. The bad news is, you go tomorrow.'

But he never did. He didn't like the deal. So he just stayed on until he was ready to go. Some people say that in order to get his own back on the Pope he did the only thing he could do to bankrupt the entire Roman Catholic Church. He gave them, as a present, his cathedral. Which was the last thing they wanted because it means they now have to look after it. You don't think that's a problem? You know how expensive it is getting a plumber or an electrician in the middle of a big city – just think how much it's going to cost St Peter to maintain a cathedral which seats 300,000 people in the middle of the bush, 200 kilometres from civilisation. I tell you, instead of hoping that Peter's Pence will look after the place they'll have to up it to Peter's Pounds pretty quickly.

Others were praying Houphouet would never ever go. For when a Baoule tribal chief like Houphouet goes, all his retinue and staff are supposed to go with him. Which must have momentarily miffed even the ever smooth and unruffled Georges Ouagnie, his faithful Lebanese director of state protocol and Mr Fix-it for over thirty years. Watching the two of them arriving at airports, going into big international conferences, tottering off together to official receptions and dinners, was like watching Africa's happiest ever married couple.

But in the end, even after thirty-three years in power, the doyen of Africa's oh-so-select club of mega-big spenders, the great baobab tree, as the Baoules say, crashed to earth. To the immense relief of the faithful Georges and no doubt all Baoules, he died the way he had lived: not like a Baoule but like a Frenchman. Even so, even after all those years, it still came as a surprise. So much so that he had to be kept in a special Swiss-made refrigerated safe, oops, I mean coffin, for two whole months while everyone ran round making the arrangements. Then they could only come up with five days of solemn ceremonies to say au revoir. Even so, the collective grief that swept the nation should warrant a mention, at least, in the *Guinness Book of Records*. Hordes of wailing women? That's nothing. With a cry of 'If Houphouet is dead, I don't want to live any more,' one guy actually threw himself to the sacred crocodiles in the moat surrounding one of the presidential palaces. Not even the great Kim Il Sung got that kind of attention. He had barely shuffled off to 'meet Marx' as the *Pyongyang Daily Gleaner* said, than he was in the hands of his Russian embalmers and that was that.

The French turned out in force to say their adieux and check, I suppose, that he took all their secrets with him. President Mitterrand, who flew in by Concorde, arrived ninety-five minutes behind schedule, a record even for him for turning up late. Balladur, wearing one of his English suits, flew in by a more economic Falcon jet with his own crocodile of former presidents, including Giscard d'Estaing, seven former prime ministers, countless ministers, and was on time. Also present was everybody who had ever had anything to do with Africa, including General de Gaulle's 'Monsieur Afrique', the mysterious and still dangerous Jacques Foccart. From the less civilised, less important parts of the world came a whole string of heads of state including the Lebanese president (who says Abidjan wasn't a safe haven for Lebanese terrorists?), goodness knows how many prime ministers, crown princes, duchesses, barons and, I nearly forgot, the unelected Lynda Chalker, who has had such a profound affect on Britain's relations with Africa.

People criticise poor old Houphouet; the way he used to wear his pinstripe suits, his big houses in France, the enormous church in the middle of nowhere. This is unfair. To me, judged in the African context, he was a good, a very good president. For old Houphouet, le Vieux, le Sage, was not just any old African president, he was part of the history of Africa – and of France as well. He was elected a member of the French National Assembly in 1945. He was a minister of state under de Gaulle and served in no less than six French governments. For goodness knows how many years, he was the doyen of French government and diplomatic life.

Going to Abidjan, which looks to me like a mini Manhattan in the sunshine, was not like going to Côte d'Ivoire. It was like going to Houphouet's place. The south of French Africa. For he wasn't just pro-French, he was pro-Pro-PRO-French. Nobody could have been Frencher. He not only insisted, for example, that all government ministers dressed like the French – they were forbidden to wear anything but the best French suits (this was pre-Balladur don't forget) – they had to act, think and virtually be French as well.

Sure, Côte d'Ivoire is facing problems at the moment. Everybody is, and Africa in particular. But the fact remains that when he was at the height of his powers and influence,

Houphouet was the most important man in Africa, and Côte d'Ivoire the most stable country. He had taken a disease-ridden swamp – not even the old slavetraders wanted to know anything about the place – and turned it into Africa's most successful country. He did what few African presidents have done: he gave peace to his people. He fed them. He gave them drinking water, telephones, a decent road system. He backed the farmers. He taught them how to farm properly, how to grow the right crops, which fertilisers to use, when to harvest, and how to get their crops to market in the best possible condition.

Most important of all, he supported his poor, down-trodden, hungry, thirsty journalists. Go on a press trip with Houphouet and he would always give you something for a drink. On one memorable trip in the 1980s, he actually handed out CFA500 million, which in those days was well over US$1 million, to the poor, down-trodden, hungry, thirsty journalists accompanying him. For which for years afterwards, I'm told, they expressed their appreciation in the time-honoured fashion.

His liberal economic policies, his political touch – light but firm – his clever management and consensus approach made it the 'Ivoirian Miracle'. To the French he was bracketed with Gandhi, Mao and even Martin Luther King as one of the great leaders of the twentieth century, and with Carlos Santana, Frank Zappa and Don Siegel as one of the great geniuses of all time. Which just goes to show how weird the French are when it comes to deciding who is a genius and who isn't. I mean, who are these guys?

To me, however, he is even greater than Jerry Lewis, who for some reason the French also hail as a genius. For it seems to me significant that within a couple of months of his dying and obviously going straight to the second most important place in the cosmos, what happens? The coffee crop in Brazil is hit by the worst frost for over forty years. Which means the price of Ivoirian coffee, which has been bouncing off the bottom of the market for years, suddenly takes off. The economy starts looking up. Everything suddenly looks rosy again. Who says building the world's largest church doesn't pay off in the long run?

Houphouet's legacy, therefore, lives on. Abidjan remains the Frenchest of all the French cities in Africa. Not just because of the camembert and the pâté and the caviar russe, but because of the French themselves. They've crawling all over the place like the mould on an over-ripe Bleu de Bresse. In other people's offices; in other people's homes; in other people's ... yes, well, we won't go into that. In fact before you've finished your first bottle of champagne over breakfast in a minister's house in Abidjan, you don't need me to tell you there are ten times as many French people in French Africa today than there were twenty years ago, including, it is said, 50,000 troops in the Forces d'Action Rapide and 15,000 Foreign Legionnaires. A third of its economy is French. Almost half its imports. In fact, it's probably more French than, say, Barbes-Rochechouart, a stone's throw from the Moulin Rouge in Paris.

But the French are all over not just Abidjan, but the rest of French-speaking Africa, far, far more than the English are over English-speaking Africa. In Presidents' offices, hardly a day goes by without the French Minister of Quelque chose ou l'Autre popping in for a chat, to deliver a personal letter from Monsieur le Président, Dieu himself, to get himself on the local television news or to receive some medal for services rendus. In ministers' offices, all the time, advisers to the president, junior ministers, anciens ambassadeurs or even representatives of l'opposition carrying little suitcases and large briefcases are popping in for a chat. In government departments, the délégué général à la Co-opération juridique et judicaire de l'Agence de Co-opération Culturelle et Technique is chatting to a professeur de la Sorbonne à Paris, before they begin another seminar on 'The strength of the CFA Zone; Why France will never devalue'.

In army barracks – in army barracks! – they are beefing up the troops, instilling that sense of discipline, helping to establish, train and equip various compagnies republicaines d'intervention. Complete with boucliers, casques avec visières, batons et fusils lance-grenades lacrymogènes pour le maintien d'ordre.

Mon Dieu, they are even meeting and having chats with all the mysterious French advisers you always find sitting in the rooms next to presidents and ministers, or even out in the corridor vetting who goes in and who comes out. Like one of those giant, soft, ripe, almost runny camemberts, they seem to just flow gently all over the place, being welcomed by everyone.

Conferences. Seminars. Jours de réflexion. Practically every day of every week I can guarantee you some French organisation, association or bunch of Masons is delivering 'un message des autorités françaises' to the president or the president's housekeeper.

French ministers, presidential advisers, former ambassadors, retired businessmen, university professors, I'm convinced, spend their lives touring French Africa as special envoys of the president, representatives of whatever federation or just plain old buddies of the minister.

On one trip alone, making my rounds I kept bumping into a delegation from the Mission Française de Co-opération et d'Action Culturelle; a conseiller pour les Affaires africaines et malgaches at the Ministère Français de la Défense; a directeur-général adjoint at the Caisse Française de Développement; a conseiller and a directeur de la co-opération militaire from the Ministère de la Co-opération; two députés from the Parlement Européen; an ancien président de l'Université de Poitiers; an ancien administrateur de la Banque de France; two gentlemen – one looked distinctly Lebanese – who told me they were discussing 'un projet qui sera unique dans le monde noir' and a mysterious young lady who looked more like a conseiller from the Mission Française de Co-opération than an administrateur from the Ministère de la Défense.

And don't they always manage to say the right thing – without saying anything? On the way in to see the president or the minister or whoever, it's always, 'Très important pour ce qui concerne les relations entre l'Afrique et la France.' On the way out it's always, 'Il semble quie le moment est bien choisi maintenant pour remonter et re-évaluer les problèmes qui se posent en Afrique.'

On television, or speaking to the press, they're always saying, 'Je pense que c'est un des rares pays où je pouvais avoir pareils contracts et relations avec les uns les autres et à tous les niveaux et dans tant de milieux, aussi bien dans tous les sensibilités. Je n'en sais rien et c'est l'avenir qui nous le dira. On commence une nouvelle procédure et chacun a son rhythme.'

Fantastic, isn't it? It sounds great. The Africans lap it up. Even though you and I know it doesn't mean a barrowload of bananas. Or does it?

And it's not just Abidjan that gets the merry-go-round treatment. In Togo the conseiller financier pour l'Afrique au Ministère Français de l'Economie is always popping in to pop corks with the minister of planning or the minister for finance. In the old days it used to be Jean-Christophe (Papa-m'a-dit) Mitterrand.

In Rwanda, the military are always popping in, you can bet your life, because of some side-deal the French have got going with either Zaire or Central African Republic.

In South Africa, who was the first president to call on Nelson Mandela after he became president? Who sent the first big government and trade mission? Who is going to get first bite at all the big contracts? You've got it in trois. And they didn't have to dress up in funny uniforms, either.

But when Mandela decided to rejoin the Commonwealth after South Africa had been left out in the cold for so many years, what did we do? Nothing, spelt r-i-e-n. Which just shows how crazy we are. Surely if there was ever a time John Major or, God help us, Mrs Chalker, should have jumped on, not a Concorde but a VC10, and flown down to shake hands with Mandela, that was it. The goodwill, the diplomatic one-upmanship, the spin-offs; they would have been enormous.

Jacques Chirac once jumped on Concorde and flew all the way to Abidjan just to have lunch with Houphouet. Some say it was to thank him for bankrolling his run at the presidency. Others say it was to ask him for more money for next time. Either way it proves how far the French are prepared to go for something that was certainly nowhere near as important as Mandela applying to rejoin the Commonwealth. But we apparently didn't think it was worth an effort, even though Mandela thought it was important enough for him to announce within a few days of becoming president.

I suppose I shouldn't have been surprised. It's about par for the course. I was in Togo once when the British Foreign Secretary announced in the House of Commons that in order to cut costs Her Majesty's Government, with great reluctance, was going to close down the British embassy in the capital, Lomé. Except there was no British embassy in Lomé. There never had been a British embassy in Lomé. Either the Foreign Office was playing games with the Treasury and agreeing to cut what had never existed, or some old biddy in King Charles Street who was supposed to be responsible for French Africa had no idea of where the place was and no interest in it either and just dished up whatever the minister wanted to hear.

On another occasion in Togo, I was with a delegation of British Members of Parliament. The president agreed to meet us first thing in the morning as soon as he arrived in the office: six o'clock. They all said it was too early. Would I tell the president that they never got up that early even for the state opening of their own parliament? They were definitely not going to do it for some ... some ... some ... French African president. If he agreed to see them at eleven o'clock, say, for coffee, or better still 12.30 for drinks followed by lunch, they might consider it. Guess which delegation didn't get to see the president?

Nor does the French influence stop at government level. It's more wide-ranging and far more in-depth than that. French teachers, doctors, nurses, vets are all over the place, explaining, helping, operating, caring for, building latrines, repairing trucks and lorries, cooking; even serving meals in bars and clubs and restaurants, which most anglophones find unbelievable.

Go into a bar anywhere in Cocody, the up-market part of Abidjan. In the corner are two French diplomats chuckling about how they are playing both sides in the Bakassi dispute between Cameroon and Nigeria: Cameroon is an old francophone buddy, even though in theory it is half-anglophone, and of course Nigeria, if it ever comes round, will be the biggest prize in Africa. No way did they want to fall out with either. Their solution: get the Nigerians to Paris, wine them, dine them, give them all the extras, then send them home with a stack of weapons and armaments. Because they're Nigerians they will sell the lot off cheap to whoever they sit next to on the plane home. The guys they sit next to, they will make certain, are Beninois, another of Nigeria's next-door neighbours who, because they can't stand the Nigerians and need the cash, will then sell the stuff on to the Cameroonians. That way the French help both sides, maintain their contacts with each, pump some money into Benin, another francophone country, and make certain that if the whole thing blows up neither Nigeria nor Cameroon can blame them for not helping.

'But wait a minute,' I said. 'Where do the Beninois get the money to buy the arms?'

They just laughed.

Go into a restaurant in the Plateau district, the business part of town. At the next table will be a Frenchman explaining subjects of vital importance to Africa. Like which is the best caviar, Beluga or Osetra. Beluga comes from the Caspian Sea; the eggs, which range from pale silver grey to black, are about the size of a pea. Osetra eggs are grey to grey-green, and slightly smaller. Lumpfish, white fish, salmon roe and red caviar are, of course, only for the likes of le monde anglophone.

Which is why today, French Africa is in many respects more French than the French. Take African diplomats. Most of them can outsmart the French any day. If it is a group meeting they do it by simply out-talking everybody. Ask them to make the speech of welcome and they will speak for long enough to ensure nobody else can get a word in. I was at a meeting once with a group of journalists. The first question was fairly general and innocuous. The minister spoke for 44 minutes 32 seconds non-stop. It was pure poetry. Nobody stirred or coughed or tried to stop him. When he finished, everybody applauded. Then he thanked everybody for such a warm welcome and fled. Nobody had a chance to ask nasty questions. Houphouet would have been proud of him.

In any meeting, as soon as the champagne is flowing they play surrealist games by giving you answers to questions you have never asked.

'Tell me, Mr Minister, are you planning to build an atomic bomb?'

'That is the question.'

'... employing Israeli scientists?'

'And if that is the question I'll try to find the answer.'

'But how can you dream of spending so much money when half the population is starving?'

'However, some questions do not have answers.'

'And the other half is dying of disease and deprivation?'

'On the other hand, some answers do not have questions.'

'Monsieur le ministre, you have not answered the questions.'

'Thank you very much for your warm welcome. It is always a great honour to meet ...'

I tried the same thing one evening on some French VIP visitors in the downstairs bar at the Hilton Hotel, which you would never think was owned by a British company. One of the conseillers – or was it one of the anciens ambassadeurs – was going on about how in the old days he and his colleagues would carry out their research into the decline in moral standards in the Cinéma Latin on the Left Bank.

I asked him about Sarajevo: 'The French, I see, are providing a lot of help in Sarajevo ...'

'We believe always in the positive approach.'

'. . . to French businessmen . . .'

'Naturally.'

'. . . to help them land all the big reconstruction projects after the troubles are over.'

'But why not? It is in our interests.'

'They say you're giving them French army uniforms . . .'

'Many of them were obviously in the army.'

'. . . appointing them lieutenant-colonels . . .'

'. . . and probably lieutenant-colonels as well. I myself . . .'

'. . . and giving them UN helmets . . .'

'There are probably also some who have served in the United Nations forces as well, when you British were . . .'

It's the same with business meetings which, in anglophone Africa, tend to be pretty direct and straight to the point:

'So have you got the money? Are you going to pay me?'

'No, my master. But I would like more . . .'

'Goodbye.'

In francophone Africa they are practically an art form. Each meeting begins invariably twenty minutes late with effusive praise for the chairman and long tributes to his wisdom and penetrating insight. Everybody then introduces themselves to each other and to the meeting as a whole. Eventually the conversation drifts towards the matter in hand. Or, at least, what you think is the matter in hand. For francophones rarely have agendas or set matters for discussion. Neither are they there for decision. People seem to be present for discussion. 'Permettez-moi de vous exposer brièvement les nouvelles orientations . . .' It is not unusual for one person, not even the most senior, to speak for maybe thirty or forty minutes. 'Comme j'ai dit il y a quelques instants, il est impératif . . .' I was at one business meeting when one of the directors for Chad spoke for forty-five minutes without notes or papers. It was a beautiful, towering performance which soared to the heights of oratory – 'La démarche vers la réalisation de cet objectif commun . . .' – and down again. 'Je vois remercie de votre haut attention. Un grand merci à tous. Que Dieu vois bénise tous et chacun.' What did he say? Nothing. Rien de rien. Rien du tout. I was ready to write down all the important points he made. But he didn't make any. He just talked.

The other wonderful ability of the francophones is to go flying off in all directions – and get lost. I was at a big business meeting once in Abidjan to discuss two completely different proposals for a big company. Eventually after the champagne had been served we got to the formalities.

'Monsieur le directeur, honorables invités, mesdames, messieurs, invités distingués . . .'

The chairman began to hint at the reason for the meeting. '. . . A échanger avec vous des vues sur les problèmes d'intérêt commun. Nous sommes très sensibles à cette attention délicate que . . .'

Suddenly I heard one of the directors saying it was important to consider the proposals in detail because they were 'comme les enfants', and 'you must have children otherwise it makes you think of taking a mistress'.

'Are you asking me to choose between having children or taking a mistress?' said the chairman.

'There are advantages in having children,' he said.

'There are also advantages in having a mistress,' said another director.

Then we were off in all directions.

'But a mistress is not so expensive.'

'And leaves you free to do what you want.'

'Which is not possible if you have children.'

'A manager is only free if he doesn't have children.'

'But with a mistress . . .'

After nearly an hour of detailing the merits of children v. mistresses, the chairman proposed lunch, 'pour hâter l'avènement du monde de bonheur, de prosperité et de fraternité auquel nous aspirons par le dialogue, la co-opération et la solidarité entre les peuples . . .' and we all headed off for more champagne and lobster.

The other thing about francophone meetings is their need to sum up the discussion and draw conclusions. Trouble is, the conclusions are never decision-orientated. They are always consensus-orientated – even when the discussion may have been about two opposing concepts.

'Well, maybe I am a little naive,' the chairman began slowly summing up our discussions one day at the Ministry of Finance in Abidjan. 'But I feel that basically we are all in agreement. On the one hand there was the argument for flexibility, the need to have a fluid structure and be able to react to events without regard to established rules. That was one view expressed, quite fairly I think, during our discussions. Quite fairly.' He nods and smiles in the appropriate direction. 'Then on the other hand we had the argument in favour of a rigid, inflexible structure reinforced by a code of rules and regulations capable of meeting every possible situation.' Again a nod and a smile. This time in the opposite direction. 'It seems to me, first – and I am sure you will agree – that we are united in our search for a solution. That is extremely important, and shows we all share the same objectives. I am sure that is appreciated by everybody here today. Second, I am pleased to say, I am struck by our common wish to succeed.' A pause. 'To share our common success. That is the second point that strikes me on reflection.'

Yes, yes. But get on with it.

'Next I am struck by the serious approach of everyone here today. I cannot let this meeting end without putting on record the depth of feeling and knowledge and seriousness with which we have all carried on our discussions. I think I can quite rightly say that rarely have I been present at such an interesting and serious debate.'

Okay, but what's the conclusion?

'Now in analysing the strands of the arguments we have heard, two points stand out: the position we have reached in the past, and the need to take a decision for the future. This I think is important. Together we have accepted the situation as it stands. That is reality. There can be no turning the corner or going back on that. Similarly, we are all in agreement that consideration must be given to the future. That is where we are all in agreement. All united. There can be no dispute about that.'

Agreed. Now what about . . .?

'The other point that came over very clearly was the need for action. Action is vital. Here again I was very pleased to hear that we are all in agreement, because the only way we can go forward is to go forward together. As a team.'

But what . . .?

'So throughout our discussions we have all been in total agreement.' Nods and smiles to all concerned. 'Agreed on our approach. Agreed on the seriousness of the matter. Agreed on the need for discussion. Agreed on the need for debate. Agreed on the need for action. These are all vital points to bear in mind when coming to a conclusion. Bearing all this in mind, the matter that is dividing us is very small indeed, almost of no consequence. In fact, looking at the matter objectively and rationally . . .'

'Zzzzzzzz zzzz zzzzzzzzz . . .'

'. . . I'm sure we can resolve the matter over lunch. If you would care to join me in a glass of champagne pour hâter l'avènement du monde de bonheur, de prosperité et de fraternité . . .'

So what is it between the French and the Africans? My theory is that whenever the French went into a country, their objective was to make that country French, in heart and mind and soul and strength. Nothing will convince me they didn't believe they had a God-given mission to bestow on as many people as possible the greatest gift accorded to mankind; the honour, the glory, the privileges of French civilisation; pink tablecloths, bone china, heavy silverware and full glasses. Of anything that's going, providing it's got bubbles. Which, you must admit, is a million times better than being colonised by somebody who insists you wear school uniforms, lose at cricket and drink tea all day.

Allons enfants de la Patrie
Le jour de gloire est arrivé.

If you haven't heard 2,000 African presidents, ministers, officials, assorted hangers-on and schoolchildren singing the 'Marseillaise' you haven't lived. It's not just any old national anthem to mumble your way through, hoping like hell you won't be recognised by anyone you know. This is the real thing. This they really mean. This is more important than religion. And why not?

Once I was in my usual place in life; in the back row of some massive *manifestation* in Abidjan with a group of foreign businessmen. Suddenly the whole place erupted with the 'Marseillaise'. An American next to me started mumbling one of the less official versions sung by expats in the privacy of their homes when bombed out of their minds on duty-free champagne. This one was all about a guy going to the 'lav-a-tor-ree'. When it came to the refrain, and we all started singing at the tops of our voices, 'Où est le papier? Où est le papier?' they practically carried us off and strung us up on the nearest *lanterne*.

The next trick was not only to make Africans French, but to make them actually part of France. Even today, all the far-flung bits of the French empire, right down to tiny St Pierre et Miquelon, a little island off the coast of Newfoundland (pop. 6,300), are officially registered as part of Metropolitan France. Then they tackled the politicians: Houphouet-Boigny, Leopold Senghor of Senegal, Mamadu Konte from Mali, were all appointed not merely members of the National Assembly, but ministers in various French governments. Any evening on French television you're as likely to see Papa Wemba as Johnny Halliday. French African pop stars are as much part of the French music scene as a can of Coke. When was the last time you heard a local British pop station playing music from Nigeria or Ghana – both English-speaking parts of Africa famous for music?

Then to hold the whole thing together, they handed out some pretty convincing insurance policies. Presidents were told that wherever they were, day or night, the French military were only minutes away. In the old days, when the going got tough and all the tough old dictators wanted to get going, they had merely to dial President Mitterrand's bedside telephone number, if they could find it – the bed, I mean, not the telephone number – and before you could say Liberté, Fraternité, Egalité the paratroopers were carrying your luggage to the waiting armoured car and, zap, you were sitting in a Mirage of your own, sipping a chilled glass of champagne and heading off to a life in the sunshine. Admittedly today the insurance policy is not so watertight. But then neither is Lloyd's. And in a continent where anything can happen to anyone any time, it's better than nothing.

Whenever the British went in, by contrast, our objective was to get the hell out as quickly as possible. You've only to think of all Mrs Thatcher's remarks about the Commonwealth. One relaxed foreign office type told me over drinks in a Lebanese bar deep in Treichville, the sleazy end of Abidjan, that Mrs Thatcher always referred to the CHGM, the Commonwealth Heads of Government Meetings, as 'Compulsory Handouts for Greedy Millionaires'. Which, he said, was absolutely out of order and deeply insulting to our Commonwealth friends and allies. Instead, he said, it should be 'Coons Holidaying on Government Money'.

When we lost our colonies we turned to the United States. When the French lost their colonies they turned – back to their colonies. In return, the Africans gave them valuable votes in the United Nations and helped them maintain the illusion they were still a world power, when the whole world and his French mistress knows otherwise. The ex-colonies were a valuable source of raw materials. Around 20 per cent of French oil comes from Africa, as does most of its uranium, cobalt and presidential diamonds.

In some francophone countries, as a result, France has as little as 60 per cent of the market. For champagne – the wealth of the wealthy – it has a surprising 130 per cent (don't forget the commissions), worth around US$50 million a year. Telephone, telex, fax; every international telephone call to and from francophone Africa goes via Paris. Which means additional revenue to the French PTT.

But, fair's fair, the French provide massive financial assistance to Africa even though maybe around 80 per cent comes back to France in the form of salaries, orders and profits. At least they give it; and it generates an enormous amount of economic activity all along the line.

Then, of course, there is the CFA Zone. Some people say it's financial colonialisation. Others say it was designed to line the pockets of civil servants and students. Not the people doing the work: not the workers in what manufacturing industry there is; not the office workers and administrators who hold a country together; and most definitely not the farmers and small landowners who are vital to feed the country. For under the terms of the grand Communauté Financière Africaine, which translated into English means Can't Feel A Thing, the francophones have to keep 65 per cent of their hard currency reserves on deposit with the French central bank. The French pay them the going market rate. Not a franc more. On any CFA borrowings they charge them the market rate. Not a franc less. To all intents and purposes they are just like an old-fashioned bank manager who smiles, says nice things, doesn't charge you for the privilege of taking him out to lunch but still charges you exactly the same rates as all the others.

Some people say it's all typically French. Unlike-the-rest-of-the-world-we're-doing-everything-we-can-to-shoulder-our-responsibilities-and-help-our-poorer-colleagues, etc., etc., when it doesn't actually cost them any more than a couple of Concorde flights to a funeral in Abidjan.

Not me. Sure, to the French it means that no less than fifteen countries keep their deposits interest-free with the Banque de France. But to the francophones, it means first and foremost they have virtually a hard currency of their own. Do business in cedis or even nairas – you might as well use bits of broken glass and torn-up copies of yesterday's speech by the president of the World Bank on structural re-adjustment. At least the CFA is freely convertible with the French franc. It has a guaranteed exchange rate. From the French franc you can go into any currency in the world. Try doing that with cedis or nairas. You might as well try dealing in hubcaps. Come to think of it, hubcaps are more useful than cedis or nairas, even if you haven't got a car.

One morning as I was coming out of the African Development Bank headquarters in Abidjan, I bumped into Mr Alhousseyni, a well-known African banker. We went into a typical French pavement café along the road and ordered coffee and croissants, just like in Paris. I asked whether he thought the CFA franc was a form of financial colonialism and a link with leurs anciens maîtres coloniaux.

He laughed. 'Look, I am a banker, not a politician. I am interested in anything that helps people to do business. The CFA franc helps people to do business. Concrètement. It's as simple as that.'

'Then why do some people say it is wrong?'

'Politics.' he said.

'No other reason?'

'Look, fifteen African countries are members of the CFA Zone. Are they all wrong? Of course not. It gives us financial stability. It is essential.' He paused. 'They say that some anglophone countries would even like to embrasser la zone CFA. Gambia . . .'

Which would not surprise me. If I was an African businessman I would rather do business in the CFA Zone than in countries with over-valued, unconvertible currencies subject to roaring inflation and enormous black markets. The sixteen-nation Economic Community of West African States – French-speaking and English-speaking – are talking about establishing a single monetary union with a single currency. But no way are the francophones going to give up the CFA. This can only mean the anglophones adjusting their currencies to the CFA, or something maybe alongside the CFA. The French will use this as a ploy to encourage the anglophones to cross sides and join them.

'Even Nigeria?'

'Even Nigeria. What good is the naira to them? If it was linked to the French franc it would transform their economy overnight.'

'And the British?'

'What have the British done for Nigeria? Nothing. They are not even their major trading partner any more. The French are interested in Africa. La France a joué et continuera à jouer un rôle significatif dans la politique monétaire de nos pays. The British are not interested. The Africans know that. The Nigerians know that.'

It was a valid point. Over the last few years, I've noticed France taking more and more interest in Nigeria. There is now a Franco-Nigerian chamber of commerce. The French government are even building a lycée in Lagos, obviously to encourage French businessmen to go to Nigeria. Nigerian businessmen are being offered French lessons for free in a French language centre which, surprise, surprise, is right next door to the Ministry of External Affairs on Victoria Island. They are being given awards and medals and honours, while the British have stopped giving knighthoods let alone green shield stamps to anybody. President Babagida now goes to Paris for hospital treatment instead of to London. And guess where Madame Babagida prefers to shop? Yves St Laurent or Marks & Spencer? The only guide to Lagos that is of any value is – you've guessed – published by the French in – right again – English and French. How many guides to francophone Africa are there published in English and French by the British government? That's right. You're catching on. And you've only got to drive halfway – no, less than a hundred metres, oops, I mean yards – into Lagos from the airport to realise that not only were the French responsible for persuading them to drive on the right, they also taught them how to drive. For not a single car, bus, van, truck or even ambulance is not crashed, not scraped and not dented. And if that hasn't convinced you of the growing influence of the French in Nigeria, and the long-term repercussions for Britain in West Africa, ask any Nigerian about le jiggy-jiggy and you'll soon see what I mean.

It's the same in Ghana. The French are building a cultural centre near the luxury Lonrho guesthouse in Accra, one of the best hotels I've stayed in in West Africa. They are talking about a chamber of commerce. They have even opened a special office for the Caisse Centrale de Coopération Economique, their official aid organisation.

In one week alone they came up with funds for an international direct-dialling system, opened Accra's only four-star hotel, built with French government money, and announced plans to completely rehabilitate Kutokoa International Airport. They are also busily examining the rubber industry and telecommunications systems in other parts of the country as well as, of course, the gold fields. On supplying French buses for public transport, they hit a petit problème. After test after test after test, the Ghanaians said the Renault buses were no good for their local roads. The French, of course, refused to take non for un réponse and came up with a loan of over FF40 million for them to buy the buses all the same. The Ghanaians, of course, gave in and bought the buses. Details about the deal were leaked to the press. There was uproar. What did the French do? They launched a programme to send Ghanaian journalists on all-expenses-paid scholarships to France. It can't be long before Flight-Lieutenant Rawlings is off for a weekend in Nice and a visit to la rive gauche to swop those battle fatigues for something more elegant.

'But would the French ever devalue the CFA?' I asked. 'That must be a big risk.'

'Sure, but it is an acceptable risk. It's been the same since 1948 and nothing lasts for ever. But I can't see anything happening yet. Maybe in 1993 with le marché uni. But la Caisse Française garantira toujours la convertibilité de la zone CFA.'

'Until Mitterrand goes?'

Mr Alhousseyni smiled. 'Look at the figures. The people arguing for devaluation say the CFA Zone is a drain on French resources. Yet it only accounts for around 4 per cent of their money supply. They say it is in deficit. It's in deficit today, but for most of the last forty years it's been in credit.

'Besides,' he continued, 'The French always put the French first. What would happen to all French debts in Africa, to French companies' earnings in francophone Africa? Are the French going to devalue them as well?' He paused. 'I doubt it very much.' Another pause. 'And will African politicians be prepared to pay more for their champagne? I doubt it.'

The trouble is, times change. Between 1970 and 1985 the CFA Zone did better than the rest of Africa: output was higher, exports were higher, inflation was lower. Since 1985 things have fallen apart: output has crashed, exports have virtually dried up, inflation has taken off, per capita incomes have fallen by over 40 per cent. The only part of the world that suffered more was Russia. The French had to do something. From the Africans' point of view the exchange rate was an importer's dream – and an exporter's nightmare. BMWs, Peugeots, a containerload of champagne – no problem. It was cheaper to drink champagne than beer. But there was no way the poor African would-be exporter could even think of exporting anything. It was cheaper to go down to the local supermarché and buy fresh French vacuum-packed haricots verts than queue at the local market and haggle over a couple of kilos of beans.

Something had to give, because all the French money that was going into the system was coming out again to service their foreign debt to other countries and foreign institutions. The Africans would not have been able to get any more credit. Their economies would have continued to collapse. The French, desperate on the one hand to shadow the German mark, knew the CFA was becoming more and more over-valued. The question was when to devalue – and how.

In the salons and dining rooms of Abidjan everybody agreed.

What did the French say? 'We will never abandon our partners.'

'Not while Mitterrand . . .'

'Jamais. Never. Pas du tout.'

Then, of course, it happened. The French devalued the CFA. Not by 10 per cent. But by a staggering 50 per cent. Overnight practically everything throughout French Africa doubled in price. Not just the basic necessities like champagne, foie gras, caviar, but even less important things like drugs and medicines . . .

Everybody took it badly. In Dakar there was an 'état de choc'. Demonstrators took to the street. Riots left six people dead: five policemen and one civilian. Cars were set on fire, streets barricaded. In Gabon a general strike was called. Everywhere there was talk of threats of more strikes, civil unrest, riots, violence. Governments did what all African governments do when they hit problems: they introduced more controls; strict price controls on everything from sugar and salt to schoolbooks. Then they did the second thing all African governments do when they hit problems: they announced a list of exceptions to the strict price controls they had just introduced on everything from sugar and salt to schoolbooks. Senegal went a stage further, and announced a 10 per cent wage rise for everyone, although where the money was to come from nobody knew.

But the Ivoirians took it worse than anybody, because to them it was impossible. It just could not happen. Again and again the French had given their word to Houphouet and Houphouet had given his word to them. Then what happened? Houphouet was no sooner on his deathbed, than wham, they devalued.

Market stalls which had been stacked high with yams and bananas, washing powder, rice, printed cloth, were now empty. Traders couldn't afford to pay the new prices the importers and wholesalers wanted so they had nothing to sell. Shoppers couldn't afford to buy whatever it was they couldn't sell so they didn't bother to come. Buses lined the streets. Taxis stood empty.

In Marcory, the middle-class area of Abidjan, everybody complained about the increase in the cost of drugs. Malaria tablets had doubled in price. 'If my children are ill, how can I afford to look after them? I pray nothing happens to them,' an old friend in the African Development Bank told me.

For the man in the street, especially in the streets of Treichville; for the struggling peasant farmers, the down-and-outs and the rest of the 99 per cent of the population, it won't make the slightest difference. They are virtually outside the system. They have to live or die on their own.

Did the Ivoirians blame the French? Not in Cocody they didn't.

'No, not at all,' a local Ivoirian banker told me over the second bottle of Dom Perignon. 'I blame – the Africans. We saw it coming years ago. Trouble was, nobody wanted to do anything about it. While Houphouet was in power, while Mitterrand was still president, they thought they were safe. It's really our fault.'

We finished the bottle and I left him working out how much more he was going to have to pay for his next Peugeot. Which just proves the hold the French have over French Africa.

But the French in Abidjan, they blamed the French.

'Of course they wait until le Vieux is on his deathbed, then they do it. They would never have dared to do it if he had been alive,' the manager of a printing company told me.

'Balladur is in power five months. What does he do? He changes the agreement, an agreement that has been in existence for fifty years,' a trader told me.

According to another banker, 'Balladur, he is the man. He forced Mitterrand to agree. If Mitterrand had not been sick he would never have agreed.'

But to be fair to the French, and I hate being fair to anyone, especially the French, they sweetened the pill of devaluation as much as they could. They cancelled all the aid debt owed them by the ten poorest countries that they didn't cancel in 1989. They cancelled all the aid debt owed them by the four richest countries. They also set up a FF300 million develop-ment fund to help the urban poor throughout all fifteen countries, which it hopes is going to be topped up by the European Union, the World Bank and the International Monetary Fund.

And what do the francophone Ivoirians think of the Brits in all this? Do they now wish they had jumped into bed with us instead of the French? Or maybe it's the other way round. Do they think they would have got a better deal with us? No sir.

The last time I was in Abidjan, I picked up the local newspaper. Houphouet's 'Thought for the Day', a regular spot on the top of the front page for over twenty-six years – it was repeated at the start of every single radio and television news bulletin – had gone. Instead across the top of the page Agence France Presse had come up with what to them was a winner. Now I don't care what the men in white coats say, I'm no paranoiac. I know that the French government, as part of their long-term strategy to conquer the world, have instructed Agence France Presse to ensure that every day in every newspaper throughout French Africa there is a wholly mis-leading story designed to make fools of the British.

– Un Britannique de 32 ans, under a law passed in 1872, condamné à 12 mois de prison for being drunk in charge of a horse.
– Une Britannique de 79 ans who had spent so much money on driving lessons that now she has passed her test she has no money left to buy a car.
– Un vicar Britannique, after 2,000 years of Christianity, has admitted that he does not believe in God.
– Le roi du porno, Paul Raymond, magnat de la presse pornographique, is for the third year running the richest man in Britain.

This time the wholly unreasonable headline Agence France Presse splashed across the front page, which trumpeted the results of some silly survey that revealed that in the 'pays de la Queen, des Lords, des Ladies, des Gentlemen' we would often go all week without changing our T-shirts, was: Britain Stinks.

Now, I ask you. Isn't that just typically French? Houphouet would have loved it.

Agadez

Malik and his wife Kande are planning to buy themselves new turbans in the New Year. Mali's will cost around FCFA 30,000 (£40). Kande's will be much cheaper, around FCFA 10,000 (£13). Which, more than anything, tells you what life is like in an upper-middle-class, land-owning, hard-working household in Niger, one of the poorest countries in the world – two-thirds of it is desert – as we approach the beginning of the twenty-first century.

Malik and Kande are Tuaregs, the legendary 'Blue men' of the Sahara. Before the droughts of the 1980s they spent their lives wandering through the desert, as their ancestors have done since the beginning of time. Today they are farmers. They have a little 10,000-square-metre garden farm in a tiny oasis fifty kilometres from Iferouane, on the edge of the Tenere desert, which with its spectacular sand dunes is one of the most fantastic regions in the whole Sahara.

During the drought they lost everything. Their pastures turned to dust, their cattle died, friends and family wasted away. But they survived. Today, when almost every household in Europe has twenty-three microchips, two linear accelerators and a cavity magnetron, whatever that is, Malik, Kande and their four children have at last all the milk and cheese they want. Their goats are thriving. The little farm is producing all the fruit and vegetables they require, with some left over to sell in the local market. When I met them Malik was building wind breaks and improving still further the irrigation system, to see if he could increase production even more.

Kande was learning how to dry potatoes, onions and other vegetables so that they will last longer in the stifling temperatures.

'In Niger everything depends on the rain,' Ousmann Assalik, an official in the government offices in Iferouane, told me. 'What we are doing now is taking advantage of the last three years when we have had good rainfall and making certain that if the drought returns we will be better prepared to survive than last time.'

Throughout Niger, the second largest country in West Africa, the Tuaregs have been encouraged to settle down and become small-scale farmers. Special mini-irrigation systems have been developed so that they can utilise what water they have. Trenches and ditches have been dug, often in the middle of the desert, to stop flash floods from developing and causing even more soil erosion. Over 75 per cent of all cultivated land in Africa is subject to soil erosion. They have even cut back on their policy of building wells to help farmers water their cattle.

'There is a balance,' Ousmann adds. 'Wells attract animals. Animals eat the vegetation. Because the wells attract so many animals, the vegetation never gets a chance to grow back. Which is the beginning of desertification, the very process that the wells were designed to prevent. In Niger we only want to build wells where we believe they will help the environment, not destroy it.'

Not all the Tuaregs like the scheme. Some, nobody knows how many, are violently opposed to it and any suggestion that they give up their desert life and become townies. But many, like Malik and Kande, are more than happy to settle down.

Africa, we all know, is a disaster area in freefall. It is the Third World of the Third World: Three hundred million people living in absolute poverty. Three hundred million! It's impossible to believe. Three out of every five people in Africa have nothing, except, maybe, a threadbare blanket, a cardboard box and,

God help them, enough energy to go on struggling to survive for yet another day.

There are no schools; if they're lucky there's a blackboard under a tree. One in three African children doesn't even have that, or any education at all.

There are precious few health care facilities; hardly any drugs or painkillers. Malaria, tuberculosis, cholera, meningitis, fatal diarrhoea – especially among babies; even leprosy: they've got the lot. Maternal mortality is 630 deaths per 100,000 live births compared to under 20 in developed countries. One in eight African children, around 20 million, are badly disabled. Average life expectancy is 51. There is only one doctor for every 25,000 people.

There is little housing as we know it. Most people have practically no shelter. Refugee camps are the size of large towns.

Food is scarce, though there is now 20 per cent more food per person than there was twenty-five years ago. A third of African children, over 34 million of them, are not just malnourished but severely malnourished in spite of – or maybe because of – headlines like: 'UN Flies in Food'. Of them, nearly 25 million are worse than severely malnourished, and every year more than four million die of starvation before they reach the age of five.

There is little fresh water. Less than 40 per cent of families in sub-Saharan Africa have clean drinking water. Today in the world of microchips and Coca Cola and Barry Manilow, people still travel sixty miles a day by camel for water. They're the lucky ones. The unlucky ones have to walk, maybe 20–30 miles. Every day. And then the water is probably so fetid it's got a thick fur on top.

Compared to them, poor old Malik is a rich man. He has his wife and family. He has a home. He has some animals. He knows where his next meal is coming from.

Yet look at the figures. Over the last thirty years more than US$300 billion in aid has been sent by poor people in rich countries all over the world to rich people in the poor countries of Africa. That is the equivalent of $26 per African person. Sub-Saharan Africa has 12 per cent of the world's population, yet it receives over one-third of the aid. It's as if, a Ghanaian economist once told me, somebody gave the US $20 million dollars and told them to get on with it. Have fun. And they blew the lot. But to Malik, his wife and the ordinary African in the desert, it doesn't look as though it's made a blind bit of difference. We might as well have blown a fortune on wine, women and horses and just wasted the rest.

So what went wrong? Why has it taken so long for Malik and Kande to buy themselves new turbans? Why isn't Africa booming? Like Singapore. Like Malaysia. Like Thailand. Like even the Philippines and Burma, the laggards of South-East Asia? It's crazy.

Africa, when you think about it, was there first. The first man was probably African. The first structure was probably built by Africans. The first society was more likely than not African. Who built the pyramids? Not the Europeans. Most definitely not the Americans. Who opened up trade routes across the Sahara, the roughest and toughest and most dangerous terrain on earth? Not the Japanese or the Koreans or the Taiwanese. Who was the first to drag a bag stuffed full of CFA francs across Berkeley Square to deposit them in a special account at the Banque Française de l'Orient; to swindle the World Bank, pull a foreign exchange fraud at the Central Bank of Kenya and stash away over US$6 billion in private bank accounts all over the world? Not the Eskimos.

Africa had organisation and structures, and presumably wheeler-dealers and fixers and civil servants, way before the rest of us. The ancient civilisation of Egypt was around long before Stamford Raffles was even thought of. Mali was one of the most important trading centres of the Islamic world. Djenne and Timbuktu were world-famous centres of wealth and culture and civilisation before anybody had even heard of revolving letters of credit. Nigeria had a social monarchy, an established court circle, a system of government as far back as the fourteenth century, a shock from which it has obviously never recovered. Even poor old Niger had its share of the action. In the tenth and eleventh centuries the Songhai and Hausa kingdoms stretched all the way round Lake Chad and back again.

But wander around Agadez, the old capital of the Tuaregs, today. Look at the mosque; go up and down the back alleys; stroll through the central market. You would never believe that in the sixteenth century it was one of the richest cities in Africa, probably in the world. It had a population of 30,000. It was the junction of four main trading routes; to the north, Tamanrasset, Tuat and Tripoli; to the east, Bilma, Tibesti and Kufra; to the south, Zinder and Kano, and to the west, Gao and Timbuktu. It was the centre of the gold trade.

One hundred years ago things were still booming; it was still a great trading nation. Fifty years ago, Malik would have had all the turbans he wanted. Over 20,000 camels at a time led by the Sultan of Agadez would set out for Nigeria on huge trading missions. There they would barter salt from the mines around Bilma for corn, cloth and everything else you can think of.

Twenty-five years ago, Malik would have had all the turbans he wanted without having had to save for them. Why is it today he has to save up for so long to buy just a single turban?

I always enjoy being in Niamey, the capital of Niger, which, for all its flashy, modern buildings and its famous Kennedy Bridge, is still a desert town. Most roads are still dust roads. Most of the traditional buildings are made of mud bricks, with the exception of the Grand Marché in the centre. Covering over six hectares, this includes nearly 2,000 shops and around 1,500 stalls. It must be the biggest shopping centre in Africa. All day long it vibrates with colour and noise and wheeling and dealing.

The population is around 250,000 and growing fast. But for me, Niamey is still full of the atmosphere of the Sahara. Life is slow, steady and measured. There are none of the hectic traffic jams of Abidjan or the busy trading of Lomé. Camels still wait leisurely at traffic lights until they turn to green instead of dashing across at amber. People still stop and say their prayers in the street. And everyone believes in ju-ju.

One evening I was in Tabakady, the only Russian restaurant I know in West Africa. I was planning to return to Kinder, the old slave capital of the Sahara. I had an invitation to meet the sultan's first minister, his minister of defence, and the chief of the army, in other words the cavalry, who still wear armour and chainmail and carry the very rifles Tanimoune the Great, one of the great sultans of the nineteenth century, ordered from Tripoli.

Over a hundred years ago, they were selling more than 3,000 slaves a year for guns and other European goods. Merchants had contacts all over Africa and deep into Europe. James Richardson, writing in 1850–51, gives a grim account of the whole sordid business. First, how the slaves were classified. Males came in five categories: *garzab*, those with beards; *morhag*, those beginning to grow beards; *sabaai*, those without beards; *sadasi*, grown-up children and *hlamasi*, children. Similarly with females: *shamalia*, those with breasts hanging down; *dabukia*, those with plump breasts; *farkah*, those with little breasts; *sadasia*, young girls; *glamasiah*, children. There was a separate category, *ajonza*, for old women. The best of the slaves were sent to Niffee and on to America. The cost: around $10 for males and $30 for females, although by the time they reached the coast the price would be perhaps five times as much.

And there was an unlimited supply. According to Richardson, whenever the sultan needed more money he sent a raiding party into one of the surrounding villages. With 2,000 horsemen and 10,000 infantry, not to mention his cannons, nobody could stop him. Richardson describes one of the raiding parties, or razzias, coming back into Zinder.

A cry was raised early this morning: 'The Sarkee is coming!'
. . . It turned out that a string of captives, fruits of the razzia,

was coming in. There cannot be in the world . . . a more appalling spectacle than this. My head swam as I gazed. A single horseman rode first . . . and the wretched captives followed him as if they had been used to this condition all their lives. Here were naked little boys, running alone, perhaps thinking themselves upon a holiday; near at hand dragged mothers with babes at their breasts; girls of various ages, some almost ripened into womanhood, others still infantile; old men bent two-double with age, their trembling chins verging towards the ground, their poor old heads covered with white wool; aged women tottering along, leaning upon long staffs, mere living skeletons . . . then followed the stout young men, ironed neck to neck! This was the first instalment of the black bullion of Central Africa; and as the wretched procession huddled through the gateways . . . the creditors of the Sarkee looked gloatingly on through their lazy eyes, and calculated on speedy payment.

Outside the Russian restaurant as I left, I saw a small, squat, elderly German in the middle of a group of Nigerians suddenly tear his jacket off and sling it on the ground. He then wrenched off his tie and pulled his shirt over his head. Around the top of his left arm was a red silk scarf.

'That's white man's ju-ju,' he screamed at a poor, scruffy-looking Hausa. 'You don't get the money here tomorrow at ten o'clock as we agreed, white man's ju-ju will kill you.'

'But he has ju-ju as well,' whispered one of the Hausa's friends.

'White man's ju-ju stronger than black man's ju-ju,' the German spat back. 'Don't you ever forget it,' he said, pointing to the scarf round his arm.

The group began to shuffle off, completely cowed. The German put his shirt back on. It was like a throwback to some Wild West film. 'If you let them get away with it they'll walk all over you. You have to make them do it your way,' he said to me, getting his breath back.

'But they could have turned on you.'

'Sure,' he said. 'That's the risk. But they don't.'

'But why is your ju-ju better than theirs?'

'Because I tell them.' He grinned.

We went back into the restaurant for a drink. He told me he worked for a French educational supplies company and had just spent three months in Chad. Now all the ministers were his friends. He also knew their brothers and sisters and aunts and uncles. He took them presents. Even lent them money. 'That way they owe me,' he said.

'You mean, they give you the business?'

'Sure,' he smiled.

'So you were collecting money this evening?'

'Of course. That's why you mustn't let them get away with it. Can you imagine what would happen if it got around that I lent people money and they didn't have to pay me back? I'd be finished.'

'And the ju-ju?'

'They all believe in ju-ju here. They've all got ju-jus.'

'But yours is better? What is it?'

'One of my wife's old scarves.'

The following evening I saw him in the hotel bar, wearing a quiet black suit, sombre tie. He could have been a bank manager dominated by his wife. I asked him whether he had got his money back. He smiled.

'So it worked?'

'Always works.' He stared at the barman. 'It's the only way you can get these people to do anything. Tell them it's ju-ju and they're scared.' The barman nodded violently and brought us more drinks. On the house.

Compared to Niamey, Agadez is a real desert town. Everywhere there is sand, sand and nothing but sand. Most of the buildings are low, single-storey blocks made of sand and mud. The mosque is sand. The tiny narrow alleyways are sand. The roads are sand. Even the food is made of sand. The only patch of concrete I can remember seeing is outside the airport. It is holding up a sign saying: 'Notre Dieu: Allah. Notre Prophète: Mahomet. Notre Livre: Le Coran.'

But however many times I go there I can't help wondering whether the whole place should, in fact, be covered in concrete.

Wander around the camel market on the outskirts of town, and there are maybe a dozen broken-down, foul-smelling, filthy-tempered, battered old camels tethered in the sand. In Hong Kong, in Singapore, in Kuala Lumpur, there would be nothing but Mercedes.

Stroll across to the Grand Mosque with its funny-looking pyramid-shaped minaret which was built in 1515 and is still covered in scaffolding. In Kuala Lumpur the mosques are spectacular modern buildings, all glass and air-conditioning.

Drop into the Italian ice cream parlour opposite. It's the best ice cream for the desert or, I suppose, the best desert for ice cream. All over South-East Asia they are making microchips and linear accelerators and cavity magnetrons, whatever they are. Not ice cream. And definitely not Italian ice cream.

Amble along the backstreets and narrow alleys. At the end of one street is what looks like a school. The door is open. Inside, a blackboard, a couple of dozen battered old desks, a mass of broken chairs. In South-East Asia the building would be one of the most modern in town, with gleaming desks and chairs. On each desk, or rather workstation, there would be a computer. In front of each computer would be another potential highly trained, highly motivated, highly professional manager ready to outgrow and outclass the West at whatever business they chose.

In Africa primary schools are practically non-existent, and those there are lack the most primary facilities. Secondary schools and universities are even more non-existent, and even more basic. In Morocco, in Togo, in Côte d'Ivoire, in Kenya, in Cairo, I've been in universities. They're run down and hopelessly underequipped. The one thing they don't lack is students. There are a hundred applicants for every place.

When I was in Togo, there were 3,200 students competing for just 30 places. And when they get there they never leave. It's a non-job for life. Partly because, since the students spend all their time protesting against everything under the sun, they never have time to study. Partly because, since the staff spend all their time protesting that they never get paid, they never have time to teach. And partly because students know that if they leave they'll never have a job to go to, so they might as well carry on not studying.

Not so throughout South-East Asia, where they're pumping out highly qualified, earnest, dedicated professionals almost as fast as they are pumping out microchips, linear accelerators and cavity magnetrons, whatever they are. And still industry wants more.

After wandering around the school I find myself in the central market. Local silversmiths are knocking out their special Agadez crosses. The Tuaregs are selling leather-work. The Bouza are wheeling and dealing in everything under the burning hot Sahara sun; cans of Coke, tins of beans, shawls, shirts. The Hausas, up from the south, are buying and selling everything else. The din is horrendous. Everybody is arguing about prices.

'Five hundred.'

'One hundred.'

'One hundred. You try to kill me, yes?'

'One hundred.'

'Is this man serious? I cannot live on one hundred.'

All over South-East Asia, people are shopping in giant, air-conditioned, computer-controlled, Western-style shopping malls like Seacon Square in Bangkok, which is so large I reckon it must have at least four time zones; mean time, not so mean time, expensive and 'If you have to ask the price you can't afford it.'

From the central market, I make my way to the local hospital. In Africa you need painkillers just to look inside a hospital. They are unhealthy – even for germs. They have precious few facilities. To have a bed is a luxury. To have even a rusty bed with anything like a mattress, sheets, a pillow is undreamt-of luxury. Medicines and food are scarce. To have an easier delivery, women believe it is better to starve as soon as they realise they are pregnant. Which is just as well. Equipment is almost non-existent. Trained staff are as rare as a bottle of disinfectant. Believe me, if you're not on a diet, avoiding fatty foods and doing regular exercise you very soon will be.

In Singapore, in Malaysia, they have probably the best medical facilities in the world. Hong Kong, of course, has its own way of doing things with needles, and snakes' teeth and rhinos' eyes. Ugh. But at least they're the cleanest needles and the best possible quality snakes' teeth and rhinos' eyes.

That evening, I was in the Hôtel de l'Air which I always think looks like a mosque converted into a cathedral. In the scruffy, dirty, dusty downstairs bar I bumped into, or rather almost trod on Theodore Monod, the tiny, wiry, grand old Frenchman of the desert. If there is anywhere in the world with two bits of sand huddled together he has trampled all over it.

I remember two quotes of his. The first: 'The desert shows us how beautiful the earth would be without men.' The second: 'In the desert we can see what this planet was like before man set foot on earth and what it will be like once the human race has been destroyed.'

A bunch of Canadian backpackers had grabbed the three or four broken chairs that were at the bar. Monod, I remember, shuffled backwards and forwards trying to catch the barman's attention which, for a Commander of the Ordre de Mérite Saharien, not to mention a member of the French Academy of Science, he seemed to find somewhat difficult. After a while he just gave up and left, presumably for the desert where he has no such problems.

In Hong Kong in the Mandarin Hotel, in the Peninsula or even in the Royal Garden, or in Bangkok in the Oriental, he'd sink into a luxury armchair in air-conditioned splendour and be served immediately by a highly paid, very professional, very efficient barman.

And yet ... and yet ... Africa has all the resources it could ever require. And more. Just down the road from Agadez at Arlit is one of the biggest uranium mines in the world. In 1980 uranium accounted for 75 per cent of their exports. Today it is around 90 per cent. Gold; cobalt; oil: Africa is overflowing with the stuff.

It has the money. Africans have – wait for it – more money tucked away in savings than the whole of the continent's entire annual output. The trouble is it's tucked away in Switzerland, in Monte Carlo, in the Cayman Islands, in post office savings accounts in Finchley, under the mattress in Paris or London or anywhere. African pension funds have money stashed away on Wall Street, in London and in Paris. African social security funds own office blocks all over the world.

It has the skills. Maybe not the skills to make microchips and the rest of the hi-tech mishmash, even though there is no shortage of mice in Africa. But it has organisational skills. Look at how the mammas all over Africa get the goods to market.

'If you rely on somebody for food, you will go without breakfast,' an old Togolese mamma used to tell me. Africans are traders. These guys were buying and selling when clever old Raffles was a twinkle in his father's eye. Damn it, some of them even traded their own people for a quick buck.

It has the financial skills. Hell, look at how so much has been lifted by so many from so few. Or should it be so much by so few from so many? Take Nigeria to the south. Between September 1988 and June 1994, US$12.4 billion of oil revenues just disappeared or, as they say, was allocated to 'dedication and other special accounts'. That's US$20 for every man, woman and starving child in the entire continent. If that is not proof of their financial skills and ability to run rings round any sophisticated financial system, I don't know what is.

The big question then is: if South-East Asia can do it, why can't Africa? It's not as if we're talking hundreds of years. Twenty-five, maybe thirty years ago, South-East Asia was nothing. Before that, between 1930 and 1960, they had no growth whatsoever. Today they are industrial giants. Their share of world trade has grown more than thirty times to over US$850 billion. In 1965 Indonesia's GDP per capita was smaller than Nigeria's. Today it is three times higher. In 1965 Thailand's was lower than Ghana's. Now it's the fastest-growing in the world.

One morning I sat drinking beer in the Hotel Telwa. A group of French tourists were piling into their Land Cruisers. Little boys were running backwards and forwards carrying their luggage for them. Two were trying to drag an enormous suitcase across the sandy track; obviously good training for later life. The French just sat watching them. When the boys finally got the case to the truck, the tourists let them struggle getting it on board. When they finally succeeded, the leader of the French group climbed out of the truck, put his hand in his designer jacket pocket and hurled a mass of coins into the air.

Is Africa in the mess it's in because of the colonists, because of the mad scramble for territory, because of the ruthless discipline, the repression, the way they were treated?

I wandered across to the ice cream parlour again. It was full of Americans. Maybe it's because of the Cold War, the rivalry between the superpowers who poured into Africa everything from guns to snowploughs in a bid to win friends and allies.

Maybe it's the aid organisations. The type of aid. Who it's given to. The trouble is, in most African countries there is nobody to give it to. Short of going around and dropping a couple of dollars into every outstretched hand, there is no established organisation capable of taking the money and allocating it to worthwhile, sensible projects. But the money has to be given to someone, otherwise nothing happens. So, in a world dominated by Western business principles and organisations, it is invariably given to a big local business, a foreign businessman living in the country concerned, or to an outside foreign company which will then move into the country to spend it on their behalf. Which is why most aid money in Africa is not spent by ordinary Africans. It is spent by outsiders running projects for Africans: Indians growing cotton and rice in Nigeria; Danes making ice cream in Togo;

Hong Kong Chinese making textiles in Ghana and the Lebanese doing everything everywhere.

Then, of course, there is what's known as tied aid. That's when a government links one damn, Pergau or otherwise, thing to another. Like not giving a certain country a great lump of cash so it won't build a dam not using construction companies not from a certain country. The trouble here again is that the donor is using elastic pound notes. As soon as he hands it over it comes straight back to him. The country gets the project, but precious little else. Okay, so the locals get the chance to drive a couple of tractors and maybe ferry the big foreign chiefs back and forth from their hotel every day. But they very rarely share in the management and construction of the actual project; they have no chance to build up their own technical and professional skills, nor to gain experience so that maybe next time they can build the whole damn thing themselves.

Little brown envelopes, of course. Little brown envelopes.

In the ice cream parlour one of the Americans was pushing a bundle of notes at the boy behind the counter. Typical American, he was trying to get the ice cream cheap by dropping the kid some readies. And, of course, the kid took it. Sure, Africa is corrupt. Anyone who has ever tried to sell even a toothbrush in Africa knows how corrupt it is. But it's not the only corrupt place on earth. Look at South Korea, Taiwan, Indonesia, Japan. What about the great United States itself. In any case, corruption is not always corruption. There are different types of corruption, or shall we say negotiating margin.

Now, if you promise not to open the little brown envelope until you're in the privacy of that tiny bank just off the Bahnhofstrasse in Zurich, I'll give you a quick insider's guide to corruption Africa-style. Or, at least, according to this man I met in a bar in downtown Agadez.

First, there's the get-the-stuff-out-of-here-toute-suite-stash-it-away-and-forget-about-it-until-you're-fired, exiled or murdered, whichever is the most convenient. This applies to people on the fringes of power: businessmen, ambassadors, government ministers and even presidents. Anyone who suddenly sees an opportunity, takes it but doesn't expect it to happen again.

This happens over and over, usually with minor civil servants, government officials, and clerks or secretaries working for companies. They get the smell of a contract, maybe from a big brother or the friend of a friend. The civil servant will promise to get the government minister to sign the bit of paper placing the order or authorising payment, or both. In return, of course, there is the small matter, cough, cough, you know what I mean? Similarly with the clerk or the secretary. Their company is about to place a big order for a small h'mm, h'mm, they would make certain it came your way. Know what I mean? In return they pick up a little brown envelope or maybe have it transferred you know where. Sometimes it's hardly enough to pay for a stamp for the envelope. But sometimes it can be enough to buy you a diamond as big as the Ritz. However much it is, the rule is get it out of the country, stash it away, keep it safe. You never know what might happen. You could get fired. The World Bank could come up with some crazy idea for a structural adjustment programme which will create employment for economists in Washington but unemployment for the poor guys in Africa they are supposed to be helping. Alternatively, the president could get out of somebody else's bed the wrong side that morning, spot the new houseboy cleaning his shoes and offer him your job as a government minister. Whoosh. You're out. You've got a house, a car, your aged mother, goodness knows how many children and, of course, all those wives to support in the manner to which they have become accustomed. It's your duty as head of the household to make certain they're looked after. So you've obviously got to make the necessary, h'mm, h'mm, arrangements.

Next stage is the no-point-keeping-it-all-in-the-bank-I'll-buy-a-flat syndrome. This usually happens with guys who manage to do two, three, maybe even more deals. They still only rate themselves as being lucky. They don't see themselves making a career out of it. So why not have a flat, maybe even a house? Somewhere to go if the heat gets too hot. In any case it would be good for the kids to have a flat in London or Paris. Maybe pick up the language. Go to school or university. Wouldn't do any harm.

The next step up – or maybe down – the ladder, according to my friend, is when the amateur decides that maybe it's not all luck, he really is pretty good at it and wants to turn professional. This usually happens after a series of deals, or maybe after just one big, big one. This generally happens to fairly senior government officials who have been left on their own by their political masters either because they are working on bigger deals themselves or because they keep being changed so they don't have a chance to knuckle in on their official's patch. Take ministries of tourism. I've lost count of the number of directors of tourism who have suddenly left their gilded offices to become special advisers or consultants to aircraft manufacturers and before you can say 'Please fasten your seatbelt' they have big houses in Hampstead, flats in Marbella and the children at finishing school in Switzerland. Similarly civil servants in ministries of defence, ministries of post and telecommunication and ministries of finance.

For most, this is as far as they want to go. But for the ambitious, especially if they're Nigerian or Zairian, this is only the start. The next stage is to become an international trading company in your own right: do the deal yourself, pocket the commissions, but take the profits as well. After, of course, all the necessary deductions for services rendered. But this is a game for grown-ups. To survive at this level you not only have to be a grown-up player, you need grown-up contracts and grown-up deals. The profit from selling on a couple of Land Rovers will not pay for the champagne. You've got to equip whole regiments. You've also got to be able to play games with figures. Want to know how it's done? Well, if you promise to cut me in, I'll tell you.

First you secure the buyer. The world is full of people selling things. The problem is the buyer. Secure him and you're off, and the only way to really secure a buyer is – you got it – fix the buyer. Get him to place the order with you direct. That way you know you've got him. If he can't or won't do that, get him to place the order with another middleman or, better still, purchasing organisation. From the buyer's point of view, it looks a cleaner deal. Your problem is you've got to fix the other guy. Usually, of course, it's no hassle. A quick four-hour lunch at the Crillon in Paris and it's all fixed. Sometimes, however, it takes two lunches, because you've got to convince this other guy that you can deliver the buyer, that the buyer will buy at – most important of all – the price you are quoting. Not the ordinary price. How do you do that? By adding on lots of extras, of course. Most government contracts, even in Africa, are strictly controlled, usually by the banks and aid organisations, because they're the only ones with the money. So all you do is say that the farm tractors have to be equipped with snowploughs, that the military vehicles should have mink-lined seats and that the government offices should be fitted with anti-bugging wallpaper. Nothing too big or too extravagant to create a diplomatic – or financial – incident. Just enough to make a difference to the price.

And how does that mean you can cream something off the top? Simple. You write the extras into the specification, but you don't do anything about them. You don't actually supply the snowploughs or whatever, you only charge for them. Second, you deliver late. The extras threw out the specifica-tions, tight schedules and so on. The job took longer. Unfortunately, you don't want to, but you have to charge extra just to cover your costs. You're sure they'll understand, thank you very much indeed.

Doesn't anybody check? Listen. You're talking about bureaucrats who broke their teeth running the Common Agricultural Policy. That's why they are now running the aid organisations. In any case there's no way anyone can prove anything. The price is higher because they wanted extras. The job, as a result, took longer. Everybody knows that, stupid. Delivery details had to be changed, cancellation charges paid. It all adds up, doesn't it?

Okay, nobody's listening, so now let's talk big stuff. And I mean big stuff. Most fraud involves single orders or contracts – a couple of bullet-proof cars here, 250 armoured personnel carriers there, maybe the occasional Boeing 737. But the real scams involve entire countries. It's possible to take a slice off the top of everything coming into and even going out of an entire country. Basically it's done two, or maybe, if you're lucky, three ways.

First, you fix the head of customs. Look for the biggest, most glorious house in any poor country and you can bet your life it belongs to him. I've lost count of the mansions I've seen in Africa looking over neatly cut lawns, avenues of trees interspersed with occasional statues, and stuffed full of Louis Quatorze furniture.

Second, you fix the rates. A few percentage points here and there nobody is going to notice. But it all adds up. Everything disappears into goodness knows what accounts. Easy pickings. If Britain's Export Credit Guarantee Department can make mistakes adding up and taking away over seventy years, why should the Africans be so perfect?

Next, if you can, and if you can depends on the dropsy, you get the rates waived altogether. I mean if a very good friend wants to bring in a shipload of whatever, it wouldn't be very friendly to charge him or his wife the rate for the job, would it? Charge Her Excellency the rate, any kind of rate, and you probably won't be in your own job for long. Then, of course, the friend has friends – and wives, and it wouldn't be right to treat them any differently, would it? Especially wives. Hence the sudden decisions to close the harbour gates on Sunday mornings and keep it in the family. Trouble is, of course, once you close the gates it's no longer in the family. Everybody knows exactly what's going on, who's behind it, and the number of the Zurich account. But you've just got to decide which side of the bread you want your caviar on.

Finally, are you ready, the biggest scam of all: the state trading monopoly designed to protect the poor and helpless, keep prices to the minimum and ensure fair shares for all.

Well, maybe all. This is not a game for ordinary mortals. It's a real-life monopoly for real-life government ministers who know they are going to be around for a long time. First you set up the state trading corporation. Next you pass legislation saying it will in future handle all imports. Handling everything centrally, ordering in bulk, will mean lower prices. Lower prices will mean a better deal for everyone. Who can argue with that? The trouble, of course, is – you've got it – hidden away in the background is your friendly neighbourhood Lebanese banker or Tunisian wheeler-dealer who is making all the – nudge, nudge – arrangements. Nobody can prove it and those who know are not saying anything, but you can bet a dirty glass of water to a presidential 737 stacked full of Dom Perignon that somewhere, somehow, something is being creamed off the top of absolutely everything coming into the country. Which, you must admit, must be big, but very big business.

Now nobody is saying that's the kind of thing Houphouet was up to in Côte d'Ivoire. Not me or two others I'm too scared to mention. But you've got to be the luckiest family doctor of all time to make enough money on the coffee futures market to build a basilica bigger than St Peter's in Rome. If you see what I mean.

I spent another evening in the Hôtel de l'Air, after all the backpackers had gone, trying to work out an African theory of corrupt-leopardskin-hat-times-thirty-years-in-power-plus-two-Concordes-in-the-back-yard-take-away-any-possible-opposition relativity. One man times thirty years in power times the total national debt not divided by any opposition plus the active support of the military combined with the quickest square root to the nearest Swiss bank equals one hell of a mess of a country. No, that's not right. What about one leopardskin hat times thirty years in power plus two Concordes in the back yard, take away any possible opposition divide what's left by the number of dollars you first thought of hidden away in bank vaults all over the world and what are we left with: less than nothing.

Or maybe it's as simple as $E = mc^2$. E stands for extortion, which is the mass of the population who do not see what's going on so they are condemned to spend the rest of their lives in tiny, squalid little hovels. Those who did see what's going on left years ago at the square of the speed of light rather than be energetically reduced to a mass like all the others.

It suddenly came to me when I was almost run over by a camel outside the mosque. The whole problem of corruption in Africa. I could solve it overnight. The World Bank should set up a Corruption Department, to advise presidents, ministers and the chauffeur's girlfriend how to lie and cheat and steal properly. At the moment, you can bet your life everyone's doing it. But they're not getting as much out of it as they should. A bit like having an affair with the boss's mistress. What the World Bank should say is, 'Look, it's wrong, and it's unjust. But we all know you're doing it. What we'll do is help you do it properly; show you how to take the money without causing all these problems for the economy, for the country, for the poor man in the street who doesn't know where his next meal is coming from. We'll show you how to invest it. Instead of sticking it in some mysterious Swiss bank which pays you next to nothing, we'll invest it for you properly, manage it for you professionally, and make you around 20–25 per cent a year on it. Which is a million times better than you're getting now. But in return, we want you to limit the amount you take. Instead of taking billions and billions, which is crazy, nobody needs billions and billions, take only, say, £50 million which, let's be honest, is enough to live on. Leave the rest behind.'

I reckon most Africans on the game would take the deal. It would be guaranteed. The money would be safe. They would be safe. There wouldn't be any risk of blackmail, it would all be legit and above board. And above all, more actual cash would be invested in Africa for the benefit of everybody than is the case nowadays. Which has to be a good idea. But, of course, while the World Bank huffs and puffs about accepting my proposal, the place continues to lurch from crisis to catastrophe to my God, what the hell can we do now?

The rest of the world is producing more food, opening more factories, developing their economies and improving the lives of their inhabitants. What is Africa doing to compete in the global economy of the twenty-first century? Nothing. Things are getting worse and worse and worse. Every time I go back to Agadez, to Lomé, to Lagos, to wherever, you can see the whole place is in an economic tailspin. It is producing less food now than it was twenty years ago, with the exception of the ice cream parlour.

On the land, food production is plummeting. It's lower than it was ten years ago. Africa is losing its share of the valuable cocoa, tea and coffee markets worldwide. Countries that were major food exporters are now major food importers. Africa's entire urban population relies on imported grain. By the year 2010, unless something drastic happens, they will have to import twice the amount.

In the towns, according to the World Bank, sub-Saharan Africa needs 350 million new jobs within the next twenty years to survive. Are they out of their minds? Africa will be lucky to get thirty-five new jobs in the next twenty years and half of them will be taken by World Bank economists. There is no way Africa can create that many jobs, unless everyone can be employed as undertakers. What factories there are are closing down and rotting away. People are leaving, both the best and the worst. Nearly 100,000 middle- and senior-level people left between 1985 and 1990. More leave every day. As for the worst, you've just got to read the newspapers; in Marseille, in Naples, in Paris.

Given what's happened over the past few years there is no way Africa can suddenly change for the better. It's going to continue to get worse and worse. Where governments and companies are operating and employing people, like governments and companies all over the world they are also looking at ways of cutting back. The last thing they are going to do is employ more people. If new companies are started, if new investors move in, they're going to be employing as few people as possible. Yet costs in Africa are horrendous and getting more horrendous by the hour. Capital and operating costs are double that of South-East Asia and increasing all the time. To ship bananas from Côte d'Ivoire to Europe costs more than from South America. That's without all the risks involved: poor quality, bad workmanship, theft, political interference, expropriation, being thrown in jail and losing the key. Africa's share of world trade has declined from 4 per cent to just 1 per cent in the last ten years. Conditions in the huge, sprawling cities like Lagos, Algiers, Kinshasa are getting worse. Even in the smaller towns – Lomé, Barmako, even Niamey and Agadez, when the sun goes down the barricades and shutters go up, the prayer mats come out and everybody prays to Allah they are not going to be liberated by some mob of marauding soldiers raping and pillaging their way through town because they have not been paid for a year or more. Roads are crumbling; railways, with one or two honourable exceptions, are falling apart. Airlines? Don't even think about it.

As if that's not enough, the whole place is drowning in debt. Over three times what export earnings they have goes in paying off their debts, which increase each year by over $6 billion. That's the average. For some countries it's more than 100 per cent.

The only growth area in Africa is in producing reports on the fact that there is no growth in Africa.

And yet . . . and yet . . . In Benin; in Burundi; in The Gambia; in Ghana; in Mali; in Tanzania; in Uganda: all these countries, Africans say, have doubled their growth rates and trebled, yes trebled, farm production. Except . . . except . . . they are playing games. How can you talk about growth rates when nobody knows how many people are actually living and dying in a country; how many villages there are; how big the towns are; how many businesses there are; how many people they employ; how many times they fill in their forms and send them back to the government to be counted; how many civil servants – if any – there are counting the forms; how the statistics are then processed? I've been in government offices in Benin. There are stacks of paper everywhere. Nobody does a thing. I've been in government offices in Ghana which had no electricity, no telephones, not even any two-way radios. All the minister was doing was stockpiling his office with sacks of rice so that he could sell them later to make money to look after his family. In Mali, I couldn't even get into the government offices because after I'd given the doorman at the hotel a present, the taxi driver a present, the policeman outside the ministry a present, I had no money left to give to the soldier on duty at the gate, so he refused to let me in.

So tell me, how can you believe any statistics that come out of Africa? Of course you can't. It's a nonsense to pretend otherwise.

Take exports. According to the statistics, Côte d'Ivoire exports US$500 million more goods than other countries import from it. Togo is a major gold exporter even though it has no goldmines. The Gambia exported absolutely nothing at all between 1967 and 1978; and Benin's biggest trading partner is – itself.

What about GDP? As far as I'm concerned it stands for Grossly Distorted Picture. You can travel all over Africa, you can go into as many government offices as you like, half of them haven't even got tables and chairs, let alone facilities for calculating whether their growth rate has doubled, trebled or just jumped over the moon. The other half probably have tables and chairs which if they haven't sold them already they will any day. The only place you see any activity is under the occasional light bulb on the wall, where a million insects are busy eating away what's left of the plaster.

Apart from maybe the president's office, the head of police, the head of the army, the chief of the radio and television and the minister of finance, government hardly exists in Africa. There is no structure, no chain of command. There is no way of getting anything done. There are practically no telephones, and those there are don't work. There are precious few typewriters. Many offices don't even have electricity.

Africans talk about being marginalised. They are not being

marginalised; they are being pushed right off the edge of the paper. For two reasons. First, the world has moved on. There are fewer resources. Everybody has other priorities. The World Bank cut back its aid budget to Africa by over US$1 billion in 1993. With Eastern Europe and now Palestine looking for hand-outs it's obviously going to cut, cut and cut again. Individual governments are cutting back. The US are talking about cutting back. Even Sweden has cut back.

Second, nobody takes Africans seriously any more. They're inefficient. They say one thing and do the other. They don't understand what the real world is all about. They are kids trying to do a man's job. Oil-rich Nigeria – one in five Africans is Nigerian – is bust. It cannot afford to pay its debts. Is it worried? Is it hell. The government says it is going to do one thing and either does nothing or the complete opposite. It said it was going to privatise its grossly inflated, enormously costly state sector. Between 1988 and 1992 the total value of its privatisation programme was less than 1 per cent of that of Argentina, Malaysia or even Mexico, and still over N28 billion worth of oil mysteriously leaks across the border somehow every year, costing the country over N77 million in lost income every single day.

For ten years Kenya said it was going to privatise, but it only sold one company. Sure, Egypt may boom. Sure, South Africa will probably hit the jackpot. Little old Togo might catch up a little. I hope so, they deserve it. Benin, maybe. It's a tiny country. It should not be as difficult to turn around as some of the giants. But Nigeria, Sierra Leone, Chad, Mali, Sudan, Somalia, Angola, Liberia, Rwanda, Zaire. No way. Nobody will admit it in public, but everybody has had enough. The way they see it, they have thrown enough money at Africa without it making any difference – to Africa, that is. It's made a lot of difference to a lot of Swiss banks. It's time to call a halt.

All I know is – and I hate saying this – I reckon Africa has missed the boat. No way can I ever see poor little Agadez or any other town or city in Africa coming within a million miles of Hong Kong or Singapore or even Bangkok, let alone catching up. Take Ghana, Ghana is supposed to be an African success story because it's growing at 5 per cent a year. Yet if it continues to grow at 5 per cent a year it will take – wait for it – another fifty years before the average Ghanaian actually crosses the poverty line. So what hope is there for the rest of Africa?

Agadez? Come back here in twenty-five years' time and I reckon it will be virtually the same – if it's lucky. Maybe the camels won't have such bad breath. Maybe they'll have renewed the scaffolding on the mosque. Maybe the smart kid in the ice cream parlour who took the money from the American will be the owner – or in jail.

Come back in fifty years' time and I'm convinced Africa will still be in the Stone Age; children will still be running around with bits of branches trying to round up a couple of scrawny goats. There will still be long, low tents. Sitting outside will be Malik, wracked with tuberculosis. In front of him will be a clean patch of sand, a heap of dog dung for fuel, some wheatflour and a little water. The dung he'll put in the centre of the patch of sand and set light to, as his ancestors have done for generations. Once it's hot, he'll push it to one side, sprinkle some flour on the sand, add water and make a dough the size of a pancake. He'll gently wave some burning twigs over the top of it until a light crust begins to form. Now he'll cover the whole bread with clean sand and put the fuel back on top of it to cook. In the distance camels will still be chomping away as they have done since the beginning of time. Behind the camels will still be open desert. The only sound will be Malik coughing up blood. In between the coughing, he will still be talking about trying to save US$200 dollars to buy a camel so that in February he can join the big thousand-kilometre, forty-day camel train that leaves Agadez for Bilma so that he can buy salt for his family and animals and sell the remainder to the rest of his village in case there is a drought.

But there is a good side. He won't have to worry about his sons wanting to go off to town in search of a pair of jeans. Thanks to the unswerving, single-minded dedication of

Africa's leaders to do everything they can to slash budget deficits, curb inflation, introduce competitive exchange rates, tariff reforms and agricultural incentives, create jobs, stimulate investment and boost the economy of Switzerland, there won't be any town left. The Tuaregs will once again reign supreme.

Dakar

You think I keep on about food and drink? You should have met Mr Diouf. He was the ultimate dedicated swallower of fashion. Like David Hume when he was private secretary to the British ambassador in Paris, he was your real tooth fairy. He believed he should eat nothing but ambrosia, drink nothing but nectar and get somebody else to pick up the tab.

His hero was not his president, also Mr Diouf, or even Nelson Mandela, but Stefan Arkadyevitch, the bon vivant brother who drifts from restaurant to restaurant all the way through *Anna Karenina* being recognised by everybody, no matter which one he goes into.

Not for him cassava dumplings, yams, chillies, white eggplant, plantains, corn, okra or any of the other strange things you see in African markets that make the world fall out of your bottom the following morning, whether you've added ground ginger or not. Neither was he the type you could take for a quick curry in an Indian restaurant in Utrecht called Mahatma Cote. Or for that matter to a traditional Chinese restaurant where the walls are decorated with dried cater-pillars, pickled snakes, ox tendons, antler velvet and so many deer penises it brings tears to your eyes.

I once went to a herbal Chinese restaurant in Singapore where I was offered a bowl of crispy black ants to cure my arthritis. When I explained I didn't have arthritis the waitress, who was more like your old-fashioned hospital sister than a Singapore girl, insisted that instead I had a dish of whip soup to begin with, followed by deep-fried scorpions on prawn toast and menthol jelly for dessert. The menthol jelly, she said, was good for the liver. The deep-fried scorpions were good for the brain. I didn't have the courage to ask her what the whip soup was good for.

'We are what we eat,' Mr Diouf would say, digging into a salad of lobster and truffles; followed by foie gras and sweetbreads; followed by roast pike à la mode de Bugey, stuffed to the gills with whiting and more truffles, drowned in lashings of butter and fresh cream and buried under a mountain of lobster tails and still more truffles; followed by lime and raspberry soufflé; followed by a selection of the most fantastic cheeses you have ever seen in your cholesterol-free life.

On which basis he was the most sophisticated, the most high church Muslim I have ever met, gastronomically speaking that is. My wife, of course, says the opposite: 'We eat what we are', especially when I'm about to dig into an enormous pork chop or even a delicious hunk of wild boar. But then she's an unreconstructed vegetarian, on a diet, obsessed with E-numbers and worried about whether the lorry driver who delivered the wrapping paper was kind to dolphins or not.

Mr Diouf knew everything there was to know about restaurants. Which ones to go to: Joel Robuchon on the rue de Longchamp in the gastronomic heart of Paris, where people are prepared to take out a second mortgage and wait two months for the privilege of tasting their most famous creation, purée de pommes de terre; Dodin-Bouffant on the rive gauche, where people would rather die than admit they passed up the daubes d'huitres et pieds de porc; The Buerchised in the park next to the parliament building in Strasbourg, where he said he had to go to meet his brother; L'Auberge de l'Ill at Illhaensern in Alsace; Girardet's in Crissier, just north of Lausanne – it was awarded three rosettes in Michelin's first-ever guide to Swiss restaurants (ask for the foie gras with grapes jellied in Madeira); the Stikliai, in Vilnius, the best restaurant in the Baltics; any restaurant in Taping County in Guangdong province, where they serve the freshest mice in the world; and any restaurant, bar or corrugated iron hut in Soweto serving sheep's intestines.

Which ones to avoid: Le Fouguet, in the Champs Elysées – it has been invaded by cockroaches; a certain restaurant in Cannes near the Petit Carlton where people not only get attacked while eating, they even, can you imagine, get maced as well; the Haughty Cavalier just under the Harbour Bridge in Sydney, because they make a big thing about using nothing but virgin hen's eggs which he didn't feel he was temperamentally suited to; Chinese restaurants in northern Bohemia, especially towards the end of the month; a particular Tunisian restaurant in Shepherd's Bush where a woman once got up from the table, went to the ladies and promptly hanged herself with her bra; restaurants in the States which make a big thing about going round cutting people's ties in half if anyone turns up wearing one after eight o'clock in the evening; any restaurant, bar or corrugated iron hut in Cotonou, Benin, serving skinned possum; restaurants which serve toast upside down and ask you to mix your own salad.

'Why I go to restaurant if I have to make my own salad? If I want to make my own salad, I stay at home,' he would say.

He also knew exactly what to order; anywhere in Central Africa, bushmeat – in other words, gorilla and chimpanzee; in Kentucky, roasted squirrel wrapped in streaky bacon; in northern Greece, sliced tortoise meat; in China, monkey in wine sauce, warm serpent's blood, python 'but only after it has been marinated in vinegar and water' and, only in Beijing, baked dog served with garlic and coconut sauce; in Rio, feijoada, their national dish, a kind of pig-trotter stew with lumps of ear and eye and nose and throat and whatever thrown in, mixed up with black beans and rice; in Johannesburg, especially in Sfuzy's, cajun-style Cape salmon. And whenever it was on the menu, starling soup, robins roasted on skewers, coated in butter and served on brown bread toast, blue blackbird pâté, pigeon stuffed with whole baby starlings with just their feet and beaks chopped off, linnet and pipit jam and, for supper, songbirds.

But even he drew the line at vanilla ice cream smeared in Coleman's mustard. I was once in some tiny village just outside Lyons. There, sitting two tables away, was this guy smearing his vanilla ice cream with mustard. 'The contrast,' he purred as I tried desperately to put my eyes back in their sockets. 'The cold. The hot. Like roquefort and Sauterne. C'est formidable.' Merci beaucoup and pass the sick-bag.

But if he knew what to order, our Mr Diouf, Monsieur Michelin himself, also knew what not to order; anything that has been vacuum-packed and cooked because it is a breeding ground for clostridium botulinum, one of the most deadly toxins known to man; alligator sausages in Atlanta, Georgia; po-po beancurd anywhere in the cosmos; suckling pig, unless it has been cooked for seventy-two hours; fat, white wood maggots; fresh gazelle or deer unless it has been buried for three days in a pit five foot deep, dug up, skinned and then roasted; and the Senegalese national dish, tiebou djen (rice and fish). He also had a particular thing against what he called scapegoats.

Champagne, he believed in drinking before, during and after meals as well as at any other time. 'J'aime ma femme,' he would always say, 'mais j'adore le champagne.' I never asked him which one. Champagne, I mean.

That's not to say he didn't go for the best Bordeaux wines and cognacs as well. The only port he would consider drinking was Taylor's 1963. And once he told me he had a particular weakness for homemade honey beer made in Kenya.

To keep fit and live to a ripe old age he religiously kept to a strict routine. Every day, he told me, he drank three bottles of champagne, two bottles of claret and half a bottle of cognac. But he never had hangovers, although once or twice while I myself was passing from the 'I'll-never-do-it-again' to the 'well-maybe-just-one-more time' stage of a hangover, he did admit he got what he called 'visual migraines'.

He was Africa's answer to Brillat-Savarin, the famous fat French bachelor civil servant, judge, expert on duelling, lighthearted pornographic writer, fiddler in New York's first professional orchestra and patron saint of gourmets, whose book *La Physiologie du Goût* has never been out of print since it was first published at his own expense in 1826. If there is ever a Nobel peace prize for gastronomy, he'd be first in line.

Me, I'm not like that. After a million years slaving away over Big Macs, frantically trading hot dogs, arbitrating French fries and arranging complicated Danish pastry swaps, I don't have such high standards. I'm happy so long as a restaurant has good food, a fantastic wine list and fairly good service. French, Chinese, Japanese, German, Hungarian, I'm not proud. My theory is simple: if foreigners have been eating this stuff for years and there are still plenty of foreigners around, there can't be anything wrong with it. Although I admit I do have reservations about restaurants which serve bacon, egg, sausage and mushroom cold for breakfast and call it a 'Heritage Platter'. Not like an old Yorkshire export manager of dubious personal hygiene I used to know who always insisted on having steak tartare 'well done'.

'With red or white wine?' waiters would ask.

'A little bit of both, lad,' he would flatulently reply.

Take him to any restaurant in the world, spend a fortune and at the end of the meal he would push back the plate and burp, 'That were reet good, lad. But as I always say, in one 'ole and out t'other.'

I first met Mr Diouf, who had a moustache, a perm and a whole wardrobe of Yves St Laurent suits, in Lomé, Togo, the one-time Dom Perignon of French West Africa. He was a member of the Senegalese delegation at the signing of the Lomé Convention, which is the EC's way of transferring money from the poor people of Europe to the rich people of Africa.

I could tell he was Senegalese. First because everyone – but everyone – in Senegal is called Monsieur Diouf. Except for one person and he is called President Diouf. If you have problems remembering people's names go to either South Korea, where everyone is called Mr Kim, or to Senegal.

Second, he was about eight foot tall and as thin as the file of successful EC investments implemented as part of the Lomé Convention. Which is the hallmark of the Senegalese. If any country is the land of walking bean posts, it's Senegal. Some people say that the Senegalese don't just feel they're superior, they knew they're superior; not just to the rest of Africa but to the rest of the world, if not the entire cosmos. Is it any wonder? Since time began they've been used to people looking up to them. Somehow it's just got into their blood. In fact, they are so tall that when the Japanese, out of the kindness of their hearts and the wish to stitch up Senegal as another commercial colony, built a radio and television centre for them in Dakar, the ceilings were too low. The Japanese had simply taken the designs off the shelf and assumed that if the world is happy driving Japanese cars it will be happy working in Japanese offices.

Third, he spent the whole Convention not in the bar, which is par for the course for anyone attending a conference or convention in Africa, especially if it is funded by an outside aid organisation dedicated to relieving famine, but upstairs in the fantastic restaurant on the thirty-fifth floor of the Hotel du 2 Février, opposite the Convention centre. And he did it without any sense of shame or guilt whatsoever.

Come the opening ceremony, the Convention centre was packed with over 3,000 delegates from all over Africa, the Caribbean and the Pacific eager to see the EC finally come across after five years of intensive non-stop negotiations in the world's most expensive restaurants.

Where was Mr Diouf? As we all tumbled out of the hotel lift on the ground floor to race across to the signing ceremony, there he was; the only person waiting to get into the lift. 'Breakfast,' he whispered. 'I must have a little breakfast.'

The ceremony began. The big guys made carbon copy speeches of the ones they made at the previous Convention five years earlier, promising the same enormous strides in development, the same increases in living standards, the same commitment to build for the future. Hidden away at the top of the hall, packed into every aisle, crammed on every flight of stairs, squeezed into every available square inch were a thousand more members of Togo's famous animateurs, the president's own official glee club. Now they exploded – the right word, I promise you – into an ear-shattering song praising their president, praising the EC and praising and praising their president again and again.

Where was Mr Diouf? The Senegalese delegation all seemed to have their heads bowed, either for fear of banging them on the ceiling or because they were beginning to suffer from champagne and caviar withdrawal symptoms. There was a single empty chair.

Now the signing ceremony proper began. On the stage was a tiny table; on the table was an enormous book; the Lomé Convention itself. The leader of every delegation signing the Convention had to come up on stage and sign the Convention on behalf of their government. Simple? No way. First the animateurs had to sing their appropriate national anthem; that country's flag appeared on the balcony and was marched down to where the particular delegation was sitting. The head of the delegation bowed to the flag and followed it at a respectful, almost funereal pace the length of the centre then oh-so-slowly up the steps. As soon as he was on stage, he bowed again to his own flag, to the Togolese flag as the host country – protocol! protocol! – and shook hands with the chief EC representative, who led him to the chair by the big book. Both then fumbled with their EC-financed expensive fountain pens. The leader of the delegation then checked the Convention, flicking through the odd couple of thousand pages and staring intently at one or two lines, presumably to make sure he wasn't signing a piece of paper agreeing to pay back all his expenses to the EC in order to finance the construction of a dozen hospitals back home. Then he signed. A round of applause. Another bow to the Togolese flag. Another bow to his own flag. A fumble to get his expensive fountain pen back in his expensive suit. Another handshake with the EC official. Another chorus from the animateurs. Then the procession all the way back to his seat.

How long did the whole thing take? Ten, maybe, fifteen minutes? No problem. But how many people had to sign the Convention? Over 70 countries times fifteen minutes! We could still be here in five years when they come to sign the next Convention.

I looked round at the Senegalese delegation. There were now thirty-two empty seats. The only person left was their deputy leader, who was presumably to sign on behalf of the leader. After all, if everybody is called Mr Diouf and everybody is eight feet tall, it doesn't make much difference who signs the thing. And Mr Diouf? He was probably checking out the menu for lunch.

Benin; Botswana; Burkina Faso; Burundi; Cameroon; Central African Republic; Chad; Comoros; Congo: still they kept coming. The flags, the songs, the processions, the fumblings with the pen, the nervous flick through the pages, the signature, the procession back, then another flag ... Except, I swear, the flags were appearing maybe a trifle more briskly than before. The processions were certainly not as funereal. The singing had lost maybe a certain edge. And there were certainly more empty seats than there used to be.

Now, I decided, was the time for me to go if I wasn't going to be trapped there for ever. I joined the scrum headed in a solid phalanx for the restaurant opposite on the thirty-fifth floor. Out of the Convention centre; across the wide open plaza which can accommodate 10,000 people; up the slope to the hotel; into the lobby; a rush for the lift. The lift opens. Out comes Mr Diouf. He had already had his lunch.

I next met Mr Diouf in Dakar, which is a bit like Paris in the sunshine. The presidential palace is like some elegant château. The National Assembly is a modern, imposing building with fountains and waterfalls. The cathedral looks as though it was carved out of icing sugar. Everywhere there is an excitement and a buzz. Things seem to move in Dakar. Whether they actually do is another matter.

Wander round the Place de l'Indépendance with its four lanes of traffic, its tall office blocks and its two and a half million street traders selling everything anybody could possibly want in the whole world and you can see why the French chose it as the seat of the governor-general of the old West African Federation. Other African capitals are almost villagey. This one is international, cosmopolitan: a professional.

Racing around town, it's sometimes hard to realise that Senegal is fighting all the problems desperately afflicting the rest of francophone Africa; disease, desertification, illiteracy, lack of resources, women walking ten kilometres a day in search of firewood, the ever-increasing price of champagne.

Take Louga, for example, close to the border with Mauritania. It was once the centre of Senegal's groundnut industry. Today it is desperately trying to hold back the Sahara. Years of intense cultivation have destroyed what was once a fertile area. The rich soil, pulled up with the groundnuts at harvest time, has been blown away. All that's left is sand and dust. Now it is the centre of an ambitious project to stop the Sahara from engulfing it, as it has swallowed thousands of similar villages throughout the sahel. The aid organisations started by throwing money at it as if a wall of dollar bills would hold back the desert. But in vain. Now, a Swedish agronomist told me, they are spending the money on educating the villagers.

'If they understand what we are doing, then it will work,' he said. 'We are trying to get them to plant the trees and then to cultivate the land – not chop everything down as soon as our backs are turned and use it for firewood.'

Dakar is also the legendary Leopold Senghor; legendary at least in French Africa. A poet and an intellectual, he stood up at the first meeting ever of foreign ministers of the Organisation for African Unity in 1963 in Senegal and called on liberation movements the length and breadth of Africa to commit themselves to – the 'poetry of action'. There was silence. No cheers. No banging of desks. No stamping of feet. It was typical Senegalese. It was dramatic, dynamic, grammatical. But nobody knew what on earth he was going on about.

Was he calling on everyone to raise their iambic pentameters aloft, hurl alliterations at the oppressors and once and for all make Africa free for sprung rhythms, paeans and outriders? It was over thirty years before the OAU ever went to Senegal again, and then because nobody else could afford to have them.

At the time I was in Senegal looking at traditional medicines. The medical faculty at Dakar University has done much to turn traditional cures to commercial advantage. But according to an American ethnobotanist (expert in primitive people's botanical remedies) at the university, time is running out.

'There are over 250,000 species in the world. Ten per cent have still not been classified. Isn't that shocking?' he told me. 'But that's not the worst of it. The plants are disappearing. Some ethnobotanists estimate that 25,000 will have disappeared by the year 2000.'

'How?'

'Fifty per cent of all plant species are found in tropical rainforests, which are disappearing at the rate of 100 acres a minute, more than 4.5 million acres a year. Do you read me? Then we have to discover their medical properties and relate them to the diseases. We estimate that only 5,000 plants have been analysed so far, so you can see how much work there is to be done.'

He was off immediately to Mali for a study tour. I said I'd go with him to the station. I've driven most of the 1,300 kilometres from Bamako across the desert to Dakar, but I've never been by train. One day, I thought, it might be fun, but not with an American ethnobotanist. We continued our discussion.

'For centuries the Filipinos treated diabetes with a brew based on the rosy periwinkle,' he said. 'We did some research on it and discovered that no way could it cure diabetes, but two of its seventy-five alkaloids have given us a hell of a lead in fighting leukaemia in children and other forms of cancer.'

From the outside, the tiny railway station looks more like an elegant town hall in a village miles from nowhere. Inside, of course, it goes to the middle of nowhere: to Djourbel; Glssas; across the Sine-Saloum and through the middle of Senegal's peanut farm; to Tambacounda, the capital of the eastern region; to Kayes, the ancient capital of Upper Senegal, to Kita; to Negala; to Kati; and finally to Bamako.

Everybody had told us the train left at ten a.m. but the ticket office was closed when we got there just after nine. I looked for a timetable but couldn't find one. Two old Muslims were staring at a brick wall saying their prayers. Three old ladies were sitting on chairs in the centre of the tiny entrance hall. I couldn't see any staff anywhere. Just like British Rail, I thought. Didn't know they had a consultancy contract with Senegal.

We wandered outside into the car park. Nobody around. We sat on a bench.

'So what about crooks and charlatans? Surely the traditional medicine business is full of them.' I asked. I'd seen doctors giving women rings to wear on their fingers to prevent them from getting pregnant.

'Don't worry,' they had told them, 'it doesn't have any side effects.'

'But will it work?' I asked the doctors.

'We have been using this method for centuries,' they told me.

'Of course there are crooks and charlatans,' he said. 'There are in every branch of medicine.'

'So how can you control them?'

'Training. Raising standards. It will come eventually.'

It was getting hot, so I walked back inside the station. Even the Muslims and the old ladies had disappeared. When I went back to the bench the American had also disappeared. Probably eaten the wrong herbs. I sat down. For the first time I noticed how many horses there are in Dakar pulling carts with rubber tyres and loaded with sand, cement, piles of wood, scrap metal. What's more I realised that all the horses appeared well-fed and looked after, not like in Egypt or other parts of North Africa.

In the north of the country animals are very badly treated, according to the Association pour la Protection des Animaux de Sénégal. But here all the animals seem well cared for. Fat, lazy cats lounge around; the dogs are well-groomed with beautiful wet noses. I've even seen Senegalese and French take their dogs to church. Even the strays around the port look healthy. There would be no work for eccentric English spinsters in Dakar. And, it would seem, no work for train drivers either.

Which is strange, because at one time it looked as if Africa was made for trains and trains for Africa. All those towns with empty spaces in between; ideal for railway lines. Cecil Rhodes dreamt of building a railway from Cairo to Cape Town. The nearest his dream came to reality was when Kitchener built over 200 miles of track across the desert in just five months in 1897 to outmanoeuvre the Sudanese and the French, especially at Fashoda. The French wanted to outmanoeuvre the British and build a line from Dakar to Djibouti so they could flood the market with French goods. Judging by the service in Dakar it's as well they didn't, although other parts of Africa have benefited from having their own railway. Zimbabwe, Botswana, Swaziland, Namibia, Mozambique, Malawi and, of course, South Africa all have their own rail networks, some more efficient than others. There is even a rail link from Zaire to Tanzania and from Zaire to Angola. From time to time the West Africans talk about railways, but nothing much happens.

Another quick check inside. Still no sign of life. I got out my history book. Senegal was discovered in the fifteenth century by the Portuguese, who explored inland as far as the Felou falls in a vain search for gold. In 1659 the Compagnie Normande founded the city now called St Louis. Shortly afterwards another French trading company started occupying coastal towns such as Joal and Rufisque. Come the Revolution and Napoleonic Wars, the French were thrown out by the British, but in 1818 they were back, and this time they decided to open up the interior with an expedition led by Molliers, one of their great explorers, who quickly discovered the source of the Senegal River.

Plans were drawn up for enormous plantations of ground-nuts, cotton and indigo. A governor, Colonel Schmaltz, was appointed to oversee operations with a host of advisers. More land was leased from the Wolof people. Experimental farms and gardens were planted. Because of problems with local labour, including most of the local prison population, the French drafted in other prisoners from Martinique. The Trazas on the right bank of the Senegal then maintained the Wolof had no right to lease their land to the French and started raiding farms in a bid to drive them out. Eventually they succeeded, with the aid of the shortcomings of the labour force as well as the climate.

The French turned to what they thought was a less risky business – gun-running, with a bit of trade thrown in to make it look respectable. But still they faced problems. The Trazas established alliances with the local kingdoms and virtually surrounded the French, who now had to face attacks on all fronts. Al-Hajj Umar, a flamboyant soldier-scholar, then tried to establish a Muslim empire, and for a while the French feared he would launch all-out war on the French infidels. The French were in two minds. One half, led by the governor, wanted to attack Umar and his followers before he became too powerful. The other half advised a low profile, heads down and fingers crossed. Not because it was sound diplomacy but because the French Treasury was too broke to finance even a token show of force.

Then Louis Faidherbe arrived on the scene. He understood Africa and the Africans. He was strict, but he was fair. If he is not the patron saint of French colonial administration he should be. First he founded a school for interpreters. Second, he instituted an extensive system of public works. The better the French were looked after, the more they would be inclined to stay. Third, he used force when he judged he had to, but in a positive way. He always demonstrated his superiority before rushing into battle. In 1855 he defeated the Walos, and three years later the Trazas. He deposed the Damel of Cayor in 1861, which opened up a direct route between Dakar and St Louis. He built forts at Medina, Joal and Kaolack. He was also very good politically with Umar. Instead of rushing in and trying to destroy him, as many old colonial administrators would have done, he balanced force and reason. Sometimes French forces were attacked and he did not retaliate. Sometimes he fought back, but at the same time called for negotiation. In the end it worked. In 1860 he and Umar peacefully agreed their frontiers and ended what could have degenerated into another long, fruitless battle. The following year Faidherbe left Senegal, which now was stronger, safer and more prosperous. France had established what was to become their strongest foothold in West Africa and their base for a glorious French empire which they hoped would stretch from Senegal to the Nile.

A taxi skidded into the car park. A Frenchman, slightly crumpled, wearing a light suit with a pullover underneath and a straw hat climbed out. 'Has it left? Am I in time?' he shouted.

'Pas de problème,' I replied. 'I'm still waiting.'

'I must get to Glssas today', he explained.

'Nobody goes to Glssas,' I said. 'There's nothing there.'

'There are special herbs there.'

'Why do you want herbs? For traditional medicines?'

'No,' he replied, 'for beer.'

'I didn't know herbs went into beer.'

'They don't. But that's what we are going to put into our beer.'

The little Frenchman in a pullover in a Dakar heatwave turned out to be head brewer at a Strasbourg brewery which had decided to make aphrodisiac beer using herbs from Senegal.

'Our business is falling,' he explained. 'We need more business. It is a good gimmick, n'est-ce pas?'

'Sure. But where are you going to find the herbs?'

'I have books about traditional African aphrodisiacs. I'm going to follow them.'

I suddenly heard a creaking from inside the station, and

leapt up. 'The train!' I said. We ran inside. There was no train. Only a tall, thin Senegalese in a white suit.

'Excusez-moi, monsieur,' shouted the brewer, 'can you tell me the time of the next train to Bamako?'

'It was cancelled last night,' he said. 'There were lions on the track at Kayes.'

'But why didn't you tell us?' I said.

'We told everybody last night.'

'Why didn't you leave a notice saying it had been cancelled?'

'Because we told everybody last night. We didn't want them wasting their time at the station if there wasn't going to be a train,' he replied oh-so-calmly and logically. 'At your service, monsieur,' he added, bowed gently and melted into the heat. We returned to the bench.

'Fancy a beer?' said the Frenchman. We went to the Hôtel Atlantique off the place de l'Indépendance. There, sitting at the bar sipping a glass of champagne, was guess-who.

At conferences; at seminars; once at a briefing on the Lomé Convention in Brussels; in Paris; in London; in New York; again in Paris; and again in Paris; and again in Paris: wherever I seemed to go, there was Mr Diouf. The moustache, the perm, the Yves St Laurent suits, Giorgio Armani sunglasses. Once in London he wore them in winter. To avoid being recognised.

He told me he was a special adviser to the president – President Diouf. He had a government house in the government compound or, I suppose, estate on the edge of Dakar. Everything was paid for: rent, electricity, food and drink. Or at least the basic food and drink. Whenever a government minister travelled anywhere, Mr Diouf could go with him: whenever a government plane travelled anywhere, he could hitch a lift. If the president travelled, Mr Diouf was up there at the front of the plane with him. As a result, he said he didn't have to go out of his way to be recognised, known or remembered by anyone. It was for others to recognise, know and remember him. This applied to everyone from presidents and prime ministers to hotel porters and head waiters. He would arrive in a country just knowing that he was going to be met by a car and chauffeur, if not by the big chief himself. If it was a small, struggling, developing country he would be happy to be met by a chauffeur. If it was a large, dynamic, go-ahead country, even one of the world's largest economies, he expected the president or, failing him, the prime minister to meet him. If they didn't turn up, he took it as a sign of their inadequacy, their lack of breeding and the fact that they were not privileged to be born Senegalese.

Introduce him to a British government minister, it didn't mean a thing. 'Not serious,' he would whisper. Fix a meeting with an American multi-multi-billionaire to talk about investing in Senegal: 'No culture,' he would whisper. 'I cannot talk to him.'

But wherever I saw him, in the Hotel Crillon, in the Hotel Raphael at the top of the Champs Elysées, in the Grill Room at the Savoy, in Simpsons, in New York, or in virtually any bar in Paris, he always managed to have an empty glass – not of water, or Coke, but an empty glass of champagne. He was obviously convinced that under the terms of the Lomé Convention, the EC was eager, with the financial support of the British taxpayer, to transfer French agricultural products to the ACP countries. And he was determined to do everything he could to assist them.

Like Louis XIV, you could just tell he preferred to eat surrounded by sumptuous gold and silver plate, tureens and candlesticks from Thomas and François-Thomas Germain, Sèvres porcelain and snow-white, hand-woven tablecloths; preferably in a room decorated with famous paintings and old prints and lit by a ten-metre-high column of candles. It took some effort, therefore, to get him to go into most London restaurants; he was convinced they served either cold quiche oozing with monosodium glutamate, or half-cold casseroles, with a fork stuck on top still gunged up with yesterday's shepherd's pie.

Wherever I took him, as soon as we sent through the door he seemed to know what was wrong with them. Whether they kept live lobsters in the kitchen to ensure they were as fresh as possible, or tried to pass off microwaved frozen lobster as fresh; which restaurants served fresh oysters and which ones opened them the previous day and kept them in the fridge. In one very famous fish restaurant in St James's, he told me the oysters had been frozen overnight. We didn't ask the manager because we both knew he would never tell us the truth. Instead we asked one of the Moroccan waiters and he admitted it straight away. The reason, he said, was that it was the chef's night off. The assistant chef couldn't open oysters without cracking the shells, so they were all opened the night before – and kept in the fridge.

The other problem was that he always wanted a lime and raspberry sorbet after the first course and a salad after the second to cleanse the palate. Which is fine in a poor, destitute, uncivilised country like Senegal – but try asking for a sorbet in London, or even a salad after the second course; you'll soon see which one is uncivilised.

Mr Diouf was very keen to talk – about politics, about literature, about philosophy, about poetry. And, of course, about food. He had a very good grasp of English – but refused to let go of it. Once he started there was no stopping him. Words would spurt out in all directions and fall in great mounds at your feet. That is, he didn't so much speak as hand down statements and pronouncements with all the authority of a General de Gaulle coming down from the mountains after he had given himself the nine commandments. The French never accept what anybody says. They only accept what they want to accept. So invariably, from the moment we met, it was one up to him and two down to me. I offered to pay the bills. Which in most cases meant opening a special line of credit with the Export Credit Guarantee Department.

Does development mean death and destruction for the people it is supposed to help? Is mass tourism harmful? What is free trade? Do multinationals deliberately make people want the things they cannot have? Do Green policies create more problems for farmers than solutions for city dwellers? Can developing countries ever get a fair deal for their raw materials? Is French post-structuralism dead? Is it right to see women's knees?

We would debate for hours on end whether in developing countries only authoritarian governments can build the institutions they require, liberalise the economies and create the educated middle class vital for successful democracy.

'Yes, they will eventually agree,' he would say.

'So why haven't you done it in Senegal?'

'Senegal is different.'

Then we're off again for another three-hour debate about why the president, the guardian of the constitution, appoints the leader of the opposition to a government post; why the president's brother is a minister and what his wife, Madame Diouf, is doing in all those construction companies. Then it would be integral multi-partyism.

'We believe in integral multi-partyism.'

'You mean democracy.'

'No.'

'You're not democrats!'

'No. We believe in a deeper form of democracy than you. Democracy is too precious to be put in the hands of people who do not appreciate it.'

Then off we'd go again, citing one political tract after another. Although as far as he was concerned the most important tract in the world was his dietary tract. He knew everything but everything there was to know about food, and would talk about it for even longer.

In Simpsons he told me the best beef was Aberdeen Angus reared in the highlands of Scotland. The iodine and salt in the sea, mixed with the nitrates in the soil, produced the best grass for fattening up pure pedigree cattle.

In the Savoy I learnt the best way to caramelise breast of pigeon and whether you should have salad during or after the main course.

In New York, I discovered which side of the bed the best oysters come from and who wrote a poem to a tripe sausage (Charles Monselet).

In Paris, he waxed lyrical about horsemeat and songbird cassoulet and insisted, but insisted, the next time I had sheep's feet in white sauce I washed it down with a 1970 Haut-Brion.

'We French,' he would say, 'we live to eat. You British, you just want to eat quickly so you can watch football.'

And because he was obsessed with food, he spoke English as if he had learnt it by studying menus and wine lists rather than boring old textbooks. Politics was always 'robust, clean and well-balanced'. Government policies were always 'firm and definite, no hint of a compromise'. Politicians had a 'big, powerful presence', and were 'supple with an assertive tone'. And as for 'well-rounded, fruity, soft and fleshy' I forget now who he was talking about. At least, I hope I do. On one glorious occasion in the middle of Simpsons he told the waiter he wanted to press me to a French tart.

When he wasn't eating and drinking with me, which was most of the time he was in London, he was eating and drinking with somebody else. Once I met him wandering across Piccadilly. He was as pleased as punch. He told me he had discovered a rare new delicacy. It was beautiful, he said. It was soft. It was succulent. It was exotic. It was one of the greatest dishes he had ever tasted in his life.

'What was it?' I asked.

'Airustu,' he said triumphantly.

Airustu? Airustu? Months later, it suddenly hit me. For him one of the greatest dishes in the world was Irish stew.

I shall always be grateful to Mr Diouf. He taught me a lot. Before I met him I thought good restaurants were those where the bill for the booze was more than twice the bill for the food. Now I know different. It's where the bill for the booze is more than three times the bill for the food.

Beirut

It's unbelievable. A whole city completely destroyed. Not a single building still standing. Nothing but great heaps of rubble and mounds of soil. No roads, no streets: all gone. Just tracks in the dust and sand. And it's not just some small patch of ground, it's building after building, street after street, for miles and miles and miles. It's like, say, the whole of the West End of London or Manhattan or the heart of Paris completely taken out. Flattened. Not just the bland, faceless office blocks that we would all like to see destroyed, but restaurants, hotels, casinos, bars, cinemas, apartments. It's staggering. Some say in all there was maybe US$35–40 billion of damage.

On television, during the war, you got the impression that, sure, there was fighting; sure, there were plenty of guns going off; sure, there was a lot of damage. But no way did I ever imagine it covered such an enormous area and involved such total destruction. I had the impression it was a bit like, say, New York, Naples, Belfast, Scotswood, Newcastle or even, I suppose, the Moulescombe estate outside Brighton. But for grown-ups.

I had no idea of the scale or the intensity of the destruction until I went there. I also had no idea of how fast they are rebuilding it. But then, the Lebanese don't exactly believe in sitting around chained to their desks, let alone their radiators. If anybody has experience running countries they have; after all, they are running so many other countries around the world. Well, maybe not officially. But from the office next door, if you see what I mean. Running their own country is a day job.

My first visit I shall never forget. Mortars were raining down on Heathrow. Northern Ireland was still red hot. I'd been thrown off the tube three times in a week – twice Victoria Station had been cleared because of a bomb scare, the Central Line had been shut down once. I'd just come back from New York. I was talking to clients about possible trips to El Salvador, Nicaragua and Vietnam.

'Unfortunately,' I began, as we all do when we're forced to go off on a trip, 'unfortunately. It's the last thing I—'

'Where to this time?' my wife said, in that tone adopted by all wives who for some reason or other think their husbands like nothing better than travelling the world, staying in luxury hotels, eating in expensive restaurants and generally having one hell of a time.

'Beirut,' I mumbled.

'Will it be safe?' she said – was that a glint in her eye?

In fact it was a million times safer than staying at home. Which was just as well because I don't for one moment think she'd campaign to get me released, if I was kidnapped, blindfolded and chained to Terry Waite for five years.

The guns and bombs and mortars had stopped. Vast areas were still sealed off, however. The lights kept going out. The water supplies were not always reliable. Occasionally the champagne was not quite as chilled as perhaps it should have been. There was still obviously an acute shortage of razor blades. But Beirut was on its way back.

The eighteen years of civil war between the Western-oriented Christians in East Beirut and the Eastern-oriented Muslims in West Beirut was over, largely because the Christians and/or the Muslims lost, leaving the Christians and/or the Muslims or, if you prefer, the Muslims and/or the Christians running the place. Which, I hope, is clear. Because I'm not going to say another word for fear of starting the whole thing off again. What's more the president, who is a Maronite Christian, the prime minister, who is a Sunni Muslim, the parliamentary speaker, who is a Shi'ite Muslim, and the chief of the armed forces, who is a Druze, agree with me. I think.

Syrian troops were everywhere. All 40,000 of them. Loung-
ing on tanks near that third pile of rubble on the right just past
what used to be Martyr's Square where it all began over twenty
years ago. Sleeping on metal beds in bombed-out buildings
near the lighthouse. Or listening to the radio in a tent high up
in some bombed-out building overlooking the beach.

On the outskirts of Bir al-Abed, the Iranian-backed Hezbol-
lah district, they seemed to be marginally a little more alert.
Out of three soldiers, one might from time to time pick up his
gun and wander along the street. But you can't criticise them.
Their mere presence, and perhaps a lot of behind-the-scenes
negotiation, has meant peace. Would that they could have the
same influence in other parts of the world. Maybe they should
take over from the United Nations peacekeeping forces in
Bosnia, Somalia, or wherever. They have certainly been a big
success in Beirut. Nobody can argue about that. I shall send a
postcard to BBG, as his friends call him in the Middle East –
Boutros Boutros Ghali, Secretary-General of the United
Nations, to you and me.

Beirut being Beirut, nobody was scared of the soldiers. Cab
drivers were already working out short cuts that involved
driving across bomb sites, doing U-turns in bomb craters and
dodging between buildings that looked as though they were
about to fall down. Especially those along what was the third
street on the right past the Syrian checkpoint near that pile of
rubble near . . . You know the one I mean. As for traffic lights,
good God they didn't take any notice of the guns, are they
going to take any notice of the traffic lights, whether they were
working or not?

'Traffic lights. Why I take notice of traffic lights?' they all say.
'In the war, you stop at traffic light, boom you're dead. Now
you want me to stop and boom I'm dead? No, I no stop at
traffic light.'

Then, with their hand still on the wheel, the car doing,
what, forty-five, maybe fifty along this potholed street in the
pitch dark somewhere between two enormous heaps of
rubble somewhere at the back of, was it Martyr's Square, they

turn right round and look you straight between the eyes.

'You want me to stop at traffic light? Yes?'

'No, no, no. Not me.' You try to keep calm. 'It's just that – I mean – at that other – we did just miss—'

'I stop. You want me . . .'

'. . . that truck by . . .'

'. . . stop . . .?'

'. . . inches . . .'

Still you're tearing along in the pitch black in the middle of nowhere. In what could still be . . . no, of course not. All that kind of thing has stopped. Trying to forget about the school bus which went careering through a red light straight into the side of a brand new Peugeot 504 the other day. The driver of the car got out, went straight up to the driver of the school bus and, in front of all the children, shot him stone cold dead. Then he got in his car and drove off. Probably not stopping at the traffic lights either, I wouldn't have thought.

'No, no, no,' you scream. 'Next time. Next lights. Zoom.' You shoot your hands across the centre of the car. 'No problem.'

As for the bars and restaurants and clubs, they were all opening up in true Lebanese style, including a new pizza parlour in what used to be the Soviet cultural centre, although who pays rent to whom, in what currency and where, I have no idea. There were even rumours about trying to re-open, as a matter of priority, the once legendary Casino du Liban. Ask anyone about the good old days at the Casino du Liban and tears come to their eyes – and mine. I only wish I had been there. Instead, for my sins, I was dragging myself up and down the M1 to Leeds of all places. Which proves to you how grievously I have sinned.

'OK,' the driver finally takes you out of his sights and turns back to the wheel. 'You're the boss. You say, zoom.' He zooms both hands backwards and forwards across the windscreen. 'We zoom through lights.' He pauses. 'But if police stop me, I tell them you said zoom zoom. I'm taxi man. You're boss. Right?'

'Right,' you mumble, searching for the worry beads, I mean, rosary, I mean hanging on to the seat in front for grim death.

On the outskirts there is more happening – because there was less damage.

'Everyone lived in the outskirts during the war,' a Lebanese businessman told me as we sat in his penthouse office surveying the whole area down to the sea. 'Even the fighters. They used to go into Beirut during the day, do their fighting, then come home again at night – to the outskirts. That's why they left the outskirts alone.'

Hotels have re-opened. Some are slightly faded and damaged, some have been beautifully refurbished. Shops have re-opened. There are even plans to build big US-style shopping malls.

'Rebuilding the centre of Beirut is one thing, but we must make certain we don't lose the business we built up during the war,' is what everybody says in the outskirts. Typical Beirut.

Whether you're in the centre or on the outskirts you only have to stay for, say, five days and you can see the rebuilding actually happening before your very eyes, as they say.

Shaky old buildings are torn down, streets cleared of rubble – some large-scale work, some small-scale. Everywhere the place is alive to the sound of jackhammers, pneumatic drills and the constant rev of enormous dump trucks.

It can only be a matter of time before Beirut is once again the business, financial and fun centre of the Middle East. Who'll take 100–1 that it will be back in business in three years? Loser buys the first round at the Casino du Liban on opening night.

Day one

'Tony, he go boom boom. Josef he go boom boom. War.' Ahmed, a fat, grizzled old taxi driver with feathers on the bonnet of his battered old cab and dead flowers inside it, told me with a cackle as we bumped along Hamra Street, the tiny narrow street that was once the ultimate in fashion.

'I have family. They go boom boom. I get gun. I go boom boom.'

Near the Maronite church, a big blue Mercedes somehow squeezes up alongside us. It's being driven by a woman.

'Moment,' he says and somehow lifts himself out of the seat, pushes his grizzled old head with its drooping moustache out of the window and practically into the window of the Mercedes to check out her legs.

We bounce along towards the American University.

'Good for me,' he says as he pulls himself back into the car. 'Good for me.' He looks at his watch which looks like an imitation Omega but is probably genuine. 'And still only seven o'clock.'

The Lebanese are among the most civilised, cultured, pleasant, hardworking, efficient people on earth. They are the great fixers, the arrangers, the guys who oil the wheels, get things – everything – done. Quickly; quietly; to the eminent satisfaction of all concerned. Lebanese is, in fact, the Arabic word for middlemen.

I've seen them all over Africa, especially in Côte d'Ivoire, which is supposed to have the biggest group of ex-pat Lebanese in the world. Their unofficial, unelected leader there was George Ouagnie, for years the confidant, doctor and right-hand man of the old president, Houphouet-Boigny. He was always at his master's right hand: at international conferences; at official receptions; tottering backwards and forwards to the presidential jets. And afterwards at Ouagnie's right hand were . . . Shall I go on?

I've seen Lebanese in Sierra Leone, which is so rich and so poor it breaks your heart. So rich because there are diamonds literally everywhere – scratch the dust and you find enough diamonds to buy a hundred pairs of shoes. But so poor, because the whole business is way beyond government's control. Licensing, legislation, all the mechanisms necessary for an orderly, effective system which would regulate the business, pump money into the government's echoing coffers and provide at least some food, some basic health care and some hope for the people are all out of the window. So who controls the whole thing? Who runs all the buying and selling, all the shipping in and out and all the pricing? Say no more.

Wherever they are, they are the guys who make it happen.

It's the National Day. The military parade is about to start. Who is that sitting just behind the president on the dais? You got it. And where is the British ambassador? Right again.

Wait one hour, two hours outside a minister's office in Africa, South America, Eastern Europe. Who comes out but a Lebanese, shaking hands, smoothing down his sleek black hair and smiling sweetly.

'A votre disposition,' he murmurs soothingly. 'Toujours.'

Or, at the other extreme. You're in a Lebanese restaurant anywhere in the world. You've run out of the local currency. 'No problem, sir. You have dollars, we take dollars. You have pounds, we take pounds. You have French francs, we take French francs. No problem.'

Imagine a similar thing in London. Once I was forced to pay a cab fare with Scottish pound notes. You'd have thought I was trying to give the driver counterfeit, radioactive Mozambiquean ten-bob notes injected with the bubonic plague the fuss he made about it.

Some people are, how shall I say, less than complimentary about the Lebanese. Not me. Sure, they take a slice of everything they handle, or think of handling. But at least they make things happen. They live in places and endure conditions that nobody else would even consider. Maybe they don't deserve the huge sums they often take. But at least they have helped, say, Africans get things done when nobody else was even prepared to listen. That deserves some reward. But how they could possibly have torn each other to pieces in a civil war that lasted eighteen whole years, I do not understand. One or two years, maybe. Everybody gets mad with somebody sometimes. But eighteen years is a whole generation. It's unbelievable. Especially for a nation of fixers. My theory is that they did it deliberately so that they would all pick up enormous contracts to build the place all over again.

How many contracts there are to go around – and how much commission there will be – is staring you in the face wherever you go. Most buildings are pockmarked. There are whole chunks missing from offices and blocks of flats. In some cases you just see a great gash; in others, you see the great gash, then loads of planks nailed somehow to the crumbling concrete. Behind the planks you see paraffin lamps and whole families still trying to survive in the rubble.

Along the streets you see large mounds of soil thrown up by the bombs, rubbish and debris created by explosions, and more rubbish and debris created by the rubbish and debris that is already there. The cinemas and hotels and bars all around Martyr's Square, the once swinging centre of Beirut, are practically flattened to the ground. One shattered skeleton is still standing on one corner. There is the wreck of another building on the other side. The rest is simply a pile of rubble.

In the old days, Beirut was France; no, not France, it was Paris; no, not Paris, it was the Left Bank in the sunshine. The hotels were French-style, French standard with, as they say, French sophistication. The corniche was Nice. Some say better than Nice. Les boîtes de nuit – no. I can't even think about it – and that's only what I've read.

We drive down a street with, on one side, the shattered remnants of once-fashionable shops and apartments. The other side is a mass of potholes, rubble, sand.

We drive along the Green Line, the dividing line between the two sides (not that there are two sides any more) then straight on through the busiest street in town. There are shops and offices on both sides as well as plenty of banks and apartment buildings. Most buildings you can see were affected by the fighting, there are giant pockmarks everywhere, but few were completely destroyed.

In addition to the Syrians, there are other uniforms and tin hats and berets all over the place: Lebanese military, Lebanese police, United Nations. In fact, the most aggressive seem to be the UN, at least when it comes to trying to get through traffic jams. They sound their horns; hands appear from every window of whatever vehicle they are in, waving at the traffic to let them pass. Of course it doesn't make a blind bit of difference. No way is any driver going to give way to the United Nations. Governments might, but out on the streets we're all equal. Yet they keep on blasting their horns and waving. Which probably tells us more about the UN than it does about Beirut.

We drove back along that third street on the right, past the Syrian checkpoint near that big pile of rubble near that medium-size pile of rubble. You know the one I mean. The pavements have been cleared of rubble. Admittedly most of it has been shovelled or bulldozed back into the derelict buildings, but at least the pavements are now clear.

Later that evening in the bar, over arak and champagne, I am talking to a French businessman who says that Beirut is one of the best, pleasantest, most civilised places on earth. Because there is not an American in sight. It's on their list of forbidden countries. While they are allowed to tramp all over China, which has done all kinds of things to all kinds of countries, Lebanon is out of bounds.

I disagree. I tell him I prefer going to countries crawling with Americans. It makes it easier to do business. With the odd exception, Americans rush in, promise the earth then fail to deliver. Which makes things easy for the rest of us.

I can't remember what happened after that.

Day two

We drive past the old American embassy.

'They get car, car goes to embassy. Big boom. That's America a gonna.'

As we pass the old French barracks, another driver tells me, 'They get car. Car goes in, big boom. That's France gone.'

Lebanon got its independence from France in 1943. The Christian Maronites, about half the population, took over.

They immediately set about running the place as a Christian European nation. The Muslims and the rest were out in the cold, even though they had more or less conquered the place well over a thousand years before when they called themselves Phoenicians. Then the trouble began. The British left. The Americans left. The Germans left. Everybody left. Except the French. They stayed. Or, at least, French businessmen and companies stayed. Which immediately gives them an enormous moral, not to mention commercial advantage. And, let's be fair, they deserve it. But now for some unfathomable reason French influence is on its way out. So is Italian. So is Spanish. Coming to the fore, wait for it, are the British. At least that's what the Lebanese say. But try buying an English newspaper in Beirut – there isn't one, while *Le Monde* is everywhere. Try ordering roast lamb and Yorkshire pudding. You'll soon see how much they love the British compared to *les autres*.

I'm in the maze of tiny alleyways just off Hamra Street, wandering up and down looking for a cab. Hey, I've just realised. All those Range Rovers. I've never seen so many in one place before. It must be the most popular car around. I knew there was something unusual about the place, but I couldn't quite make it out. They ought to put their Lebanese agent in charge of worldwide sales. They'd overtake every other car on the market within three weeks. Happy dreams.

Still no cab. That shows you how busy it is. A car stops in the street beside me. The driver, who looks like a retired kidnapper, asks where I want to go. 'No problem, sir. I take you there. Jump in, please.'

I must admit, I hesitated. I didn't really fancy getting the Terry Waite Award for Taking Unnecessary Risks. But in the end I got in. The driver, who I now realise is a kind, considerate man who obviously loves dogs, looks after his mother and is nice to foreigners in distress, takes me straight there. I ask him how much.

'No, no, sir. It is gift. I help you. A good day, sir.'

On the way back, I notice somebody along my favourite

street has cleared out part of a shop front and is selling soap.

Day three

Outside the hotel, I spot the world's greatest living expert on the Middle East. I had met him on the way to Beirut, in Vienna, where he gave me the benefit of his 153 years' experience selling red-and-white checked tablecloths to the Arabs.

When I first saw him he was jumping up and down in front of the departures board cursing everything east of Leeds. 'Look.' He jabbed his finger up at the board. 'Aleppo. That must be German for Delayed.'

I decide to dodge up the sidestreet to avoid him, and ended up near the American University. All along the street almost every door and window is advertising or promoting or selling something; ice cream machines, mobile telephones, classical guitars, special lessons given by a medical student, a dental surgeon, a beauty institute, Flora margarine. Everyone is doing some kind of business.

During the war, of course, a lot of business went underground. Literally. The war was so long and so devastating that the Lebanese, being Lebanese, didn't just retreat to their cellars, they enlarged them, reinforced them and turned them into upside-down office blocks.

Many's the time I've wandered around an enormous pile of rubble with a business card in one hand and my briefcase in the other looking for the front door. Once I was wandering up and down the third track on the right after that pile of concrete blocks just past the spot where the Syrians always stop you and ask where you are going. There was nothing but derelict, bomb-shattered buildings all around me – not a front door or street number in sight. A bit like New York. A gleaming new silver-grey Mercedes swung round the corner on to the rubble. What made the driver, an elderly, smooth Lebanese, wind down his window and ask if I was lost I cannot imagine. I showed him the business card and explained my dilemma.

'Jump in,' he said. 'I'm going there myself. I'll take you with me.' I jumped in. 'Put your seatbelt on,' he said. 'Otherwise the police will think you're a car bomber looking for a quick escape.'

He swung the car off what was once a road and drove gingerly between piles of rubble which were once a prestigious office building, then straight down a great hole in the ground. There beneath the rubble was the company I had been looking for. They had built a three-storey-deep bomb-proof shelter. On the top floor was the car park. On the second floor were their administrative offices. On the bottom was the director's suite. It was just like any other office, with computers and coffee machines, telephones and a television set. The only thing they didn't seem to have was rubber plants in the reception area. Which is probably what enabled them to continue operating successfully throughout the war.

At lunchtime, as we drove back down that street to the hotel, I noticed a young man repairing a burst waterpipe that looked as if it had been running since the very first day of the civil war; four of the gaping apartments on the first floor had been boarded up, admittedly with rough old timber; people had apparently moved in. This was better than *The Archers*.

At lunch I'm with a group of old Lebanese businessmen. They start boasting of their old nightclubs the way other countries boast of their cultural heritage, their churches or, if they're Americans, the size of their baseball stadiums or shopping malls. 'Hey buddy, put all our shopping malls together and they would fill half of Wisconsin. Hey, I just knew you wouldn't a known that,' a proud American shopkeeper in Champaign, Illinois told me once.

But ask old Beirut hands what it was like in the old days, and their eyes will mist over. They will smile that smile of utter happiness. They will take a quick deep breath and say . . . Well, nothing actually. They shake their heads; if they are Lebanese they will shake you by the hand and whisper slowly, 'My boy. My boy. Ah . . . if only . . . Listen, I can tell you. Never in my life . . .' Or they will mutter, 'Unbelievable. Do you know I still even now dream of . . .' They will wave their hands in the air, then collapse into the nearest chair where they will sit for the rest of the day gazing vacantly at their memories.

The nearest I've ever come to Beirut's nightlife was a travel agent I had years ago who played football for an airline team. Wherever in the world they played they used to win – except in Beirut.

'It was fantastic,' he would burble. 'I only used to wake up when they blew the whistle for the second half.' That's all he would say.

On a trip to Jakarta I met a Dutchman who went on and on about Beirut in the old days and the things people used to get up to with swans and donkeys and goats dressed in velvet. Swans? Goats? Donkeys? I tried to express what I thought was the mildest form of surprise.

'Sure,' he said. 'Why not? Frederick the Great once discovered one of his cavalrymen had formed a somewhat unnatural attachment with his mare. He had him thrown out of the cavalry. He said a man like that should be in the infantry.'

Gee, and I used to think the Colony Room in Soho was daring, with its louche collection of dipsomaniacs, cross-dressers and Robin Douglas-Home relating stories about playing the piano for Princess Margaret in the nude.

I never go to nightclubs, in Beirut or anywhere else. Well, apart from maybe the occasional visit when I'm forced into it. I don't really know much about them. But if I ever find out about the ones in Beirut in the old days, I promise you'll be the first to know.

That evening, at a reception up in the hills way out of town, I met an old Lebanese ambassador who told me again about how during the war nobody lived in the centre of Beirut; everybody lived outside. In the morning they would come in from the suburbs, the Christians from Jounieh to the north and the Muslims from the south. They would fight like mad. In the evening they would go home again.

'Jounieh,' he said. 'You should have seen Jounieh. During the war, it was beautiful. The hotels, bars, clubs, casinos.

We've never seen so much money. Now,' he shrugged, 'it is a disaster. There's no money, no people. The hotels and bars, they are closing. The casinos close. The peace – it is not good for us.'

'So where did all the terrorists go when they stopped fighting?'

He shrugged again. 'Back home. Back to their jobs. Making money.'

My guess is they all got jobs as taxi drivers or merchant bankers.

My confidence boosted by accepting lifts from total strangers in bombed-out areas, I decide to go for the Terry Waite Award for Taking Precautions. I decide not to get the official bus back from the reception to the hotel; instead, I hail a cab. I want to see how they are getting on along my favourite street.

'If you get hijacked,' says one of my so-called colleagues, 'it's your own fault. I'm not going round to your place every week to cut the grass.'

Day four

In Beirut everyone wants to make money. Everyone is looking for a deal. Everyone wants to do business – any kind of business, any which way you like: the waiters at the hotel; the manager at reception; the guys who call the cabs; the cab drivers; people you bump into in the street.

You're trying to get through to someone on the telephone. You get a wrong number, which is not difficult, and instead of shouting at each other you end up doing a deal. You're in a lift going up to a meeting. The lift stops at three floors. By the time everybody gets out they've done half a dozen deals. Meet somebody at a meeting. By the time you get back to your hotel, he is waiting for you. He's got a better idea. Do it his way and you'll both end up making more money.

I've got to go to Tripoli, up in the north. In the old days you could take the train along the coast, which must have been spectacular. But no more. Before we set off, I drive along you know where. A young boy is sitting by the edge of a pile of rubble. In front of him is a pair of bathroom scales. He is charging people for weighing themselves.

Tripoli, the second largest city and the sweet capital of the country, doesn't seem to know whether it wants to be one thing or the other. Old men were smoking their hubbly-bubblies or playing what looked like a grown-up version of draughts, slapping the pieces on the board whenever they made a move. Little boys were dragging huge bags full of empty Pepsi cans across the streets. Wherever I went the shops and offices seemed to be barricaded behind huge steel doors. I went to one company selling paint. I promise you it would have been easier getting into the Bank of England than into their storeroom. But it was worth it. While I was waiting for them to open the steel doors, I picked up a newspaper lying on a desk. The front page headline said 'Iraqi head seeks arms'.

Yet for their flats and houses they had no security at all.

'Twenty-four hours a day, you call me. No problem. In the office, at home, no problem. We do business together. Yes.' Everybody says the same thing. Trouble is, if you do business on your terms they send you a bunch of flowers. Do business on their terms and you get a big hug and a kiss as well.

We decided to do the next best thing: have lunch. We went to this fantastic, obviously traditional Lebanese restaurant on the edge of a housing estate, the kind of place you usually find Chinese restaurants. But inside it was spectacular. An enormous room, all the trimmings, tremendous service. And as for the food, we had lamb – starting with its feet and ending up with its eyes, ears, nose and throat. There was just one dish I didn't recognise. Foolishly I asked what it was.

'That's its spinal cord,' the waiter said.

I never learn.

The guy in the paint business told me he was also bringing in secondhand cars: BMWs, Mercedes, Peugeots, and for some reason white Jaguars from all over Europe.

'Secondhand or stolen?'

He grinned. 'In this country they are secondhand.'

'But in Europe they are stolen.'

Secondhand or stolen, they are a steal. On almost any backstreet in Beirut you can pick up any halfway decent car for around US$2,000–3,000. Which is amazing. But be warned: the police have a list of every stolen car in the country. A top UN official was arrested trying to ship his Mercedes back home. It was on the police computer file.

Over more strange-looking dishes, he told me he was buying an apartment on the famous Corniche in Beirut for US$700,000. But he was going to tell the taxman it only cost US$7,000.

I laughed. 'You'll never get away with it. Such a big difference. They'll—'

'But I have lots of cars,' he smiled.

Some politicians, he told me, were making so much money from drugs – he called them narco-politicians – that they were also buying property along the Corniche for US$1 million and claiming it was only worth US$100,000. If they could get away with it, so could he.

On the way back I had time to spare, so I went to the big new cathedral of Notre Dame, high in the hills overlooking Jounieh. On the way I stopped at a tiny church, no bigger than a large garage. It was obviously old, although it looked as if the stone had recently been sanded down. There was an old lady sitting at the back. I asked her how old the church was.

'You visit Lebanon, yes?'

'Yes, I'm here for a few days. I was . . .'

'You stay in Beirut?'

'Yes. But I was wondering if—'

'You like Beirut?'

'Yes, I do, very much, but I was . . .'

'I have land. You see this land.' She waved out of the chapel door across to the Mediterranean.

'Yes, very nice. But tell me, do you—'

'I sell land. You want land. I sell to you.'

'No. No thank you, I'm . . .'

'I give you good price.'

'Is it, what, a hundred—'

She put her arm around mine. 'We do business, yes. Good price. I give you . . .'

I never did find out how old it was. But I learnt never again to talk to old ladies in churches. I reckon I was there well over an hour. She showed me the chapel. Then we waddled across the road and looked at the church and the church buildings opposite. We sat down together in some kind of covered shelter. All the time she was pushing the land she had for sale. How it was beautiful. How you could build things on it; a hotel, shops, apartments. How, above all, she would let me have it for a good, a very good price.

I get back to the hotel. A poor, pathetic skeleton of a figure is huddled up on the steps. It suddenly occurs to me that after eighteen years of civil war you would have thought you wouldn't be able to move for people begging for money, for people chasing you down the street on their crutches, for even, as you find all over Africa and India, people dragging themselves on dirty planks with three wheels underneath. Not a bit of it. This was the first time anyone had stopped me begging for money. Who was it? An American student. She'd hit hard times. Her parents didn't understand her. Her boy-friend had left her. There was no embassy to go to. It was all the fault of the system. I agreed with her and gave her ten dollars.

In the bar, somebody tells me they are now organising hijacking tours of Beirut: where they were lifted; where they were held; where they were released. Apparently they show you the actual radiator which Terry Waite was chained to for all those years.

Me, I feel sorry for the radiator.

Day five

I have a meeting at Solidere, the US$1.8 billion company set up by the government to rebuild Beirut the private enterprise way, not the government way. Already most of the money has been raised from private investors.

I'm now hooked. I drive along my favourite street. Another old shopfront has not only been cleared out but somebody has painted it white, filled it with refrigerators and is in business. An old man is balancing precariously on top of an extremely dangerous pair of steps painting a sign outside a shop selling furniture. You can bet your life in two days every shop in the block will have a sign. By the end of next week they'll probably all be millionaires.

I have a meeting with one of the old Lebanese ambassadors still on the circuit. We talk about setting up a fund, similar to Solidere, to help finance the industrial development of the country. They even want to build their own Silicon Valley with the help of US-based Lebanese professors, researchers and engineers working in the real-life one in California. I mean, how can they go wrong?

I rush back to the hotel, pack and head for the airport. Except – okay, call me soft – I can't resist a final look at Lazarus Street. A van selling coffee is parked by the pavement. Maybe for only five minutes, maybe for half an hour, but it's another small step forwards. Across the road I can see two men coming out from a building, each carrying something. They turn towards the beach. The taxi draws up alongside them. I can see now. They are carrying fishing rods.

Twenty years to rebuild! These guys will do it in twenty months. Drinks on me at the new Casino du Liban if I'm wrong.

Taipei

Now let's hear it for the Taiwanese, those genuine inventors, wheeler-dealers and scrupulous international businessmen who gave us Rolex watches, number-one-quality Ralph Lauren polo shirts and Ronnie Walker Black Label whisky.

My lords, ladies and gentlemen, if you would please be upstanding, raise your glass of shampagne and join me in a toast to the finest, the most dedicated, the most trustworthy, the most genuine counterfeit nation in the world. Probably since time began; for never before in the history of mankind have so many dodgy products been produced for so many by so few.

Almost as much as they love counterfeiting luxury goods and products, the Taiwanese love drinking toasts. To you; to me; to the future harmony and peace of mankind; to record sales next week, next month, next year. To the Patent Office; to the Fraud Squad; to the manufacturers of long-range telescopes, mini-cameras and photocopying machines.

In offices, with Java coffee (genuine), I have drunk to the integrity of the Taiwanese businessman. In restaurants, over fresh Maine lobsters (genuine) flown in daily direct from the United States (fake), I've drunk to the genius of their creativity. At an official banquet in Taipei, after coronation chicken (some lumps were genuine chicken, some were not), I once drank to the sheer incorruptibility of the Taiwanese with glass after glass of the very best King Victoria Finest Scotchman's Whisko.

Not, of course, that they did anything wrong. Drinking

toasts, I mean. Even to the Patent Office. Or the FBI. But in a world where it is increasingly difficult to know what is genuine and what is not, you just have to admire them for it, don't you? Counterfeiting, I mean.

Not that they call it counterfeiting, of course. Unreal is their word for it. Genuinely.

'The results are real, but the way we get there is unreal,' they will say. Not a few Taiwanese will even admit they are up there at the top because of their unreal skills.

'Unreal, unreal,' I once wondered aloud to a businessman I thought was a genuine Taiwanese friend at the Grand Hotel in Taipei, which is itself a copy of a Chinese palace in the once Forbidden City of Peking. 'Do you say unreal because you know what you make is unreal, therefore bogus, counterfeit . . .?'

Which was when I very quickly realised he wasn't a genuine friend at all. He went bananas (genuine). 'Look at us. In less than ten years we turn shabby, dirty country into one of the world's booming most economies. We build companies that stretch the world. We make product people want. You.' He jabbed an imitation genuine Chinese chopstick at me. 'What you done? What? You tell me.'

Which you must admit is a genuine point. Well, a genuine Taiwanese point. In a Taiwanese sense, of course.

It would be deceptive of me if I did not admit that I've seen plenty of counterfeiting going on all over the world – in Italy, in Yugoslavia, in Lithuania, and in every car boot sale I've ever been to from Edinburgh to Warsaw. Once, up in the Lebanon hills, I looked round this small factory miles from anywhere producing pharmaceuticals. Half a dozen machines were punching out tablets non-stop. Another machine was mixing a gluey, yellow liquid.

'French perfume,' the owner grinned. 'Genuine.'

Further along they were printing boxes which said 'Packed and sealed in France.'

In Kinshasa in Zaire I once met a counterfeiter who was sending his son to Oxford with the money he made dealing in cassettes, watches, even passports.

But the Taiwanese are genuinely the best in the world. Before they got involved and turned their professional skills and dynamism to it, counterfeiting was something cheap and nasty, a backstreet activity for backroom boys. Now they've turned it into an art form, and taken it to undreamt of heights:

– Tear-apart dolls dressed as lawyers, doctors and even – and especially – bank managers that you can tear apart and crush underfoot whenever the real-life equivalent makes you hopping mad.

– A special Mafia crucifix. Ask your victim to kiss the crucifix. Squeeze the sides of the cross. Out of the top shoots a deadly thin stiletto blade. All for just US$9.95.

– Velly funny Chinese puzzles in Christmas crackers like: Q. 15, 27, 33 and 69. What's the odd one out? A. 33; all the others come with rice.

You want half a million of each by lunchtime? No problem. All packed and ready for shipping, with or without the necessary counterfeit customs documentation, shipping papers and false invoices.

Then there is the small stuff. Some people say that computer fraud alone is costing the US around $750 million a year in lost sales. Some computer programmes are on sale in Taiwan and around the world before they have even been released in the US.

'Microsoft were losing so much money here,' an American told me, 'because of counterfeiting – the counterfeit Windows programme was so good it even fooled their own experts – the company decided to put holograms on their products to protect them.' And you can guess what happened. 'They started counterfeiting the holograms.'

In fact, in many cases, the counterfeit is far better than the original; well, if not far better, far better value for money. Ask yourself, what would you prefer to buy for the wife: a £10,000-plus original Rolex, or a £25 counterfeit Rolex which looks practically the same, tells exactly the same time, will last almost as long and leaves you £9,975 in your pocket to spend on whatever the hell you like.

But it's not just Rolex watches, number-one-quality Ralph Lauren polo shirts, Ronnie Walker Black Label and little Scottish dolls which you bang on the head to make their kilt fly up that have contributed to their counterfeiting success. Taiwan also has a black market stock exchange, a black market futures market, a black market foreign exchange market, a black market banking system. Probably the only black market they don't have is a black market black market. If you see what I mean.

Over a third of all private sector lending is black market lending. Many small and medium-size companies in Taiwan never borrow from the banks; they borrow from the black market. Rates are high. Depending on the risk, depending on the security, if any, they could be anything from 6 to 15 per cent – wait for it – a month. Which is not doing anyone any favours. But there is no shortage of business. Partly because the official banking system is so bad. Bankers don't like taking any risks whatsoever; they say they can't rely on the figures they are given. They also don't have any interest, if you see what I mean, in a loan they arrange at work. But a loan arranged by a friend is a different matter.

Then there is the restaurant loan. During one visit I went out to dinner with a Taiwanese businessman, who paid for the meal by credit card. Twice. The first was for the meal. The second was, well, you know. He signed the counterfoil. The restaurant manager gave him a bundle of money. He stuffed the money inside his jacket pocket.

'In England,' I said, 'we normally give the restaurant money for the meal. Here it seems the restaurant gives you money for the meal.'

'Taiwan custom,' he grinned. 'Good for business. Very good.'

Are you ready now? What happens is, the restaurant pretends they provided you with an enormous banquet; they give you the credit card voucher to sign, and you sign it. The restaurant then gives you back half, three-quarters or even the whole amount for the counterfeit meal, depending on how good a customer you are or whether your big brother is bigger than their big brother. Then they bill the credit card company for the total amount. Clever? But just try swinging that one down at your nearest Happy Eater.

Even the entire cable television industry is illegal, and Taiwan has over 400 cable operators, nearly 50 channels and over 2 million subscribers. BBC, CNN, Hong Kong's Star-TV, you name them, they are all in Taiwan, and all have enormous followings. But not one of them, you will not be surprised to hear, is legitimate. The government has never passed legislation giving them permission to operate. Not one television licence has ever been issued. They just installed their cables wherever they wanted. No asking permission or anything. They just stuck them up.

So big are black market activities in Taiwan that most people I spoke to admitted it must genuinely be at least half the official economy. Which must warrant some kind of counterfeit award.

One genuine (I think) US businessman told me that Taiwan was the counterfeit capital of the counterfeit world. Not the real world, because he said the Taiwanese have obviously counterfeited that as well by now and sold it off to the highest bidder. In a kilt, of course. Which flies up in the air if you bang it on the head.

But who can argue with their very genuine success. In less time than it takes for the DTI to come up with yet another report on improving the competitiveness of British goods in export markets, Taiwanese businessmen, or golden oxen as they are called, have turned their little island, which is about the size of a printed circuit motherboard (the main circuit board inside a computer – they make eight out of every ten produced throughout the world) into the world's twentieth largest economy and fourteenth largest trading nation with over US$84 billion of foreign currency reserves in the bank, the second biggest in the world. Its GNP per person is double that of Portugal and Greece and bigger even than that of Saudi Arabia.

But they don't owe their enormous success just to counterfeiting; they owe it to counterfeiting *their way*. You and I know that, for them, counterfeiting was easy, because they had the one thing that absolutely guarantees success, anywhere in the world. They were all Chinese. And wherever you get genuine Chinese blood you get genuine Chinese sweat and genuine Chinese guts and genuine Chinese success. Take Hong Kong. Take Singapore. Take Malaysia. Take the Golden Dragon Chinese Restaurant in Heathfield.

Straight in in the mornings. Straight at it. No coffee. No discussing what they fell asleep watching on television the previous evening. Work through lunch. No afternoon tea. Work practically through night until job is done. In States, in England, everybody come into office, start talking about what on television last night. Not in Taiwan. In Taiwan everybody come in office and start work. In office we work. At home, watch television.

'Chinese culture says we help each other. We work as group. Western culture says, to hell with group. We on own to beat everybody else,' a Taiwanese golden oxen told me in his office about 9.30 one evening. 'Chinese proud of work. We like work. We want produce best quality work.' Two hours later I was still there.

But they do it their own Chinese way. In one company I visited in Tooyuan everybody brings their slippers to the office.

'It's like visiting a temple,' I said as I pulled my shoes off at the door, wished I'd put on clean socks, and rummaged around in the visitors' slippers cupboard for a pair that would hide the hole in my big toe.

'It's like being at home,' the manager, a Chinese who had trained in the US, corrected me. 'At home, everybody relaxed.

In office, if we wear slippers we also relaxed. If we relaxed, we work better. Also not mind working longer.'

I once visited a company in Taiwan's Silicon Valley, the Hsinchu Science Industrial Park, an hour's drive from Taipei, which is home to over 150 hi-tech companies each dedicated to destroying their competitors around the world (genuine). The owner, who was as smooth as a Japanese lacquered bento box, looked as though he would be pushing his technical skills to the limit if he switched on a television set (counterfeit).

He told me he had started out making washing machines for Chinese laundries. But he didn't think the business would wash its face. He switched to electronics, beginning as a sub-contractor to a sub-contractor. Now he was part of Taiwan's US$10 billion information technology industry making keyboards, image scanners and millions and millions of tiny plastic switches.

'I tell you, boy,' he said to me, 'for making money, this is best damned country on earth.'

We went into an enormous aircraft hangar of a factory that was doing nothing but punch out plastic switches. The noise was deafening. Nobody was wearing earmuffs.

'How do they work in this?' I screamed at him over the din. It's so . . . it's so . . . it's so noisy.'

'They all deaf,' he shouted back at me. 'Everybody deaf. No problems.'

They also deal with their customers in a Chinese way. They don't bother with credit checks or bank references, they just know they are going to get paid.

'But what happens if you don't get paid?' I asked a manager in yet another electronics company in Hsinchu.

'Always get paid,' he said. 'Always. Not problem not to get paid.'

Which was obviously true because he told me he had just bought a house in England – in Dipswitch in Lunstaple country. The only risk they seemed to have was if the client died.

'If client dies, new manager takes his place. New manager has his own suppliers. But we have to try and get him to buy from us because old manager buy from us.'

'And do they?'

'Some do, some do not.' He shrugged. 'That is business.'

Taiwan, which is Chinese for 'come back at five and I'll have a copy waiting for you', was Formosa until 1949 when General Chiang Kai-Shek arrived out of the blue with two million soldiers, bureaucrats and other hangers-on who had been driven out of mainland China by the Communists. For which, I suppose, we have to be eternally grateful to Mao Tse-Tung. Can you imagine the damage that China would have done to world trade if Mao had lost and Chiang Kai-Shek and his merry band of workaholic counterfeiters had been running the place for the last forty-odd years. We wouldn't be able to walk for Rolex watches. Ralph Lauren shirts would be piled as high as the Empire State Building and there would be enough Ronnie Walker to fill the Atlantic Ocean. But luckily for us, Mao won a genuine victory and saved the world from being buried ten foot deep by counterfeit goods. Instead we've only been buried in counterfeit goods one foot deep.

Instead of Formosa, Mao called it a 'rebel province'. Everybody else called it a counterfeit country (genuine) and refused to have anything to do with it. At least, while Mao was around.

But while their backs were turned, little old Taiwan set about becoming a genuine success. First they put agriculture on a proper basis. Land was sold to farmers at a price they could afford: 2.5 times the money they got from their annual harvests. Farm leases were set at six years, making it worthwhile for a farmer to work his land. Rents were calculated at around one-third of the average yield the farmer had obtained over the previous three years. Farmers, as a result, began producing. They also began building their simple processing, canning and production operations. Taiwan was beginning to work.

Second, they encouraged industry and exports. In order to raise the money to invest in industrial development for export growth, the government decided to pay bonus interest rates to savers, especially the farmers. This money they then lent on to industry at subsidised rates. Again, it worked. New factories were thrown up faster than the accusations hurled across the Taiwan Strait at mainland China. Before the paint was dry they had moved in. Production was breaking records before it even began. Everybody believed in work. Work was their salvation. Work they did, and save them it did. It soaked up the surplus funds that would otherwise have been wasted on the type of silly consumer goods with which Taiwan has flooded the world. It enabled industry to expand. It soaked up unemployment.

Next, they set up their own export processing zones specifically designed to attract foreign investors, create more jobs and boost exports further.

Finally, they put in the heavy industries to provide all the raw materials for the companies in the export processing zones. Once they had established their heavy industries, and the machine was operating at full steam, they began their drive to go up-market and into new technologies.

But not everybody liked what they were doing and the success they were achieving. Especially not Chairman Mao. The result was that if their president went visiting abroad, no country was prepared to accept him as the leader of an industrious, hard-working, peaceful country, for fear of upsetting the Chairman. The president had to pretend he was on holiday and that his team of advisers were his travel agents. Any serious discussions had to be done either by the side of the pool, driving around in unmarked cars, or behind closed doors with the lights off and the curtains drawn. And denied afterwards.

Now, of course, everybody wants to know them because of their amazing success at turning out virtually anything faster and cheaper than anybody else.

Taipei, Kaohsiung, Taichung and Tainan, as a result, are an

intricate mass of wide streets, thousands of baseball caps, hundreds of posters advertising Madonna doing something which looks terribly uncomfortable, huge McDonald's signs and masses of notices in English – or American – saying, Plane ride, Freeway, Automobile Parking Lot, Baskin-Robbins Ice Cream or even, To the Embassy of El Salvador.

Whatever the time of day or night, Taipei looks as though the whole three million population is out there at the same time, lined up at the traffic lights on their motorbikes and scooters waiting for the start of the Grand National. Some scooters have three people on them: the driver, usually a girl side-saddle on the back, and in front on the platform either a child or a little old lady. As for bicycles; other people ride bicycles to get from A to B, for delivering midwives in country villages and for delivering your newspapers to somebody else's house. The Dutch ride them like it's a religion. In Taipei they ride them like a political statement. They line up together at the lights, then at Go they triumph by sheer force of numbers, just as they stitched up the world market for genuine plastic table-tennis bats and so many other products vital to our needs as we face the demands of the twenty-first century.

Today, when the hallmark of civilisation is to get CNN twenty-four hours a day on your hotel television set, I think it's unfair that in spite of the millions of anti-Communist dollars they've received from Washington, the Taiwanese keep stressing their 5,000 years of culture to prove how shallow the Americans are. In fact, the way they go on about their history you'd think the Chinese invented television in the third year of the Twang Dynasty, and that it was only because the shallow Americans were not clever enough to invent Coca-Cola at the same time that there was not enough advertising revenue to enable them to develop the idea.

Taipei is still as Chinese as a spring roll. With barbecue sauce on top. There are millions of little alleyways, like the microscopic electric circuits on a PCB, with hundreds of thousands of mysterious little corrugated-iron shacks or houses huddled under groups of trees where, hidden away out of sight, life probably continues as it was before the Twang Dynasty and the invention of television. In between, like huge capacitors, are ancient temples, the giant modern factories, vast hotels and enormous exhibition halls.

I was once in Taipei with an Englishman who was based in Singapore and who'd visited Taiwan, he said, thirty or forty times.

'What's that big building with the Chinese roof?' he asked me one evening as we drove through town.

'That's your hotel,' I said.

Though he'd been in and out of Taipei so often, he had always stayed inside the Grand Hotel, which has to be one of the world's great hotels. He was scared to venture out because the place was so Chinese. Not me. I have always been fascinated by it, by its history, its success and the culture that produced that success. Whenever I'm in Taipei, I spend all the time I can outside the hotel. Now, just as the printed circuit board is changing to meet the ever-increasing demands for miniaturisation, so Taiwan is also facing change, I reckon – and becoming increasingly worried about its future.

In the old days the golden oxen practically had no time to breathe. When they weren't working and building up their empires they were studying for their MBAs (My Business Above all others) and PhDs (Please to Hold Down your sales so I can have the largest market share). They didn't even have time for eating and drinking. Clients they entertained once a year, unlike the Japanese, who go out and get bombed with clients nearly every night.

'At New Year we entertain client, not usually other time. Nobody has time for drinking,' I can remember being told again and again.

'In the clubs?'

'No, club too expensive.'

Now they don't even have time to go to the restaurants once a year. Like the PCB and the whole electronics industry, Taiwan is worrying about becoming unplugged. So business-men spend their free time at their local neighbourhood temples, throwing sticks on the ground. Trying to find out what the future has in store.

Gone are the days when Generalissimo Chiang and his merry men threw a handful of sticks on the temple floor and came up with the magic formula of turning a patch of dust squeezed between the South China Sea and the Pacific into a worldwide success story. South Korea, Singapore, Malaysia, perhaps Thailand, maybe even Indonesia – and, of course, their old enemy China; as the big players all around begin their own spectacular Taiwan-style dash for growth, will Taiwan be able to stay ahead of the pack? Can they step up production still further, go up-market, increase their value-added, go overseas, or even deep into China itself, and still maintain their number one spot, or will they begin losing out?

In Hong Kong, most Chinese speak Cantonese, which is fine for doing business in, surprise, surprise, Canton, the province just across the water which is now known as Guangzhou. In Taiwan, most Chinese speak Mandarin or Putonghua, the 'universal language' which covers the rest of China. Inevitably, most Taiwanese businessmen, whatever the politics, want to get into China, which is only seventy miles away across the Taiwan Strait.

Chairman Mao and the great leap forward to backwardness and disaster has gone the way of all leaders. All the 'old thieves' as the Taiwanese called them, have gone. New men are in charge. Maybe they are still 'young thieves', but they are different. Low costs; few controls; virtually no competition; huge market; minimum financial risks: businessmen are always chasing the lowest costs and the highest return, and China now offers everything. It has cheap land – one-hundredth, maybe one-thousandth the price back home. It has cheap labour, one-tenth the price. It has an enormous, wide-open market. Are the Taiwanese going to look the other way? Not on your life, especially as China has started eroding Taiwan's share of major foreign markets. In the US, in Japan, China already outsells them; elsewhere China is slowly creeping up behind – admittedly in the T-shirt, tennis shoes and candleholder end of the market, but China's there, and increasingly so.

Five, six years ago there was no contact between Taiwan and mainland China. They practically filtered the air between them. Telephone calls between the countries could be counted on two hands. Today it would take 6,000 pairs of hands including the thumbs. Flights were minimal. Today direct flights are still banned but Hong Kong's Kai Tak airport is a revolving door as over one million Taiwanese a year flock into China to do deals with friends and relatives left behind over forty years ago, and to see for the first time the land of their fathers. And just as Hong Kong businessmen are moving into Guangdong, Taiwanese businessmen are linking up with their tongbao, or fellow citizens, and moving into the special economic zone of Xiamen in Fujian Province opposite. Taiwanese electronics, toy and textile companies, some with the machinery shipped in from Taiwan, are popping up all over the place. In some areas more than 25 per cent of workers are working for Taiwanese companies.

In and around Pingtan for example, which is only two hours away on their Megal speedboat, five hours by Megal cruiser and ten hours by illegal fishing boat, across the Straits from Nanliao on their north-west coast, already there are supposed to be more than 12,000 Taiwan-backed and financed companies. One of them exports not cameras or hi-fis or videos to China, but tiny pedigree lapdogs, especially to Beijing.

'Beijing,' I wondered when I met the manager. 'Why Beijing? I thought dogs were not allowed in Beijing.'

'They're not,' he grinned. 'That's why I want export to Beijing. That way I make more money.'

'Of course, how silly of me ... So how much can you sell them for?'

'Four thousand, five thousand, six ...'

Some companies are even seeing beyond China and talking of turning Taiwan into the finance, transportation and technology centre of the West Pacific.

But are they happy with the genuine success coming their

way as, inevitably, Taiwan and China work out a way of living closer together? No way. They, of all people, suspect the whole thing might be – how shall I say? – counterfeit.

How they will structure the reconciliation remains to be seen. Will China forgive the Republic? I doubt it. Will the Republic say it was all a mistake? I doubt it. Will each side recognise the other as a sovereign independent state? My guess is, China would be prepared to accept a suitable form of words – Taiwan has already taken part in the Asian Olympics in Beijing as Chinese Taipei – if Taiwan will promise to be good boys and help them in their development. Which, of course, they will.

Inevitably everyone is nervous about the future, like two companies eyeing each other up when they can see both chairmen have their hearts set on a merger. Only a few days in Taipei surveying the scene – it's difficult not to survey the scene because you are automatically head and shoulders above everybody in sight, including the police – and it's not difficult to see the different effects it is having on people.

A railroad worker in Hualien on the east of the island was so worried about the future that he turned up for work one night and tried to get his own back by setting fire to a five-kilo gas tank. An opposition politician who wanted to set political discussions alight turned up at the ruling Kuomintang Party's headquarters with a petrol can and two gas lights. And a woman standing as an Independent threatened to go around baring her breasts for democracy. This obviously didn't appeal to the Taiwanese because she wasn't elected, although for which particular reason I couldn't discover.

The stock market is worried. Because everyone is dithering about their future and trying to find better outlets for their money, they are forcing down still further the level of their existing investments. In the old days, before they had second let alone third and fourth thoughts, the Taiwan stock exchange was as high as one of their cheap Taiwan-made tennis balls. Today it's been smashed into the net by one of their new hi-tech super-tough Taiwan-made tennis rackets. Prices are down, daily turnover is down, the overall index is down. With over 70 per cent of the turnover coming from individuals rather than companies or institutions, that means something. Individuals tend to think longer and harder about playing games with their own money. When they play, they tend to play long-term. Professional fund managers, however, will flip if they get even a blip on their computer screens.

Foreign investors are worried as well. Will the Big Hands or Big Guys who sit on the Taiwanese parliament's finance committee keep the market to themselves, or will they allow more foreign play, insider-speak for allowing more foreign companies in. At present, their stock market is the tightest in Asia. A foreigner is not allowed to own an ashtray let alone a chunk of stock. At present only around 5 per cent of the total market capitalisation of US$90 billion is foreign-owned. Since 1991 overseas investors have pleaded to be allowed to invest another US$5 billion, half the amount Taiwan has itself invested in China over the last ten years. Not possible, say the Taiwanese. They have allowed in less than US$ 3 million.

Even the Kuomintang, which has run the place for the last forty-four years, is worried. 'Its brain has gone, its heart is weak, its legs are crippled,' I was told by a second-generation mainlander who sees himself more as a first-generation native-born Taiwanese.

Inevitably the Taiwanese government is nervous. It's only had three full-scale riots in the National Assembly to debate the issue when the result was, for the Ayes, two broken legs and six cracked ribs, and for the Noes, three broken legs, five cracked ribs, and a summons for assault from a clerk who had her hair pulled so much to stop her from reading out the results that her only hope now of being welcomed in polite society is to become a Buddhist monk.

The government, therefore, does not want to rush into things. It wants to take its time. Presumably to let the clerk's hair grow back.

In the old days life was easy. They only had to worry about building still more factories, increasing production, cutting costs, opening new markets, out-manoeuvring Chairman Mao every which way they could, and being presented with a peach, the Chinese symbol for a long life. Whatever they did, tiny little PCB Taiwan outstripped, outgunned and outran everybody in every way: life expectancy, schooling, health care, calorific intake, the number of karaoke bars and the number of patent infringement warnings in the post on Monday mornings.

Now the whole thing depends on good luck sticks. And if the sticks don't come up with the right answer, they play a kind of heads-and-tails game with two pieces of highly polished wood. Mix them up and drop them on the ground at your feet. If both come down heads up you win. If you get one head and one tail, you'll be all right. But if both come up tails . . . We'll call you. Sometime.

One manager in the Whu Whei Industrial Company told me the temple in the middle of Taipei was having its busiest time ever. All day every day it is packed, not just with the little old ladies you normally find in temples and churches all over the world, but with businessmen, businesswomen, and even young people all throwing handfuls, armfuls of sticks on the ground all day long until they hit the right combination.

'Temple received so much money it is now building its own hospital,' he added, throwing his bits of stick yet again, hoping against hope to get a double header.

Nor is China their only worry. Everybody worries about drugs. Everybody worries about the environment. In spite of all the statistics and the displays of wealth – one in seven owns a car, four out of ten own a motorcycle – Taiwan is still a poor country. One morning in Taipei, what am I saying, half an hour in Taipei and you realise that although in the sixteenth century the Portuguese named it Ilha Formosa, the Beautiful Island, it has appalling pollution problems. Its housing is, well, Chinese. Hardly anyone has a modern sewage system.

According to the paintings of Kuo Hsi which I saw in the National Palace Museum, the eleventh century was about the last time Taiwan was pollution free. Ethereal Parks, they seem to have had as far back as the Chou dynasty, which was about the time we were leaving the Garden of Eden. By the time of the Wei, Chin and Northern and Southern dynasties, when the Emperor first gave the order to Chinese restaurants to go out and multiply all over the world, they were planning garden enclaves where the fashionable literate could, they claim, indulge in the 'arcane philosophizing of pure conversation'.

By the Ming and Ching dynasties the pollution was obviously getting pretty bad because the smoky, dusty district records of Soochow clearly show that people had been forced to give up the idea of spending weekends in the country and, instead, were 'digging out ponds, cultivating plants and piling up earth and stone into mountains and rockeries ... adjacent to their own urban residences so that they could feel they were standing at the edge of a lake or in a mountain forest far from the mundane world.'

Today the ponds are full of oil drums, abandoned cars and umbrellas. In between them the roads are so choked with traffic that right in the middle of Taipei I've seen people get out of their cars and vans, do their morning exercises and get back in before the traffic has moved on.

One of the reasons for the pollution, I was told, was that there were so many ordinary, humble, hard-working, dedicated, efficient, totally incorruptible policemen driving to work in luxury foreign cars; cars they could no way afford to buy on their ordinary, humble etc. wages. The government was eventually forced to take severe measures in order to avoid a public outcry. With inscrutable Chinese logic, they introduced strict regulations, backed by the full authority of the state, banning the police from driving the cars to work.

Now, however, they are launching the biggest clean-up programme ever undertaken by any government anywhere. A special environmental commission has been established. Factories are being told to clean up. They are even worried about the traditional Chinese funeral. In the West we keep being told we can't take it with us. In the East, if you want to take it with you, you do. Except, of course, in Taiwan, where there is no way you can take the real thing with you. What you take is a counterfeit: a papier mâché model. Of your favourite car; of a television set with, attached to the screen, your favourite scene from your favourite programme; of your mobile telephone, even of your house and, inside the papier mâché house, papier mâché models of your family and friends. If all that is too much, your friendly local undertaker will arrange instead for you to depart this life with a bundle of bank notes (counterfeit) tucked inside your pretty pink silk shroud (counterfeit). Did you think they would put a genuine one in? Come on.

I once actually managed to attend on the same day a typical Chinese wedding and a typical Chinese funeral. One was exciting and colourful, flowers and garlands everywhere, people clustered in small groups, laughing and joking. There was a light, happy atmosphere about the place. The other was the wedding.

At the funeral, I stood at the back, expecting to see a long line of black limousines. Instead I saw a small open-air truck decorated with garlands as if for a carnival procession. On the front of the truck was a huge black-and-white photograph of the poor man himself. On the back was the coffin. The wedding was much more solemn, much more well-that's-it-fella-that's-the-end-of-the-world. Everything was heavy, heavy, heavy. There was certainly no laughing and joking.

The problem with funerals – something else to worry about – is that with so many people dying and taking so much with them the crematoria can't cope. Taipei some mornings is like Sydney in the middle of a forest fire. The authorities are looking for ways of solving the problem. In South Korea they actually publish a blacklist of people guilty of what they call 'excessive embellishment', who have arranged too flash funerals or put up too ornate ornaments or tombs for their dear departed and, therefore, pumped too much smoke into the atmosphere. In Taiwan they have different ideas. They are trying to persuade people, would you believe, that instead of taking all their worldly goods with them (counterfeit) they take a counterfeit credit card with them (genuine).

Will it catch on? One velly, velly old man at the wedding – this was not a subject to talk about at funerals – told me he would put his money (genuine) on the idea. 'It is velly, velly good idea. Chinese people they like taking goods and money with them, but they like even more taking card. Card gives you unlimited credit, no expiry date, no spending limit and no date for paying money back.'

Funerals, weddings, and, of course, the other tragedy in life: children. The Taiwanese are also worrying like mad about their children. Or at least, everybody I met kept criticising them. Other people's, of course.

'They're lazy. They don't believe in studying.'

'They drink too much, Some are even on drugs.'

'No way is the current generation going to work anywhere near as hard as their fathers.'

That's what I was told between leaving the plane and collecting my luggage. Sure the young people of Taiwan might still be Chinese. Sure they might still be products of their culture. Sure they might still adhere to their Confucian principles. But today they have Coca-Cola in their blood, pictures of Madonna inside their PCs and Doc Martens on their feet. At least that's what I was told, which struck me as odd because I got the distinct impression that the only thing that really counts in Taiwan apart from the good old yankee dollar is good manners and a good education.

In the high streets, up back alleys, driving through factory estates, in the middle of nowhere, children and young people most definitely do not display that one quality that identifies young people throughout the West; a healthy disrespect for their elders. And at all times of the day – even the night, the place seems to be swarming with kids, all shapes and sizes, who might not know who Chiang Kai-Shek was, or who invented the Walkman, but who are going very willingly to school, college or university, great bundles of books under their arm, pages bulging from their briefcases.

In Singapore you see enormous office blocks completely

crammed with kids studying everything from nuclear physics to how to make a toilet that rings a bell if you don't pull the chain. In South Korea there is a whole industry devoted to cramming for examinations. Not content with spending all day at school, the kids spend their evenings packed into cramming colleges to pass even more exams more quickly. In Japan, I've been out at seven o'clock on a Sunday morning in the middle of Tokyo. What do I see? Hundreds of kids in their smart, military-style uniforms racing off to school.

Taiwan is exactly the same. Education is everything. Creep unwillingly to school? Never on your life. At the same time, the pressures are enormous: on parents, to make the one kimono do instead of twenty-seven, just to help little Tsai Chin get his degree in nuclear physics before his eleventh birthday; on the children. Help with the washing up? Watch television? No way. There is Einstein to master before supper. On the schools. They don't have enough schools for the number of children, let alone enough teachers. What do they do? They share the buildings. One school uses the building in the morning and another uses it in the afternoon. In the evening, it looks as though both lots come back again to sit on top of each other and cram in yet more work.

As for teachers, apart from the near obligatory karaoke nights, all over South-East Asia, I kept coming across business-men who excused themselves politely from an evening trailing round the bars, not to rush home to the wife, but to rush round to the local school to fill in an hour or two as a teacher.

At a reception in Taipei I was introduced to what I thought was a Taiwanese yuppie. He had an expensive suit, a jazzy sports car and was obviously rolling in it. I thought he was either a serious, honourable politician or the local millionaire. He turned out to be a teacher at a juku, a Japanese school for crammers. He was rolling in it because, as with everything in Japan, they were paid by results. He was getting more students through their examinations, and so was the school, so that they were able to charge the earth and parents were prepared to pay it. Exactly the same thing, he told me, happened in Taiwan. The crammers rule. The parents pay.

If anyone cracks under the pressure, it's a visit to the local shrine. A handful of sticks. Candles. Some fortune cookies. Then back to the books. No namby-pamby counselling here.

And if they fail – if they fail! Very few fail – it's immediately back into battle. Another round of cramming. Perhaps two visits to the local shrine. Double the number of sticks. A private tutor. Defeat is unknown. Victory is everything.

I asked the millionaire crammer why children in the Far East seem to be better at maths than the semi-illiterate, totally innumerate morons in the West. Is it in their blood? Were they all born with a silver abacus in their hand?

'No, no,' he said, 'it because we have large family in the East. Father must be good at figures. If not, he forget son number seven, nephew number nine or great-aunt number seven. Figures help you remember.'

'What about all their birthdays? How do you remember them?' I wondered.

'Birthdays not important,' he said. 'Wife remember birthdays. She write it all down.'

When the kids have finally got their degrees, everybody worries about what they are going to do with them. Will they get a job? Will they get properly paid? Will they get married? Will their children be successful?

Even for the odd two or three whose training is not academic, but technical, there is intense competition. I was there when Taiwan was host to the International Youth Skill Olympics. Teams of young people came from all over the world to demonstrate their skills in such practical things as bricklaying, plumbing, breaking and entering, beating up old ladies and how to wear a smart suit when you go to court so that the judge puts you on probation so you can go and do it again. The Taiwan team – now, now, no smirking in the back row – came first. Their team demonstrated their age-old traditional skills of copying and getting the goods onto the market quicker than the company who first thought of the idea. Next came South Korea, who demonstrated their age-old traditional skills of copying the Taiwanese copy and getting it on the market quicker and cheaper than the original inventor. The British – this is true, I'm not kidding – demonstrated the skills that have made us internationally famous: bricklaying, plumbing, and how to drag a ten-minute job out to last all week. Everybody was given medals. The British were given three silver, six bronze, five diplomas of excellence and a stopwatch. But Taiwan being Taiwan, you can bet your life they were all counterfeit.

I asked one of the Taiwanese organisers why they organise such an event.

'We need to skill our young people,' he said.

The result of all this is that the good luck lions, the symbols of happiness and money that have been protecting the Taiwanese since their first genuine counterfeit came off the press, don't know whether to break into a wide smile or grit their teeth.

If they break into a wide smile it means opening their mouths. Opening their mouths will make it easier to catch all the money thrown their way. Taiwan will continue to be rich. If they grit their teeth, it means closing their mouths, and if they do that they'll never catch any money. Taiwan will be poor.

Most Taiwanese I met expected the lions to grit their teeth. Not a full-scale, tooth-breaking grit, just maybe a slight clenching of the jaw. But a true grit nonetheless.

Whether they are worried or not, the mere fact that they are worrying about whether they have anything to worry about is making things worse – for themselves, for their existing investments, and for their future investments.

So what is the future for Taiwan? On my first trip, I thought it was the black hole. Everybody kept talking to me about the black hole. Black hole,' they would say.

I would half nod and half not nod, slowly. If you see what I mean. After all, you cannot be too careful.

'Black hole,' they would repeat. 'You see black hole?'

'Yes, of … No, what I mean is …' Then I would have a coughing fit.

'Now I know, I understand. You not want anyone to know about black hole, yes?'

'No. I mean yes. No, I …' I would mumble.

'You frightened everyone know you like black hole. You not worry. Everybody know you like black hole. Everybody like black hole. You not like black hole everybody think you …'

Black hole? Black Hole? Black hole to the Taiwanese means golf. That's what it is.

So what is their future? Like it or not, China is bound to be, even if there is no change in their current leadership, more socialist-capitalist than socialist-socialist. Hong Kong will be part of China, which is bound to mean more rather than less democracy in China; maybe only in Guangdong and similar areas infected by proximity to the one-time colony, but it will be a start. And once democracy takes hold, like Chinese restaurants in the world's high streets, it will be virtually impossible to destroy, Tiananmen Square or no Tiananmen Square.

Will Taiwan gradually – maybe even rapidly – become Chinese-Chinese under the impact of booming trade with the mainland? Will they be able to keep up their counterfeiting operations? Well, maybe not counterfeiting as such. The latest trick, I mean strategy, adopted by the Taiwanese, I'm told, is to express interest in placing a huge order for whatever it is they're interested in. The company president and a whole gang then turn up at the factory to sign the agreement of intent or provisional order form – complete with cameras. Before signing the contract, they say, 'The president would like to tour the plant.' The company says, 'Yes, of course. Delighted. If the president would like to …' And if the president is going to tour the plant, could they all come as well to take photographs? Bingo. It's a Taiwan stand-off. If the company says no, it's goodbye Mr President, big order and money in the bank. If they say yes, it's goodbye every secret in the joint. Of course the Taiwanese will photograph the president standing next to Sid Braithwaite and shaking hands with Flo, the tea-lady since Brunel hired her. Of course they will also photograph everything else, including the contents of the wastepaper basket.

Back home – what am I saying? Outside the plant, round the corner, under the trees – they will immediately analyse every picture to discover exactly how the products are made. Having done that, they will immediately – don't forget we're talking about Taiwanese – think up a hundred new developments and techniques for everything they saw and, here's the clever bit, patent the whole lot the following morning. It has to be the following morning because with the best Taiwanese will in the world it still takes all night for them to fax everything back to Taipei for their development engineers and lawyers to prepare the necessary papers so that they can be refaxed back to London and submitted to the Patent Office as soon as it opens.

What does the poor company do? It prays. Because once the order has been filled, whatever they do, they're dead. Everything from the doorbell to the factory hooter has been patented and registered in every country under the sun.

Will Taiwan be able to continue drinking toasts in genuine Ronnie Walker Black Label? The Taiwanese claim that the record for drinking toasts (genuine) the Taiwanese way (counterfeit) is held by President Clinton. When he was Governor of Arkansas he was constantly in Taiwan.

On one occasion, I was told, he drank no less than forty-two toasts with the president, Lee Teng-hui. Which means he was obviously drinking King Victoria Finest Scotchman's Whisko – but not swallowing it. In fact, based on my experience of Taiwan's Finest Scotchman's Whisko, I'm amazed he gave up at forty-three. The only reason I can think of is that he was beginning to gag on the colouring.

When he got back home apparently Hillary was furious,

and the only way she could stop him from going back to Taipei was to make him run for president.

Now look at the mess (genuine) we're all in, thanks to those fantastic Taiwanese inventors, wheeler-dealers and scrupulous international businessmen (counterfeit).

Ho Chi Minh City

I hate to say it, but the Vietnamese are preparing for war. Again. And they're doing it with all the single-minded ruthlessness, determination and dedication which they have perfected over 2,000 years of almost non-stop fighting. Except in this case it's a trade war.

Look at the statistics. Talk to the experts. Engage British diplomats in polite conversation over *cha gios* at the Rex Hotel in the centre of Ho Chi Minh City, which is now called the Khach San Ben Thanh Hotel, which is Vietnamese for 'We're going to bury you in even cheaper products than you can get in Taiwan.' They will all tell you the same thing.

Vietnam is a desperately poor country. Over 50 per cent of the population are below the poverty line. Average income is less than US$200 a year. Over 50 per cent of the population are under twenty-five years old. It has an enormous amount of ground to make up. It is run by Communists. They have to overcome the legacy of their latest series of wars against the French and the Americans. They are making valiant efforts. Under Doi Moi, their perestroika-style reform programme, they have switched from the old Soviet-style command economy with its regular quota of breakdowns, shortages and revolutionary slogans to a more open, business-oriented economy. People are better off. Some more so than others. A few, especially those with any type of property and those buying and selling, are even better off. The country has no real legal system, no commercial law, no property law, no foreigners in advertisements, and as for criminal law, ask a policeman. Freedom of the press, speech, religion and assembly are, how shall we say, tolerated. Instead of the World Cup semi-final, Vietnamese television ran a long tribute to Kim Il Sung, the dead Stalinist leader of North Korea; and according to the newspaper *Hanoi Moi*, 'the most glorious event of the twentieth century' was the Bolshevik Revolution in 1917.

'It will take time, believe me: maybe ten, even fifteen years, certainly no less. Now about the cricket, old boy, did you see the latest score?' British diplomats have told me again and again.

Nonsense. You've only got to stand for two seconds on the corner of Nguyen Hue Boulevard and Leo Loi Boulevard, the two main thoroughfares running through Ho Chi Minh City, one of the most densely populated areas in Asia; see the hotels, the lights, the shops piled high with goods; look at the commercial stormtroopers, well-dressed, smart, fashionable; and gasp at the traffic – millions and millions and millions of bicycles and mopeds and rickshaws; in a city of 4.5 million people there are only 40,000 private cars – to realise this place is already mobilising – and fast.

Go down to Cholon, the Chinese quarter at four o'clock in the morning and the place is packed. Some people say it's the powerhouse, or engineroom. The Chinese are always the workers, the traders, the wheeler-dealers, the people who make things happen. Others say it's the source of the country's enormous black economy. When the Viet Cong moved in, way back in April 1975, the Chinese buried their money and valuables in the ground, kept their heads down and kept at it. Now they are slowly digging up their goodies, using them and putting them back into circulation. On top of that there is an enormous amount of money coming in from Chinese overseas. Unofficially, of course. A few will even whisper about things like drugs coming down through Laos, across the border at Lao Bao into Quang Tri Province and into secret processing and refining plants in Cholon and out into Europe, the States, wherever. One or two, shh, will even whisper things about a more dangerous and more lucrative business altogether; edible birds' nests from Koh Si Koh Ha island. Apparently they come down into Cholon through southern Thailand and out into Hong Kong where the best can fetch up to US$3,000 a kilo. But I wouldn't know anything about that kind of thing.

'It's even worse than Hong Kong,' a British architect living in Hong Kong and working in China told me one evening as we stood on the pavement outside the massive Chinese electronics market on Hang Vuong Boulevard, squeezed on one side by millions of people desperate to spend money which, according to the statistics, doesn't exist, and on the other by millions of bicycles and mopeds and rickshaws. That's Cholon. But it's practically the same all over the city, in every street, in every alleyway, all day, every day.

At six in the evening, for example, Ben Thanh, Ho Chi Minh City's five-star street market, is still packed with people buying and selling, wheeling and dealing. As late as midnight, Le Thanh Ton Street, the flower market, is still solid with people.

Hanoi, the capital, over 1,500 miles away up in the north, is the same. But different. It is full of bicycles and mopeds and rickshaws – but not so many. There are shops and stalls all over the place – but not everywhere. And it is crowded with people, but not to bursting point. It is more the second son, the poor cousin, the government and business centre.

The city centre is fantastic. Many people, not just those who saw it from 30,000 feet or who have watched their ladies football teams playing in the mud, rave about it; its history, its elegance, its culture, its beautiful but fading fifteenth- to nineteenth-century architecture, its boulevards, its big French colonial houses, its beautiful French colonial plumbing which you find everywhere – in France. And its pagodas. It's full of ancient pagodas: Ngoe Son, the Jade Mountain Temple in the middle of Hoan Kiem Lake; the Ambassador's Pagoda, the official centre of Buddhism in the city; the famous One Pillar Pagoda, Chua Mot Cot, near the back of – oops, I nearly forgot – the Ho Chi Minh Mausoleum, the Ho Chi Minh Museum and the famous Ho Chi Minh House on Stilts where he lived and worked from 1958 to 1969 which, as far as I'm concerned, proves beyond any doubt whatsoever that he was not, repeat not, like the rest of us. There is no bathroom or toilet in the place. Honest.

But my favourite place is the Van Mieu or Temple of Literature, which covers a whole block somewhere near the Ho Chi Minh Mausoleum. In fact, everything is pretty much dominated by the Ho Chi Minh Mausoleum. At first, I must admit, I didn't feel I should go near anything as grand as a Temple of Literature. Then I decided it certainly wouldn't do me any harm. And, of course, it is fabulous. I should have gone there years ago. (Okay, okay, you don't have to agree.) Originally built in 1070 – think about it; four years after all that business with the Normans – it was Vietnam's first university. Even in those days, it was a centre for scholarship and writing. Today it's been beautifully restored to almost National Trust standard. Paths have been laid, gardens are looked after; the buildings – the portico, the different gates, the sanctuary and the pagoda, are in superb condition. It practically makes you want to become a Buddhist.

But for all that, or maybe because of all that, Hanoi seems to lack the buzz, the verve, the fun, the excitement of Ho Chi Minh City. Hanoi's old quarter, squeezed between the lake, the Citadel (which dates back to 300 BC), the Dong Xuan market, famous for its range of snake medicines, and the Red River, has been a hive of activity for over 1,000 years. Some of the property, especially around Ho Tay or West Lake, is the best and certainly the most expensive you'll find in Asia. With a grain of earth costing practically the equivalent of a grain of gold – all property in Vietnam is bought and sold with gold – almost but not quite luxury apartments are fetching up to US$8,000 a month. Plus service charges.

The people are nice, friendly. Maybe a little quiet, a bit reserved. But that's not a bad thing. Especially if you've got a million reports to write. The local Halida beer is good. It's produced by a local company, run by a woman, which used to export fish paste all over Eastern Europe. When the Wall came down and Eastern Europe began to fall apart she switched to beer and hasn't looked back.

The only reason I can think of for Hanoi lacking that buzz is the local diet: dog. If people want to spoil themselves, or celebrate, especially towards the end of the month or coming up to the new moon, they go to the dogs. You see them in shops and stalls; on benches by the side of the road; in cages on bikes leaning up against walls. Cho Mua: We buy dog. Cho Ban: We sell dog. The price: about US$1 a kilo – more at the end of the month because it's more in demand. And how would you like it, madam? You can have dog liver or, if you prefer, dog intestines. Goes down a treat with green beans and onions. I could let you have it chopped up ready for the barbecue. I could do you spicy dog sausages. Or, if you're planning a special treat for the family this weekend, how about a complete roast dog. It'll go down fantastic, I guarantee. It gives a whole new meaning to the phrase, a Rover dealer.

The one thing I couldn't get anyone to tell me was the best wine to accompany dog. My own suggestion was something Alsatian, but I may be wrong.

The live dogs in Hanoi, I must say, all seem remarkably well-behaved. Well, those that you see sitting obediently at their masters' feet, keeping an eye open for strangers, eager to leap up as soon as they are called. Not like our three dogs. Years ago I wanted to take them to obedience classes. But they wouldn't go. My guess is that Hanoi dogs must be constantly worried they are going to find themselves on the menu the next time they sneak into the kitchen.

I obviously didn't see every single town and village in Vietnam, but those I saw were more capitalist Ho Chi Minh City than socialist Hanoi. In Tay Ninh Province, the end of the Ho Chi Minh Trail, where there is the most amazing multi-coloured, almost psychedelic temple you've ever seen, the market is packed from 5 a.m. until 6 p.m. every day.

In Hoa Long, the scene of fierce fighting during the war, where wave after wave of US troops cut through the countryside using napalm, phosphorus and Agent Orange, the land is lush once again. Rice and other crops are growing in abundance. A pretty little gaily painted pagoda stands in the town centre surrounded by – you've got it – more shops and stalls selling everything you can think of and many things it is probably better not to think of.

All along the border with Kampuchea (they say), Cambodia (we say), there are more stalls and shops and markets, enormous markets, some the size of football pitches, everywhere, all piled high with clothes, shoes, cosmetics, birds in tiny bamboo cages, elaborately carved chairs, massive embroidery pictures of peacocks, strange-looking foods, bottles with dark grey contents, cheap plastic buckets and a million other unmentionable things that come flooding through the Friendship Gate with China now that all the mines – all 700,000 of them – have been cleared and the 1,000-mile border is open again after the short but bitterly fought war between them in 1979. But the stalls are also piled high with everything hi-tech and electronic, not only from Japan but from Taiwan and South Korea as well. One shop had a sign saying 'Video. Hi-fi.' Another had a banner, 'Entrez dans le mond meilleur de Walt Disney', which can only mean that the French government's campaign against the cultural imperialism of the Americans has yet to reach the outback of Vietnam. There was even a sign that said 'Photocopie'. The sign outside another shop I couldn't see: it was blocked out by an enormous wall of television sets piled in front of it. The shacks that were not piled high with goods seemed to be making or selling either full-size billiard tables or those old-fashioned heavy white – is it brocade? – wedding dresses. The shops might not all have electricity, but they are all generating a great deal of business.

The Vietnamese might not dine off caviar and drink champagne as much as their socialist cousins in other countries, but nobody is starving. Nobody is going hungry. There is more than enough to go round. They might not all be wearing Boss suits or Versace safety pins but everybody is adequately, if not well, dressed. The styles, the clothes, the standards, the fashions are as good as anywhere in the world. And everybody looks as though they wash their hair twice a week in coconut milk although, funnily enough, I don't know why, it's only the women, especially those in Ho Chi Minh City, who seem to have saved up enough money to buy a house.

The fields and paddy fields are practically manicured. It's not surprising that in three years Vietnam has become the world's third largest exporter of rice and will soon be the world's second largest producer of coffee. The cattle, which would win prizes at Smithfields, are clean and well-fed. The water buffalo, plodding along dragging their enormous loads, almost wink at you as if to say, 'Thank Goodness I'm here and not in a more developed country in Africa.' There are chickens scratching around; calves that can hardly stand up are being looked after by children who can hardly stand up. Even the dogs are round and fat and racing around. No, not because they're about to give someone a lot of pleasure. That's in the north of the country. Don't you read your Michelin?

And are they working? Men are, day and night, repairing trucks so broken down all that's left is the seat, the steering wheel and the engine; or unloading huge chunks of charcoal from rickshaws; or squatting on the floor welding sheets of metal, sparks flying off in all directions; or spraying the fields or heaving huge sacks onto bicycles, mopeds or, if they're lucky, trucks.

Women are working in the fields or piling up mountains of watermelon by the edge of the road; or leading cattle to fresh pasture; or squatting on the ground surrounded by ducks, stuffing what look like great lumps of jelly down their throats, presumably for the Vietnamese equivalent of foie gras.

Even the kids are rushing around with jars and cans and plastic bottles full of petrol which they sell at the roadside to the never-ending throng of motorcycles, or riding on buffa-loes.

And they are at it non-stop, seven days a week, practically

twenty-four hours a day. Repairing buildings, machinery, fences. Building/restoring/renovating shacks, huts, houses, outbuildings. Shifting, transporting, delivering everything you can think of. Late one evening, I don't know where, I even saw a man cycling into town. Rolled up inside a great sheet of wire fencing on the back of his bike was an enormous live pig going, no doubt, to you know where.

It's the same story with factories and offices. I spent a whole Sunday going from one brick production plant to another. Some were small, broken-down, still in the Middle Ages. Others were larger, more streamlined, maybe in the late nineteenth century. But they were all operating, all busy, all able to sell as much as they could produce. Their textile factories, which employ 250,000 people, are selling US$500 million worth of products a year and still growing at 40 per cent a year. The big Vietnam Motor Corporation Co. just north of Hanoi can't produce enough. South Korea's Daewoo, Japan's Mitsubishi and Malaysia's Proton are already planning to set up plants. Peugeot and Nissan are on the brink and Daimler-Benz, Ford, Chrysler and Toyota are thinking about it. Even their monkey breeding and export business – one farm in Dong Nai province has over 15,000 rhesus, pigtail red-faced and other types – is going up in leaps and bounds.

The only time they ever seem to stop working and selling is to celebrate their New Year or the patron saint of their village. Then it's three days of non-stop sacrificing pigs and buffaloes, non-stop eating and drinking, non-stop praying and burning incense and non-stop dragon dancing. After that it's back to non-stop work.

I tell you, these are not poor, undeveloped, down-trodden people desperately struggling to survive. They're already on their way. Ten, fifteen years before they're up there with the Asian tigers? Ten, fifteen months, more likely.

If you don't believe me there is only one way to find out the truth. Ask the British embassy – and believe the opposite of what they say. I guarantee it's the fail-safe way to find out what's going to happen anywhere in the world.

'No, no. You can't take my word for it, old chap,' I was assured by a seasoned FO buff over dinner in Maxims, which some people swear is the best restaurant in all Indo-China, although to me it seemed more like a motorway stop for coach parties. 'Ten, fifteen years. At least. Maybe longer,' he said.

Now do you believe me?

Down Dong Kohi Street, along the banks of the Saigon River, up Nguyen Hue Boulevard, into Lam Son Square. Round and round they go every Sunday evening on their Honda 100cc motorcycles. Thousands of them. The image-conscious fellas in their Levi's, Nike tops, a packet of 555 cigarettes in their pocket, and sprayed from head to toe in French perfume; the girls, who all seem to be about eleven and a half, in their traditional *ao dais*. Sometimes it's one to a bike, often two, in many cases three or four. If families join in, I have seen up to five people travelling on a single motorcycle; child, father, child, mother, young girl riding sidesaddle on the back.

Crossing the street is impossible. It's like trying to dash across to the Arc de Triomphe in the middle of the Friday evening rush hour. If you make it you're the luckiest man alive. If you don't, every hospital in the country will be treating the injured for weeks.

Then at 9 p.m., zap, they're all gone. Until next Sunday.

The Vietnamese must be the roughest, toughest, most determined, most stubborn people in history. Can you imagine, they've been at war pretty well non-stop since the Chinese moved into the Red River delta in the second century BC and the Trung sisters killed the local lord. Through the third century. Through the Ly dynasty. Through the Tran and later Ly dynasties. And so on through Trinh and Nguyen to when the French attacked Da Nang harbour in 1847. Then, of course, on March 8, 1965, the first unit of the US Expeditionary Force also came ashore in Da Nang.

It's difficult trying to be objective about the Vietnam War – especially in Vietnam. But wandering around the country visiting battlefields and war zones, talking to Vietnamese, Chinese, French, it's impossible to imagine how on earth the Americans thought they could win. I mean, everything was against them. The battleground; the ground rules; the people themselves – their singlemindedness, their cold-blooded, ruthless dedication, their absolute determination against all the odds, against all logic, against the greatest power and the greatest resources the earth has ever known.

Just outside Ho Chi Minh City, the new name for Saigon, are the Cu Chi Tunnels. Now I read the newspapers as well as the guy falling asleep next to me in the train from Buxted to London every morning. I knew the Vietnamese were great tunnellers. I knew that at Dien Bien Phu one of the reasons the Viet Minh were able to inflict such a glorious defeat on the French, the last in a long unbroken line of defeats they have suffered since 1815, was that instead of trying to drag their heavy artillery and anti-aircraft guns through high mountain passes they tunnelled through the hills surrounding the French camps and attacked them mercilessly without fear of reprisals. But I had failed to appreciate the size and scale of tunnel operations during the Vietnam War itself.

At Cu Chi, about twenty miles from Ho Chi Minh City, I actually climbed down into the tunnels, crawled along them and saw the eating quarters and the emergency hospital and where the generals sat and ran the operation. It's mind-boggling. Over 200 kilometres of tunnels, dug three storeys deep, accommodating over 5,000 men eating, sleeping, drinking, underneath one of the biggest airbases, covering hundreds of acres, that the Americans ever built outside the US.

'Americans, they send dogs down after us. But we steal soap from Americans. We wash in American soap. We wash clothes in American soap. Dogs find us, they smell soap, they think we are Americans. They go away,' one of the guides, an old soldier, told me.

All around the tunnels you can see the craters left by the wave after wave of B52s which tried but failed to destroy them. You can see where they scored a direct hit. You can also see how, when there was a direct hit, the Vietnamese built new tunnels and entrances and exits.

Wander round the Crimes in Aggression War in Vietnam Museum in Vo Van Tan Street – the building was once home to the US Information Service – and you'll see what else they survived. If you've got the courage.

Now I've been to the concentration camps; I've been to old KGB headquarters and interrogation and torture blocks in Eastern Europe; but they're nothing compared to this. Called originally the Exhibition of Chinese and American War Crimes in Aggression War in Vietnam – the 'Chinese' was dropped in 1990; the 'American' in 1994 – it tells the story, obviously, from the Vietnamese point of view.

I know all wars are wrong. I know that in wars there are atrocities on both sides. And I know the Vietnamese are masters of – is it persuasion or is it propaganda? – and that every army unit was accompanied by painters, writers, photographers, film-makers as well as even singers and dancers. And I am quite prepared to accept that it wasn't just the Americans who did such horrifying things to the Vietnamese people; after all, the French, the Chinese, the South Vietnamese under Ngo Dinh Diem, were not exactly on the side of the angels. But, God help me, this is one of the most shocking, horrifying, terrifying, stomach-churning exhibitions I've ever seen. It almost makes you wonder how an American could dare set foot in Vietnam again. Which is obviously why not many of them do and those that do claim, in their New York, Boston and Mississippi accents, to be Australian, Canadian, Danish, Swedish, or whatever.

Outside in the rough, sandy yard are a guillotine used by the French, an American aircraft shot down during the war, a collection of armoured vehicles, some heavy artillery, some bombs and weapons.

Inside one low wooden hut after another is the most unbelievable collection of photographs and exhibits concentrated on the Americans' behaviour during the war. There are scores of graphic, detailed photographs of atrocities. There are photographs of US soldiers setting houses on fire, leading prisoners away, laughing at a heap of torn-up, mangled bodies, dragging a mutilated body by a length of rope through the bush and, of course, that picture of the body being dragged along behind a tank.

There are pictures of US airplanes spraying toxic chemicals; B52s saturation-bombing Hanoi and other parts of the country; and all types of bombs, shells and mines ranging from the orange and guava bombs up to the seven-ton seismic bomb which could devastate an area the size of a football pitch and seriously injure anything within three miles.

There are pictures of people sprayed by a steel pellet bomb being thrown out of a helicopter, pictures of napalm bomb victims, and phosphorus bomb victims. And, of course, there are photographs of the My Lai massacre on March 16, 1968, when 504 people were slaughtered.

This is what went under the name of constant vigilance, dry-season offensives and delaying actions.

During my visit an old Vietnamese showed me a phrase-book produced by the Vietnamese Ministry of Foreign Affairs for government officials during the war. On the one side it told you what happened; on the other was the official description. Regimental combat teams were called small groups of soldiers. Intensive was an offensive. And the scorched-earth policy was to be described as a wave of machinegun fire.

When I came out there were three very quiet Americans standing by the War Times Souvenir Shop which was selling, among other things, imitation US uniforms and hats. They told me they were from Georgia. I often go to the States, and only in the last few years have I found Americans prepared to talk about Vietnam; either those who took part or those who didn't. It's as if they wanted to blot the whole thing out of their national consciousness. Strangely enough, it's usually only in Georgia I find people really ready to talk about it. Whether that's because Georgians did not latch on to the Canada trick or the teacher dodge until too late, or whether they were just more prepared to fight than anybody else, I don't know.

I asked the three of them what they thought. One was big and burly, with a great bushy beard and a violent pink jacket. He said he was from Savannah. During the war he was with the helicopter rescue service.

'Whenever they shot down one of our choppers, we had to go out there with another one of those big babies and bring it home,' he drawled.

'Bring it home?' I wondered.

'To try and repair it. Get it back into service. If not, use it for spares. You'd be amazed how many of those choppers we patched up and put back into service.'

He told me he served two terms: 1967–68 and 1968–69.

'Two terms. How come two terms?'

'I volunteered.'

'So what made you volunteer?'

'I was waiting to be shipped out. I was at the airport. This other bunch of guys arrive. The officer is one of those tough guys, built like a tank. He's almost bald. What hair he's got is grey. I ask him how long he's been out there. He looks at me and says, How old do you think I am? I look at him. He looks old enough to be my father. Gee, around forty, forty-five, I guess. He tells me he's nineteen. He's a farmer's boy from Tennessee. He's been living out in the bush for eighteen months. For Chrissakes, I think, if this is what it does to a nineteen-year-old, I'll sign on again just to stop them sending out another nineteen-year-old. That's as true as I'm sitting here.'

He looked at the queue of Vietnamese waiting to go in. 'Yessir, I was one of the lucky ones. Came back with everything I went with. Still got my arms, my legs. Not too crazy. Least no more than I was when I went.' He said he was horrified at what he had seen. He knew atrocities had been committed on both sides. He'd lived through all the anti-Vietnam feeling in the States. He'd even pretended for a time he had not been to Vietnam. But this was the first time he had seen it like it was.

The second one was from Augusta. He looked fit, suntanned, the kind of American who jogs before breakfast and runs mini-marathons to keep in shape. He told me he was in the Marines. 'You know the picture of the South Vietnamese guy holding the gun to that VC's head and just killing him there like that? It was in all the papers, on television. I was there. I saw it. What they don't tell you is that moments before, that VC wiped out that guy's whole family. His wife, his kids, his mother and father. I mean, you'd want to kill him if he did that to your family, wouldn't you? But they don't tell you that.'

We stood by the guillotine. 'I remember another thing,' he said. 'We get into this clearing. There's nothing but trees. Then we hear this voice: IBCs. You're dead. We freeze. Then at the edge of the clearing we see a VC. He's got a loudhailer. IBC, you're dead. Nobody moves. We just look at him. He's standing there all by himself. No weapons, nothing. We're carrying more weapons than they had in the whole of World War Two. Then once again, he said: IBCs, you're dead.'

'So what happened?'

'I'll tell you what happened. The trees opened up. Those damn VCs had carved hiding places in the inside of trees. They fell off the branches. They came up from out of the earth. They were everywhere. We didn't have a chance.'

The two of them then started going on about China Beach near Oanang where at least once in every thirteen-month tour Americans went to rest, relax, swim, get bombed out of their minds, or whatever.

'So what was the worst thing you came across?' I asked as we started walking.

'The worst thing? We're operating with the South Vietnam-ese. We get to this village. The South Vietnamese guy says they are hiding Viet Cong. He goes up to the village chief, tells him if they don't give us the Viet Cong, he'll level the village. The chief says they're not hiding any VCs. Our guy says he'll give him ten minutes to come up with them. Ten minutes are up and there're no Viet Cong. The South Vietnamese move in and they flatten the place. Everything . . . everybody.'

'The worst thing?' the second guy said. 'We're on patrol. We get to this village. The Viet Cong have been there. There in the middle is one of our boys. They've nailed him to a tree. He's stark naked. He's slit from here,' he points to his throat, 'to here.' He points to his groin. 'And they've cut his balls off and stuffed them in his mouth.' He gulps. 'Nope, I don't reckon I've come across anything worse than that.'

All the time we were talking, Vietnamese were queuing up to go in. At 7,000 dong per ticket, around 70 cents, it's about the equivalent of a day's wages for many of them.

The third American was lean and tall, over six foot. He had dark grey hair, glasses, looked a bit like a college professor. He told me he had been in Vietnam throughout the war. He was a child at the time. His parents were missionaries way out in the country. They had refused to leave. He stayed with them.

I asked what he thought about the exhibition. He didn't say anything.

Having decided to go for it, the Vietnamese now, I reckon, are using the same ruthless determination that they used to wage war against their old enemy – China? France? the US? – to kickstart their present moped economy, expand it and take their rightful place, heaven help us, alongside the other Asian Tigers.

First, they have drawn up their objectives. In 1925 Ho Chi Minh founded the Vietnam Revolutionary Youth League. His objective: freedom. At the time it was an impossible dream. But they did it.

Today, no matter who you talk to; the Ministry of Trade, the Chamber of Commerce, the local office of the State Committee for Co-operation and Investment, or the rickshaw driver who hangs around outside the now-closed Majestic Hotel who speaks English, French, Chinese and Japanese and was twice thrown in jail by the South Vietnamese for supporting Ho Chi Minh during the war, everybody is singing the same song. We are a nation of 72 million people. We are way behind the rest of South-East Asia. We want to catch up. We are going to catch up. There are enormous opportunities in the country for foreign investors. We will do everything we can to encourage, cajole, virtually blackmail foreign investors to come in. And they do.

Production costs are low. Overheads are low. Salaries are low: as low as US$20 a month for labourers; US$80 for drivers, US$200–300 for junior executives. In order to make ends meet many people take to the streets – buying and selling. One old lady who spends all day wandering the streets with two fruit baskets balanced either end of a long pole, told me – in French – that she was doing it to help her sister get her first diploma. Another woman, selling vegetables along Mai Thi Luu by the corner with Dien Bien Pha Street told me, this time with a little help from a customer, that she used to work in an office. She earned 200,000 dong per month. But she couldn't survive. Now she is up at four o'clock every morning to go to the big wholesale market at Ong Lanh Bridge. From there she makes her way to her spot along Mai Thi Luu where she stays until she has sold everything. She makes enough money not only to survive; her children are also getting a better education.

Companies are not just coming in for the low production and overhead costs and the low salaries, however, they are also coming in because Vietnam will one day soon be a booming consumer market – just think of the fridges, washing machines, food mixers and cars they will need. Some are also coming in, I'm convinced, because they believe that the sooner they can absorb Vietnam into the Asian Club, raise their standard of living and get them hooked on consumer goods, the less chance there is that there will be any more problems. Much the same way, I guess, as west Germany regards east Germany.

Second, the Vietnamese are mobilising behind the cause. Wherever you go, they are more than prepared to welcome foreigners – even Americans. Which I must admit surprised me, for two reasons. The second being that I would have thought Vietnam had such nightmare memories for them that Americans would want to stay away. I mean there's the most famous embassy roof in the world, just down the road from the presidential palace. There's the Binh Soup Shop in Ly Chinh Tang Street, two minutes walk from the railway station or twenty minutes by rickshaw, the secret headquarters of the Viet Cong during the war but today a pretty nondescript café. There's what used to be District 8, built by the US for the privileged few – civil servants, government officials – to make them love Uncle Sam and support the war, as well as to show to visiting American VIPs, which was destroyed when the Viet Cong hit Saigon in April 1975. And there's all those blue-eyed, blond little kids running after them shouting, Daddy, Daddy.

But some quiet Americans are back in what was not so long ago a war zone crawling with dragon ladies and suicide squads, obviously eager to let Saigons by bygones. Not many. But they are there. So are the Japanese, half of Singapore, three-quarters of Taiwan, a bunch of Koreans, a smattering of Europeans and even a single Argentinian.

Sit in almost any hotel in Ho Chi Minh City tucking into a hearty meal of pig's brains, ducks' feet and sea slugs washed down with snake wine to the strains of Gounod's 'Ave Maria' played on a cello in the background, and you can see them traipsing through reception up to their rooms; and before you hit the liver salts to the strains of Gounod's 'Ave Maria' played on a clarinet they're out again looking to sign up whatever deal is going. And they are all getting the maximum support from the Vietnamese – the government; all the state organisations and committees. It's unbelievable how fast they can move if the deal is right and they are convinced you are the right person.

The problem is getting the deal right. I spoke to an Australian architect who had submitted and re-submitted plans for a big hotel/office development no less than twelve times. Every time it was rejected. He had followed all the correct procedures; a statue of Ho Chi Minh in the reception area; a donation to the local children's home; a couple of trips to Paris for key officials and their wives or whoever. Then, he said, it suddenly hit him. The reception area was going to be supported by seven enormous beams. Seven means death to the Vietnamese. He threw in another one – bingo. With eight beams, it was approved straightaway.

So how do the Vietnamese decide if you're the right person? Easy. Hold your hands out flat. Close your fingers tightly together. If you can see daylight between them, you're out. It means bad luck, you're not to be trusted. If your fingers fit tightly together, like mine, you're in. Put the deposit down on that Rolls-Royce straightaway.

In the très très swish restaurant at the Hotel Metropole one lunchtime I met a Taiwanese property developer who told me he had big problems when he first came to Vietnam because there were gaps between his fingers big enough to build a couple of office blocks. But he solved the problem.

'How?' I wondered. 'Plastic surgery?'

'No,' he grinned, waving his hands in front of my face. 'Rings. Today in Vietnam I always wear lots of rings. You cannot see any gap between my fingers. Today I am very lucky.'

The French, of course, are in a class of their own, as usual. Because they never really left. To us, Dien Bien Phu was yet another glorious French defeat. To the French it was merely a *divertissement*, an opportunity to pretend to hand the place over to the Americans who, they knew, would make a mess of the whole thing so that they could come back later and claim their rightful slice of the action. Which is exactly what they've done. They've stitched up the government, written off a whole load of old debt, granted them a whole load of new debt, signed them up for the Francophone Club and even undertaken to arrange the next big gathering in Hanoi. They have moved in in a big way at the provincial level as well, and French businessmen have renewed all their old contacts and invited anybody who's anybody to Paris for le weekend. Now they are sitting back, waiting. They're even pouring in as tourists and, ever the diplomats, dressing up like Vietnamese noblemen and women during the French occupation, holding 'royal' banquets and inviting as their guest of honour Nguyen

Phuoc Bao Hien, grandson of the Emperor Thanh Thai, who ruled Vietnam from 1889 to 1907.

Third, logistics. Listen, there is nothing you can tell the Vietnamese about distribution and delivery systems and getting the goods to market on time. These are the guys who built, ran and operated the Ho Chi Minh trail, who built, ran and operated the Cu Chi tunnels, who ... shall I go on? Shipping raw materials in, shipping goods out is child's play to them.

Fourth, they have cranked up the old propaganda machine again. All over the world the message has gone out: Vietnam wants to do business; Vietnam is going to do business; Vietnam is going to do big, big business, so you'd better watch out.

I was surprised, however, at how little propaganda there was in the country itself. Sure you see big pictures of Ho Chi Minh in government offices, railway stations, university waiting rooms. In the main post office in Ho Chi Minh City which was designed by the towering Monsieur Eiffel himself, there is a big portrait. There are a couple of big posters here and there in the town. But nothing obvious, nothing dramatic. Out in the countryside, I think I saw only two or three posters, which looked as though they had been there a million years.

There is certainly no cult of anything at all, which in some respects is surprising, bearing in mind everything Ho Chi Minh did for them. There are no thoughts of Ho Chi Minh. There are no picture books. There are no songs. And there are no loudspeakers in the streets. Which is a pity, because even a few bars of the 'Red Flag' would make a change from Gounod's 'Ave Maria', the constant phut, phut of motorcycles and the sound of dogs barking all night as if they've heard what's on the menu for lunch the following day.

Now and then you see the police driving around in their scruffy yellow trucks. Or trying to drive around. They are smothered by bikes and mopeds and rickshaws, like the rest of us. Now and then you might spot a soldier. Trying to cross the street; leaning up against a wall; stuck on a moped in a traffic jam. Like everybody else.

I must say there's not much sign of the war either. In Ho Chi Minh City they tell you that, though they dug out so much earth to build the tunnels, they used it all to fill in the craters left by the bombs. The only bunkers you see nowadays are in golf courses. Neither are there huge areas destroyed by Agent Orange. The areas I saw that had been sprayed were covered with scrub and, in many cases, young woodland.

I did, however, read a newspaper article that went on about the need to 'build a clean, strong, well-organised party'. The failure of perestroika in the Soviet Union proved beyond doubt that 'a socialist-oriented society must have renovation'. But that was about it.

The result of all these efforts is, of course, good news and bad news. Good news because it means greater investment, more jobs, greater stability, less risk of people deserting the countryside and making for the already severely over-populated towns, and less risk of anything starting again in the future. Bad news because in the rush to build factories and offices for foreign investors, and hotels for everybody who follows in their wake, including the inevitable tourists, great chunks of the country are disappearing faster than if they had been bombed. In fact, in some ways the new urban guerrillas are the speculators and property developers and construction companies.

Take Hanoi. Gone are all the old French-style colonial buildings next to the Mansapal Theatre. Gone are the nice old houses next to the Grand Department Store on Hang Bai Street as well as those on Ly Thuong Kier and Phan Chu Trinh streets. In their place is a multi-storey hotel and some nondescript office blocks. Gone are the huddle of old buildings alongside the Temple of Literature. In their place, bland, faceless offices for the State Committee for Co-operation and Investment. Gone also, though no doubt not so much lamented, is the famous Hanoi Hilton, the old Ho Loa which served as first a prison for Vietnamese nationalists under the

French and then for the Americans under the Vietnamese. It's being replaced by a massive US$20 million office, hotel and apartment complex. Hilton are planning their own hotel nearer the commercial area. The association was probably too much for them. The famous Westlake, which covers over five square kilometres in the centre of the city, should in all honesty be renamed the Western Lake because so many old buildings have been torn down and replaced with fancy modern villas and apartment blocks. In only a week, you see old homes being torn down and new, larger, more insipid ones built in their place.

Quick – there's a spot worth developing. Let's move in. When nobody is looking, in come the boys. Overnight, a small house can be levelled ready for the bulldozers the following morning; a big house will have the top two floors taken off. The following morning, because it is now a dangerous structure, the job can be completed in broad daylight.

'I see photographs of Hanoi. I want to come here. When I come here everything has changed,' a French tourist told me when I spotted him wandering about looking for the Ho Loa, which to him was the Maison Centrale. Indeed, things have got so bad that a whole host of preservation and conservation societies have sprung up to try and save their national monuments before it's too late.

So will the Vietnamese make it? Will the qualities that enabled them to win one war enable them to win another?

'It's the final day of my trip to Vietnam. I'm in Ho Chi Minh City in the Caravelle Hotel, the old Foreign Press hotel, which is now called Khach San Doc Lap, which stands for 'You ain't seen nothin yet, Uncle Sam.' I'm ready to leave. My luggage is piled up on the roof waiting for the helicopter. I'm sitting in the restaurant playing with my food, wondering whether to eat it. I'm talking to another FO buff. The skies outside are black.

'Looks as though it's going to rain,' I mutter.

'Not at all, old chap. Rainy season's not for another couple of months. Take my word for it.'

The following day – you got it – it rained.

Havana

I don't know about To Have. This is most definitely To Have Not country.

The clocks stopped at twelve noon, January 1, 1959. Nothing, but nothing, has happened since. Everything has been left to crumble slowly into the ground. Nothing has been painted. Nothing has been repaired. Nothing has even been dusted. The whole place is covered – buried – in cobwebs, poverty, despair and decay.

The children of this 900-mile-long, fertile tropical island, who thirty-five years ago were told that they were going to be the only privileged members of the new social order, are today expressing their undying gratitude by surviving on 1 bread roll a day, 2 eggs a week and $2\frac{1}{2}$ ounces of beans, 4 ounces of coffee, 4 pounds of sugar and 5 pounds of rice – a month. And a delicious helping of cat stew whenever they can get it. So efficient has twenty years of state planning been that Cuba cannot grow enough food or catch enough fish to stop them from going blind from diet deficiencies.

The rest of the less privileged population, facing death in the afternoon if not tomorrow morning, is reduced to begging for just about everything. Even for soap. Not just the poor guys who are living and dying in the streets, but barmen, taxi drivers and shopkeepers as well. Even schoolteachers. I told one schoolteacher that I was sorry, but soap was not something I usually carried around in my briefcase.

'Please can't you go back to the hotel and get some?' he said. 'We haven't had soap for months and months.'

Havana and Beirut are similar, I suppose. Both are nothing. Both are completely ruined. Both look like demolition sites. The difference is that Beirut did it by waging civil war. The Cubans did it my waging peace. Wandering around Havana is like trying to remember the last time your brother-in-law bought you a drink.

Everything is falling to bits – some things more than others. Some government buildings look halfway passable, like islands in the stream of decay. What is holding the rest of the place together God only knows. And I don't just mean the odd building in the centre of town, I mean every single building. Even the buildings supported by wooden scaffold poles that themselves have been gently rotting away for twenty years. Even the buildings which were being constructed all those years ago and are still surrounded by cranes. Maybe they're held up by the rubbish and the refuse inside; maybe by the sheer survival instinct of every man, woman and privileged child in the place.

The Malecon, Havana's six-lane promenade, still looks graceful, but today it's empty and crumbling. The once swish, fashionable Fifth Avenue, lined with foreign embassies, is the same. Outside disintegrating buildings, ambassadors' cars sit forlornly on concrete blocks, their tyres long since removed and probably sold on the black market for bread. Even the Russian embassy, which looks like a cross between a Palace of Culture and a giant Aztec totem pole, is collapsing as fast as the Soviet Union's support for the country which, after twenty solid years, is now practically zero. Even the Masons' headquarters in the town centre is falling to bits. The Spanish lodges still send some money, I quickly discovered with a handshake, to an old man sitting inside by a broken window. Not, of course, as much as they would like, but something.

The streets are more potholes than street. Traffic is almost non-existent, except for bicycles. Cubans may not be the healthiest people on earth but they must be the fittest. Nearly everybody cycles everywhere. Even government ministers cycle to work, their bodyguards on either side, also on bicycles.

Some people told me they cycled two, maybe three hours a day to work and back. And most people have someone riding with them: men with women, men without women. I saw wizened, shrunken old ladies riding sidesaddle. Young girls seemed to ride anywhere. I even saw a joyrider sprawled out across the handlebars.

I met an accountant in a government office who told me he cycled two hours to the office and two hours back every day. In winter he gets up at five o'clock. The wife and two daughters get up at 5.30. The son also rises about the same time. The rest of the year it's an hour earlier because of the torrents of rain in spring and the humidity and pollution in summer.

You see the occasional motorbike, and even sidecars, some carrying up to five people at a time.

Wandering around Havana is like wandering round an empty, fuming, chugging, broken-down motor museum, or watching an old late-night gangster movie on television. If you see a car, it is one of those big old American cars: A Chevvy or a Dodge or an Oldsmobile or even a Packard Eight 1100 with its original radio. The wings have gone, the windows have gone, most of the inside has gone. I swear I saw a Chevrolet Belair Convertible, which Noël Coward used to drive around Jamaica until it ran out of petrol and he couldn't find the petrol cap. Inside there were no seats, only wooden crates. The driver was sitting on one in the front and everybody else was sitting on others in the back. I saw rusty, broken-down old Ladas. I even saw old cars and trucks I never knew existed. I promise you, while I was there I only saw one Toyota and a couple of Nissans.

The people are obviously thriving on the combination of their privileged diets and long periods exercising on their privileged bicycles. They are certainly some of the fittest, healthiest rakes I have ever seen. Most families seem to share a single tiny room, about 10 feet by 15 feet, where they eat, drink, sleep and go to the toilet. Salaries are nothing. What am I saying? They are less than nothing. Ordinary workers, secretaries, office staff, earn US$1.50, maybe US$3 – a month. A nurse earns around US$8 a month.

In order to stop them getting flabby and putting on weight the government doesn't believe in softening them up by allowing them to amble across the road to the nearest supermarket and gorge themselves on tins of goodies. Instead everyone is issued with a super keep-fit privileged ration book, which they have to take to the nearest super keep-fit state ration shop, which is deliberately miles away, and queue for long hours to buy a single special super keep-fit high-protein tin of beans which is supposed to last an entire family until Christmas. Next year. Breakfast, lunch and dinner. That is if they are unlucky enough to have three privileged super keep-fit meals a day.

Bread is common food – not for the privileged. Similarly eggs. So the privileged people of Cuba can go months on end without seeing either. Instead they experience the joys of melting down plastic gloves as a cheese substitute and eating sandwiches stuffed with the strands lovingly extracted from floor mops.

During one trip, I was told the government had been discussing the health of the nation. With practically no meat in the shops, no milk and precious little bread, they felt – surprise, surprise – there was a threat of people wasting away for lack of vitamins. What should they do to solve the problem? Give the people more meat, said one minister, who is now an ex-minister because he obviously didn't understand the needs of the privileged in a Marxist society.

But below the grime and the rust and the sheer miserable privilege you could see why a million would-be Hemingways once raved about the place. Havana is full of once-beautiful squares, once-fabulous Spanish-style buildings, once-lovely old houses and once-long colonnades. In its heyday it must have been beautiful, like Beirut or Alexandria. The rich and super-rich flooded in. It was, I was told by an old hotel porter with a long memory, an ABC country, full of Americans, Brits and Canadians, who all went around together. If the Brits were having a golf tournament, the Americans would kill to get invited. If the Canadians were organising a tennis tournament the Brits would do anything to be there. The bars, especially Sloppy Joe's, were famous the world over for daiquiris and planters' punches and *jamon y queso* sandwiches. The casinos were always packed with the beautiful people. The Tropicana was legendary. Many's the time, he told me, grown men would fight duels for the honour of smoking a Cuban cigar rolled on a virgin's thighs.

In the old days in the tabaqueros they would sit on row after row of wooden benches and roll 100 cigars a morning while listening to the rector read out loud from the newspapers. In the afternoon things were more relaxed. The rector read them novels and short stories. But they still rolled their standard twenty-five cigars an hour. Now there's no reading. Not even any muzak. The cigar factories have all closed down. What tabaqueros are left are in storefront factories in Miami tuned in all day long to one of the Cuban exile radio stations. As for the virgins, your guess is as good as mine.

Whenever I go to Havana I stay in the Hotel Inglaterra, a wonderful if dilapidated traditional Spanish hotel, with high cool ceilings, tiled floors and mosaic walls. It still advertises commodious stables for guests' horses. In the bad old days it was part of the circuit. Now it's not even a model of socialist efficiency. In a country which is desperately counting the cost of everything, I notice, for example, that the lights are on in my room all the time, day and night. Because the switch is broken and nobody repairs it. The furniture is luxurious, compared to an underground Chechnyan air-raid shelter. The bathroom, well, kinda works. On my first trip, in one corner, hidden under a pile of cobwebs, was this giant upside-down ice cream cornet with a long green tube coming out of the end. It took me three days to realise it was a Kirghizstan hairdryer. Anyway I couldn't get it to do a thing for me the whole time I was there.

There was a bath, but no bath plug, which struck me as odd. I know the Russians don't have bath plugs, because they probably don't have any baths either. But when you think of the electricity that must be consumed pumping water to at least the hotels and maybe one or two select parts of the city, and the cost involved, it seems crazy they are prepared to see it flow straight down the drains again. At the very least, plugs would mean less water consumption, less electricity and presumably less cost. But maybe that's being too capitalist.

What did strike me as revolutionary was that the bathroom floor was higher than the rest of the room. So what happened? One morning the top of the East German shower unit blows off. Water shoots straight through the Uzbekistan shower curtain, sprays the Kirghizstan hairdryer, short circuits the Tajikistan fuse, blows all the Kazakhstan light bulbs and floods the room. But at least the lights went out. What happened as it was beginning to get dark that evening? They came round and repaired the lot.

The rest of the hotel was, as they say, interesting. The food was interesting. The drink was interesting. The service was interesting.

There was nowhere to escape to outside. Almost all the bars have disappeared. In a city that kept Hemingway busy writing in the morning and drinking joltos, Cuban Havana Club rum and dry martinis the rest of the day, there are only three bars left. There's the one round the back of the Cathedral Square, which has photographs of Papa, as he is universally known, on the wall and a blow-up of his signature behind the bar. There's the one way out at the Hemingway Marina, from where he used to go fishing for blue marlin. And there's La Theresa's, the beach bar down on the bay. Except I could never find a cab driver brave enough to take me there. It's crazy, when you think there is a whole industry waiting to be built around the bars Hemingway drank in: Drinking Times of Old Havana, For Whom the Bells Tolls.

What do people do? They despair. Because everybody knows the mess they are in; everybody knows something must be done; everybody knows nothing can be done. While you-know-who is still around. It's shocking.

The only trading company I could find was round the back of Revolution Place, which didn't look quite right. Maybe it's meant to be symbolic. A bit like the Revolution itself. Either way it doesn't seem to fit together. There is this big, big, well I suppose you'd call it a monument, in the centre, like four giant, blocked-in stepladders leaning against each other. Around it are some of the most faceless statues I've seen for a long time. Then there is this huge open square for spontaneous demonstrations of unity and national gratitude, which doesn't look as though it's ever been used. On one side is a pretty nondescript office building. Scrawled all over the front of it is a giant outline portrait of Che Guevara. On another side is the National Library. On another the National Theatre. But to look at them you would never guess. I thought they were just more offices. Over at the back is Fidel's office although I was told nobody ever knows when or if he's there.

When I finally got to the company I discovered it was engaged in highly treasonous operations. At enormous risk to life and limb they were importing toilet seats from the United States.

I couldn't find any factories or workshops, hardly any garages. Even the banks, or the banks that were open, looked desperate. Windows were broken, doors hanging off their hinges, floors were pitted. What furniture there was was twisted and rusty. They looked like the only banks in the world which desperately needed people to break in in order to give them money. Give, not lend. None of them looked as though they could afford to buy a pane of glass, let alone repay a loan.

Telephones hardly ever work. All the wires are in the open, so when it rains, the rain gets in and breaks the connection. When it's sunny, the heat melts the wires and breaks the connection. If you want to call the US, ninety miles away, the call has to be routed via Italy.

There are power-cuts all the time. Suddenly during the

morning the lights will go out and you spend the rest of the day with one half of your face cleanshaven and the other half looking like Che Guevara. Or suddenly in the afternoon, zap, the lights go out and if you're listening to a classical concert on Cuba's serious music channel you rush down to the car to hear it on the car radio. Or even in the evening. Once I was told the lights went out halfway through *Tosca* at the National Theatre and everyone just sat there waiting for the power to come back on.

Out in the country you can drive for hours without seeing another person, let alone another car. There are still farms, but none of them operate nearly as efficiently as they should. The sugarcane is as thin and fragile as dried grass. Men still plough with oxen. Russian tractors are rotting away for want of diesel.

After thirty-five years completely insulated from the rest of the world they also have no experience or knowledge of business. They don't understand basic business concepts, not even the yummies, the young upwardly mobile Marxists, who are supposed to be inching Cuba oh-so-slowly back into the real world.

One yummy asked me what was the date of the most momentous event in modern history.

May 8, 1945? September 2, 1945? January 1, 1959? I wondered.

'June 15, 1994,' he grinned. 'The first time in thirty-five years that Fidel Castro left off his military fatigues and wore a business suit.'

Which struck me as doubly significant. It was the first time I heard anyone refer to him by name. It was usually 'El' (him) or 'La barba' (the beard). He also felt that swapping the fatigues for a suit was obviously not just the whim of a dedicated follower of fashion.

But talk to any yummy about basic things like costs, earnings, profitability, their eyes glaze over. They start dreaming of that girl in the 1830 Club in the Malecon where they hang out and do their partying and disco-ing in private, away from the privileged classes.

Talk to a proper Cuban businessman, if you can find one, about the simplest form of buying and selling.

'Well, I think the initial priority is to raise some capital . . .'

He looks at you.

'. . . so that with the capital we could consider a feasibility study, a cost analysis and a marketing assessment . . .'

He can't make up his mind whether you're mad or whether you're mad.

'Then with the results we could consider approaching various sources and putting together a package . . .'

He's off. He's dreaming of the other girl in the 1830 Club in the Malecon with the legs that go up to her shoulder blades.

On one trip I arrived just as the government was taking its first tentative steps to rejoin the world. After thirty-five years they had decided to accept the hated yankee dollar as legal tender. They also decided to open up their economy to private enterprise. Just 186 different types of jobs would no longer be the preserve of the state, and could be undertaken by ordinary private individuals. Trouble was, as far as I could discover all 186 jobs were to do with cleaning cars. Park your car anywhere in Havana and immediately you are descended on by 186 different car-cleaning specialists, 180 to make it filthy, five to clean the car itself and one with the unenviable task of cleaning out the exhaust.

I tried explaining what I was saying about business, but it was no way sufficient to make any difference. They didn't understand a word. They just do not understand the nature, the thinking, the concept of private enterprise, what is needed to generate it, what is needed to stimulate it, what effect it will have on society.

Obviously there is going to be change. How slow or how fast, depends on how long you-know-who hangs on. A slow catching up will probably take years. But once it begins, everybody, every government, every aid organisation in the world will be eager to help. Especially the Americans. For all the obvious reasons. A fast catching up could take, knowing how fast the Americans can move when they want to, maybe four or five years. Especially if the more unconventional American organisations get involved. I won't put money on it, but if they do you can bet your life one day there will be a Papa Hemingway Theme Park just outside Havana complete with casinos, bars, bullrings and everything else the old boy believed in.

In the meantime, while the architect of all their fortunes is too modest to acknowledge the gratitude of his privileged people and drives through the streets of Havana only late at night surrounded by a battalion of AK-47s, the only options seem to be death or exile.

Death I saw at the Columbus Cemetery off Zapata Avenue practically in the centre of town. It's clean, neat and tidy. The hedges are clipped, the grass is trim. All the mausoleums, some of them bigger than the homes some people are still living in just two minutes walk away, are all clean, neat and in good repair. Obviously the dead get more fuss made of them than the living. There was this poor guy sitting on a bench, staring blankly into space.

'Death is a big moment for people in Latin America,' he said.

Exile and the enormous threat of death as well, I saw at Cojimar, just east of Havana, the tiny fishing village in the book by what's-his-name about some old fishermen. Every day you see people setting sail for Florida on incredibly precarious rafts. Rubber tyres, bits of old plywood, a broken door, lumps of polystyrene, old beds, car chassis, packing crates, even single inner tubes, all bound together with string and clothes-line and chewing gum. I wouldn't risk floating them in the bath let alone sail them ninety miles across the Straits of Florida, three times the width of the English Channel, at the mercy of the tropical sun, ten-foot high waves and Zoma, a black-eyed fifteen-foot shark which, I was told, cruises just off the coast, waiting . . .

I saw one family arrive, their raft tied to the roof of their car: mother, father, two teenage sons. They untied this flimsy raft, carried it across the beach, put it in the water and were off. All

I could see them carrying were two green cans.

'What's in the cans?' I asked some guy standing watching. 'Water for the voyage?'

'No,' he said. 'Petrol. To keep off the sharks.'

My God, can you imagine how privileged people have to be to do that?

Bruce Chatwin, that great eater of prehistoric eggs, made a big thing about songlines in Australia. All I can say is, I hit the Cuban equivalent – as soon as we landed in Havana.

A whole DC10 hobbles and staggers into a tiny immigration area designed and built to handle biplanes. There are six immigration boxes to handle everybody. Invisible lines are everywhere. What happens? Two of them immediately close down. Not a word to anyone, no attempt to get replacements. One of the officials, a woman, then spends all the time we are queuing up the other side of the line playing pat-a-cake with some kid outside on the tarmac. After about two days, it is finally my turn. Any longer and I wouldn't have had time to get into Havana and back again for the whole process to start again on the way out. I hand over my passport. Big stare. Am I the guy in the passport? I try to look casual. Maybe I should fill in another form, refer the case to my superior officer or telephone Moscow for instructions? I hand in my travel card. The Cubans issue travel cards, not visas, so you don't have to tell your friendly capitalist government where you've been. Again I try to look casual. Bang. The guy stamps all over my passport, so what the hell was the point of the travel card in the first place? Then I'm through.

Straight out of the box, round the corner and – wham – I'm bang up against the whole DC10-load desperately trying to put all its hand luggage, its duty-frees and everything else it has collected through a single X-ray machine. You think that's crazy! Are you ready? As each bag, box or sack comes out of the machine, a single security man grabs it and examines it. What should take, what, thirty seconds per person now takes two to three minutes. Does anyone say anything? No way. Would you say anything to a security man in a country covered with invisible lines?

But fair's fair. Praise where praise is due. As he sees the mass of people jamming up around the machine, and the mountain of stuff waiting to be pushed through, what does he do? He switches off the electronic security archway so we can spill out across the other side. If that is not considerate, what is? The result, of course, is – chaos. Everybody is trying to get through the arch, get their luggage through the arch, get their friends' friends' luggage through the arch. Other security men are standing by, but they do nothing. They stay their side of the line. Obviously it is not their job. Their turn comes next. Either that or they are mentally fixing the dodgers so they can pick them up later.

I'm relaxed, I take it steady. A million years travelling in Africa has taught me that there's no point in rushing because – you get it – there's bound to be another two-hour wait before the luggage arrives. And was I right? The distance from plane to luggage hall could not have been more than 200, well let's exaggerate like mad, 300 metres. There was not another plane scheduled to land for hours. So how long did it take before the first battered suitcase arrived? A whole hour. I timed it. I was trying to see if I could get them in the *Guinness Book of Records*. By the time the luggage started coming through I'd almost forgotten if I had a suitcase to wait for and if I did, what it was like. But eventually we recognised each other and were reconciled.

Was that the end of my entry problems? Not at all. Next came the how-the-hell-can-I-find-an-honest-taxi-driver routine. Through the final customs check. Through the arrivals hall. And then – wham – I'm in the open, hit full in the face by the heat. It's about 90 degrees and climbing by the second, and I'm surrounded by a million people all shrieking, Taxi, Taxi, Taxi. It's rough. But on the arrivals-at-airports-disturbance-scale it still only registers 97. Lagos, for example – not that I'm one to criticise – is a million times worse. This is kids' stuff.

'No. No, gracias,' I mumble using up most of my Spanish. I cross the invisible line and head for a nice, motherly-looking lady taxi driver at the back of the scrum. I tell her my hotel, the Inglaterra, and within two minutes we're on our way. And she charges me much less than I was prepared to pay.

It always works. But don't tell anyone. You could ruin the system.

The following morning I am wandering across the San Rafael y San Miguel, a big square in the centre of town, when I come across a group of medical students from Ghana, in the green hills of Africa. My Evé is not brilliant but I understand the odd word. I couldn't help wishing my brothers well, could I? Immediately I am adopted by them. They promise to show me the unofficial, non-tourist part of Havana.

'What do you mean, non-tourist part?' I asked.

Then it all came out. The centre of town is designated a tourist area. Inside that area, tourists are safe. There is supposed to be a policeman on every corner. Taxi drivers are tourist taxi drivers, and are supposed to charge official tourist rates. Hotels and bars are official tourist hotels and bars. They are also supposed to charge official tourist rates.

'So how do you know what is the official tourist area and what is not?' I asked. 'There're no signs, no barriers.'

There are tourist lines, they told me. Invisible tourist wrong lines. Known to the police, to taxi drivers, and to everybody else in Havana.

'So show me,' I said.

Suddenly they all remembered things to do. One had to queue up for his daily bread ration. Another had been promised some dried milk. He hadn't seen dried milk for a month. He couldn't afford not to go. The rest had cars to clean, and cars to clean and cars to clean. The only one who stayed was from south of Accra. His parents had gone to Cuba over twenty years ago to study. He was very tall and very thin. He was wearing the standard pair of old jeans and a T-shirt. He was studying to be a doctor, he told me, and had only two more years to do on the famous Isla de la Juventuel (Island of

Youth), which had originally been a notorious prison, the Isla de Pinos. When Castro seized power he closed the place down and built a complex of schools and training centres for students from all over the world. He told me he had never been to Ghana, but had read everything he could find about it in newspapers at the British embassy. He wanted to know everything I could tell him about the place. In return, he agreed to show me the invisible wrong lines.

We crossed the square and turned towards Baptista's old palace which is now the Memorial of the Revolution. Inside are all the things connected with their final liberation: the boat that brought Castro back to Cuba, the tanks that liberated the people from destitution under capitalism to destitution under socialism, and probably a couple of old capitalist razor blades as well.

I stepped off the broken pavement onto the roadway.

'No, don't,' he cried in a loud whisper. 'I can't come with you.'

'Why?'

'It's the tourist area. I'm not allowed.'

'But why?'

'It's the law. If I'm found inside they will stop me, ask for my papers. They might take me to the police station for questioning. You walk there. I'll follow.'

I decided to stay with my brother on his side of the square. Together we walked around the far end of the building and turned back up the other side.

'No, don't,' he whispered again.

'You mean. . .?'

'Yes. I'll cross over the road. You follow me on this side.' He shot across the road. What should I do? Follow him and risk getting him into trouble with the police? Or do as he said and hopefully avoid any problems? I did as my brother said. He darted along the other side of the street. I tried to keep pace with him on my side, dodging the tourists hanging around outside the Hotel Plaza. At the corner he suddenly shot back across the road to the plaza in the centre. He turned and nodded towards me. I shot across after him. It was like a chase scene in some third-rate spy movie.

'It's okay now,' he said when I caught up with him. 'This is inside the tourist area. But you must speak to me. I mustn't speak to you.'

'My brother.' We Ghanaians talk to each other like that. 'My brother,' I said, 'you're kidding me. It's not as bad as that, is it?'

I'd seen hardly any police and even fewer military in Havana, which, I must admit, surprised me. I had thought the place would be crawling with them.

'They are everywhere,' he said.

'But you don't, or at least I don't, see any.'

'That's because you are not looking. Every street has somebody working for the police.' He pointed to a young girl in a fancy Lycra outfit leaning up against a doorway. 'What do you think she's doing?' I was about to guess. 'Working for the police. How else can she see what's going on?' he whispered.

'Sure, but. . .'

'Then there are people all the time going around, checking up on them, making certain they are doing their—' He grabbed my arm. A man appeared out of the shadows, wearing filthy jeans and an even dirtier T-shirt. We stood still. The man went up to the girl and the two of them disappeared into the doorway.

'There,' he whispered. 'What did I tell you?'

As we walked back towards the Capitolio, modelled on the hated Capitol building in Washington, he told me the Cubans did not like 'niggers'. He said it in a deliberate Southern accent.

'There are about 600 of us. Most of us were born here. Our parents came here in solidarity with the Revolution. But that's all forgotten now. The only time they need us is when Mandela comes or Jerry Rawlings. Then they wheel us out to cheer. Afterwards they forget all about us.'

By now we were walking past the big flight of steps up to the Capitolio. I went to step off the pavement and walk down towards the railway station.

'No, don't,' he whispered again. 'This is non-tourist area. You are not allowed into non-tourist area.'

I looked around. There were no signs, no barriers, nothing to indicate I was passing into any different type of area.

'But how do I know?' I began.

'You don't. But they do. If they discover you here with me, they will blame me. I will have to show them my papers.'

'But what can they do?'

He swung his eyes up to heaven and swivelled round on the spot. 'My brother, I will tell you what they will do. They will ask for my papers. They will write my name down. Then they will come and ask me questions.'

'Just because. . .?'

'Just because I am talking to you. Then they will take me to the police station.'

'But they can't.'

'They can't! Listen, my brother. You try and tell them they can't.' He spun round again and washed his face all over with his hands. 'Of course they can. They can do what they want. And then I tell you what happens, they say they want to check my records. You know what that means?'

I shook my head.

'It means they call the British embassy and ask them.'

'But why the British embassy? Surely there's a Ghanaian. . .?'

'My brother,' he shook his head in sorrow, 'my brother, you know nothing. In Cuba they think Ghana, Zimbabwe, Zambia, they are all members of the Commonwealth. The Commonwealth is British. Therefore, they call the British embassy. My brother,' he sighed, 'I could be there for weeks before they can check my records.'

What could I do? 'Okay,' I said. 'You walk, I'll follow.' And I followed him across the mysterious lines and into forbidden territory. We went down a broken-down side-street leading to the railway line. Halfway down we turned right; two blocks, then left; along a bit, then, all of a sudden, through a tiny wooden door. There was hardly any plaster on the walls, the floor was sand. Facing us were two solid doors. He banged on the doors. They opened. In we went. It was an unofficial, illegal private bar.

'They find you here,' he wiped his face all over again with his hands, 'I am in big, but I mean big, trouble.'

Then why did you bring me here?' It was my turn to whisper.

'Because you are my brother. You are from Ghana. You know my home country.'

'But there's plenty of bars in town,' I said. 'I've been to the—'

'They're all tourist bars. We're not allowed to go to tourist bars. That's why we have to have our own private bars. In any case, how can we pay tourist prices?'

The bar was tiny, the front room of a house that should have been condemned a million years ago. A stack of beer cans stood in one corner. There were three rickety tables, about six equally rickety metal chairs. Practically no light. The windows were shuttered. The doors were kept bolted. It felt like being on the run. For I don't know how long, I drank unofficial Hatvey beer in an unofficial bar the wrong side of the line with people who don't officially exist. Most of them were Africans, or looked as though they were. They told me about living in Havana, trying to survive what they called El Tirano and what they thought of El Verdugo, which, though I may be wrong, I think has something to do with a pig.

'There is no food, everybody is hungry. We have ration books. One piece of bread a week, no milk, no meat. How can we live?'

They showed me their ration books. In the gloom I could just about see the details: 2.5kg rice, 250g beans, 1.4kg sugar, 30g coffee, one bar of soap. No mention of meat. Another one said: 2kg rice, 200g beans, 200g oil, 3 packets of cigarettes. Again, no mention of meat.

They told me horror stories about the hospitals and health care facilities, or rather lack of them. There were pharmacies, but they had no aspirin, no medicines, not even cream to rub on sores. There were hospitals, but the hospitals didn't have sheets or towels or soap, let alone syringes, swabs or even batteries for heart pacemaker machines. They had all vanished. Most hospitals didn't even have enough blood. People were too weak to give blood. Instead they had to rely on dextrose.

Yet Cuba has a worldwide reputation for medical research and technology. One evening in the Inglaterra I met a doctor from the Dominican Republic who had come to Havana to study fibre-optic surgery for four weeks and was paying handsomely for the privilege. On another occasion I met an American expert on biotechnology. Cuba, he told me, leads the world. Apparently because of the training a number of key Cuban scientists received in the old Soviet Union, and the virtually unlimited resources the government gave them, today they have a string of world-beating biotechnology firsts.

But had they been able to promote their technology worldwide? No way. Not that they hadn't tried. They built no less than four factories to produce the stuff. They had it coming out of their eyeballs. But did they think of how they were actually going to sell it? Not at all. When, in spite of their efforts, outside pharmaceutical companies heard about what they had been doing and politely asked for samples, the Cubans said no.

'Why should we give them samples? They will only copy our process,' I was told firmly by one Cuban.

'But if you don't give them samples, they will refuse to consider your products and refuse to buy,' I said.

'What difference does it make? We make the best materials in the world.'

'Sure. But if you don't let them examine them and test them. . .'

'Let them buy samples. If they want to buy samples, we will sell them samples,' he said.

'But it isn't like that. If a big company asks a small company for samples, and you give them some, they will increase the order bit by bit until eventually. . .'

'If they are going to increase the orders why don't they buy the samples instead of asking for them free?'

'Because that's not how it's done.'

'Why not? It's not right.'

'Maybe it's not right, but that's the procedure.'

'Then they should change the procedure.'

And so stalemate. The Cubans have spent millions building their four plants; they are desperate to sell at least something. But will they play by the rules and give free samples? Will they hell. So the four plants stand idle. All that research and effort and skill is wasted. Their chances of getting any money back are blown to Kingdom Come.

'How much do the samples cost?' I asked.

'Around US$3.00,' he said.

Another example of Cubans just not understanding the real world.

We drank more beer and I heard more stories. They told me how they worked the black market; how they siphoned petrol from cars; how they shifted coffee in hollowed-out medical dictionaries; how they stole satellite dishes tuned to Mexican television from homes one side of town and sold them to homes the other side of town; how they transported illicit rum from one end of Havana to the other inside bicycle frames. With the dollars they made they could go either to Almacenes Lux store and buy soap from Mexico, food from Venezuela, meat from Denmark, tomato purée from Brazil, even Omo from Britain, or to the big Pan-American Market on Third Street and get crushed to death trying to get their hands on fresh meat.

'It's dollar apartheid,' one of them said. 'If you have pesos you have nothing. To survive you need dollars. Some people get them by post from family and friends in Miami. We get them by working the black market.'

But it was not easy. The police were against them officially and unofficially. Officially they would seal off not only single rooms or houses but whole streets looking for what they claimed were stolen oods. If they didn't find what they were looking for they would still carry off jeans, trainers, videos, CD players or whatever they fancied. There was nothing anyone could do to stop them.

When I finally staggered out of the bar into the passageway a shrunken little old lady was hobbling down the stairs one at a time. Through a gap in the ceiling I could see another old lady tottering along the landing. Two equally wizened old men were sitting on the step outside.

'How many people actually live here?'

They shrugged.

We said our goodbyes, then for safety's sake – theirs, not mine – I staggered back up the street alone. A man was pouring petrol out of a plastic barrel into his car, a battered old Chevvy. Further along, I saw two young boys wrestling with a satellite dish. I turned left past one of the state ration shops and out into the square with the Coloseio in the distance. If what my brothers had told me was true, I was still the wrong side of the invisible tourist lines and on my own. I had only another 50 paces to go: 49, 48, 47. I could see the invisible line: 32, 31, 30 – not far now; 17, 16, 15 – nearly there; 5, 4, 3, 2, 1. Safety.

That evening I decided I had taken enough risks. Instead of crossing the invisible lines again I reckoned it was time for my cultural experience. I would go to the Gran Teatro next door to the hotel.

Like the rest of Havana, the theatre had obviously seen better days. The red velvet seats were still red, but not as red as they used to be. Which is probably also symbolic. The gilt was no more. The series of paintings which circled the stage had long since faded. So had most of the audience. I sat about six rows from the front surrounded by a load of Comrade Darby and Joans. They hobbled in, in once-smart suits and dresses. Behind me were small family groups. A few beads, lots of open-neck shirts, and I noticed three ties, one of them worn by a ferocious looking woman with what is known in polite society as a salty little moustache, who kept whispering in German.

What we were going to see, I had absolutely no idea. I

couldn't make head nor tail of the poster outside the theatre.
One half seemed to say it was a concert, the other half said
something about Cultera. I kept asking people but they didn't
seem to know either. The three women at the ticket office only
seemed interested in getting my money. Especially when they
saw I was prepared to pay in dollars. When the curtain finally
went up, I was amazed. It was a sugary-sweet musical set in
some Ruritarian castle complete with ill-fitting evening suits,
tiaras, elegant ballgowns, dancing girls and three quick bursts
of the Can-Can. Anything less Cuban I could not imagine. At
one stage I thought it was a straight lift of some Ivor Novello
number which had been staged to highlight the weakness and
decadence of the bourgeoisie.

I tried to ask the little old lady I was sitting next to what it
was about but she just kept giggling and squeaking with
delight at the costumes and the music and singing. At the
interval I offered her a glass of beer – no champagne at the
theatre in Havana – and we hobbled to the courtyard at the
back of the theatre. It turned out that she had been a chemical
engineer. She had studied in Minsk in Belorussia for five years.
She spoke Russian, and had frequently been to the ballet and
opera when she was there, even to the Bolshoi. She had come
back to Cuba, and was now retired, scraping along on her
small savings.

I never did discover what the show was about, but social
realism, a plea for a proletarian paradise and an exposé of the
corrupting influence of the bourgeois élite it was not.

When I came out, I noticed, standing outside, a young girl
in a fancy Lycra outfit.

Hemingway. Hemingway. Should I go across the river and
into the trees to Hemingway's place at San Francisco di Paolo,
where he lived with his sixty-four cats, four dogs, Royal
machine-gun and battered old stand-up typewriter?

Half of me said no, it's daft. You don't judge somebody by
where they live, how many books they have on their shelves,

or whether they cut the grass. In any case, while some of his stuff was great, some of it was a bit, well, corny. On the other hand, going to Havana and not going to Papa's place is a bit like going to Spain and not going to a bullfight.

Originally the site of an old Spanish fort, I was told it was only open on Wednesdays, when presumably he did his writing. The rest of the time he spent doing his drinking around the bars of old Havana. I couldn't afford to wait until Wednesday so I went on Monday when, I discovered, it was also open. But since it is now owned and run by the state, they keep quiet about it because the last thing they want is actual visitors.

Set in the middle of nine rambling hectares of brush, scrub and bits of woodland, it looks today more like the home of a cosy writer of boys' own stories. The house itself, the tower in which old Papa kept his cats, and the guest wing, or rather wooden shack, are nothing to write home or anywhere else about. The house is supposed to contain his hunting trophies, but we were not allowed to see them. The rooms are supposed to be adorned with pictures and photographs of every possible type of bullfight, but we were not allowed to see them. He was supposed to write every morning, barefoot and in loose-fitting clothing, at his desk. But we were not allowed to see it. From the top of the tower you are supposed to be able to see the whole of Havana. But – you guessed – we were not allowed to see it.

What I was allowed to see was his empty swimming pool; the graves of his four dogs, two of which he dug himself (the other two were dug by the staff); his all-wood fishing boat which was parked in a special open shed with a wooden walkway all around it, and the visitors' shack, oops, I mean wing, where the likes of Gary Cooper, Grace Kelly *et al.* slept off their hangovers.

On the way out the two women who signed me in and listed my details – name, passport number, car registration plate, mother's maiden name and what I had for breakfast the day before yesterday – stopped me again. They had forgotten, they said, to ask my nationality.

'Chinese,' I said. I thought the old free-wheeling, devil-may-care, boozy hellraiser would appreciate my bravado.

The older one, who looked a bit like Che Guevara's mother-in-law, then tried to tap me for a tip. For the first time, I refused. It was time, I thought, for a farewell to alms.

Dhaka

Floods. Mudslides. Cyclones. Ferries sinking. Trains crashing. Every possible disease known to man. And Lynda Chalker doing her throwing-chocolates-to-the-starving routine.

Not only is Bangladesh one of the poorest countries, and one of the largest poorest countries, in the world, if you see what I mean, it also seems to be first in line for any really big disaster waiting to happen.

If there is a flood going, Bangladesh will get it. Hundreds of thousands of people will be swept away, their homes destroyed, and most of the country will be left under water. Other countries get mud-slides. In Bangladesh, they get them the size of Mount Everest. Nor do they ever get just your ordinary cyclones. They get the cyclones of cyclones. If a ferry sinks in Bangladesh, hundreds of people will die. Their bodies will be washed up on the banks of the delta for months afterwards, black, bloated, and smelling to high heaven. If a train crashes, thousands will be killed. And as for the diseases rife in the country, my medical dictionary has only heard of half of them.

Then I went there – and discovered the truth. It's far, far worse than I imagined. Poor old Bangladesh, with over 120 million people – 70 per cent Hindu, 30 per cent Muslim – and still counting, squeezed on to the East Bengal River delta, on one side the Bay of Bengal, on the other, the Gangetic plains of India, and on the rest, the forests of Myanmar – Burma to you and me – must be the unluckiest country alive, and not just because the unelected Baroness Chalker has been there several times.

No wonder they get floods. The whole country is a mass of ditches and brooks and streams and rivers. The worst flood of all was in 1988 when over 100,000 died. What's more Dhaka, the jute capital of the world, is flooded – with rickshaws: black, plain, coloured, multi-coloured, multi-multi-coloured. I have never been anywhere, and that includes huge chunks of Asia, where I've seen so many rickshaws and so many different types of rickshaws: manual, auto, mini-bus, maxi-bus, van, truck, lorry, even refrigerated rickshaws. They're literally everywhere. The streets are flooded with them. They come swirling round corners in a huge mass, sweeping everything out of their way. They block entire streets and intersections. They choke all the tiny backstreets. There is no escaping them. And there is none of the gentle pop-pop-pop of the rickshaws you find in Bangkok, in Jakarta, in Colombo or anywhere else in South-East Asia. They belong to the kamikaze school of rickshaw driving. You think Nigel Mansell takes risks, you haven't seen these guys. They can carve up a Ferrari; they can turn corners at speeds you wouldn't believe possible; overtake in spaces less than half their size and do a U-turn on less than half a sixpence. Which is probably all they earn in a year.

Even more amazingly, the drivers are not exactly your regular ton-up merchants. They all look like either your regular ton-up holy man: long grey beard, a Mahatma Gandhi wrap-around, flimsy sandals and as thin as anyone could be, or they look as though they were left behind when the original ton-up Mughals turned and ran.

But there they are, all day and practically all night, carrying everybody backwards and forwards: serious businessmen in their city suits, many with umbrellas (to keep off the sun); housewives with their shopping; shopkeepers, traders, deliverymen; and shifting everything you can think of: bread, sacks of rice, cement, enormous reels of textiles, huge stacks of sheet metal, piles and piles of bamboo poles. Outside the Textile Engineering Institute, I saw one auto-rickshaw which had a flimsy aluminium barrier between the passenger and the driver. Presumably to protect the passenger from the rays of holiness. Believe me, this is pre-Henry Ford country, with a vengeance.

Dhaka is not just packed with people, it is swarming, crawling, overflowing and flooding over with people. There is not a square inch left that is not crammed with people. The rickshaws are bursting with people. The buses are jammed with them. What few cars and trucks there are, are packed worse than sardine tins. Even the trains are full to overflowing. One morning in Gazipur I saw a train so overloaded with people, inside, outside, on the roof, hanging on to the outside of the carriages, hanging on to people hanging on to the outside of the carriages, it would give the entire Health and Safety Executive the most enormous collective heart attack in history.

And the shame and the pity and the horror of it is that most of them seem to be eating, living, sleeping and dying on the streets. I tell a lie; not all of them. I saw one family which had just taken over the roundabout in the middle of the big junction leading to the university. Another I saw was living in the flimsiest hammock I've ever seen strung up between the side of a building and a tree, over this stream of flowing black stuff.

'Every time I come back, it seems to get worse,' I was told by a Bangladeshi professor of biochemistry who gained his MA in London, now lives in Toronto, and comes back to Dhaka with his wife every three years to visit the family. 'The traffic, the noise, the conditions. The people. There are so, so many people. They must do something about the number of people.'

Which struck me as odd because he told me he had spent his life studying ways to prolong people's lives.

His wife, who was also a doctor, told me that whenever he came back he would sit for hours in their house just outside Dhaka, his eyes closed, his shoulders slightly bent, his hands together in his lap as if he was deep in prayer. But he wasn't. 'Religion. I don't believe in religion. It causes all the trouble in the world,' he would say when he came round.

She was more resigned, or indifferent, as wives usually are. 'I don't mind,' she said. 'I just sit in the car. They take me to my family. I am happy. In any case,' she tucked her sari around her, 'as I see it, Bangladesh is one of the top 150 countries in the world.'

The old town, a maze of tiny streets and alleyways, is so packed with people you just cannot imagine how they would fit any more in. Most are tiny, shrivelled scraps of human beings. You can't believe people can be so emaciated. If they took tablets you'd probably see them going down. But there they are. And some of them are pulling enormous carts piled three, even four layers high with sacks, boxes and even oil drums; and carrying enormous crates and sacks and boxes on their head.

'Dhaka, sir, is only 50 per cent as good as it used to be, sir,' Mr Kala told me every time I saw him selling newspapers at the traffic lights on the way to the Shashkamal Hotel, which is an experience to remember.

I kept wanting to tell him about the health club and beauty parlour round the corner where, for probably the equivalent of what he makes in a year, you can have yourself strapped into an electrical muscle stimulator for an hour in order to lose a couple of white corpuscles. But he wasn't interested. For some reason he seemed to want to dash off and sell newspapers to the car behind.

Walk down just about any street – in the town centre, way out by the port, opposite Mujunder and Brothers shop, anywhere. Sitting outside a shack the size of a sentry box where about twenty people are making bicycle frames will be a skeleton of a woman. How old she may be, you couldn't begin to think. In her arms will be the tiniest, most shrivelled-up baby you have ever seen, its eyes as black as soot.

Further along will be a shop the size of a telephone box, selling all the latest cassettes you don't want to hear. Unless, of course, you speak Arabic and are not fussy about recording quality. Sitting on the step will be a man who spends his life polishing shoes. With his fingers.

Walking straight across the road, rickshaws swerving to left and right of him, bells ringing like mad, is a man with a complete wooden double bed upside-down on his head. Behind him is a shrunken midget of a girl on crutches, legs dangling helplessly beneath her.

All along one street there are nothing but sewing machines. Early one morning I saw, standing by one machine, this Muslim picture of loveliness in a dazzling, shocking pink ensemble with a tiny, delicate, white lace hat, shiny black boots – and an enormous beard down to his waist. Curled up underneath the sewing machine, under the flimsiest of sacks, was a pile of bones. Whether it was dead or alive I couldn't tell.

Turn the corner. Past the man doing shaves and haircuts in the street are two rickshaws mangled together on the pavement. The drivers are exchanging names and addresses, although God knows how you have an address in a place like Dhaka. Sitting by the wall is a stencil writer. Or rather a stencil stenciller. You want a sign stencilled? Bring him the bit of wood or the board or even the door and he will stencil the sign on it for you, there and then. But you'd better be quick. He's been doing it for about a million years already and some of his stencils are wearing pretty thin.

Across the road, sitting in the gutter which is flowing with either oil or something I'd rather not think about is an old woman, bent over, a stick in her hand, just staring into nothing. Further down, across a couple of open drains, just past this enormous black puddle of whatever, is a shop selling heavily stylised, slushy, large-size chocolate-box portraits of people with babies, of people sitting on chairs grinning at the camera, of people holding awards or certificates.

A boy pushes past carrying three live chickens upside-down in each hand. A tiny girl – I don't know; five or six years old – comes up to me carrying what looks like a dead baby in her arms. Suddenly, just opposite, I see coming out of a tiny, muddy, filthy alleyway – a Ralph Lauren sweater. I look up. On the roof is a satellite dish.

Try and do anything in Dhaka and you are immediately surrounded by people. You've got to roll this rubber tyre down the alleyway, across the street and into Mobarak and Sons. Five people will help you. You've got to carry all these bamboo poles up four flights of precarious stairs to build another extension onto the extension you've already built on the roof. Ten people are waiting to help. You want to lift this huge coil of barbed wire onto the back of this tiny, fragile rickshaw and deliver it to Basha Bari Road. No problem; there are fifteen people to help you. You are trying to offload these great twenty-foot loops of steel reinforcing rod by that sign saying Islam PVC Pipes. There are twenty people to help you, no problem.

You want to re-confirm your ticket at Air India or Indian Airlines so that you don't turn up at the airport again and they say you're not on the list. This time, of course, there is only one man at the front desk completely surrounded by a million ticket-waving, queue-jumping, to-the-hell-with-the-rest-of-them people all with the same idea. Where are the other twenty when you need them most? Out helping that guy offload those dirty great loops of steel reinforcing rod? What do you think?

But for all the people packed into Dhaka – listen, if you yawn, twenty people will put their hands up to your mouth to save you the bother – I still reckon there are more rickshaws than people and, what's more, they are multiplying at a faster rate, even though as far back as 1989 the government banned new ones from taking to the streets because they were 'posing a threat to the traffic system in the densely populated city'. Posing a threat? Believe me, you can hardly move for them. Try crossing the road outside the North-Sooth (sic) Company and you'll be run over by a rickshaw carrying two soldiers sitting bolt upright, rifles at the ready, going off to war somewhere. One evening as I was leaving the Pubali Bank near the National Museum, I saw rolls of textiles stacked on a rickshaw maybe ten feet high. Sitting on top of them was a young man in a suit, smoking a cigarette. Pushing the whole thing was a holy man ten times his age. Another day, opposite the Bazaar and Hawkers Co-operative Society stalls, I saw another rickshaw with a refrigerator standing in the back.

Take your life into your hands and attempt a dash across to Mollah and Sons? No way. If they're standing still, and most of the traffic in Dhaka has been standing still most of this century, there is just a solid, solid mass of them. All the front wheels are twisted and jammed-up tight against all the special anti-jamming bars across all the axles of all the ones in front. It's impossible. I once spent thirty years stuck outside Sadar Ghat, the port terminal, in the biggest jam of all time listening to some Fatima singing 'Ticky, Ticky, Ticky' on Bangladeshi radio in the kind of voice that gives scratchy old 78s a good name.

If they're on the move, it's worse still. They are still all one solid, solid, mass. Except now they're a moving solid, solid mass – and somehow weaving and twisting and skidding and swirling in front of each other at the same time. The inside of the atom is pretty tame by comparison.

Nobody reacts. Nobody does anything. Not even the police in their pale blue shirts, their white helmets and their hands in their pockets. That's Dhaka.

Mudslides. Just five minutes in Dhaka – no more – and you realise how much mud there is there and where it's all going. Political mud, I mean.

Now in case you think I'm in any way prejudiced, let me say straight away that the fact that they are always squabbling and shouting at each other and can never agree on anything has nothing to do with the fact that the prime minister is a woman, and the leader of the opposition is a woman. The last time I was there the whole country was at more of a standstill than it usually is because of this enormous political mudslide blocking everything.

Mrs Leader of the Opposition said that Mrs Leader of the Government had rigged the elections. Mrs Leader of the

Government said Mrs Leader of the Opposition was talking out of the back of her sari. The elections were fair, the people had spoken. She was just a bad loser. Why didn't she stop making a fuss and go back to washing the dishes and ironing and cooking and doing all the things women do best. Mrs Leader of the Opposition then went bananas and, with all the members of the opposition, resigned from parliament. Parliament was now invalid, she said. Mrs Leader of the Government should call new elections. So there. Not so, said Mrs Leader of the Government. The elected members were elected. They did not resign. The government was perfectly entitled to continue governing while it had the support of the elected members who were there. Which it did. What's more she didn't like the colour of Mrs Leader of the Opposition's sari. It made her look fat.

In the meantime the poor villagers out in the middle of nowhere are still trying to dig themselves out of the millions of tons of real mud that buried them, their families, and what homes and possessions they had. It's almost too much for words.

'We are very poor, sir. We are very poor country, sir. It is our leaders, sir. They do nothing, sir,' an old farmer told me in Gaipur. 'Please, please to tell them to do something. This is my request, sir.'

If that's what a poor farmer thinks, sir or madam, you can guess what the rest of the country thinks. Yet the two – I nearly said it – leading politicians continue to, how shall I say, debate the niceties of constitutional law.

'We have one foot in the oven and the other foot in the fridge,' a government official told me solemnly one morning. True or not, I don't know. All I know is that the only place where it's impossible for mud to stick is parliament itself. Not because there have not been all kinds of allegations. But because the parliament building looks like – what do I mean, looks like? – it is a single, solid, shiny, concrete block with one or two bits missing, practically surrounded by water. A bit like the South Bank looked in its early days. All around the parliament building are all the ministers' official homes and garages and wall-safes and beautifully landscaped gardens. But that's another story.

As for cyclones, the biggest cyclone going through Asia at the moment has got less to do with the weather than it has to do with religion. Bangladesh is already a Muslim country, but somehow it gives you the impression it wants to be even more Muslim than it is now. The whole attitude, culture, philosophy of the country is Muslim. There are mosques everywhere. Everyone says the Baitul Mukarram mosque in the middle of town is magnificent and modern, but to me – I trust I am not risking a *fatwa* by saying this – it seems neither magnificent nor modern. It is certainly in a very commanding position, and it is quite imposing, but it's more parish church than cathedral, if you see what I mean. The Satmasfid mosque with its seven domes certainly looked impressive from the outside. What it looks like from inside, I don't know because this particular guy I saw there had this thing about infidels. So the Star mosque gets my vote. I admit it's more chapel than even parish church but it looks so nice – small, warm, almost family-like – not at all big and imposing. Nine out of ten.

Everyone goes around saying 'As salem Alaikum.' Immediately you set foot outside the airport door the beggars give you the 'As salem Alaikum' then bang on your car windows. Which shows you their order of priorities. The beggars sitting in all the government offices you visit say the same thing, except they usually add, 'I'm a very poor man, sir. Big family, sir. Anything you can do, sir, most grateful, sir.'

Cattle, goats, even pigs, roam the streets. Or try to, if they can get in between the rickshaws.

Lots of women wear the veil, which is something I personally would encourage many women to do. Except, it seems, when taking a shower. Then they take the veil off, although they remain fully clothed – at least according to the posters for showers that I saw all over town. I even saw one woman whose face was completely covered. How she could see where she was going, God – oops – Allah only knows.

Bangladeshi television broadcasts more prayers than soaps. Which, you've got to admit, is something. They even break into their regular programmes for evening prayers. Their national airline, Biman Bangladesh, has one channel just for 'Recitations from Holy Quran'. All hotel rooms boast the Koran, and the Holy 'Bible' as they say in quotes, and guess which one gets pride of place. Bars and restaurants give you a choice between American Club Sandwich and Arabian Club Sandwich, and heaven help you if you choose the wrong one. And the New Year is no longer the New Year. It is the English New Year.

Nor is it just floods, mudslides and cyclones – any kind of calamity, catastrophe or disaster, poor old Bangladesh has either already got it or they've got it coming.

Take water-holes. What could be more innocent, more useful, more practical for the health of the population than digging water-holes? So what's happened? Out in the villages, the wells that were dug to give them and their cattle fresh drinking water are turning poisonous. Traces of arsenic have started seeping into the supply causing, for the villagers, inflammation of the eyes, all kinds of strange growths and even gangrene, and for their cattle, death.

The chemical fertiliser and insecticide they've been using in a desperate bid to boost food production has somehow got into what water supply they have left and killed off the frogs which, when they finished eating their own tadpoles, used to go for mosquitoes in a big way. Result: malaria is once again a big problem across whole areas of the country which had been clear for years. And when they can't afford to use fertiliser or repair the tractors or spraying equipment, pumri-pokas, mazrapokas and even gumpokas start attacking the paddy fields and turning them yellow.

Students. Everybody has students. But Bangladesh has

students that fight hour-long gun battles across the university campus in the middle of Dhaka. Last time I was in Dhaka one gun battle was still going on. Still, you have to admire the literary quality of their graffiti. No mindless slogans for them. All along one wall by the main dark-brick university building was scrawled, 'Liberty. What crimes are committed in thy name?' Trouble was, nobody could tell me which side was responsible for it, whether it was pro- or anti-government, or whether it was directed at the government at all.

What about the Ganges? Twenty years ago it brought death and destruction to over thirty million people in the south-west of the country. Today it's drying up, so that the River Gorai, which brought fresh water from the Ganges to that whole area is also drying up. The result, no fresh water, a fall in ground water levels and increased salt levels in what's left, which could spell disaster for people, plants and wildlife.

So what about making the best use of the plants and wildlife they've got left? No way. There are no longer any good restaurants, or public eating places as they call them, in Bangladesh. Well, maybe apart from Niiblo's along Nazim Uddin Road, but that's between you and me. Why? Because, would you believe it, all their best chefs have gone to England.

I met a Bangladeshi chef, home from Leicester, who gave me the low-down on Indian restaurants. Now I'm no expert. To me there are only three types of Indian curry; hot, very hot, and when-will-the-steam-stop-coming-out-of-my-ears? Frequently, however, I get dragged to Indian restaurants. In Calcutta I once had something in which everything was hot; the cucumbers, the tomatoes and that little green thing on the edge of the plate. Allah, help me! Where is the nearest cold bath? In Colombo, Sri Lanka, I once had some traditional Indian desserts which were so sweet I was frightened to shake my head in case my teeth dropped out. The most memorable Indian meal I think I've never had was in Walsall. I went to meet a client in Crewe. We couldn't find anywhere to eat. Then he remembered this restaurant in his home town, so we drove practically 100 miles to go there. Was it worth it? I can't remember the meal but I can sure remember the drive.

But according to my friendly Bangladeshi chef from Leicester – he told me to read *The Satanic Verses*. Not because its a good book, but for all the Indian restaurants Rushdie mentions – there is no such thing as an Indian curry. They are all Bangladeshi curries. Most Indian restaurants are apparently not Indian restaurants at all. They're Bangladeshi restaurants. And most of them are run by Bangladeshis from Sylhet, way up in the north-east of the country.

How can you tell? Easy, according to my friend. Bangladeshi Indian restaurants tend to concentrate on fish and vegetables such as potol, a type of courgette and lal sag, a kind of blood-red leaf spinach, biryanis and morag pulao with rezala or chicken and the usual borharis. Punjabi Indian is kebabs and karabi cooking, lots of meat and lots of spices. Pakistani Indian is usually from Mirpur, just south of Kashmir. It is practically nothing but meat; massalas, biryanis and kebabs. Gujarati Indian, which came to us via Kenya and Uganda, is lots of rice, crispy vermicelli, chickpeas, lots of coriander and chilli sauces. Go into any Leicester restaurant and you'll have a fantastic Gujarati meal, he told me. Leicester has the biggest concentration of Indians outside India and most of them are Gujaratis. South Indian is all big pancakes stuffed with spicy vegetables and lots of coconut sauce.

Most Indian restaurants serve Bengali or Bangladeshi dishes. Therefore, most Indian restaurants are, in fact, Bangladeshi. If you please, sir or madam.

So what happens to the poor Bangladeshis when they manage to escape to other parts of the world? They end up living in appalling conditions in Brick Lane, London, or if they join the United Nations peacekeeping force they end up besieged in Bihac by the Serbs, reduced to smoking tealeaf cigarettes and eating rice and compo curry. While everybody else back in Sarajevo is on four square meals a day.

Is all that too much for one country to endure? Not at all. As if Bangladesh has not suffered enough accidents and catastrophes, you've only to throw some salt over your shoulder, hold the rabbit's paw tightly in your fist and look out of the window to see a million more just waiting to happen.

That broken-down old double-decker Ashok Leyland bus with almost all its windows missing, a metal grid where the windscreen should be, packed to the very edge of the platform with 2,507 people, careering out of control down Sang Sud Avenue; one day it's just going to – to – to. . .

That auto-rickshaw mini-bus outside the high court with ten people packed in the back, two more each side of the driver. It's so close to that cart being pulled by those two tiny little ponies with nothing but bits of rope, no bridle or anything, to keep them in check. If they're not careful they will – will – will. . .

That man on the bicycle outside Molloh and Sons. If he's not careful, that rickshaw with the steel rods sticking out the back is going to swing round and – and – and. . .

And yet, and yet . . . suddenly the skies clear, the clouds part and there is a burst of unbelievable, beautiful Bangladeshi sunshine.

One day, having finished my rounds, I was coming back past Lalbagh Fort which is tucked away in its own immaculately kept grounds, behind high brick walls on the south-western part of the old city. It was another typical Dhaka day. We kept getting stuck behind, before and between every type of rickshaw. My head was ringing with a million bicycle bells. Once we stayed long enough outside a butcher's shop to see the strangest looking animal hung, drawn and quartered while the blood quite hygienically flowed off the bench, across the floor, down the step and straight into this open sewer outside. We edged our way past more shops, with raw meat piled high outside; past another shop full of different skins. We turned a corner. Some goats were tied to a lamp post casually admiring the scenery. An old man hobbled past. On his head was a tray of the freshest, cleanest and most beautiful-looking vegetables I have ever seen – and I don't like vegetables.

Further forward we edged, through the maze of streets

barely wide enough for two rickshaws to pass let alone a car and three rickshaws – three, because none of them would give way. By now every kid in Bangladesh was banging and thumping on my car window. In the end I got out and wandered across to a sign saying Real Computer Garden. Which is a dangerous thing to do because you're always immediately surrounded by hands. One of them belonged to a smart-looking, ordinary kind of kid of nine or ten, who had been leading the banging on the window.

'You interested in computers, sir?' he asked me as I was carried along by the crowd.

'Vaguely,' I mumbled.

He didn't look exactly smart. But he didn't look exactly filthy either. 'Please, sir,' he said. 'I am very interested in computers.'

Would you believe, for the next twenty minutes this kid told me everything about computers. Who makes them. What they do. How they work. What the problem with the Pentium microprocessor was all about.

'Please, sir, the Pentium can only operate to eight digits. This is big problem.'

'But isn't eight digits enough? I mean, how big are your expenses?'

'Normally, yes, sir. But not always. Financial analysis depends on accuracy.'

'But didn't Pentium say it only means you make a mistake once every 27,000 years?'

'Yes, sir. But it is still not accurate, sir. Is it, sir?'

Then he was off. Reciprocals of y, multiples of x, approximate values of the other, spreadsheet calculations. It was all way beyond me. I mean, I can't even boil the water to make a cup of coffee. At least, that's what my wife says.

'But not to worry, sir.' He finally came back down to earth. 'All our problems will be over by 1997.'

'Why 1997?' I wondered.

'Because then, sir,' he smiled confidently, 'Pentium will produce their next generation chip, the Nx586. That, sir, will solve all our problems, won't it, sir?'

I was about to thank him for his assurance when another car edged round the corner and off he went with all the other kids banging on the window begging for pennies.

Goodness me, if only the Nx586 would solve all Bangladesh's problems, it would have been worth all the floods and mudslides and cyclones and ferries sinking and trains crashing and even the visits by Lynda Chalker.

Mexico City

What a difference a day makes. Especially if it's December 20, 1994 and you're Mexican. Because December 20, 1994 – it's engraved on every Mexican's sombrero – was D-Day, Devaluation Day, when at a stroke, as they say, the peso plunged around 40 per cent and with it all their dreams of being the biggest enchilada in the world.

Before, it was all Viva Mexico, Viva los Mexicans. They were just about the biggest, most successful, most dynamic country in the world. At least, according to the talk in the bars around the Plaza Fiesta San Agustin in Mexico City, and in the smart restaurants in Colonia Polanco on the northern side of Chapultepec Park, where everyone seems to eat giant open ravioli overflowing with tons of huitlacoche, some kind of corn fungus, which is the Mexican equivalent of truffles.

Trade barriers had been lowered; dozens of state-owned industries had been sold; private industry had been given a string of incentives; free markets were the order of the day. Business was booming, employment was up, incomes were up, domestic growth was up. Foreign investment was flooding in: over US$50 billion in five years. Monterrey, Mexico's second city up in the north, was so full of US companies setting up shop nobody had time to think of what happened a long time ago. Saltillo, a tortilla chip's throw away, in the dusty Coahuila desert, was being hailed as the future Detroit of Mexico, so many car manufacturers were moving in.

Everyone was going hog-wild and looking forward to the good times. The fat cats, huddled together in San Angel, the swish up-market end of Mexico City, and in Polanco, which boasts probably all the best and most expensive hotels, shops and restaurants in the city, were smoking their pungent Mexican puros non-stop, buying all the foreign consumer goods they could find in Masaryk, known locally as Rodeo Drive, and going off to Rocky Mountain ski resorts every weekend.

The middle classes, in Coyoacan, a pleasant, relaxed, charming, quiet suburb, were buying more middle-class things, dreaming more middle-class dreams and applying for membership of Perisur, the massive Aztec temple to the god of shopping in Mexico City.

Wage earners were flocking into El Puerto de Liverpool, would you believe, the biggest department store group in the country, and buying everything they could lay their hands on.

Only the poor were out in the cold, and there are plenty of people in Mexico who have no shoes or socks and hardly anything to wear. No, not the shy, quiet, modest, retiring young couples who flock to glitzy super-swish Cancun on the Caribbean coast to get married wearing shorts, no shoes and no shirt (her), and tiny white bikini (him); nor the middle-aged swingers (him and her) who still tell you Acapulco is where it's at. I mean the families living in tiny breeze-block shacks in San Miguel Teotongo on the outskirts of Mexico City, trying to survive on a diet of tortillas, beans and hope. They still had it rough. But not as rough, maybe, as before. At least that's what I kept being told.

Gee whiz, their President Carlos Salinas de Gortari, the Harvard-trained technocrat who had made it all possible, was practically packing his bags and heading off for Geneva or Bonn or Singapore or wherever to become director-general of the new World Trade Organisation to teach the rest of the world how to do it the Mexican way. Then – caramba – it happened. The whole place just screeched to a halt. The mariachis popped their buttons. All of them. Everyone in Zona Rosa went white. The fat cats in Colonia Polanco choked on their crunchy little fried grasshoppers, an Oaxacan delicacy.

The whole country stopped dead in the middle of the third verse of 'Guadalajara'. Just like that, the peso in their pocket was no longer worth a fistful of dollars. It was worth 60 per cent of a fistful of dollars. Nobody could have been more stunned. The mighty Mexico had fallen. Crash. They were in a bucketful of guajillo chillies. Right up to their necks. Nobody could believe it.

Then – wham – everything shot up in price. Soft drinks, for many poor families part of their diet, soared 20 per cent. Tortillas went up 15 per cent. Milk up 17 per cent. Cornmeal up 20 per cent. Bread up 25 per cent. Eggs and chickens, for those who could afford them, shot up 29 per cent. Coffee a massive 36.6 per cent. Sugar, 56 per cent. Petrol, electricity, electrical goods, even car repair bills, they all soared sky high.

Before, the shops had been packed – the family-run corner shops, the US-style discount stores, the huge new Santa Fe shopping centre out to the west of Mexico City, the largest shopping mall in Latin America. Now, overnight, in Monterrey, in Mexico City, in Merida, in Cancun, everywhere I went, shops were empty. No chocolates, which are pretty well part of their daily diet. No cakes. No microwave popcorn. No nuttin', as they say. Even in Sanborn's, one of Mexico City's famous department stores, nobody was buying their up-market electrical goods, their household appliances. Nobody anywhere was buying or selling. Shops were not even ordering from wholesalers or importing. Nobody was doin' nuttin', as they also say.

Even the vast, rambling Mercado de la Merced, some say the biggest market in the world, was at a standstill. Now vegetables – I'm sure this will not surprise you – are not my favourite subject. For three reasons. First, my wife is a vegetarian. She keeps insisting I give up meat and go back to her roots. Second, my wife is a vegetarian. And you can guess the third reason. But now and then, if I have a chance, I will admit, on condition you don't tell her, I actually wander round the Mercado if I have three hours to spare between meetings and lunch or dinner. Now and then I will also admit, again if you don't tell her, I am momentarily, but momentarily, moved by the vast array of everything that I am told again and again is good for me; for my weight, my white corpuscles, and the general future of the universe. Now I hallucinate a lot about vegetables, so maybe I'm not exactly objective, but I can honestly say that whenever I go there I am always amazed at the fantastic array of shapes and sizes and colours. Most important, the colours. To me chillies are what I have to fight through to get to the meat. But here they are not only the usual greens and reds, they are every shade under the Mexican sun, even deep, rich, leathery browns, like highly polished riding boots. Then there are those strange-looking mamey fruits, weird black zapotes, not to mention deep red, plump toma- toes, practically the size of footballs, plus a mass of funny- looking shapes I never dreamed existed even in my fevered meat-starved imagination. But even the Mercado had come to a standstill.

In Tepito, a sprawling open-air market, I saw a stallholder trying to sell television sets, music centres, videos, and everything else I don't understand. He was almost crying. He told me he had struggled for years to build up his business. He was doing very well. Just before D-Day he had bought more goods than ever before, expecting his business to increase. Now he was dead. Because of the devaluation he had to find twice as many pesos to pay for them than before.

'How can I pay, señor?' he said. 'Nobody is buying. Nobody will pay my prices. But still I have to pay. Tell me, is that right?' What can you say? 'The rich, they will be all right. They are always all right. But what about me?'

'So what will you do?'

'Mexico canta y aguanta. Sing and put up with it. Some- how.'

It was the same in the swish, up-market Bazar del Sabodo craft market which opens Saturdays only for the rich and super-rich in an enormous old mansion next to the San Jacinto Monastery in San Angel. Again nobody was buying. Normally you can't keep track of the textiles and lacquerwork and engravings and gold and silverware and glassware going backwards and forwards. This time nothing. Not even one of their famous paper flowers. In the bar it was a good day for the worms. Nobody was knocking back the tequilas or the jamaicas, chias, tamarinds or margaritas either. Which shows you how badly they were taking it.

In the plants and factories I visited things were just ticking over or, worse, at a standstill. Monterrey was practically a ghost town. Ford, Volkswagen, Nissan, Mercedes-Benz all shut down immediately. Even Dina, Mexico's own truck and bus maker, closed down. Partly because suppliers stopped supplying, because they didn't think they would get paid. Partly because dealers cancelled their orders. Partly because the manufacturers themselves just lost their nerve.

The roads were almost empty. Before, you could hardly cross the road for giant Mack trucks hurtling backwards and forwards from the States. Now they had practically dis-appeared. But still you couldn't cross the road. Instead of trucks there was a non-stop stream of protest marches and demonstrations. Even the green laser in the top of their huge Beacon of Commerce in the centre of town, which was originally designed to zap anyone who did not have faith in their success, began to flicker.

Foreign investors just turned and ran. Before, productivity may have been fairly low, the infrastructure pretty basic, the cost of capital high, the law a bit fudgy and law enforcement dependable – it depended who the policeman was – but it had what they wanted: low costs a busride away from the biggest market in the world. Now they had about as much faith in Mexico as they had in English footballers behaving themselves and saying please and thank you.

Normally, so long as he gets his enchiladas, the man in the poncho is pretty relaxed and casual. Now everybody had steam coming out of their ears as if they had been hitting the jalapeños, the saba and the tabasco all in one go.

In Las Mañanitas Hotel in Cuernavaca, up in the mountains, an hour's drive from Mexico City, a favourite Wednesday-to-Tuesday weekend get-away for the élite, they were playing with their tortilla chips and wondering whether they could still afford to take the kids to Reino Aventura, the biggest theme park in Latin America, and if not what they were going to say to the neighbours. In the Price-Costco warehouse clubs they were agonising over more basic things, like what they were going to say when their rich neighbours told them that, of course they could still afford to go to the Reino Aventura with the kids, but they thought this year was the year to stay at home and paint the kitchen instead.

Wherever you turned there were not only these guys wearing black balaclavas and ski helmets, carrying assault rifles, banners praising the Zapatistas and life-size papier mâché figures of the president, Ernesto Zedillo, at the mercy of Uncle Sam, but also, in a world first for protests and direct action, rich housewives in their Gucci and Versace suits, designer sunglasses glinting in the sunshine, mobile telephones at the ready, marching to the presidential palace to complain that in future they would only be able to spend somebody else's hard-earned money on 60 per cent of the necessities of life such as Salvatore Ferragamo scarves, Giorgio Armani shirts and hormone replacement tablets by post from Boots in the Brompton Road. Which was the more frightening I hesitate to say, in case I end up with a diamond-encrusted icepick lodged in the middle of my head.

Even Mexico's famous band of merry kidnappers called it a day. Before, they could grab pretty well any moderately well-known businessman off the streets and get up to US$30 million for his return. Now, nobody had the money to pay even if they wanted to. The last thing the kidnappers wanted was US$30 million in pesos, used notes or not.

What amazes me is that if, all those years ago, just by ripping out a couple of hearts and drowning virgins in sacred wells, these guys could read the stars, write complicated books on astronomy and astrology, paint, build, play basketball with human skulls using only their elbows and thighs, and foretell the future, how come devaluation was such a big surprise anyway? If, of course, you ignore all the stuff about budget deficits, an over-valued peso, corruption, assassinations, a one-sided, grossly inefficient judicial system and electoral fraud. Call me innocent. Until I started going to Mexico I thought tacos were something you had if you couldn't get hamburgers. Now I know better. They are two or more ballot pages folded together to look like one. What's more, a pregnant vote has got nothing to do with pregnancy. It's all to do with hiding one ballot paper inside another. At least, according to this very nice man I met one evening near the Alameda while I was trying to bribe my way into Los Girasoles, this fantastic, bright yellow colonial-style restaurant famous for its camarones a la nao, shrimps swimming in hot dark pasilla chilli sauce with lumps of spicy mango and cinnamon-flavoured Mexican sweet potato.

I'm no expert on Mayan culture, but I only had to see the big pyramid-like El Castillo temple at Chichen Itzá to realise that all you had to do was count the number of empty Coke cans between the Temple of the Bearded Man and the Temple of the Jaguars, multiply it by the number of times you heard an owl hooting – an owl hooting is a sign of bad luck; tut, tut, don't you know your Mayan mythology? – take away the square root of the tree at the bottom of your garden and add the date of the last time your brother-in-law bought you a drink and what have you got? December 20, 1994. And I didn't have to rip out any hearts, virgin or otherwise, in the process.

So how come nobody else worked it out? Don't the Mexicans believe this stuff about the Mayans?

Okay, amigo, I know it's easy to get the impression that Mexico, the land of siestas, burros, rhinestoned sombreros and mañana, is a first-world country up there with the rest of them. And I'm not just talking about after an evening on the margaritas.

It's big. It has a population around 90 million. It stretches all the way from the enormous Walmart distribution centre in

Laredo, Texas, which always seems packed with Mexicans, across the much polluted Tijuana River, the biggest border crossing in North America, which always seems packed with Mexicans, especially late at night, trying to get into the US, down across the black mountains that look like giant piles of coal dust, across Mexico City, one of the biggest urban land sprawls in the world, all the way down to the remote Chiapas jungle, birthplace of the masked Zapatista guerillas and home to the rare quetzal, the legendary bird of the Mayans, and to more Indians and illiterates than anywhere else in the country.

It's very American. You think Canada looks American, you should see Mexico. It's got all the trappings of first-league status. Big luxury hotels, as good as any anywhere in the world; fabulous resort areas; enormous world-class companies. It has style, it has fashion, and – potential kidnappers look the other way – a bunch of billionaires. Forbes estimated twenty-four at the last count. Some people even say that it ranks number four in the world league for billionaires.

But it's all muchacha. Sure it's big. Sure it's got 90 million people. But it's often impossible to get in for the mass of people trying to get out. On foot, from some of Mexico's big successful fruit and vegetable operations up in the north-west near the US border. By road, from Jalisco and Zacartecas in the centre of the country, you see broken-down cars and trucks and even farm wagons making for the Rio Grande. By plane, from all over the country. Even by free-phone. Call certain farms in California, or even certain firms in Los Angeles not a million miles from the docks, and I was told they will even send a truck down to collect you. Late at night, of course. Make another call and for US$400 you can get a forged US social security card; another US$500 and you get the Green Card; another couple of grand and you get the tops: a gringuita, an American woman. Long, short or tall, it doesn't make any difference. You take what you're offered. Because once you marry her, amigo, your problems are over. They can't send you back home. You're an American.

Not that there is anything new about it. It's been going on since the 1920s when the US railway companies were desperate for cheap labour but the US government was not.

So where do the takers come from? From the countryside. Mexican farms, which usually grow only corn and beans, are tiny and barely able to support a can of worms. Land Reform was at the heart of the Revolution, was it eighty years ago? But it is still mañana. From the towns. Many small and medium-sized companies have been squeezed to death, not only by the big companies, which is not unusual anywhere, but also by the need to adjust to NAFTA. Many have laid off staff. Some have closed some operations. Some have closed down altogether.

Today, depending on whom you talk to, there are either 2 million or 200 million Mexicans working in the US. In San Joaquin, just over the border, or further north and more up-market in the Napa Valley, you see them, front teeth missing, a greasy bandanna around their heads, working as grape pickers for a season. In up-market, bankrupt Orange County, which used to be big fund raisers for the Ku Klux Klan, just two hours south of Los Angeles during the rush hour or thirty minutes on Sunday afternoon, I have also seen them working as messengers or cleaners or truck drivers.

Sure, Mexico has got world-class companies like Cemex, the enormous cement company, and billionaires like Carlos Slim Helu, US$6.6 billion and climbing, head of the national telephone company, and Emilio Azcarrago, US$5.4 and climbing faster, head of the leading television station. But for all that, Super Mex, Latin America's most stable political system – they have had a long history of free and fair elections, although never at the same time – is no way one enormous industrial estate churning out millions of cheap products for the States. It might think it is, but the reality is something else. I once spent a happy day visiting what I was told were major Mexican electronics companies, which turned out to be plastic toy manufacturers using batteries to make dolls blink and model trains go round in circles; a shaving-mirror manufacturer and a student who wanted to borrow US$10 million to build a factory to make Mexico's first computer chip. The fact is, Mexico as a whole does about as much business a year as greater Los angeles; many towns still have open sewers; pollution in some areas is horrifying, particularly in railway stations early in the morning; dogs still get to the garbage before the monthly truck arrives; and policemen still slouch around with Viva Zapata moustaches and paunches the size of beer barrels. Cockfighting is as common and as popular as, say, bullfighting – all over the country there are cockfighting clubs, cockfighting leagues and even special cockfighting stadiums – and big, smooth, handsome, successful, 32-year-old lawyers still live at home with their mother and their 28-year-old sister. You don't believe me? You should watch the soaps on Mexican TV.

In some ways, in fact, Mexico is two countries. A bit like Italy. In the south, and that includes Mexico City, things are still pretty slow and relaxed. Managers don't so much manage as put off taking decisions, do everything they can to avoid sticking to deadlines, and have long lunches. Meetings begin whenever people decide to turn up, and end whenever anyone gets a phone call they think is more interesting. And most phone calls, even from the wife, are more interesting than most meetings. As for targets, cost controls, deliveries, customers – they're not important. It's who you know that counts. And how well you look after him. I know the managing director of one big Mexican company who every month writes off three days just for wining, dining and entertaining his biggest customer.

In the north, it's Milan. They're hard-working, dedicated, real professionals. Meetings start on time. There are agendas. Decisions are taken – and implemented. Some Americans told me their plants in places like Aguascalientes and Hermosillo are among the most efficient and productive they have anywhere in the world. Including the US.

But there are problems. For one thing, in both north and south, but especially in the north, everybody is fighting all the time with one hand tied behind their backs. Telephones don't always work; external calls are all right, internal ones are the big problem. The post hardly exists. Faxes are beginning to make their mark but not yet because of the problem with telephones. This doesn't just slow everything down, it creates other problems. Paying bills, for example. Because the post is so bad and banking services so poor companies have to go out and collect their own cheques from customers. Which, of course, not only means additional costs but additional problems. Some companies have tried to get round this by paying their salesmen extra commission for the cheques they collect. Which again sometimes works and sometimes creates still more problems.

Few banks have proper computer systems. Most operate on a hunch. Similarly airlines. I once waited seventeen minutes at the Taesa Airlines desk at Cancun airport while three girls played with the computer, wrestled with the American Express machine and finally wrote out my ticket by hand.

In one government office after another you find desks and chairs are still to be delivered, computers have not yet arrived and even coffee machines without any coffee. One ministry official practically broke down in tears when he told me he had already waited three months for a single bookshelf to keep all the statistics he had gathered proving that Mexico was now a fully developed, mature economy. When Bombay Palace, the international chain of up-market Indian restaurants, decided to open in the Zona Rosa in Mexico City, they had to import everything: ovens, incense, brass elephants, even all the spices and vegetables.

Mexico City is much, much bigger than I expected. Tokyo, Seoul, Buenos Aires, Jakarta, Dublin on a Saturday night – I thought I knew all the world's big cities. But I didn't realise Mexico City was up there with them. Over 500 square miles; over 17 million people; it just goes on and on and on. Nestling between twin volcanoes, Popocatépetl and Iztaccihuati, it is built on the site of Tenochtitlan, the old waterlogged Aztec capital discovered by Hernán Cortés and his Conquistadors in 1519. The new Venice, they called it, presumably because even in those days with all its canals and lagoons it was overrun by tourists who would rather die than pay the price the locals were demanding for a cup of coffee.

Flying, you come in practically across the centre of the city, which gives you an idea of the area it covers. Inching your way across town in any of the millions of broken-down, battered old taxis, with four bald tyres, leaky radiator, overheated engine and long clapped-out air-conditioning, you feel you know intimately every square inch of the place. Sure, there are one or two major roads. Most of them, or at least most of the ones I know, are about three cars wide jammed with four lanes of traffic, all inching their way forward.

Bars and restaurants are open more or less day and night, especially in the Zona Rosa. In some of them, you'd think you were in Paris. Until you get the bill. It's nothing like you'd get in Paris. It's so cheap you think they forgot to charge for the champagne.

And, probably more important, it has that buzz, that *je ne sais quoi*, and those three- and four-hour lunches of happy memory. In fact, I reckon the number of restaurants is limited by the number of people who can play the piano, the electronic organ, the guitar, the accordion, and the ancient Aztec art of banging coconut shells together. I've never been anywhere where it's so impossible to hear yourself eat. It's as if they are deliberately trying to drown the screams as people suddenly realise that in Mexico hot chilli sauce is hot, Hot, HOT. Whatever type of restaurant, from one chock-a-block with chandeliers and mirrors in, I'm not kidding, Liverpool Street, to the grubbiest cantina off the Plaza Garibaldi, it's always the same. I've forgotten how many tortillas I've eaten to the strains of 'Guadalajara' played on pianos, electronic organs, guitars, accordions or those damn shells.

Mexico City is also much higher than I thought: over 2,240 metres above sea level. The headquarters of the Mexican navy, for example, is over one mile above the ships it commands. Which must mean something or other.

On my first trip, all the way across the Atlantic I was warned by an eager Indian businessman who kept repeating, 'It'll take you a long time to get used to it. You mark my words, dear sir, you will have to take it easy. Have a rest every half of the hour. You might not think so, but I can assure you. . .'

When I finally made it, puff, puff, I was amazed, not just at how high it was but how ancient and historic and broken-down everything was. The huge sixteenth-century cathedral in the Zocalo, the big square in the city centre, is not just falling apart, it is actually slowly sinking, which I suppose is what happens if you insist on building on a swamp in the middle of a lake, all because some Aztec god saw an eagle sitting there on a cactus eating a serpent and decreed it should be the site of a temple and the Conquistadors decided that what was good enough for the Aztecs was good enough for them. Already it is a couple of feet below street level, and still sinking. Inside it is full of scaffolding keeping it together, which is a good thing, because as soon as you see the altar is three metres higher than the entrance you want to get out as quickly as possible. The president's office on the other side of the square looks as though it is sinking as well. But under a sea of debt.

The only building I saw that looked as though it stood any chance of getting a building certificate was the Hospital de Jésus, standing, they say, on the very spot where Montezuma, complete with headdress, met Cortés and his fellow ecotour-ists for the first time. Built in 1524 to look after the Spanish soldiers wounded in battle, it is still a hospital today. And some soldiers, I was told, were still waiting to see a doctor. The massive Jesus of Nazareth Church next door, however, has, I'm pleased to say, only one door, hardly any windows and fits in perfectly with the local environment.

The only places not crumbling to pieces are, strangely enough, the archaeological sites. The three famous pyramids representing the sun, the moon and water, the three gods of the Aztecs at Teotihuacan, about an hour out of Mexico City, are in good shape, given their age. Admittedly vast chunks of them were used to build the cathedral. But what's left is in good condition. Even the grass around them is neat, and worthy of some certificate or other.

As for the Mexicans, aren't they serious? I thought they were going to be like the Spanish, but worse. Partly because of the sun; the more sun you have, the livelier you are, at least that's what my wife keeps telling me. And partly because, well, of the Spanish. No way. The Mexicans are about as Spanish as a left-hand-drive pair of castanets. They don't have that zest and zing. Probably too many chillies en Nogada, or constantly living with the threat of having your heart torn out and thrown overboard to appease the gods. They seem to be slow, almost ponderous, more like an elder sister or an aunt than a Carmen Miranda. They're not even like, say, the Argentinians who think nothing of tangoing all night and playing polo the following morning. Nothing like the Brazilians, who will do absolutely anything, anywhere, any time, if the spirit moves them. Which it does most of the time. Gee whiz, even the Uruguayans, if that's what you call them, are more laughs.

All the Mexicans I came across were quiet, sober, hard-working, eager to eat early and quick to finish and rush home. Maybe it's something to do with being colonised by the Jesuits. Or maybe once they made Lee Trevino, they broke the mould.

On one trip I landed early on a Saturday evening and checked into a small, typical Mexican hacienda, the Hotel Monte Carlo, slap bang in the Centro between the Zocalo and the Alameda Central. I try to avoid the chains and international groups. Some guys when they hit Mexico City make for Plaza Garibaldi, where you can knock back the tequilas to non-stop mariachi music. Others go for La Tirana, some say the trendiest bar in town. Not me. I slip on a balaclava helmet – well, you never know if the Zapatista National Liberation Army are going to be successful – and make for the Zocalo. It's the only way to look inconspicuous in Mexico nowadays. Sometimes the square is full of Aztecs in all their gear, or in some cases lack of it, reliving the battles they lost which destroyed their civilisation. Underneath all the warpaint, I know there are doctors and dentists and professors of philosophy who should know better, but I don't care. I'm more at home with failure.

This time the place was packed. Loudspeakers were blaring, balloons going off all over the place. At the far end by the cathedral, broken-down old buses were parked in a solid block, each carrying placards and slogans. On a makeshift stage on the other side, speaker after speaker was screaming about something or other. The amazing thing was, nobody seemed to be taking much notice of what was going on. People were walking up and down; some were just staring vacantly at either the platform or the row of buses. One old man was stretched out on the side of the road. He could have been dead for three days. Nobody was taking any notice. All around him women were shouting and screaming at children who were either doing or not doing what they were told.

A soldier marched up and down with a dainty pink umbrella. The only sign of excitement seemed to be coming from a row of what looked like confessional boxes outside the cathedral. When I strolled across to them they turned out to be mobile toilets.

In most poor, desperate, undeveloped countries they rush up to your car when you stop at traffic lights and splash dirty water over your windscreen. Pay them a little something and they wash it off for you. In super, modern, stylish, sophisticated Italy they are more professional. They spit all over your windscreen. If you pay them they'll splash it with dirty water and hopefully wipe it all off before the lights change. In Mexico City they've gone a stage further still. At zebra crossings, kids with their faces painted weird colours put on an acrobatic show for you. As soon as the car stops at the lights, they leap out at you and start performing conjuring tricks. You see this empty bag. There! Nothing inside, right? Right. Now one, two, three. They put their hand in the bag and out comes a defenceless, pathetic old rabbit who looks sick to death of being pushed into a bag and dragged out again in clouds of exhaust fumes, God knows how many times a day. Quick, give the guy some money before the lights change so we can get the hell outta here.

Then there is parking. There are over 17 million people living in Mexico City and, whenever I'm looking for a parking space, over 17 million cars. What happens? You spend hours driving round and round. There's never, ever a space. But there are hundreds of little one-way streets, cul-de-sacs and back alleys roped off by scruffy-looking policemen, leaning up against brick walls either smoking or staring into space, obviously trying to work out how the Mayans invented the zero.

In the end, in sheer desperation, we park the car in a slow-moving stream of traffic. I go up to the policeman. 'Buenos dias, señor,' I grovel. 'I wonder, por favor. Park. In there. Possible. Si?'

He shuffles along the wall obviously still trying to work out what $2 + 2 \times 0$ is. 'Si.'

We have to unhook the rope ourselves, back in, and hook it up again. We park the car. I then have to drop the policeman, who has barely shifted from his spot on the wall, the equivalent of a week's wages – mine, not his – for the privilege of doing his dirty work for him. Don't get me wrong; I'm not expecting anyone to grovel. Damn it, I don't even expect my wife to say thank you when I bring her back something she doesn't want from somewhere she thinks I should never have gone to in the first place. But there is such a thing as 50–50. If I do this, you do that. In Mexico, I get the impression they're quite happy for everyone to be rushing around doing their half. But doing their own half, that's something else.

By the time I got back to the hotel it was late – almost 8.30. I had to rush into the restaurant because everybody was eager to close on the dot of nine and go home. But I had to fight off everybody in sight to be allowed to carry even my newspaper through the door myself. Before I set foot inside the door I practically had to wrestle a porter to the ground just to get him to take his hands off my paper. Was he going to run off with it? Was he going to swing it round and smash it in my face because I was a bourgeois, foreign reactionary intent on exploiting...? No way. All he wanted was the honour of carrying it up to my room and the privilege of a 'Dollar, amigo. Give me dollar.'

Once in the restaurant, I gulped back a couple of plates of your ordinary, run-of-the-mill chillies en Nogada, poblano chillies stuffed with meat, dipped in batter, fried and then drowned in a rich cream and walnut sauce before being rolled in pomegranate seeds and cilantro leaves followed by something that sounded exotic in Spanish but turned out to be cold jelly when it arrived in English. I was out of there by five minutes to nine. At one minute past I was in my room, having fought off two porters who practically wanted to carry me upstairs for the privilege of a 'Dollar, amigo. Give me dollar.'

The following morning the sun came up at the cost of who knows how many hearts ripped out by the Aztec priests at the Pyramid of the Sun at Teotihuacan. This obviously meant I had to take my pick between visiting Xochimilco, an old Chichimec Indian word for 'where the flowers are', which is really 120 miles of floating gardens of flowers, vegetables and fruit with probably the biggest flower market in the world (it covers over thirty acres and has more than 1,250 stalls selling everything from water-lilies to orchids), or Chihuahua, the home of Pancho Villa, the great Mexican revolutionary, and the world headquarters of those funny little dogs, or Trotsky's hideaway. I picked Trotsky. I mean, I selected Trotsky's hideaway.

All I can say is the Mexicans were not doing anybody any favours. For years poor old Trotsky roamed the world like some refugee from an alien ideology, looking for somebody to take him in. An old contact fixed it with the Mexican government. They gave him number 410 rio Churubusco, which I can tell you is no Chartwell or Colombey-les-Deux-Eglises where a tired old political leader could relax, catch Alzheimer's disease and see out his days surrounded by a loyal staff all busy scribbling their memoirs of the snivelling, incontinent old has-been and negotiating film deals. Even allowing for the year, 1937; the fact that half the world was thinking of tearing the other half apart; that the Mexicans didn't particularly want to upset Stalin too much and that Mexico as not exactly one of the richest nations going, it is pretty basic. Far from being a grand château or even an elegant if dusty townhouse, it's more like a rambling old grey cement farmhouse, after twenty years of collectivisation, set in about half an acre with a brick wall round it.

There is precious little furnishings, and what there is is State Furnishing Co-operative No. 58 stuff. There are no floor coverings. Nothing on the walls. Just the basic, and I mean basic, necessities according to Regulation 1007 Section 2, paragraph (d), Command Paper XXIII, Overseas Dachas, The Furnishings Thereof. The study and his desk, which looks more like a large kitchen table, are just as they were that fateful morning. There are a couple of pens left carelessly around, a magnifying glass and a book on Stalin on the right. Which I thought was significant. In the corner is a bed where presumably he retired after he had bored himself to sleep with another long article justifying whatever it was that made him fall out with Stalin.

The floor, I noticed, was painted a heavy, thick red. Whether that had any significance I couldn't discover. My guide looked like a Russian Orthodox monk on his day off. He had a long beard, was dressed all in black and had a large wooden cross around his neck. He was only interested in talking about Trotsky's library. Well, I say library. There was one wall of shelves with all kinds of books stacked haphazardly together.

They say, show me your bookshelves and I'll tell you what kind of man you are. All I can say is, Trotsky's bookshelves seem pretty much to represent the man. Who else, for example, would have sitting together, *The Big Money* by John Dos Passos, *The Game* by Jack London, *Labour in Ireland* by James Connolly and Lawrence's *The Plumed Serpent*? On the next shelf, side by side were *An African Survey* by Lord Hailey, which I also happen to have on my shelves, *Seeds of Destruction* by someone called Blair, and *A World I Never Made* by James T. Farrell, which sounds like a bundle of laughs.

The garden was collective farm stuff with more paths than plants. Obviously Gertrude Jekyll was not one of his favourite authors. In one corner were a couple of open rabbit hutches and a run for his chickens which looked as though it had been thrown together by the state chicken co-operative. Apparently the old boy used to breed them. Until they came home to roost.

The only encouraging thing about the place was that there was no Trotsky souvenir shop called Take Your Pick. Although I suppose, as Mexico becomes more developed and the economy gathers more and more speed, some bright capitalist will come up with the idea. What form the souvenirs will take I shudder to think.

On the way out, the Russian monk showed me Trotsky's glasses, his passport and the letter his widow wrote to the Mexican President, a month after he was killed, thanking him for allowing them in.

I asked him how many visitors they got.

'Two or three,' he said.

'A day?'

'No. A week.'

Nobody picks Trotsky any more.

Outside Mexico City, or at least the bits not controlled by Sub-Commandante Marcos and his merry band of Zapatistas, the place is littered with chewing-gum trees; mile-long swarms of swallowtail butterflies which can block out the sun as quickly and as effectively as a swarm of locusts; old world courtesies such as rich benefactors caring for the needs of poor policemen, judges and politicians; temples, old Spanish cities – don't ask why, but one day I want to go to San Miguel de Allende where every September bulls run through the streets as they do in Pamplona – and ropes or speed bumps.

I've never known – oops – a country to have – oops – so many – oops – speed bumps. Blindfold me, put me in a car, and I guarantee within two seconds I'll tell you if I'm in Mexico. Driving around the countryside, I don't think we once managed to get into fourth gear, whereas in towns, where for some strange reason they don't believe in speed bumps, I don't think we were ever out of fourth gear – oops.

I haven't been to Veracruz, which is supposed to be like New Orleans after dark; or to the Copper Canyon, which is bigger and deeper and more spectacular than the Grand Canyon; or to hot-spots like Ixtapa, Puerto Vallarto, Cozumel or, I suppose, Acapulco. Not because of the speed bumps, but because there are some things you just can't swing on expenses. I have, however, been to Cancun, which many finance directors and chairmen of executive remuneration committees say is better than all the rest put together. All I know is, to me, it was hotter than a chilli-spiked tomato juice which, I can tell you from bitter experience is hot, Hot, HOT.

I went there not because of that but because it was the nearest spot on the map to visit the temples at Chichen Itzá, the old Mayan powerbase in the Yucatan peninsula out in the east. That's my story and I'm sticking to it. I arrived late one Friday night, having practically hedge-hopped all the way from Monterrey, and couldn't believe my red eyes. It was one enormous luxury hotel after another, beside mile after mile after mile of beautiful sandy beach. It was like Florida without the danger. Well, the danger of being shot, maimed or killed. There were plenty of other dangers around, particularly when the mariachi music started drifting through the palm trees. But I can take it.

The Mayan ruins at Chichen Itzá – see, I did go there after all – are spectacular; well worth the time, effort, agony and heartache of getting there. Worth the battle through thick, lush ferns and bamboos, the desperate struggle against the mass of overhanging creepers, the hot, humid atmosphere, the screeching parrots, the vicious mosquitoes. That's just to get out of the hotel on to the bus. After that the journey is three hours of absolute hell. The buses are invariably full of American tourists, chasing the cheap peso.

On planes, I always get the fat lady and the kid who insists on dismantling the whole thing from the inside out the moment they come thumping and screeching on board. On buses I get the earnest, dedicated, middle-aged feminists who just know that I am personally responsible for everything that has ever gone wrong in the whole world. Sure enough, on the trip to Chichen Itzá I got lumbered with earnest, dedicated, middle-aged feminist Number One, from Boston. Before she even sat down, so that I wouldn't think she was just an ordinary housewife, she told me she was something terribly big in 'industrial hygiene'.

'You mean you put the soap in the washrooms?' I wondered. My god, did she go bananas! I was being racist, sexist and every other kind of -ist. I was a pathetic, low-minded cheap little male European who deserved ... cheap jibes ... need help ... blah blah screech blah.

I mean, I ask you, how was I to know that industrial hygiene was some newfangled yuppie Boston word for a works manager. But try as I might to convince her it was an innocent slip of the tongue, she wouldn't listen.

'Surly ... Trouble with men today ... always trying to ... blah ... blah ... blah.' She then suddenly switched to the Austrians. They should return the headdress of the ancient Aztec ruler, Montezuma, to Mexico. It doesn't belong to them. They stole it. It's the Mexicans' cultural heritage ... blah blah blah.

'Why don't you give us back our tea then?' I said, in all innocence. Caramba. Did she go spare. She tried ordering the driver to throw me off the bus, until I pointed out that Mexico was a sovereign independent state and the Americans had no right to come marching in, throwing their weight around and giving orders to everybody. After all they don't do it in Panama. In Grenada. In Haiti. In ...

By the time we got to Chichen Itzá, I can tell you, I was in the mood for human sacrifice.

So was it worth the aggro? On a scale of 1–10 I would say it's around $4\frac{1}{2}$. About the same as Mrs Mollony's bar in Newmarket on Fergus. In terms of size and brute force the temples are certainly up there with the Pyramids. But bearing in mind they were building the Great Wall of China over 1,000 years before the first Mayans even noticed the stars, they have to be down the line when it comes to the Wonders of the World. Which surprised me. For some reason, maybe because of the pyramid shape, I thought the Mayans flourished round about the same time as Tutankhamen. No way, José. The temples are only around 1,000 years old, which makes them pretty primitive when you think what we were building at the same time and had been building before then. But, credit where credit is due; the Mayans were the original Americans, at least that's what everyone told me, so eight out of ten for effort. For Americans.

Two things struck me as I wandered around (apart from praying to the Mayan gods that they would demand as compensation for our visit the heart of an industrial hygiene manager from Boston – if she had one). First, if the Mayans were such clever mathematicians and astronomers, how come they only came up with one spectacular building: the pyramid, the Temple of Kukulcan, with its four lots of 91 steps making 364? Hey! Don't forget the one at the top making 365; one for every day of the year.

The other buildings, the Temple of the Jaguars, the Observatory, the Temple of Venus, and so on, are okay, but there is nothing particularly mathematical about them. They look as though they were pretty much put together as they went along. The Mayan basketball stadium, for example, looks fairly bizarre, to put it mildly. Imagine this enormous, oblong field. On either side are huge stands for the spectators. In the centre of each wall, just below where the spectators are presumably sitting and hollering and singing the Mayan equivalent of 'Here We Go', is the tiniest stone circle. Somehow the poor players had, not to throw some human skull through the circle, which would have been difficult enough, but with both hands gripped together to punch it through, otherwise they would lose not only their sponsor but their lives as well. I mean, is that making things easy?

Second, how genuine is the actual pyramid and all the other stuff? I mean, I've seen prints showing them as nothing but a heap of rubble; now suddenly they are the real thing. No rubble, no trees growing out of them halfway up; all clean, squared up, mathematical: 92 perfect steps each exactly 8.85 metres wide, the base exactly 55.3 metres long on each side and the whole thing exactly 30 metres high, allowing 6 metres for the temple on top. The pyramid has four sides: the four seasons of the year. Each side has nine corners. Multiply by two: 18. So how many months were there in the Mayan calendar? You got it. Each month had 20 days. So, your starter for 10, 20 times 18 equals what? The number of days in the year. Plus, of course, one on top: 365. I kept trying to ask the guides, who all looked as though they were hooked on pulque, Mexican firewater distilled from cactus, how all this arose from the rubble, but they just grinned and thanked me for my 'comprehension'.

Call me old-fashioned, but to me a ruin is a ruin, not something that's been rebuilt. Nobody would suggest putting the roof back on the Parthenon, or tidying up the Pyramids, so why play games with Chichen Itzá? Worse still, why play games and not let us join in. Don't you agree?

What I tried not to notice, because I was well brought up, were the actual descendants of the Mayans. They're all about five feet tall, slightly hunched, have jet black hair and slit eyes.

'They're about as in-bred as the Institutional Revolutionary Party, the PRI, that has ruled Mexico for over sixty-five years,' a Mexican student whom I swear I first met when he was wearing a balaclava helmet in the Zocalo one evening told me.

But I'll tell you what I did notice, as plain as the salt around the top of a margarita. I noticed that if you count the number of small square holes in the tiny upper chamber of the Caracol or Observatory; multiply it by the number of steps leading to the Temple of Kukulcan; divide it by the square root of the number of times some Mayan kid tries to sell you a sombrero; add the number of headless statues sitting cross-legged outside the Iglesia and subtract the number of Coke cans thrown around, what do you get? You get October 3, 2001. Which, if I'm not mistaken, is the date Mexico has to start repaying the debts it ran up as a result of the devaluation. Don't say I didn't warn you.

For all that, I will admit Mexico City is one of the few places in the world which has truly moved me. By about three and a half inches, to be precise. I was actually there one Sunday morning during an earthquake. It might not have been as big as the one in 1985, which I was told did extensive damage, although looking at the place today you would never guess. Not because everything looks so beautiful, but because you don't know whether the damage was created by the earthquake, by the Conquistadors or by Montezuma himself. I don't care. In Mexico City, for me the earth moved. Which has to be better than an icepick in the back of the head.

Managua

Armed men with beards spouting Lenin and Marx. Priests writing poems about Marilyn Monroe. Salman Rushdie popping in for a few days to write a book. Olly North hiding in the bushes with a shredding machine. Terry Waite looking the other way. Ronald Reagan denying all knowledge of the place.

What did I find when I got to Managua? Evangelists.

The place was crawling with them. They were outside the pharmacy just up from Bolivar, the one big street that runs through the centre of town; opposite the bicycle shop, way past the big Mercado Roberto Huembes; outside the Mechanical Engineering Academy, or rather outside the house which calls itself the Mechanical Engineering Academy; going in and out of one precarious-looking corrugated-iron shack after another; in the square, outside the huge blackened remains of the Cathedral Santo Domingo.

The place was packed with people – young and old, but mostly young; poor and not-so-poor, but mainly not-so-poor. Everybody was looking intently to the platform and the speaker, who wasn't ranting and raving, but speaking clearly, forcefully and persuasively.

We parked alongside a collection of broken-down, dusty old cars, trucks and buses on the far corner. There were kids everywhere, standing alongside, I guess, their parents. None of them were running around.

'Socialista?' I mumbled in my made-up Spanish to a young man with long hair, beard and a black beret.

'Evangelista,' he said. 'Alianza Evangelica Nicaraguense.'

Which amazed me. The tone. The hollering. The oh-so-sharp difference between the big smooth fatcats on the platform and the poor guys in the crowd. I would have bet anyone an old worn-out Neiman Marcus catalogue to a brand new, unread copy of *Das Kapital* that this was a demonstration in favour of equality between all men.

Then I looked again. All of the old, broken-down cars at the back of the crowd had posters in the windows proclaiming Jesus Vienne, or Christo Vienne, or simply, Jesus. The buses and vans, all heaps of metal balancing precariously on three bald tyres and faith in the Almighty, were covered in religious paintings and slogans. One filthy old truck looked as though it was piled with rotting carcases of meat. On the side in huge letters it said, 'Dios Te Ama'. Which must have been a comfort if you were planning to go anywhere near the van let alone the meat.

The speaker was in his shirtsleeves. It was one of those vivid white shirts, the type you only see on television commercials. His trousers were that electric-blue shiny material. He looked a bit like a boxer or a wrestler, with big heavy shoulders. He was stooping slightly in front of the microphone, his mouth close up to it. Every now and then he would pound his left hand into his right. I couldn't understand what he was saying but it sounded pretty impressive and convincing. The stage was bare: no posters, no slogans.

To his left stood four or five young men wearing dark electric-blue suits. All looked smart, well-groomed; white shirts, serious ties. In front of the stage was one of those flashy cars – a big Peugeot or a Lexus, something like that.

I walked slowly through the crowd. Everybody was staring, listening intently. It was a bit unnerving. Like the beginning of one of those old science fiction movies when everybody stands staring at the spaceship. I stood listening for a while. Whatever he was selling, he was good at it.

I walked back through the crowd. There was a group of businessmen types standing by an old battered dirty yellow bus, the type that was probably a school bus in the US before the war. The War of Independence.

'Politicos?' I gestured towards the stage.

They shook their heads. 'Evangelista,' the one nearest me said.

'Si, si,' they whispered. 'Evangelista.'

You see them all over the place nowadays. In Eastern Europe: in Budapest outside Deli Palyandrar station, clean-cut, well-groomed, trying to stop and talk to anybody who will listen; in Tallin, in Estonia as well as in Riga, in Latvia, they stand self-consciously in the main squares. Some I have even spotted in Africa. Once in Lomé I got caught up in a visit by Morris Cerullo, the big American evangelist who promises miracles by the dozen.

'Lorsque vous quitterez ce bâtiment, vous ne serez plus les mêmes gens,' he told us almost the moment we arrived. And he was right. Until then I had a soft spot for evangelists. When I left the bâtiment halfway through his show it was gone. I wished the minister who baptised him by total immersion had held his head under a bit longer. Not that I mean to be unChristian.

I have even seen them trooping off to the Vineyard Christian Fellowship Chapel in Toronto airport for what they call the Toronto Blessing, which is designed either to protect you from the effects of eating too much airline food, or to give you patience if, like me, you always end up sitting next to the fat lady and the kid.

But this was my first sighting of evangelists in central America which must be worth, what, 10 points, 2.37 million air miles or a life without tea, coffee, alcohol, dirty shirts, greasy ties and long hair.

Each to his own beliefs, but I still find it difficult to go bananas about the evangelists as some people do. I mean if we agree there should be freedom of speech, freedom of choice, freedom of religion and everything else, I can't see how one can say it only applies to one side and not the other. Providing, of course, that everybody follows the same basic rules. Like agreeing with everything I say and do. Some hope. But certainly listening to this guy, watching the people around me, it would have been difficult to find a more staid, sober, dignified, serious gathering. He wasn't raving or telling little jokes. He was obviously speaking concisely and convincingly. You could feel he had his audience with him. When he finished, he just finished. There was no build-up, no peroration, no calls to arms. He obviously just finished what he had to say and stopped. Everyone then went to their cars or buses or trucks or just wandered off. The guy on the platform put his jacket on, jumped off the stage and walked to his car.

As the buses pulled away I could see the names of towns and villages around Managua; Masaya, Rivas, Matagalpa. But some people had come a long way; from Leon, Nicaragua's second largest city, famous for its graffiti and still a big FSLN/ Sandinista stronghold; from Esteli, the scene of heavy fighting during the war and still a flashpoint between Sandinistas and the government; from Granada, on the western side of Lake Nicaragua, and on the opposite side of the political divide.

I've got nothing against Nicaragua. I've got nothing against evangelists either. In fact, some of my best enemies are not evangelists. It's just that it was not quite what I expected to find as soon as I fell off the plane. Not in Managua, the hotbed of Jesuit-inspired revolution.

Mention evangelists back home, especially on the third Saturday of every month when they seem to descend on our village like a flock of locusts, if I'm not mixing my Old Testament metaphors, and everybody will tell you they're only in it for the money. Give them 10 per cent of your income they say. Where do you think all that money goes? Into their pockets, of course. Where else? Not me. First of all you've got to admire their dedication and, I suppose, their courage. I mean, it takes me all my courage to ask someone the way to the nearest champagne bar. Well, before lunch it does. To stop people in the street and hammer them with the ins-and-outs of Deuteronomy, or to stand on street corners in the rain elaborating on the implications of the Sermon on the Mount for late twentieth-century man is something I could never do.

As for leading the life of Riley, you don't see any signs of it. I mean, no smoking, no drinking, no tea, no coffee, no alcohol. There's not much left, is there?

As far as I'm concerned, if they're in it for the money, they're crazy. First, because I can think of easier ways of making money than standing on some rickety platform in front of a bombed-out or rather earthquaked-out cathedral with giant posters of revolutionary heroes staring down at me from the front of the National Assembly on my left.

Second, because they are obviously doing some good. Whether they are doing an enormous amount of good, some good or just a little good is a Jesuitical distinction I cannot make. They are definitely doing some good. And judging by the state of Managua, I'd have thought that if the Devil himself suddenly arrived and swept up a couple of leaves they'd be grateful.

Third, because you have to admit they're always welcomed. Some people say it's only the Indians, the poor, the unedu-cated who welcome them. That's certainly not my impression – and I've seen them in action all over the place. But if it was, it doesn't make any difference, even if they are taking business away from the Jesuits. The Jesuits, I'm sure, being more Jesuitical than the rest of us, would not deny anyone the freedom of choice: even if that freedom of choice went against them. Not that the Jesuits are giving in, or losing.

Managua is first, second, third and fourth a religious city. Not European religious; not Middle East religious, but South Amer-ican religious. There are religious paintings, posters, slogans on buses, on cars, scrawled all over walls. In other countries you see pictures of pop stars on the buses; not here. One painting of Christ actually filled the whole of the back of the bus. Be distracted for a second by a señorita and run into the back of that bus, and God knows what will happen to you.

In the Far East I do the pagodas and the temples. In Venice or Cracow I do the churches. In Managua, I decided to do the evangelists.

My last Sunday – well, you can't let them see you're enthusiastic, can you? – I woke up to this deep, heavy rumbling sound. The earth hadn't moved so I assumed it must have been gunfire and bombs going off on the other side of town. Everybody said they were fireworks, but nobody organises a firework display at 7.15 on a Sunday morning. I waited for a cab to come ambling up to the hotel.

'Evangelistas,' I mumbled nervously, trying to suggest that naturally I wasn't one of them, perish the thought, but from a purely sociological point of view I was. . .

'Sure, buddy. We go. No problem.'

The driver had just got back after three years in Miami. He was practically a multi-millionaire – in Nicaraguan terms.

As it was the first day of the week, I decided to start with the Seventh-day Adventists. From there I went to a tiny, rusty, corrugated-iron hut of a church near the back of a steel mill which, I couldn't help noticing, was next door to the Ministry for Foreign Affairs. Then it was on to tiny neat brick churches in obviously up-market shanty areas where the corrugated iron had been painted delicate shades of green; then brick churches surrounded by brick houses, and finally a proper stone church tucked away behind a couple of neat villas.

All the churches were full. Not St Paul's Cathedral-type churches, mark you, but ordinary St Paul's, Stow-in-the-Wold-type churches. Everybody was singing and enjoying themselves and joining in whenever they wanted, shouting out amen or alleluia or whatever. They all seemed smart, Sunday-morning-well-dressed. Admittedly I didn't see any sports cars; nor did I see one electric-blue suit all morning. But these were not your poor, down-trodden Indians being exploited by some smart bunch of redneck out-of-towners in it for the money. These guys were believers. What exactly they believed in, God only knows – if you see what I mean. Every time I tried to ask them I got a different answer.

I once spent a whole morning in a New Age bookshop in a crumbling courtyard off a crumbling street near the not-so-crumbling Vabaduse Square in Tallinn, Estonia, jammed with everything you could possibly want to know about way-out, way-way-out and very-funny-now-change-me-back-again religion. Did I find out what the evangelists believe in? Did I hell.

I do know that the world only has another 350-odd years to go. Who told me? This evangelista doing his thing in the Mercado Roberto Huembes near the university which, would you believe, is run by a Jesuit who trained at Cambridge.

'The clock,' he said. 'The answer is in the clock. Right?'

'Right,' I said.

We shook our heads together as if that was the key to the universe.

'The clock,' I said.

'Si, señor, the clock.'

We shook our heads together again. He then just looked at me in silence as if that was that. I thought I might have missed something in translation. He smiled at me.

'How do you mean,' I began, 'the clock? I'm afraid I don't...'

He shuffled round to me. Obviously he wasn't used to dealing with coffee-drinking, alcohol-swilling dumbos with dirty shirts, greasy ties, long hair and only one wife.

'The clock,' he said. 'It's obvious. Look.' He pointed to his watch. 'Everything is governed by time, yes?'

'Well, yeah, I suppose...'

'The year of Our Lord was AD 1, right? On the clock that is 00.01. Right?'

'Well, I sup—'

'So the end of the world is 2400. Right?' He clapped his hands together. That was it. No hesitations, no doubts, no second thoughts.

So pass the word on. There's only four hours to go.

Nicaragua means 'Here near the lake' if you're a Spanish scholar, an expert on the Nahuatl language, and a gentleman, or Nickers if you're in the Foreign Office. Hence all the old jokes you hear in White's and Boodles: when was the last time you were in Nickers? I like Nickers. You can't beat Nickers. Nickers are going down.

And the people in Nickers? They're known as Nicos, of course.

The country itself, the largest in Central America, is nothing but two coastlines separated by a load of volcanoes: nearly thirty, not to be too precise, eight of them still active which is probably why they have all those earthquakes. Practically the whole population lives either on the slopes of a volcano, the lava, or the debris left behind after an eruption.

In spite of that and the fact that it is only 175th in the list of richest nations in the world, it has a certain sense of order and solidity about it.

Some countries are a mess. Without wishing to upset anybody, they are invariably in Africa and are run by military dictators. Nothing works, everything is falling apart. Lay electricity cable or telephone wires in the morning and by the afternoon they have been dug up and either sold or melted down. In one country whose capital city begins with L and ends in S, they even rob the planes as they are taxi-ing to take off from the airport.

In Nicaragua, by contrast, you get the feeling it could be up there with the rest if they hadn't been so unlucky. The Nickers, I mean Nicos, may have their ups and downs, but they seem to have a sense of discipline – maybe another spin-off from the Jesuits. Taxis arrive when you book them, not just on the right day, but at the right time. Meetings start on time. Everything is ordered and logical. The people are friendly and always prepared to avoid any discussion of politics, human rights, re-forestation, land management, public health and why the school bus is parked right in front of the driveway so we can't get out.

If people have to wear suits, they wear suits. If they have to wear uniforms, they wear uniforms. I've lost count of the offices, factories, even hotels in Africa where the staff are slopping around in greasy T-shirts, stained jeans and flip-flops because they've forgotten to put their uniforms on or, more likely, sold them to buy food or medicine for their family.

For fifty years the Nicos were twisted as well as mercilessly exploited and almost destroyed by the Somozas. Daddy Somoza seized power in 1937 by assassinating their big national hero, Augusto Cesar Sandino, who was violently anti-American, and had absolutely dominated the place for nearly twenty years. Somoza soon amassed a huge fortune, as well as practically all the land throughout the country. 'He may be a son of a bitch,' Franklin D. Roosevelt once said. 'But he's ours.' Which tells you everything about US diplomacy. Theirs he remained until 1956 when he was assassinated by a radical young poet dressed as a waiter. Elder son, Luis, took over and followed in papa's footsteps till he died in 1967 when baby brother, Anastasio, took over. Which was too much of a bad thing even for the long-suffering Nicaraguans. Come 1961, Carlos Fonseco Amador, a long-time opponent of the Somozas, finally joined up with an old sparring partner and fellow opponent of the Somozas, Santos Lopez. The Sandinistas, named after Augusto Cesar Sandino, were in business. Not that it seemed to make much difference to baby brother – until the night of December 23, 1972, the night an enormous earthquake devastated Managua.

Down came the cathedral. Down came no less than 250 office blocks and mini-skyscrapers. Down came just about every house, shack and lean-to in the city. Six thousand people were killed. Over 300,000 were made homeless. Before, Managua had not exactly been the most beautiful city in the world. After the earthquake, it wasn't even worth entering it for the competition. It was well nigh flattened.

'It was worse than being bombed,' an old evangelista I met in the Inter-Continental told me. 'There was nobody we could forgive.'

Aid poured in from all over the world – and went straight into baby brother's pocket. Opposition mounted. The government resorted to assassination and mass killings. Carlos Fonseco was assassinated. After a long, bloody struggle the

Sandinistas seized power on July 19, 1979. It was a dream come true. The streets were flowing with political faith, hope and charity. At last the good guys, the idealists, and the good Jesuits – mustn't forget them – were in power. They were going to create heaven on earth. This was going to be liberation theology in action.

The vice-president was a novelist; the Minister of the Interior a poet and writer; the Minister of Culture was a poet, a writer and a priest, first a Trappist monk and then a Benedictine who ran his own island commune on Lake Nicaragua.

Immediately they did what you would expect anyone to do who took over a country racked, since its discovery by Gil Gonzalez de Avila in 1519, by vicious repression, torture, poverty, disease and mysterious disappearances: they tore down all the Somoza statues and in their place they put up the world's biggest murals telling everyone how to look after chickens.

Having got the important issues out of the way, they started on the less important. They gave all the land amassed by the Somozas back to the peasants. In other words they nationalised it. They launched an anti-polio drive, cutting infant mortality by a third. And they launched a massive education campaign which cut illiteracy from over 50 per cent to just under 13 per cent.

Some people hailed it as an example to the world. Others said it was just a clever ploy by a bunch of writers to boost their royalties. Even today, you're hard pushed to find a book shop in Managua selling anything lighthearted or frivolous. About the easiest read I came across was *Marilyn Monroe and other Poems* by Erneste Cardenal, the ex-Trappist, ex-Benedictine and now ex-minister, and *Liberation Theology* by James V. Schall, this time still a practising Jesuit.

At first, nobody could have had more international support than the Sandinistas. The Poles sent them all the unpronounceable cartoon films they could find. The Swedes sent them all their incomprehensible movies. Salman Rushdie dropped in for three weeks and did an in-depth book on them. Edward 'Red Ted' Knight flew out to bring them greetings from the people of Lambeth. But still they were neither discouraged nor deflected.

And did they create heaven on earth? They did. Except it was in Miami and Costa Rica. The bright guys left for Miami where they promptly became fund managers, bankers or drug smugglers and made a fortune. The rest headed for Costa Rica where wages were double what they were at home. Life was good. And they could send money back to their nearest post office. Whether the money got from the post office to their families was another matter.

As for creating heaven in Nicaragua, after fifteen years in power the Sandinistas hadn't done one-eighth of what they promised. Some people blame the Americans. The Americans didn't want a popular revolutionary government in power in Latin America. It was a dangerous precedent. So they started arming their opponents, the Contras and other counter-revolutionary groups, to oust them. They also imposed a trade blockade. Then came the Iran–Contra affair.

Others blame the Sandinistas themselves. They had the right ideas and the right objectives, but they couldn't govern. They didn't understand politics. 'They banned everyone from leaving,' an old government official told me, 'which was silly. Castro, for example, let everyone go. The result; he had no opposition. The Sandinistas stopped everyone. The result was they had to deal with an opposition. They never understood that.'

In 1990 the Sandinistas submitted themselves to the will of the people on the basis of Unity, Stability and Direction. They had given the country unity: just about everybody was united against them. They had given the country stability: the rate of inflation had been stable at around 30,000 per cent the whole time they were in power. They had given the country a sense of direction: everybody wanted to find out in which direction their friends and relatives had been sent when they were escorted from their homes at three o'clock in the morning.

The Sandinistas were thrown out on their necks. To be fair to them, as soon as they realised that the people in whom they had placed their trust had been manipulated and bribed and blackmailed by bourgeois, capitalist concepts like the freedom to walk the streets without being shot in the back by a Kalashnikov, and they had lost the election, they left office. Just the office. Everything else they took with them, including the carpets, paintings off the walls, electric light bulbs, even the electric light fittings.

For their supporters, they decided to have a whip-round. They whipped round all the luxury houses and ranches and grabbed the lot. Now everybody is trying to get them out. But you know what it's like in August trying to get your mother-in-law to leave when she only popped in for lunch on Christmas Day.

Most of the big guys with the real big houses have left anyway. Better to spend the rest of your life queuing up to get into Tavernier's in Miami than stay around hoping the new government you voted in will get round to throwing out the head of the local Sandinistas who's got this Russian tank, a stack of Kalashnikovs and something that looks like it could take us all to Kingdom Come lined up on your front lawn.

The new government of Violetta Barvios de Chamorro, the widow of Pedro Joaquin who was assassinated by the Somozas, is desperately trying to solve the problem. Which is obviously why they asked Jimmy Carter, who was president when the Sandinistas took over, if he could help. I was told that when somebody asked him if it was going to be easy or difficult, he said that as far as he was concerned North Korea was a sovereign independent nation under a great historic leader. Which amazed me. I didn't think he had understood the question. But that's the Contra view.

The problem is that until the land dispute is settled, nobody is going to go to Nicaragua, let alone do business or invest there. I mean, if you buy land from somebody, how do you know they actually own the land they are selling to you? The only solution I can think of is another earthquake. Then there'll be nothing left to argue over. But maybe that's being a little too extreme.

Now that they are not only in opposition but also property owners, the Sandinistas have themselves split in two: those living in the really, really big houses and those living in the ordinary big houses. In the far, far left-hand corner of the chapel is the old president, Daniel Ortega himself. Still breathing fire and brimstone, still preaching Marxist-Leninism, still pushing the old hardline left. With him are one or two acolytes. In the right-hand corner, tucked away between the Yamaha organ and the collection plate, are the modernisers, the old vice-president, Sergio Ramirez, and the ex-Trappist, ex-Benedictine, ex-poet and now ex-Minister of Culture, Erneste Cardenal.

The military, who some people said were as bad as the Sandinistas, have gone back to the barracks. Not to study theology, but to study boring things like constitutional government, accountability, rule by civilians, that kind of woolly left-wing stuff.

Managua today is just as much a non-city as it was when the Sandinistas took over. Some places you visit you would never believe were hit by earthquakes. Elsewhere you can still see some damage. There can be absolutely no doubt, however, that Managua has been hit by an earthquake. There are hardly any tall buildings in the place. The tallest is the Inter-Continental Hotel, known locally as the Ugly American, even though it's loosely based on some Mayan pyramid design and is owned by the Taiwanese and run by the Japanese. And that's only six storeys high. After that comes the Bank of America building, the presidential palace, or rather house, the Texaco petrol station and the Comedor Sara which looks like an aircraft hangar but serves a shrimp curry hot enough to lift you twenty feet off the ground. The Central Bank is only one storey, which must mean something.

The rest is low, squat, sprawling, and desperately poor. There are shacks and hovels all over the place. Children, some horribly·crippled, run, skip and drag themselves across roads to scramble over any car or truck that has to stop at the lights or the crossroads. I actually saw a tiny boy with a withered leg clambering over the bonnet of an enormous Russian-built truck at the crossroads by the president's house. Which might be one reason why there are so many horses and carts.

Managua also has lots of huge open spaces. It's as if they've just cleared away the rubble from the earthquake, swept the streets and thrown some grass seed all over the place. It's the only city I know which is more country than town. Drive from one end of what you think is the town – it's difficult to tell because you don't know where the town/country meets the country/country, if you see what I mean – to the other and you spend more time looking at grass and cattle happily munching away at it than you do looking at buildings.

A week in Managua and you can practically tell one blade of grass from another. Two weeks in Managua and you are talking to the stuff.

'So how are you today?'

'Not bad.'

'Planning any holidays?'

'Yeah. I'm thinking of moving across to that block over there. Reckon it's about time that was grass as well.'

'Hey, that'll be fun. Enjoy.'

The whole place – apart from the grass – is slow, dozy, second gear. The streets are almost empty; maybe the occasional Russian truck or tiny pony and cart. And you can guess which overtakes which.

Now and then you see the old yellow school buses which the US threw out when Olly North stopped riding them to school; taxis that look as though they were on the way to the scrapheap, but the owner couldn't bear to be parted from them, and occasionally one of those big old American cars held together by faith and chewing gum.

Everyone seems to sit around on boxes, chairs, piles of old tyres, oil drums: old men chewing something and spitting it into the dust; young men curled up on window ledges; women just staring out of windows. If they move, it's as if they're frightened of moving too quickly in case they trigger another earthquake. Rush around? Never. They know that would definitely trigger another earthquake.

Everything is scruffy, dirty, dusty and made of car tyres and oil drums. Managua must be the car tyre and oil drum capital of the world. The atmosphere seems to be held together with car tyres and oil drums. The fences are car tyres. The steps are car tyres. Walls look as though they are lined with car tyres. Even outdoor signs are made with car tyres. As for the oil drums, they're in garden walls, in garages, in houses. If, instead of car tyres or oil drums, you use car batteries, you're a rich man. I saw one house almost entirely built of car batteries. What the charge was I couldn't tell you, but it was the most impressive house on the block.

All the same, things are not so bad as they were. At one stage the country was on its deathbed, ready to receive the last rites. Today it's slowly recovering. Inflation is only 7,000 per cent a year. And most villages have television. But it is going to take years, some say twenty, maybe thirty years before things get back to where they were. If ever. There is still hardly any industry or business. Even in Managua there are only a couple of factories, a few garages and a collection of repair shops.

Practically everything has to be imported. Even machetes, the most basic of all tools, have to be imported from El Salvador next door, which is no industrial giant itself. There's not an awful lot of coffee in Nicaragua at the moment either, but they're hoping there is going to be. At present it brings in around US$100 million out of total exports of US$400 million.

All along the west coast, from San Juan del Sur to Peneloya and Corinto, the sea is chock-a-block with lobster. But the fishing boats are so badly equipped, filthy and dangerous that even in the vast so-called Miskito Camps Protected Area, divers, who are usually the poorest of the poorest, are catching lobsters by hand for export to US restaurants. These restaurants make a big thing, not about the filthy, overcrowded, dangerous working conditions of the divers, or the fact that the diving tanks they go down in are so old and unreliable that the gauges don't tell them how much air they've got left and they are constantly in danger of blowing up, but about the fact that they don't use diver-caught lobster.

As far as I'm concerned, and I enjoy eating lobster as much as that poor pathetic guy over there with the shaven head, the real-wool fisherman's smock and plastic open-toe sandals munching tofu sandwiches, I can't honestly see much difference between eating a diver-caught lobster, a trap-caught lobster or a waiter-caught lobster from the tank over there by the kitchen door.

As for the security situation, depending on who you talk to, either all the old Sandinistas or crooks posing as Sandinistas have laid down their arms, shaved their beards and gone back to studying liberation theology instead of practising it, or they are still roaming around shooting people up and causing trouble, especially in the north. Either way, everybody tells you it's best not to go out after eight. At night, if you're in Managua. In the morning, if you're anywhere else in the country.

During one trip, a bunch of old Contra-rebels who had laid down their arms managed to shoot up a town less than 100 miles from the capital, killing seven people. Probably by throwing their theology books at them. Which is obviously why there are not too many outsiders – their word, not mine – in Managua at the moment. I was almost the only one in the hotel. Not because the word got out; more likely because there are one or two marginally more exciting things to do in life than visit the empty offices of Nicaraguan government ministers and spend all day talking to fat, slobbery men with beards. It's like spending a week on the set of *The Good, the Bad and the Ugly*.

One morning I had to go to the Ministry of Finance. The director was around forty. Years, not stone. Although I suppose he could have been that as well. I waited almost an hour to talk to him. When he arrived, we shook hands. Then he had to go to another meeting. One afternoon I saw another official in the National Assembly. He was tall and thin and had a pair of those long, black, slinky leather boots on. And a beard. In the evening, at the university, I had another meeting. The director of business studies had a black beard flecked with specks of grey. And she was a woman.

And tourists, God help us, that's the last thing even the present government seems to want. It would corrupt the purity of the revolution. Even though it failed. It would jeopardise their integrity. It would compromise their aspirations to build a New World economy based on Old World ideas like factories, workshops, offices, warehouses.

So determined are they to keep tourists out of the country they have done the one thing guaranteed to keep them out for ever. They have established a state tourism office, Inturismo, which has the full support of the government.

They are also planning to build their own Disney World, 125 acres of boating lakes, motorcar and go-kart tracks at Jinotepe, about an hour's drive from Managua. So confident are they that they will draw the crowds that currently flock to Disney Worlds that, I was told by a fat, bearded, slobbering official in the Ministry of Tourism, they are drawing up plans for a 45-room hotel for visitors as well. They even blew US$40 million turning the seaside villa of their former President Somoza at Montelimar into a huge hotel complex. Except nobody wanted to go to a converted seaside villa in Montelimar, let alone a former president's. The whole thing was a disaster.

If tourists do get in, the government has come up with the cruncher. They have made everything so cheap nobody could possibly believe the prices are for real. A hotel in Managua is about the price of a Big Mac with chips. To cross the whole country by bus costs about the price of the chips. To get a train from Managua to Isla de Maiz Grande costs the same as a prime rib. Plus a couple of daiquiris.

Not that the Nicos are to blame. Until now, the only experience they have had of tourism and foreign travel is driving loads of guns in unmarked vans down from California through Mexico, through Honduras to the border and then running like hell. They have also concluded that the only way they can restrict the growing number of ecotourists threatening to descend on them is to make it difficult for them to get in, so they have decided to stop tearing down trees and building enormous roads. So concerned are they, that the government actually sends the military into the fields to guard the trees and stop them from falling into the wrong hands. It also, of course, keeps the military out of the capital, far away from government offices and a million miles from causing trouble, but I'm sure that has not occurred to anyone.

You don't believe they're anti-tourism? You try going into an Inturismo office and asking the time, let alone directions to the Centro Nicaraguense de Derechos Humanos, the Centre for Human Rights, and you'll soon see who's right. If, that is, you can find the tourist office.

Now I've been around, and I know that finding a twenty-storey office block or a factory covering 2,500 square miles is not always easy. In Ho Chi Minh City I once lost a whole university with 14,000 students. In Dallas I spent three and a half hours driving up and down Carrier Parkway looking for a factory I'd visited twice before. In Managua it's a million times worse. Some people are operating pre-earthquake. Ask them the way to the Tica bus station and they will tell you how you got there before the place was flattened. When you get directions, therefore, you don't know whether they are speaking pre- or post-earthquake. On top of that, if you've got a driver you don't know whether he is pre- or post-earthquake. Similarly with street names. If you have a street name you don't know whether it's pre-earthquake, post-earthquake, pre-Sandinistas, post-Sandinistas or just the wrong name.

Confused? Practically everybody I met got their arnbas mixed up with their abajas. As a result you don't know whether you're going left, right, up, down, round about or back to where you started. It took me two taxi drivers, three maps, one guidebook and a glass of champagne in the Inter-

Continental Hotel to find the Inturismo office. (Out of the Inter-Con; one block south; one block west. There you are. Unless they've moved it.)

Outside Managua you can travel through town after town for days on end without seeing a house, let alone a street. Most places are virtually the same as when the Spanish left; sandy tracks, wooden shacks, big wooden shack which is the church, even bigger wooden shack which is the hotel, hostel or doss-house. The occasional bullfight. And karaoke evenings every Friday. Some parts, especially down around San Juan del Norte on the border with Costa Rica, are even worse. They have karaoke evenings on Wednesdays as well. In fact so poor and so desperate are parts of the country that when the new government of Mrs Chamorro took over and started handing the land back to the peasants, the peasants gave it back to the government.

'We no wanna this. You have it. We take your cars and big homes instead.'

'No, no. You gotta have it. We promised you. It was in our manifesto.'

'In your manifesto. And you're doing it. You sure are crazy politicians.'

It's difficult to remember that Nicaragua was once the centre of world attention, a prize to be fought over. No, I'm not talking about Olly North and the Contra we-didn't-cover-it-up-very-well cover-up. I'm talking about the sixteenth century: Britain, Spain, world domination, linking the Atlantic and Pacific. You didn't know? Before Panama got the canal, there were a whole heap of feasibility studies carried out by Ye Olde Worlde Banke to see whether they could extend the big river to the huge Lake Nicaragua.

I may be wrong. But last time I was in Washington, I heard a rumour that the World Bank would soon be making up its mind and deciding whether to go ahead with the project. Apparently they've just found a memo from Charles V asking them please to pull their finger out, because if not Spain could not guarantee to keep Japanese cars out of the area. I hope they give it the go-ahead. At least it will prove they don't just commission feasibility studies and fly first class all over the world.

I am heading back to the airport. What's blocking the empty streets? Another religious demonstration! This time it's the turn of the Catholics. And this time it's against abortion.

Marching through the streets came thousands of students wearing white shirts and ties or crisp white blouses. They are clean, well-groomed, polite, orderly. It's difficult not to agree with them because at the end of the day abortion is, well, murder. One second there is this living being. The next second it's flop, a lump of gunge in a bucket. Dead.

I don't care how you argue it, it's got to be wrong. If it isn't wrong, how come everybody keeps quiet about it and pretends it doesn't exist? I mean, if it was okay everybody would be announcing their abortions in *The Times*, having parties to celebrate another successful zap and giving medals to the guys in Harley Street for their contribution to the balance of payments.

I know nothing about babies. But, gee whiz, did the students put their case, even though I didn't understand a word they were saying. Poster after poster showed tiny, perfectly formed babies, smeared in blood. One was being cradled in a hand. Hovering just over a bucket. I mean if somebody somewhere not a million miles from Auschwitz was doing this kind of thing, all hell would be let loose. But because it's happening all over the place all the time nobody takes any notice.

'Hitler, he kill babies. Abortion kill babies. That right?' a young girl said to me.

'Animals not tear their young from mother. We not tear young from mother,' a boy of about sixteen added.

'No number, no name, no family,' said another.

'How can we have peace when we are so violent in the womb?'

'Babies get in way of big houses, cars, boats. So kill babies. Yes?'

'Criminals have rights. Animals have rights. But baby in womb not have rights.'

What can you say?

Panama City

In Panama City, I'm in ecstasy. I'm in another world. It's as if there is something in the atmosphere that goes straight to my head. Maybe it's the shock of being in a country where the taxi drivers are so honest they don't have meters, and you have to keep insisting they take half the contents of your wallet for a three-minute trip from the Ministry of Justice to the National Theatre. Maybe it's because people keep trying to sell you a brand new Cadillac for anything between US$2,000 and US$5,000 because it got ever so slightly scratched being unloaded at the docks and has to be sold off cheap for insurance purposes. Maybe it's because the national lottery is so clean, efficient and above reproach that when the president's wife hits the jackpot nobody even thinks of saying a word, except congratulations.

On the other hand, maybe it's got something to do with those little packets of white sugar you see all over the place and that white blancmange you see them digging into all the time.

In the days of old Pineapple Face, as His Excellency General Manuel Antonio Noriega was known affectionately by everyone including his employers in Washington, things were completely different. There were standards. Everyone knew the standards. Everybody abided by them.

When you got a taxi you knew exactly how much the fare was; how much you had to pay and how much went to you know who. If you wanted to buy a brand new Cadillac that was – hmm, hmm – not accidentally but deliberately scratched being unloaded at the port, you knew the price was exactly US$2,500. Not a dollar more, not a dollar less. And you knew who got the $500. And no way, not once, did the president, the president's wife or anyone involved with him ever win the national lottery. They didn't have to. They got their share every week.

Today, that's all gone. There just aren't any standards left. Nobody knows what to do or what not to do any more.

Businessmen complain that if they charter private planes to fly to any of the country's hundreds of long, fabulous, deserted beaches or thousands of remote landing strips for a quick business meeting, they never know whether they are going to be stopped by the police or the army on some minor technical offence. One evening in Hollywood – no, not Hollywood, Hollywood; Hollywood, Panama City, or Panama, as we call it – I met a local businessman with a strong Italian accent who told me that in the old days if you paid your insurance money, you knew you were insured. Today you still paid, but there was no longer any insurance.

'Nobody is snatching anything from the US airbases any more,' he said, 'because there is nobody around to insure them. How can that be right?'

In the old days if businessmen did not maintain the standards, the whole of the Chamber of Commerce building was painted black; presumably as a warning to keep out of the red, and that was that. Today the only business communities you find with standards are up in the northern mountains, and further north still in Miami and Washington.

Another businessman, or rather ex-businessman, I met who was on his monthly shopping trip to Panama City, told me he had grown so used to life as a farmer in the mountains there was no way he would go back into business. It was too risky. In the old days if you put up an office block or an apartment building you knew who your sleeping partners were. There were no unknowns, no risks.

Today the Panamanian banks are so busy looking after all those people who come in day after day to deposit the life savings they have collected in little brown paper bags that they haven't had time to set up departments to provide such things as building loans. As a result, businessmen and developers were being forced to pay for the building of one tiny 17-, 23- or even 57-storey skyscraper office, apartment block or hotel after another out of their own pockets, or raise the cash from their friends. Which is a shocking indictment on the country.

I know it's true, because once when I called in to see the vice-president of the Panama branch of Merrill Lynch, he was not around, and nobody could tell me when he would be back in the office, although one person did mention something about ten years' time, but I may have misheard.

But what is even more shocking is that, as far as I can tell, hardly any of the buildings they put up are occupied. How do I know? A trick I learnt from a Dutch investment banker who made millions buying up empty offices and factories in the UK during Mrs Thatcher's time as prime minister. Look at the offices during the day. Check the number of cars in the car park and the number of plants in the windows. See, you can tell he was a Dutchman. It saves a fortune on estate agents' fees and accountants' in-depth property analyses.

Similarly apartment buildings and hotels. How many of those do you know that only have a couple of lights on at night, and they are on the top floor. Come on. There is either one hell of a good cockfight going on in town or the place is empty, right?

So why do they keep on building them if they can't let them? Because they can pretend they're full, use the profits from you know what to make up the rent or pay for the luxury suites and, hey presto, the cash is legitimate. It's in the system. They can use it whenever they want. This is Panama, don't forget.

In Colon, out on the Atlantic coast, I always feel as if my head is in the clouds, I don't know why. To old South America hands it's known as the Colon of the world. It's old, filthy, dingy, steaming hot. It's full to overflowing with every disease you can think of. In other words, it's a stinking backwater in need of a good irrigation.

In the old days, you can imagine ships and luxury liners calling in there on their way up the coast or through the Canal: passengers eager for a quick spin around town; every crook under the southern double cross waiting to grab them. A bit like Brighton on an August Bank Holiday.

Today not even the vultures bother to call in there. What few buildings there are seem to be crumbling into the boiling hot, steaming mud. The trees and shrubs and creepers seem to be growing as you look at them. I'm not saying the hotel on Avenida del Frente has dirty linen, but it's the perfect venue for an annual convention of international launderers. Big rooms, high ceilings, slightly you-know-what.

Out in the garden, sipping pastis, I met your typical drunken British export sales manager in a stained white suit.

'The moisture, the humidity, the soil, the heat,' he said, mopping his brow with an enormous red handkerchief and smoking what looked like a long thin cigarette. 'I used to sell agricultural machinery to these guys years ago. They'd hack everything down. Two months later I'd come back and it would all be twenty-feet high again. The stuff has a life of its own. I don't bother any more.'

Now, he said, he was in the service industry and doing so much business it would make a Conquistador jealous.

But the place that gets my head really spinning is the Free Zone, the biggest duty-free zone in the West, the world centre of wholesale purchasing, the second most important city in Panama. It is some joint, I can tell you. It seems to start about five, maybe ten miles out of town, as soon as I see all those enormous posters advertising everything under the sun. The nearer I get, and the more lurid and extravagant the posters become, promoting products like Permit and Request and Suspense and Guess, the more my head begins to buzz. They say that Atlanta, Georgia is the world capital of outdoor signs and posters. They should see the highway leading to Colon and the Free Zone.

Then suddenly there's a long grey wall, a giant pair of heavy metal gates, a small squat brick building, a shaky canopy, what looks like a guard wearing some kind of security-type uniform. We drive through what is obviously the smallest loophole in the place.

'Welcome, amigo, to the first and largest free trade zone in the western hemisphere and one of the most successful in the world.'

'Well, thank you. . .'

'It's the investment centre of the Americas. Within twenty-four hours we can ship anything anywhere in Central America and the Caribbean.'

'Really. That's. . .'

'Over 350 million people. That's how many people we serve throughout the region. From right here.'

Their enthusiasm is infectious.

I'm no expert on free trade zones, except that for one reason or another – mostly business – I've dragged myself through one free trade zone after another all the way from Rotterdam, the biggest in the world, to Singapore, which also claims to be the biggest in the world, and back again and all I can say is this free zone is big, Big, BIG.

Most free zones are nothing but a row of warehouses surrounded by barbed wire. This one is like being trapped in the centre of a mid-western US town dedicated solely to fake invoicing, oops, I mean shopping. At first sight there is nothing but shops, shops and more shops. Shops selling children's clothes; shops selling women's clothes; shops selling men's clothes. Everything freshly laundered, I guarantee. In theory, that is. Because the shops are not supposed to be shops at all. They're only there to take orders.

Hidden away behind the shops are enormous warehouses stocking in cardboard boxes, in wooden crates and in enormous forty-ton containers everything on sale in the shops. You want three container-loads of electronics? No problem. A hundred containers of fresh fruit? No problem. A million car spares with a few Scud missile parts thrown in? No problem.

In 1948, when it first opened for business, it covered just five hectares and contained only three companies. Today, it covers 300 hectares, the size of your typical offshore tax haven; boasts over 1,400 companies and contains 27.53 million miles of overhanging telephone cables that run along the streets in such tight bunches you can hardly see the pollution created by lots of little bonfires that seem to be being lit all day long.

By the year 2000 it will have its own port, its own airport, maybe 2,000 companies and happy customers all over South America, the Caribbean and perhaps the United States as well.

'You want make jeans here? No problem. We make jeans for you.'

'You want to build factory? We build factory, yes. You and me together. It's a deal.'

'Taxes? You don't pay taxes. Here nobody pay taxes. Here, I introduce you to my friend.'

Up and down street after street I go, every one lined with shops not selling everything from everywhere. And really not selling. Outside each shop there are about twenty forty-ton container lorries: ten collecting goods for delivery and ten delivering new products.

Then I notice the shops are no longer shops. They are the size of department stores, and not selling everything department stores sell – and more. The warehouses behind them are no longer your ordinary industrial estate warehouse, they are now the size of aircraft hangars. And instead of twenty of those huge container lorries outside there are now 200.

Down another no way mean street I wander, and across a bridge. Now I am surrounded by the most enormous warehouses you have seen. These are not just aircraft hangars, they are aircraft hangars for bunches of 747s.

What do they contain? Everything. And more.

Some of them have names up outside: Worldwide Distribution; Global Transport; World Logistics; Inter-Galactic Lorry-drivers – that kind of thing. Most have nothing at all. But the business they do must be phenomenal. It's no wonder everyone's eyes are the size of dinner plates.

I'm exhausted. I stop and take a deep breath. Whoa. My

head starts spinning again. My eyes are buzzing. Suddenly I'm seeing stars. Lots of bright red, green, yellow stars. Funny, that. A few minutes later, they're all gone.

I wander around the warehouses. Some are surrounded by wire fencing, ten, twelve feet high. At first I thought it was to keep the canaries in. Then I saw the guard dogs. But they looked so dodgy and sleepy they needn't have bothered.

I go back to the Free Zone's offices to be bombarded with facts and figures.

'Panama has commercial preferential bilateral agreements with Costa Rica, Guatemala, El Salvador, Nicaragua.'

'Panama also has non-preferential trade agreements with Germany, Rumania, Russia, the Czech Republic.'

'Panama is the centre of the world. It is the point between the eastern and western hemispheres as well as between the north and south. If you climb 11,000 feet to the top of Volcan Baru, you can see something few people have seen anywhere in the world. You see both the Atlantic and the Pacific Oceans at the same time.'

I thought he was going to say you could see a Panamanian policeman, which is definitely a rare sight, although I once actually saw one helping an old lady across the road. How much he charged her, I don't know.

'So how much business does the Free Zone do?' I asked.

'Last year we did over US$10 billion. Maybe US$15 billion. And already this year we're over 15 per cent up.'

'But that's a hell of a lot of business for a single free zone.'

Smiles all round. 'And it's all tax free.' More big smiles all round. 'No sales tax, no import tax. You can transfer your dividends out of the country no problem.' Even bigger smiles.

'Gee. No wonder everybody wants to come here.'

'Everybody wants to come. From Far East, from Europe, from South America: Chile. From Chile we get fresh fruit. From Argentina we get food. From Venezuela, we get meat. From Colombia, we get...'

Of course, that's why my head is spinning.

'You mean any type of goods can come in? No problem?'

'No problem. No checking, no customs. We are a free trade zone.'

'And they can go out again, no checking, no customs?'

'No. We're a free trade zone.'

'So it doesn't make any difference to you what comes in, or what goes out? Or where?'

'No sir.'

'And there's no exchange controls, nothing?'

'Nothing. People just have to fill in one document. That's it. Costs them three dollars, that's all.'

'So who are your big customers?'

'Colombia, Venezuela, Argentina. . .'

'Colombia?'

'Colombia.'

'This document. It is a bill, an invoice?'

'No. It's to prove ownership of goods.'

'So how does everybody pay: letters of credit, bankers' draft?'

'Usually, it depends. Some people pay cash.'

'How much of your business is cash?'

'Around 10 per cent.'

This was interesting. 'You mean people can just turn up with a briefcase full of dollar bills and pay cash, no questions asked?'

'No questions asked.'

'No proof of identity?'

'No proof of identity.'

'From Colombia? From Venezuela? From China?'

'From anywhere. It's business.'

Wait a minute . . . Ten per cent of the business is done in cash. That's over US$1.5 billion. How many banks are there in the Free Zone? Twenty-five. That means each bank handles an average US$60 million dollars a year. In cash. US$5 million a month. It's not possible. There are plenty of banks in London which would give anything to be doing that kind of business.

Then there is the question of security. They won't allow taxis into the Free Zone in case they are carrying what they call contraband, but they are quite happy for US$1.5 billion in cash to go walking around the streets every year and the only security is that policewoman over there, leaning up against the wall, a gun slung over her shoulder, eating chips.

I mean, I know Panama is Panama, but one container-load of Johnnie Walker Black Label plus fifty-seven small packets of white stuff doesn't exactly make two does it? If the Free Zone does everything it says it does, big though it is, I reckon it would have to be at least twice the size. Either that or there is more money flowing in and straight out the other side than there is water flowing through the Panama Canal.

I hitched a lift back up to the mega-mega-warehouses. I wanted to have another sniff around, if that's the phrase. They were all deserted. Nobody was in sight. There were no lorries either anywhere to be seen.

'So where's the traffic?' I asked this dozy-looking doorman.

'Traffic! What you mean traffic? There no trafficking here.'

'No trucks,' I said. 'There are no trucks. Where have the trucks gone?'

'They're all inside.'

'Inside? You mean inside the warehouses?'

'Sure, why not? They're big.'

'But if all these lorries are inside, where's all the staff?'

I can't remember what he said. By now my head was spinning round and round as if I was on some kind of funfair ride. The lights were brighter than usual. Everything seemed . . . seemed . . . I can only think it was the atmosphere.

Everything became clearer the further I got from the Free Zone and the closer I got to Panama City. Actually, halfway between the two, I was fantastic. I could see everything quite clearly.

First, Panama is obviously a dodgers' paradise. They say there are so many shell companies in Panama that if you put your ear to a Panamanian Certificate of Incorporation you hear not only the Atlantic but the Pacific as well. Everybody you meet has a string of Panamanian Mickey Mouse companies, Minnie Mouse corporations and Donald Duck subsidiaries.

Then there is the Panamanian way of doing business. You've got a customer who wants to buy something typically Panamanian, like . . . like . . . like . . . anything. You've found a seller who wants to sell whatever it is the buyer wants. Right. You sit in the middle and buy so much at so much and sell on at so much plus whatever you can get away with.

Right? Wrong. You've forgotten all the Mickey Mouse companies, all the Donald Duck invoices and the Goofy bank accounts you've got to pass the deal through before it happens. You don't believe me? Look, do you want to make a hundred thousand and pay tax on it, or do you want to do it the Panamanian way, make a million and stash it away anywhere you like, tax free?

Okay, then you do it the Panamanian way. Quite clearly, forming one company or opening one bank account is not enough. You've got to open millions of them so that if they ever check you out they get so confused, so tied up in knots (to investigate a single cross-border transaction needs a million people to agree and half a rainforest to process) they just give up in despair. And you've still got your ill-gotten gains stashed away tax free. End of story.

Well, not exactly. It depends how much we're talking about, where it is and whether you want just to leave it there to gather dust or to make use of it, or part of it, perhaps for other deals. If so, you've got to get it back into circulation without raising any eyebrows.

How do you do that? According to this man I met in a bar along the big street running through the centre of town called Tumba Muerto, the Tomb of the Dead, which slightly puts you off until everyone assures you that the last person you're likely to see along there is a policeman, you've basically got three choices.

First, dummy runs. You cash the lot. You check the minimum cash levels for putting money into whatever bank you want to put it into. You then spend the rest of your life going round the different bank branches queuing up and putting in as much as you can below the minimum cash level.

Put in any more and you risk the bank trying to find out where the money came from. Alternatively you can go to a special distribution agency, take your life in your hands, and give them the money to dribble into the bank for you.

Second, dummy companies. You set up a dummy company which buys and sells goods that don't exist – every time paying a supplier, which is another of your dummy companies, hiring a transport company, which is another of your dummy companies, paying insurance on the load to another . . . you got it.

Third, dummy claims. Are you sitting comfortably? Then I'll begin. Company A buys a couple of shiploads of cement from Agent B. Agent B does all the paperwork real legal and gives the order to Family Friend C who – surprise, surprise – delivers only half a shipload. Company A is happy because by paying the full amount he gets some funny money out of his pocket and back into the system. Agent B is happy because he picks up the full commission for only half an order. Family Friend C is happy because he gets the deal, he offloads some cement, and he knows Company A will be back again soon. Everyone's happy.

But that's still not all. At least, not according to this other guy I met in another bar further up Tumba Muerto.

You've done the deal. Now, how are you going to deliver the stuff? DHL? Forget it. You've got to have your own ship. Of course it's stupid. Of course it's expensive. But this is Panama. Right? Right! Buying a ship means losing money, right? Right. That means whatever money you make is immediately down the drain. Right? Wrong! This is Panama. How many times do I have to remind you.

First you form half a dozen transportation and shipping companies to buy different bits of the boat for different companies in different parts of the world. Next you start about two and a half million finance companies to come up with the money for the damn thing. Except if you do it right, open the right bank accounts with the right banks and shuffle money from one account to another so fast nobody knows what you're doing, you'll end up by owning a boat which some-body somewhere has actually paid you to sell them.

Confused? Good. You're supposed to be. This is ... you're right. Panama.

Marcos, the old Filipino president of happy memory to banks worldwide, was said to have had almost as many companies as his wife had shoes, so that in the end, what with all the cross-share holdings and double-cross dealing that went on between them he just lost track.

So now you've got the boat you let somebody else sell you with their own money, your trading companies have to negotiate with your transportation companies for the hire of the thing, which of course is so booked up you're going to be forced not only to buy out a raft of previous shipping contracts, you're also going to have to pay out way over the odds for the privilege of using your own transport. Right? Right.

And of course, once you've got your own boat there's plenty of other tricks you can play. Put the word round you've got half a boatload, twenty containers, three-quarters of a warehouse of something or other. It doesn't matter. Sooner or later somebody will bite. Then all you do is ask them to give you a letter of credit made out to one of your Mickey Mouse companies. They send the letter of credit. Wham, as soon as it hits the bank you take the money straight out and shuffle it into any one of a dozen other Mickey Mouse bank accounts you control all over the world, wrap the original company and disappear. What's the poor guy who sent the letter of credit going to do? What can he do? Sue the company that owned the boat? If you've done your job properly he'll spend twenty years going from court to court until he finds out that he actually owns the boat as well.

Funnily enough, now you mention it, I actually saw the kind of boat you're looking for. It was down by the port of Cristobel, just outside Colon. It was perfect. It was about, I guess, 100 feet long. In order to disguise how modern it is, it was very cleverly covered, from stem to stern, in this expen-sive, rust-coloured paint. Its engines were coughing and spluttering, but that was to make the taxman think it had diesel engines instead of the super high-power rocket engines it really has. The crew were deliberately old and dumb and deaf, so they couldn't communicate with the customs inspector. It's a steal. I'll get my finance companies to get in touch with yours to arrange the financing you need to do the deal. On the best possible terms, of course. No point falling out over it, is there?

Okay. So now you've got all this money, what are you going to do with it? Keep it under the bed? That's risky, especially with all the crooks and thieves about nowadays. Somehow you've got to get it back into the system. You've got a number of alternatives. You can either put it in a sack and join the queue at any bank in the country. Panamanian banks are so flexible, I'm told, that when the government recently paid off all US$700 million of their arrears to the IMF, the World Bank, the Inter-American Development Bank, the International Fund for Agricultural Development and that PO box number in Palermo, the banks arranged for it all to be delivered in three suitcases, two brown paper bags and a couple of handfuls of those little packets of sugar or whatever that white stuff is.

The danger, of course, is you might then have problems transferring it to other banks in other countries. You know how smallminded and petty some people, especially regulators, can be. Instead, you've got to get it into the ordinary, boring, safe banks. Trouble is the Uckfield branch of NatWest is not exactly used to accepting money in teachests. Which means you've got to trickle it back into the system.

Here, according to another man I met, you've got a number of options: set up a chain of restaurants or hotels that refuse to take credit cards. That way you can fiddle the books, sell more meals or let more rooms than you really do and use your money to make up the difference. Or run fleets of empty buses in Liverpool. Every time I go to Liverpool the buses are empty, which must mean somebody is using them to pump illegal money back into the system; or, if you've got real big money to shift, start your own bureaux de change. Money exchange is a money-in-no-questions-asked-money-out operation. So if, say, you wanted to push a couple of million dollars into the system for a not very good rate, would you have problems doing it through your own money exchange shops? Which, come to think of it, might be one of the reasons why there are so many bureaux de change in Panama. It can't be because there are so many tourists around eager to change their pound notes and their French francs. Because there aren't.

The other more exciting, grown-up way of getting money back into the system is to take up gambling. Win or lose, it doesn't matter. All you've got to do is go into any casino, good/bad, reputable/disreputable, they're all the same. Order a bottle of champagne. Buy US$100 in chips. Put them all on number 13 if you like; give them to the hat-check girl; flush them down the loo: it doesn't make any difference. The following morning, go to your friendly local bank manager, give him all the money you've got stashed away and tell him to put the lot into government securities because you don't believe in taking risks with your money.

Ninety-nine bank managers out of a hundred won't say a word. They're not stupid. Well, apart from mine. They need the business. They'll do exactly as you say. If you get the one in a hundred, all you say is, 'Had a good night at the casino. Must have been my lucky day.' Which usually does the trick. Get the one bank manager in a million who asks for proof, you have two options. The second is to tell him you'll get a note from the casino confirming your win. Which is as easy as losing a fortune on the tables. There's not one casino in the world that will refuse to help anyone who's having a spot of bother with the banks. It's just not in their nature. In any case, if the word ever got out, what do you think would happen to them? Professionally speaking, I mean.

By now I am getting closer and closer to Panama. My head is beginning to spin. I'm seeing colours. Red. White. Green. Purple. There's dense, hot, steamy jungle on both sides. We swing round the corner and there ... right in front of me ... is a ship ... A giant enormous tanker ... Moving slowly ...

through the ... At first I thought I was hallucinating again. Then I realised. It was the Canal, which I've always maintained was a brilliant ploy all those years ago by the French to ensure that if they couldn't control the Americas, then neither would the British. Which is why Ferdinand de Lesseps, the great builder of the Suez Canal, obviously with the support of the French government, came up with the idea of linking the Atlantic and Pacific and was prepared to sacrifice hundreds of promising young soldiers and engineers and tens of thousands of workers to yellow fever, malaria and a string of other deadly diseases, to ensure that the Taiwanese would destroy any chance Latin America might have of establishing a shoe industry, the Japanese would destroy any chance they might have of building up an electronics or automobile industry, and the Chinese would destroy their textile, raffia-mat and anything costing less than 55 cents an item industry. They were even prepared to throw in Gauguin as well, but after fifteen days working as a labourer he packed his easel and quit. What was even cleverer of them was the way, once they started the project and made certain it would have to be completed, they all disappeared and left it to the Americans to come in and at great sacrifice to themselves finish the job. Of course, the French government denied all such intentions. But we all know how much credibility to attach to what the French government says about anything ranging from, say, hijacking Ben Bella to, say, hijacking Carlos.

If you don't accept that theory, the only alternative one is that the French built the Canal because they arrogantly thought that when God created Panama he didn't exactly make a good job of it so they had to come along and finish the job for him.

Either way, the Canal really is spectacular. It is honestly one of the modern wonders of the world. I mean, how could any ordinary mortal man – you see, I'm excluding the French – even think of building such a thing? It's unbelievable. The sheer size and scale of it: 50 miles through dense jungle and mountain; locks 1,000 feet long by 110 feet wide; not to mention building the world's largest dam and creating the world's largest lake. It's crazy.

Then it's not just the size of the thing, it's what it does. At Miraflores, one of the three sets of double locks on the Canal, you can actually see huge tankers rising and falling fifty-four feet in as many seconds. I'm no fanatic about boats, but this is truly spectacular.

At first ships used to go through all the time. Some ships booked in advance, others just turned up and went through whenever there was a gap. When I first went there they had decided to improve the system by suspending bookings and letting everyone through on a first-come basis. The result: chaos. More and more ships just kept turning up, practically blocking the entrance. At one stage there were over 100 ships waiting to go through. The Panamanians said they had problems overhauling one of the giant locks, which meant they couldn't handle so much traffic; there was a big jump in the amount of fruit being shipped from South America to Philadelphia and other east coast ports; the US was sending a hell of a lot more grain back through the Canal to Asia. And, on top of everything, it's supposed to be silting up.

No, not with drugs being dumped by people frightened of being caught with them by the police. They're not as silly as that in Panama. In any case, the police would never allow them to do anything so stupid. Apparently the combination of intensive logging all along the banks and intensive rain has meant that enormous amounts of soil, no longer held back by tree roots, have been sliding into the water and clogging the thing up. So desperate are the Japanese, because it is so vital to them in breaking into South and Central America, they are already talking about paying to dredge it, or even build an extension. Which seems crazy to me. Instead of taking their money and keeping it open we should allow it to silt up until the Japanese open their markets to our goods.

None of this is good news for the Embera and Cuna Indians deep in the Darien jungle, which straddles the border with Colombia. For every delay getting through the Canal brings

nearer the day when thousands of acres of one of the world's
most biologically rich rainforest will be ripped up to provide
the missing 67-mile link in the Pan-American Highway which,
at present, runs from Fairbank way up in Alaska down to the
southern tip of Chile.

'Petrol, iron, steel, cotton. It is crazy, we cannot ship goods
direct by road to Mexico, the US, all because of some trees,'
one trader told me.

'We send fruit from Chile to Philadelphia. For three days it
is in queue waiting to go through Canal. It gets to Philadelphia
late, it costs more money. It is crazy, yes. If we have road, fruit
can be in the US market in three days. Guaranteed.'

Trouble is, there is the cost, although Colombia says they'll
pay for the thirty-three miles their side of the border if Panama
picks up the tab for the rest. Then, of course, there is the
environmental question. Is it worth pulling down all those
trees just to help the Koreans sell cheap Chilean fruit and
vegetables in their grocery shops all over the States?

My guess is it'll go ahead because, rightly or wrongly, it has
to. For the sake of trade. For the sake of politics. The more
South America is integrated, doing business, shipping goods
into the US, the safer things will be throughout the region. For
the sake of the Indians as well. At present they are poor,
hungry, jobless, desperately struggling to survive; so much so
that the forest is already subject to massive illegal logging.
With the new road, the illegal logging will cease. There will be
regulated logging, regulated re-planting, professional forestry
management. Plus, of course, all the jobs and all the spin-
offs.

What also amazes me about the Canal is the number of fully
trained combat troops the US government keeps in Panama to
look after it, even though for over eighty years nobody has as
much as sent it an anonymous letter. At the last count, I was
told, there were over 30,000 squeezed on to just 80,000 acres
of land containing 4,287 buildings including military barracks,
community centres, offices, six bowling alleys, twelve hobby
shops, nine swimming pools, eight post offices, seven the-

atres, five sports centres, three stables and two golf courses.

My only guess is that years ago they picked up a rumour that the French might want to grab it back, so they've been on the look-out for them ever since. Who started the rumour? The French. Because they wanted to tie up US troops in Panama so that they could get on with running Africa and the Far East without interruptions.

As for the American soldiers, every one of them I met told me it was the best posting in the world. 'Womb to tomb, you don't have to do a thing,' one major said. You can't help wondering, however; if all 30,000 troops are battle-hardened killers ready to lay down their lives for the sake of a canal, how come it took another 26,000 battle-hardened troops to reward one of their employees by taking him back home to live a life of luxury without any worries about security or where his next meal would come from. It either means one Panamanian is worth 26,000 Americans, or the Americans are not used to invading other people's countries, riding roughshod over concepts of sovereignty, destroying whole areas of cities and smashing innocent people's homes to Kingdom Come.

Some people say they really came to rid the country of drug-trafficking, money-laundering and rampant corruption. But that can't possibly be true, because it is still going on as much as, if not more than, before. At least according to this guy with a crewcut I met one evening in a bar in the San Felipe area, after I'd done the tourist thing and driven about fifty-seven times backwards and forwards over the Bridge of the Americas which links North and South America, dreaming one day of driving the length of the Pan-American Highway. He told me they had to bring in another 26,000 troops because the 30,000 already in the country were bombed out of their minds on blue flake.

'What's blue flake?'

'Cocaine.'

'But I thought everyone was tested.'

'Sure. But only for marijuana.'

'But that's. . .'

'And they tell us when they're going to test us, so five days before, we all stop taking it. Five days after you've had it, there's no trace of the stuff.'

He said they were not actually there to protect the Canal, but to run spy flights over the Andes to detect drug smugglers and, being good soldiers, they could never know too much about the enemy. Then he crashed out on the floor and had to be carried out.

Another guy, with earrings, white shoes and one of those whooffy-do haircuts came up to me and apologised. Such behaviour, he said, was not good for Panama's image as a tourist destination. He himself was running regular trips to cute little landing strips along the sparkling, deserted beaches on the Atlantic and Pacific coasts. Within minutes, if not seconds, of arriving, people could be having the time of their lives racing fast boats up and down delightful little back-waters. Soon he was hoping to expand and offer this same kind of service to the thousands of little jungle hideaways scattered all over the country. So far, he said, the Canadians were the only people who had discovered the potential of Panama and were flocking in in anything like appreciable numbers. But that, I thought, had more to do with the attractions of Canada than anything Panama has to offer.

Hell, I've just realised. Do you know what I didn't do? I didn't form even one Panamanian company, let alone open a string of Panamanian bank accounts. Everybody kept telling me I should, but I kept putting it off. To be honest, I couldn't think of the right name. I mean, nobody opens a company in Panama called Peter Biddlecombe Ltd. It's got to sound big and dramatic and important. Like Worldwide Global Enter-prises of Inter-Galactic Exploitation or Universal Trading and Technology. I just couldn't think of anything.

Then I couldn't decide which type of company I wanted; how many subsidiaries it should have; whether they should open branch offices in their own right; whether they should be joint ventures with this other string of dummy companies I was going to set up in Liechtenstein; whether I could get away with a set of Articles of Association that said once they had been agreed they could be thrown away, that the directors would be appointed by telephone, that the minutes of company meetings could be agreed by post and that the managing director was whoever paid the telephone bill. All of which indecisiveness is n-n-not l-l-like me at all at all at all.

I can only assume it was something to do with the atmosphere. Either that or the white blancmange I had at that meeting in Colon. Because after that whenever I felt like doing anything I kinda came over all ... Whoa ... There, it's happening again. Quick, get me a chair. Otherwise I'll ... I'll ... I'll ...

FRENCH LESSONS IN AFRICA

Travels With My Briefcase Through French Africa

Peter Biddlecombe

Having travelled across Africa for over ten years, Peter Biddlecombe's often hilarious account of a long and lingering *liaison dangereuse* with the 60 per cent of the continent that is French-speaking is a highly readable, hugely entertaining introduction to the *je ne sais quoi* of French Africa.

In countries such as Togo, Mali and Burkina Faso, Biddlecombe encounters old-fashioned camel butchers, modern witch doctors who run mail-order companies, gold smugglers and counterfeiters who send their sons to Oxford. He also experiences a delicious *foie gras* of places: from eerie voodoo ceremonies in the old slave port of Ouidah to Italian ice-cream parlours in the middle of the Sahara desert . . .

'This astonishing book is all highlights, an incident on every page'
Daily Mail

'The funniest, yet most serious, book about contemporary Africa on the market'
Guardian

TRAVELS WITH MY BRIEFCASE

Around the World – On Expenses

Peter Biddlecombe

It is a great truth of modern life that businessmen are today the world's most accomplished travellers. Like Marco Polo, the business traveller has a purpose; he is a man with a mission. Not for him a simple trawl through tourist hell – his experiences are authentic, driven by career rather than courier. Consequently, the adventurous nature of such trips is never forced – the Hindu Kush, Amazonian jungle or Kalahari hold no fears for those who have braved the Tokyo underground in rush hour.

In *Travels With My Briefcase* Peter Biddlecombe introduces us to the world of the business traveller, stumbling across the humorous and bizarre in the most unexpected places – like Switzerland – and generally proving that you don't have to be a student, aesthete or one-eyed skate-boarder to experience the thrill and excitement of exploring the world.

Now you can order superb titles directly from Abacus

☐ French Lessons in Africa	Peter Biddlecombe	£7.99
☐ Travels With My Briefcase	Peter Biddlecombe	£7.99
☐ Around the World – On Expenses	Peter Biddlecombe	£7.99

Please allow for postage and packing: **Free UK delivery.**
Europe; add 25% of retail price; Rest of World; 45% of retail price.

To order any of the above or any other Abacus titles, please call our credit card orderline or fill in this coupon and send/fax it to:

Abacus, 250 Western Avenue, London, W3 6XZ, UK.
Fax 0181 324 5678   Telephone 0181 324 5517

☐ I enclose a UK bank cheque made payable to Abacus for £ ....

☐ Please charge £.............. to my Access, Visa, Delta, Switch Card No.

☐☐☐☐☐☐☐☐☐☐☐☐☐☐☐☐☐☐☐☐.

Expiry Date ☐☐☐☐   Switch Issue No. ☐☐

NAME (Block letters please) ....

ADDRESS ....

....

....

Postcode ....Telephone ....

Signature ....

Please allow 28 days for delivery within the UK. Offer subject to price and availability.

Please do not send any further mailings from companies carefully selected by Abacus ☐